PURITANISM
IN THE PERIOD OF THE
GREAT PERSECUTION
1660–1688

PURITANISM
IN THE PERIOD OF THE
GREAT PERSECUTION
1660-1688

BY

GERALD R. CRAGG

CAMBRIDGE
AT THE UNIVERSITY PRESS
1957

PUBLISHED BY
THE SYNDICS OF THE CAMBRIDGE UNIVERSITY PRESS
Bentley House, 200 Euston Road, London, N.W.1
American Branch: 32 East 57th Street, New York 22, N.Y.

Printed in Great Britain at the University Press, Cambridge
(Brooke Crutchley, University Printer)

CONTENTS

PREFACE

This book is an attempt to interpret an experience. While Oliver Cromwell lived, the Puritans possessed political power; when he died, they rapidly lost it. Seldom has a reversal of fortune been so complete. In the course of a few months a régime which its foes had failed to overthrow disintegrated and collapsed. Militant Puritanism had no answers to the political problems of the English people; a nation drifting toward chaos hailed the house of Stuart as the only alternative to disaster, and King Charles II won by default the throne which he had been unable to regain by force.

The story of that strange abdication of power has often been told. What it meant to those who chiefly suffered from its consequences has generally been neglected. Even the histories of nonconformity (many of them old, most of them now obsolete) have concentrated on events and have taken for granted the kind of life that unfolded within the framework that the history of the period provided. It is obvious, of course, that experience cannot be divorced from the events that shape it, and in the first chapter of this book I have tried to provide a brief outline of the period of persecution. The purpose of the chapter is merely to supply the background necessary for an appreciation of the life of the Puritans in the Restoration era. I believe that the story merits retelling in greater detail, and at a later date I hope to do so. Here, however, I have been concerned with narrative only in so far as it may help the reader to understand the social life of a distinctive group at a particular time. My chief concern has been to describe the life of a people under persecution. They were harried in their homes and in their meeting houses; they were arrested, tried and imprisoned. A few were transported; many died. To meet an ordeal so searching and so severe they could call on certain distinctive resources. They were keenly aware that suffering was as much a test of their spiritual fortitude as it was a trial of their physical endurance. Persecution was not continuous; in the intervals, the nonconformists maintained a life, individual as well as corporate, which was marked by strongly defined characteristics. We can reconstruct the pattern of their daily experience; we can see how firmly it was set within the framework of a type of worship: deliberately selected, then earnestly and faithfully performed.

'Puritan' is a term notoriously difficult to define. Richard Baxter found the essence of Puritanism in two things: a serious effort to live a godly life, and a desire to achieve further reformation in the church. After the Restoration (though far less than before the Civil War), there were many within the Church of England who retained attitudes characteristic of the Puritans, but for the sake of convenience I have restricted the term to those whose views were sufficiently pronounced to drive them into nonconformity. Some writers have distinguished between nonconformists who were Puritans and those who were not, but I have preferred a more inclusive usage. Though the dissenting groups differed among themselves on many matters, they shared a common heritage and were united in their protest against the demands imposed by the established church. Admittedly many of the Puritans regarded the Quakers with suspicion, but the pattern of their lives was strikingly similar; they differed on various points of doctrine, they testified to the truth in different ways, and they worshipped according to different forms, but in the experiences of a persecuted people they were at one. I have used the terms 'nonconformist' and 'dissenter' indifferently; in this I believe that I follow the practice of many of those most intimately concerned.

One small point requires explanation. The Puritans were a vocal people, eager to express their views in print. Most of their works have never been reprinted, but the writings of many of their more eminent representatives have been reissued (in whole or in part) in collected editions. When I have referred to a book which has reappeared in this form, I have enclosed the title in brackets; then the pagination is to the composite volume, not to the individual work.

My obligations are many; it would be tedious to enumerate them all, and invidious to distinguish among them. I must acknowledge, however, the unfailing courtesy of the patient race of librarians, without whose help this study could not have been completed. In preparing the typescript, Miss Glenna Smith deciphered my palimpsest with great patience and skill, and I am deeply indebted to her for her assistance. I wish to thank the Syndics of the Cambridge University Press for their kindness, the members of the staff for their constant co-operation, and the craftsmen of the Press for the skill and accuracy with which they have produced this work. It is customary for authors to acknowledge their obligation to their wives; only other authors understand what this means—and perhaps only other authors' wives fully appreciate all that it implies.

G. R. C.

MONTREAL
October 8, 1956

THE NOTES

Superior figures in the text refer to the
appendix of notes beginning on p. 260

CHAPTER I

THE BACKGROUND OF PERSECUTION

THE collapse of Puritan power was a political event which had far-reaching spiritual results. In retrospect it is easy to see why the Puritans failed. The acquisition of power confronted them with problems too intricate for them to solve. Political and constitutional difficulties emerged to which they had no answers. They believed in the voice of the people, but they constantly defied it. They paid lip-service to parliamentary principles, but they were forced to rely on the power of the sword, and military government proved as expensive as it was unpopular. They tried to establish the rule of the saints, but were discredited by the frailties of their own followers.

All this was apparent only in part to the men most immediately concerned. What the Puritans realised clearly enough was that lack of unity was the primary cause of their downfall. While Cromwell lived, his immense prestige had been sufficient both to check the conspiracies of his foes and to neutralise the contentions of his followers. When he died, there was no one strong enough to arrest the disintegration which set in at once. Each of the major parties within Puritanism struggled in turn with the problems which Cromwell himself had failed to solve; all alike proved only the measure of their incapacity. The protectoralists, the republicans and the army officers successively presided over the increasing chaos which marked a society in dissolution. None of them had the political skill or the moral authority to control the confusion into which the country was subsiding.

Meanwhile the ineptitude of those who tried to lead was matched by the ineffectiveness of those who might have followed. The Independents, more closely committed to the régime than any other group, had little internal cohesion, and were chiefly fertile in irrelevant and impractical suggestions for change. The militant sects, which had once provided the dynamic which had carried the revolutionary movement so far, showed no signs of rallying in the face of the new crisis. They could still awaken fear in others; in themselves they were bewildered and confused. They were discredited in the eyes of their contemporaries and were fatally divided amongst themselves. If they could have found a leader, they might have repeated the achievements of an earlier day; no leader emerged.

Some Puritans felt that paralysis on the left wing of their movement was matched by disloyalty on the right. The conservative elements within Puritanism—the Presbyterians, the lawyers, the merchants of the city of London—increasingly favoured a restoration of the monarchy. They shared a growing alarm at the multiplying signs of social disintegration, and in kingship they saw a symbol of continuity and order. By its restoration the country might perhaps be able to recover some measure of political stability. Beyond proposing a return to tried and tested forms of government, they had no remedy to offer for the nation's ills. Though the sectaries raised the cry of treason, it was with a clear conscience that the Presbyterians advocated the restoration of the house of Stuart. They had always deplored the execution of King Charles I; they had long been impatient of what they regarded as sectarian excesses. And many members of the smaller groups were already looking in the same direction. The Anabaptists and the Quakers were beginning to make overtures to the man who apparently would soon be king.

The confusions of the closing months of the Interregnum revealed far more than the bankruptcy of Puritanism as a political force. They showed that it had no inner cohesion. They proved that it could not translate its ideals into objectives capable of commanding general assent. Even those in whom the experiment in godly government had raised the highest hopes saw little prospect of redeeming it from futility. Extremists might querulously complain that a great betrayal had forfeited a glorious opportunity, but the easy expedient of vilifying others was no answer to the perplexities of the period. For some reason the power of godliness had proved more limited than the enthusiasts had expected. It had not disciplined those of like purpose into a common mind; it had provided no answers to the political problems that clamoured for solution. Among the pamphlets which appeared during the final phase of the Interregnum, the notes of perplexity and disillusionment were often sounded. Why had sincerity achieved such a disappointing measure of success?

Without an awareness of this bewilderment and frustration it is impossible to appreciate the perplexities with which, after the Restoration, the Puritans were beset. They had experienced persecution in the past; they had known it under Queen Elizabeth and under the early Stuart kings. Never before had it come as the sequel to a dramatic reversal of fortune. Persecution was inevitably embittered by memories of failure and defeat. If the possession of power had posed certain problems, the loss of it created others, no less acute though wholly different. Henceforth the Puritans were required not to act with wisdom but to suffer with patience. Under circumstances of exceptional stringency they were called upon to apply to their own situation those religious resources which they had always extolled as the answer to every human need.

As the inevitability of the Restoration became daily more apparent, many men of Puritan outlook regarded its approach with something closely resembling relief. Monarchy seemed to be the only alternative to chaos; any form of government was preferable to none. Yet as they awaited the return of the king, they realised how precarious their own position would be. The men in authority would have little sympathy with Puritan aspirations. The godly must expect ridicule. In all likelihood they would be called upon to endure reproach. Probably persecution and suffering lay ahead.[1] 'I must confess', wrote Oliver Heywood in his diary, 'we are in a precarious state, being afraid lest the supreme governor should prove wicked, frown on the faithful of the land, obstruct the work of reformation, set up the abrogated ceremonies, subject us to the tyranny of an insulting hierarchy, corrupt God's pure worship, and turn gospel discipline into courts of formality.... But shall our surmisings hinder our rejoicings?... Let us wait on God, keep his ways, and trust him with events.'[2]

Faith was all the more necessary, since foresight could offer little help. It was impossible to forecast the future. The signs of the times were confused and contradictory. There could be no doubt that many of the royalists were bent on revenge: if a vindictive spirit prevailed among the justices of the peace, what quarter could their opponents expect? But it was equally apparent that the king had no desire to see the recent cleavage perpetuated among his people. He made no secret of his hope that a conciliatory spirit would govern the settlement of the kingdom. He not only promised an act of oblivion, but insisted that the dilatory House of Commons should pass it without delay—and with as few exceptions as possible.[1] Some of the regicides were executed as retribution for their share in the death of Charles I; a few notable Puritans were left in doubt as to their status, and feared for their lives as well as for their liberty, but on the whole the great upheaval was accomplished at a singularly modest price in blood.[2] Charles II knew that the religious problem was as complex as it was urgent, and he carefully avoided rash commitments. He made it clear that the church would be ruled by bishops; its members must expect to worship according to the Book of Common Prayer, but he encouraged the hope that grievances would so be remedied that with few exceptions his subjects could find a place within the national establishment.

Such a prospect might seem remote, but it was not entirely unreasonable. Some of the Puritans, it is true, intended to make no concessions and they asked for none from the Church of England. Those who belonged to the Independent tradition did not desire comprehension; they merely hoped for liberty to live and to worship as they chose. But the Presbyterians—and they were the largest single group—were convinced that if certain defects in the government and worship of the church could be remedied, any reasonable man would be able to conform. Since they believed that their demands were modest, they did not consider their hopes extreme.

Yet the confidence of the Presbyterians lagged far behind their hopes. The initiative was obviously slipping into other hands; those who had so recently controlled affairs were afraid that they

4

would find themselves relegated to the role of impotent spectators.[1] Events soon showed how accurately they judged. From all parts of the country came reports of ministers subjected to abuse or driven from their livings.[2] The Presbyterians suspected that the king's advisers were actually pursuing a policy widely different from that which they professed to follow. Unquestionably these suspicions were well-founded. Hyde and his friends intended to pacify the Puritans until they could safely repress them. Meanwhile the Laudians were determined to gain possession of the establishment, and they could run no risks until their control of it was complete. The events of the first few months of the reign fall into a perfectly consistent pattern. Promises were freely made; they were never implemented unless the development of a crisis showed that a timely concession must be offered. It was sometimes necessary to soothe the fears of a party which it was still inexpedient to alarm.[3]

Negotiations regarding a religious settlement began without delay, but for some time there was little prospect of rapid progress. The king himself was easy of access and conciliatory in attitude. He insisted that peace could be achieved only if both parties were prepared to make concessions; an intermediate position must be found acceptable to both sides. His counsellors, on the other hand, were non-committal and evasive. Discussions virtually ceased. But meanwhile the Presbyterian members of the Convention parliament, alarmed at the mounting evidence that the episcopal party was steadily tightening its hold upon the church, decided that the time had come to make a stand. The official reaction was prompt. Parliament was recessed; steps were taken to fill the vacant bishoprics without delay, and negotiations with the Presbyterians were resumed. The time was obviously ripe for a conciliatory gesture, and the king's Declaration of 25 October 1660 was issued. The Presbyterians were amazed at the generous terms in which it was couched. Baxter felt that if this was a faithful reflection of the government's intentions there was no reason why 'any sober honest minister' should not conform, and he determined to use his influence to persuade as many as possible to do so.[4] The offer of high

5

preferment to the Presbyterian leaders seemed to justify their hopes, but a nagging scepticism persisted. Could they be sure that the responsible bodies would ratify the royal Declaration? It was soon apparent that they could not. When a bill to that end was introduced into the House of Commons, it was defeated at the instigation of the king's own ministers.[1] Yet those who had best cause to feel that they had been deceived were satisfied that the Declaration had served a useful purpose. It now stood on record that the king had once offered the Puritans terms which would have satisfied most of their demands. Henceforth their suggestions for reform could appeal to the authority of the king's own words.

The next important concession (and the last of any account) was likewise prompted by signs of Puritan discontent. Venner's irresponsible rising had shown how easily royalist fears could be raised, but of far greater significance than that wild enterprise was the united action by which the Puritans of the city of London returned to the new parliament four Presbyterian members. Intercepted letters showed that this was part of a concerted effort to gain control of the House of Commons, and the government was alarmed.[2] Clearly it was time to offer a further concession to the Puritans. For months the king's promise of a synod to revise the Book of Common Prayer had been studiously ignored; within a week of the London elections the warrants for the Savoy Conference appeared.[3] The summons to the meeting was gracious and conciliatory in tone, and for a moment the flagging hopes of the Puritans revived. There was little possibility, however, that any constructive results would emerge. Debate by syllogism did nothing to place the significant issues in their true perspective. The temper in which the participants approached their task made it unlikely that agreement could be reached on any subject of genuine concern.[4] The presentation of documents degenerated into an exchange of recriminations. The discussion rapidly became a source of exasperation to the disputants and an occasion for mockery to everybody else.[5]

Even before the Savoy Conference ended it was apparent that the important decisions would be taken elsewhere. Convocation

6

was already busy with its own revision of the Prayer Book. It would determine the pattern of uniformity; parliament would then lay down the terms under which it would be enforced. The changes made by Convocation were fewer in number and less drastic in character than the extent of the Laudian triumph might have pre-supposed. Whatever may have been the reasons for this moderation, the Puritans failed to detect any signs of a conciliatory purpose. Many of the minor changes seemed designed to offend their susceptibilities, and it became a part of their tradition that the alterations now introduced were intended to alienate them and drive them from the church.[1]

Responsibility for the next step in the religious settlement now passed to the House of Commons. The Corporation Act had shown that parliament knew how to strike a shrewd blow at the centres of Puritan power. With the revision of the Prayer Book complete, the way was open to lay down the conditions which would henceforth govern membership in the established church. The Act of Uniformity required that prior to St Bartholomew's Day 1662 every one who held any ecclesiastical office was to read morning and evening prayer, and then 'openly and publicly, before the congregation there assembled, declare his unfeigned assent and consent...to all and everything contained and prescribed in, and by, the book entitled "The Book of Common Prayer"'. The Solemn League and Covenant was to be explicitly renounced, and the lawfulness of any attempt to change the government either of church or state was to be repudiated in the most explicit terms. Only those who had received episcopal ordination might henceforth officiate in the Church of England. Not only incumbents of parishes, but also schoolmasters and even private tutors came within the terms of the Act. The nature of every possible offence was carefully defined; the appropriate penalty for every breach of the law was clearly indicated.[2]

The passing of the Act of Uniformity ended a long period of increasing uncertainty and doubt. Though the Puritans had been promised much, their apprehensions had steadily mounted. Now they knew the worst. But the full knowledge of their fate created a new kind of problem. Even when they clearly saw the alter-

7

natives before them, it was not necessarily easy to make a choice. Were they foolishly magnifying their scruples, and so jeopardising their vocation?[1] Preoccupation with a delicate ethical dilemma might blind a man's eyes to the duties immediately before him— for example, to the elementary obligation to provide for his family's needs. With anxious care, deeply troubled men began to investigate the whole controversy afresh. They not only searched their own consciences, but sought help wherever it might be found.[2] Some—and they were the fortunate ones—had no doubt what their decision would be. With a sense of immense relief, men like Joseph Alleine saw at once that the terms of the Act removed any uncertainty as to their future course.[3] For the handful of Anabaptists who were affected, the arguments against yielding were both sweeping in scope and detailed in character. The same was true for most of the Independents. For many of the Presbyterians, however, the perplexities which they faced were all the greater because the barriers in their way seemed less insuperable. They often found that they could go a considerable distance toward meeting the requirements imposed, and it was legitimately a matter of doubt whether the remaining obstacles were such as to compel them to forsake the national church.[4] The most serious impediment to conformity was the clause requiring 'assent and consent' to everything contained in the Book of Common Prayer,[5] and this was aggravated by the fact that few ministers had an adequate chance to study the new book, and many had no opportunity at all.[6] To various elements in the liturgy the Puritans took exception; objections were not always the same, nor were they all regarded as of equal weight. No less serious was the demand that ministers who had not received episcopal ordination should now submit to it. The various oaths which were imposed were also an obstacle. So was the required abjuration of the Solemn League and Covenant.[7]

'The Act of Uniformity', said Oliver Heywood, 'struck all nonconformists dead on St. Bartholomew's day, Aug. 24, 1662.'[8] On that day nearly two thousand ministers chose to be ejected rather than to conform, and thereafter, year by year, they solemnly observed the anniversary as it recurred. It was impossible for them to ignore a day whose consequences had been so serious. As a result of their decision most of the ministers found that persecution had ceased to be a theoretical possibility and had become an imminent likelihood. Those for whom it became a painful reality soon discovered that it entailed spiritual problems as serious as the physical discomforts it involved.[1] For the most part the ejected ministers were thrown upon the world without means of support. They could not continue the work for which they had been trained, and the alternatives to which educated men would naturally turn were closed to them by the ingenuity with which the Act of Uniformity had been framed. Many were the expedients to which they were driven. A few had private means. Some possessed skills for which the community was glad to remunerate them. Many turned to secular callings until they could find some opportunity of exercising their ministry once more. Some discovered that wealthy friends were willing to support them. Gradually the ejected ministers began to preach to little groups of followers and received from them such support as predominantly humble folk could offer. Unquestionably some suffered severely, but in retrospect the nonconformists gratefully recorded that relatively few had been brought to actual destitution.[2] But there were other problems beside poverty. Idleness could be an intolerable burden to men who believed that they should be up and doing, and it bred its own kind of bitter frustration. The routine which had governed a minister's days suddenly became irrelevant.[3] Meanwhile he could see a need, but could not meet it. He had been called to preach, but a ban of silence had been laid upon him. Some of the ministers seriously weighed the possibility of undertaking missionary work;[4] some went to the colonies, and found scope for their gifts in the New World.[5] Most of them decided to remain where they were; they would wait for a day of wider usefulness, and meanwhile would accept whatever fate the providence of God might ordain.

The persecution of the Puritans was the policy on which the men in power had decided. It therefore seemed reasonable to expect that severe repression would begin at once and that it would continue indefinitely and without respite. Events belied

9

such expectations. Persecution was certainly the Puritans' fate, but it was fitfully and often ineffectively applied. A great variety of forces combined to ensure an uncertain but not an unimportant measure of protection. Both the tides of public opinion and the cross-currents of political life considerably affected the position of those who had chosen to become dissenters. At times the factors which govern human relationships modified their situation for good or for ill. Fear and desire for revenge might work in one direction, but good will and the reluctance of decent men to persecute their neighbours worked in the other. At times the nonconformists seemed little more than pawns in the game of high political intrigue, and here again the consequences were sometimes favourable, sometimes the reverse.

No sooner had the Act of Uniformity become law than the nonconformists had their first experience of the unpredictable effect of political forces. In spite of the recent legislation the king encouraged them to hope for lenient treatment. If they petitioned him, his royal clemency would protect them against the full impact of the law. They followed his advice, though they got little for their pains except public abuse.[1] Charles was unable to carry his Council with him; Sheldon's resolute opposition blocked any chance of a general amnesty, and the hopes which the king had encouraged were effectually dashed. Charles, however, did not abandon his attempt to gain the nonconformists a measure of relief. A variety of motives prompted his attitude. Repression was not congenial to his easy-going nature. Ordinary prudence had taught him the folly of exasperating a party that could be as formidable as the Puritans had shown themselves in the past, and Charles had no intention of setting out once more upon his travels. A sound political instinct told him that it might be advantageous to cultivate some group that could provide a counterpoise to the resurgent Anglicanism of the House of Commons. Moreover, an important constitutional issue was at stake. The limits of royal authority were ill-defined. The Civil War had destroyed Stuart absolutism, but in the first flush of the new reign there were many champions of kingly power. Few denied that some kind of dispensing power was inherent in the monarchy, but no one could say how far it extended or what it could achieve. Charles had no intention of abdicating rights if he could safely maintain them.[1] It soon became clear that though the House of Commons was fervidly loyal in its protestations, it would be quick to challenge any infringement of what it regarded as its prerogatives. For a decade Charles made cautious and intermittent attempts to establish his dispensing power, and the intended beneficiaries were the nonconformists. He never pressed the matter to an issue. When opposition became too formidable, he always made a timely and graceful withdrawal. But his efforts gave a measure of unity to the decade which followed the Act of Uniformity, and to the nonconformists they afforded a measure of intermittent and unpredictable relief.

In December 1662 the king renewed his attempt to protect the nonconformists against the persecuting laws. His first Declaration of Indulgence was astute in its phrasing as well as conciliatory in its aim.[2] Parliament, however, was alert to its hidden implications, and had no intention of giving legislative sanction to 'that power of dispensing which he conceived to be in him'. The House of Commons assured the king that his earlier promises of toleration had been wholly contingent on parliamentary ratification, and consequently need burden his conscience no longer. His present proposals, they pointed out, were entirely impractical and would merely create confusion in the state. When a bill was introduced into the House of Lords to give effect to the king's wishes, it encountered strenuous and fatal opposition.[3] In this direction there obviously lay little hope for the nonconformists.

The king might favour lenient courses, but the members of the Cavalier Parliament did not, and the initiative now rested with them. The Corporation Act had removed Puritan magistrates; the Act of Uniformity had silenced Puritan ministers; the Conventicle Act of 1664 struck at the rank and file of nonconformity.[4] Any one over 16 years of age apprehended at a meeting held under pretext of religious worship but not conducted according to the liturgy of the Church of England became subject to the penalties of the Act, provided that more than five persons other than members of the household were present. In the first instance the punishment was to be three months' imprisonment or a fine of not more than five pounds; for a second offence the penalties were doubled; on the third occasion, after trial by jury, the accused was to be sentenced to transportation for seven years to one of the American colonies, Virginia and New England excepted.[1]

Legislation of this kind was partly inspired by revenge, but in equal measure it was prompted by fear. The spectre of the Roundheads constantly haunted the authorities. Royal Proclamations, issued at brief and regular intervals, ordered former Cromwellian soldiers to keep at a safe distance from the capital. To an amazing degree the army of the Commonwealth had been quietly absorbed into civilian life, but the government was reluctant to believe that there was no immediate cause for alarm. Its fears, of course, were fed by a constant stream of rumours, and every important development in the programme of repression was closely related to a fresh outburst of excited reports. Late in 1661 the 'Presbyterian Plot' was disclosed; the sequel was the Corporation Act. In the following year the government announced that it had uncovered the existence of a revolutionary council which was ready to overthrow the monarchy; the excitement thus aroused hastened the passing of the Act of Uniformity. A plot more authentic than most was the northern conspiracy, known as the Kaber Rigg or Farnley Wood Plot. The projected rising was a fiasco, but amid the alarm it created the government pressed through the Conventicle Act.

In sifting the rumours of such revolutionary movements, it is unusually difficult to distinguish between fact and fiction. The temper of the times and the fears of the authorities encouraged rumour-mongers and agents provocateurs, and much of their evidence was plainly worthless. The nonconformists indignantly denied that they were implicated in these conspiracies; indeed, they dismissed both the plots and the proofs of their existence as royalist fabrications, cynically manufactured to serve political ends.[2] The government put forth every effort to establish the guilt of the dissenters, but they found singularly little evidence of the kind on which they could base a prosecution.[3] Even when they brought conspirators to trial, the result did little to clarify the situation. The picture that emerges is as confused as the legal outcome was inconclusive, but there was nothing indefinite about the consequences that accrued to the nonconformists. Everywhere persecution was intensified. Even in places where they had hitherto been relatively undisturbed they found that the pressure upon them was steadily mounting.[1] The stigma of disloyalty was irrevocably attached to them, and with many an Anglican squire it became an article of faith that 'it was impossible for a dissenter not to be a rebel'.[2] This was the sole result achieved by a band of plotters so few in number and so divided among themselves that they had little chance of endangering anybody but their friends. In their own blind way they multiplied the miseries of all nonconformists, and deepened the chasm between churchman and dissenter.[3]

In the year 1665 a further step was taken to perfect the instrument of persecution. The king proposed that all nonconformists should be permitted to purchase freedom of worship by the payment of sums of money which would be regulated by a stipulated schedule. The Anglican retort was the passing of the Five Mile Act. It forbade any ejected minister to live within five miles of any corporate town or of any place where he had formerly exercised his calling. In addition, an oath, framed in particularly drastic terms, was imposed on all nonconformist ministers. Many men who had already suffered severely were driven from their homes. Others concluded that the Act imposed demands to which they could not submit, and they braced themselves to meet the consequences of their disobedience.[4]

The situation was modified, however, by unforeseen events. The Great Plague, which had compelled parliament to meet in Oxford, persuaded many of the conformist clergy to fly from London. The churches stood empty amid a population haunted by the fear of disease and death.[5] This was a challenge which the ejected ministers felt they could not ignore.[6] They took possession of the vacant pulpits, and the people listened meekly to their message of judgement and mercy. In the wake of the Plague came the Fire of London. To the nonconformists it was apparent that they were living in exceptional times. When God had 'a controversy with his people' those who had heard his call could not be silent. It was therefore right that they should meet more publicly than heretofore. The increased congregations they attracted seemed to justify a bolder policy. With remarkable industry they began to erect new meeting houses in which to worship, but sometimes when the building was finished it was seized for the benefit of a parish which had lost its church but had shown no comparable zeal in replacing it.[1]

The increased activity of the nonconformists inevitably attracted attention, but their devoted service during the recent troubles had temporarily checked the persecuting spirit. The posture of foreign affairs brought them further respite. War with Holland reawakened the government's apprehensions about the nonconformists.[2] The Dutch were Calvinists; so were the dissenters. Strong sympathies, created by loyalty to a common faith, already bound them together. To declare war on the Dutch while maintaining persecution against the dissenters would inevitably strengthen the ties which united them, and would consolidate a nucleus of disaffection at home.[3] Moreover, there was a strong Puritan tradition in the navy; repression at home might easily breed disaffection afloat.[4] On all counts it seemed expedient to suspend the pressure against the nonconformists. Other factors also favoured greater leniency. Clarendon, conscious of the forces arrayed against him, had tried to strengthen his position by co-operating with the resurgent Anglicanism of the Cavalier Parliament, and the price of the alliance had been a persecuting policy.[5] With Clarendon's fall, new leaders had come to power. The members of the Cabal were quite prepared to use religious factors in the intricate game of political manœuvre, but their sympathies were not the same as Clarendon's.[6] Their attitude was much more flexible than his; for a variety of reasons they were predisposed to provide a larger respite for the nonconformists.[7]

The temporary immunity which they enjoyed was reflected in the greater confidence which they displayed. In towns where they had traditionally been strong they discovered that they could circumvent the Corporation Act. Gradually they regained something of their former influence. Anglican complaints of their impudence multiplied.[1] From Yarmouth, Gloucester, Taunton and Dover came variants of the same story; nonconformists were increasing their activities in all directions. They were meeting publicly and in large numbers, and the local authorities were either unable to check them or unwilling to do so.[2] Often the reports were forwarded by informers who hoped that their zeal would be suitably rewarded, but when every allowance has been made for exaggerations inspired by cupidity and self-importance, it is apparent that the nonconformists were turning to good account the respite they were enjoying. Some talked confidently of the imminence of toleration; others were convinced that before long they would once more be members of the established church.[3]

The time seemed opportune to raise the wider question of their relationship with the Church of England. An influential wing of nonconformity had been reluctant to regard ejection as irrevocable. Baxter and his friends considered it a duty not to cut themselves off from the services of the established church, and they were scrupulous to arrange their private meetings at times which did not conflict with public worship.[4] Though they could not fully conform to the ways of the church, they did not consider themselves wholly divorced from its life. Nor had they abandoned the hope that circumstances might yet arise which would make it possible for them once more to occupy the places which they had relinquished.[5] Within the church itself there were many leaders who hoped that recent events could be reversed and the broken unity of the nation's religious life restored. Early in 1667 an approach was made from the Anglican side. The initial steps were taken by Lord Keeper Bridgman, but it soon became apparent that the moving spirit in the matter was Bishop Wilkins of Chester. He and his chaplain held a series of conferences with Richard Baxter, Thomas Manton and William Bates. The proposal under consideration aimed at the comprehension of the Presbyterians; they would be instituted to livings by a formula which might be regarded as reordination but need not be interpreted as such. Certain ceremonies would be treated as optional, and modifications would be made in the liturgy. Baxter, who had been particularly fertile in suggestions, remained dissatisfied on various points, but the bill which Sir Matthew Hale drew up (and showed to Baxter) would have brought back to the church (so Baxter believed) the great majority of those who had left it.[1]

The measure was still-born. Without a word of warning, the negotiations were abruptly suspended. Anglicans who had promoted the scheme hastened to disown it. Public opinion veered sharply in a different direction. When parliament assembled the House of Commons forbade the introduction of any bill designed to promote comprehension, and before long it was eagerly discussing more effective means of punishing dissenters.[2] The fury of the members was so vehement that the Secretary of State felt obliged to warn them that their enthusiasm was out-stripping their discretion.[3] The prorogation of parliament tem-porarily checked this outburst of Anglican zeal, but it was obvious to the nonconformists that their respite would be brief. They had found the whole episode a sobering and disillusioning experience. Perhaps Baxter was right, remarked Manton, to regard all Anglican offers with suspicion.[4]

Parliament made slow progress with its new act against conventicles. Adjournments and prorogations caused frequent interruptions, and the debates were spread over many months. They reflected a more generous temper than the first heat of Anglican indignation might have promised, but their general tenor neither affected the final vote nor influenced the character of the bill itself.[5] The Conventicle Act of 1670 was widely regarded as a particularly severe measure. Andrew Marvell described it as 'the quintessence of arbitrary malice', and it is clear that a number of other members of parliament agreed with him.[6] The king showed no enthusiasm for the Act, but was powerless to prevent its passing; he well knew that it was 'the price of money'.[7]

'An Act to Prevent and Suppress Seditious Conventicles' aimed at providing 'further and more speedy remedies against the growing dangerous practices of seditious sectaries' who used the plea of 'tender consciences' as a screen behind which to plot revolution.[1] One or more justices of the peace, by confession or on the oath of two witnesses or 'by notorious evidence and circumstance of the fact', could make a record of each offence which would in law be equivalent to a conviction. Legal procedure was considerably simplified; one man, acting on what might be little more than hearsay, could impose a sentence that might easily ruin the victim. It is true that the initial fines were relatively small—five shillings was the penalty for a first conviction for attendance at a conventicle and for subsequent offences the amount was doubled. But the Act also provided that the fines of those who could not pay might be imposed on those who could, provided that on no single occasion was the amount to exceed ten pounds. But those more directly responsible for holding the conventicle were subject to far higher penalties. The minister himself was to be fined twenty pounds for the first offence, and twice that amount on each subsequent occasion. The person at whose house the meeting was held was also liable to a fine of twenty pounds, and these larger amounts, like those levied for mere attendance, could be reassigned to those deemed able to pay them. A nonconformist of substance could quickly be ruined, and the Act provided that any offender who could not pay the required amounts should have his property seized and sold. Most sinister of all was the power which the Act placed in the hands of informers. The dregs of the community were not only encouraged to ruin their nonconformist neighbours but were enabled to compel the officers of the law to act as their accomplices.

The Conventicle Act of 1670 was a serious blow to the nonconformists, but they did not meekly submit to it. Nothing could illustrate their resurgent confidence more clearly than the vigour with which they resisted the pressures of the Act. In some places the magistrates reported that the opposition of the dissenters was so resolute that it was virtually impossible to enforce the laws against them.[2] Even in London the authorities were apprehensive about the probable results of applying the provisions of the new Act.[3] Such resistance might be courageous; it was certain to be ineffective. The forces arrayed against the dissenters were too strong to be successfully challenged. It soon became apparent that the new law was skilfully framed to impose the severest penalties that were likely to be enforced. Probably no other single act caused as much suffering among nonconformist communities as the Conventicle Act of 1670.[1]

The outlook appeared unusually gloomy, but the sequel showed how largely the fate of the nonconformists was determined by the cross-currents of political life. While parliament was in session they had little respite; at such times the persecuting acts were most likely to be strictly enforced, and the House of Commons even began to discuss the need of yet more stringent measures against dissent. But in the ensuing months the attention of parliament was often distracted by other issues. The two Houses were engaged in an unseemly and unprofitable wrangle regarding their respective privileges, and the king had an excellent excuse for frequent prorogations. And whenever parliament rose, the pressure on the nonconformists tended to relax. It was becoming clear that many of the magistrates had little enthusiasm for their persecuting duties; unless prodded from time to time they were apt to be remiss. For the moment the desire for revenge had spent itself. Oppressing inoffensive neighbours was a distasteful task, and the justices fully realised that they could look for little encouragement from the king.[2]

At this stage the king's attitude seemed likely to exert a particularly decisive influence. It was widely rumoured that he intended to grant religious freedom on terms more generous than any contemplated heretofore, and there seemed no reason to doubt the reliability of the reports.[3] Charles had his own reasons for the course he now adopted. His secret treaty with France committed him to war with Holland, and war abroad could not be reconciled with persecution at home. He believed that constitutionally he had the power to grant the nonconformists exemption from the penal laws irrespective of the attitude of parliament, and he decided to put the matter to the test. In March 1672 he issued his second Declaration of Indulgence, and almost simultaneously declared war on Holland. The opening sentences of the Declaration stated in the most cogent terms the futility of persecution.

Ample experience had proved its utter ineffectiveness, and Charles announced by virtue of his dispensing power all penal laws against nonconformists would be suspended. Roman Catholics would be free to worship only in their own homes. Protestant dissenters, provided they secured licences both for their minister and for their place of worship, might meet in public.[1]

Among the nonconformists the reaction to the Declaration was mixed. The concessions granted to the Catholics caused some concern, and there was considerable doubt about the validity of the king's use of his dispensing power.[2] And whatever might be the rights and wrongs of his constitutional position, the House of Commons would certainly dispute his claim, and would probably victimise the beneficiaries of his Indulgence. But whether the king was legally entitled to do so or not, he had offered the nonconformists an opportunity which it seemed foolish to decline. Even those who were most critical of the Declaration itself decided to make use of the liberty it afforded. And many—perhaps a considerable majority—were not in the least disturbed by constitutional qualms.[3] To them the supremely important thing was that after enforced silence they would now have full liberty to preach. From individuals and from congregations grateful addresses of thanks began to pour in to the king.[4] Then, with little delay, the nonconformists applied for the licences which would protect their meetings against disturbance. The Quakers, of course, ignored the Declaration. In their eyes the king had no more right to concede freedom of worship than he had to withhold it, and many of the Anabaptists shared their view.[5] But most of the nonconformists adopted a less uncompromising attitude. What the king offered they were glad to accept.

From the records of the licence office there emerges a clear picture of the character of dissent. Most of the ejected ministers were among those who received authorisation to preach, but new leaders had also arisen. The congregations were usually small enough to be accommodated in private homes, but the licences specify a great variety of meeting places. Some groups had buildings specially erected for the purpose; others met in oast houses or in barns. Occasionally the nonconformists worshipped in private chapels. In a few instances they had actually secured the use of various kinds of public buildings.[1]

The Declaration of Indulgence had important consequences for nonconformist life. Many societies which had hitherto maintained a precarious existence now felt that they were justified in organising on a more permanent basis, and the records of many of the older nonconformist congregations date from this period.[2] The sense of sharing in a distinctive corporate life grew stronger; for all their differences among themselves, the dissenters were becoming more conscious of themselves as a body distinct from the national church and organised apart from it. Even the Presbyterians, who were reluctant to do anything that might suggest that their separation from the Church of England was permanent, began to admit (by implication at least) that they must take steps to perpetuate their existence. For the first time since the Restoration they began to ordain men to the ministry.[3]

The nonconformists realised that their immunity from persecution was precarious and would probably be brief. On that score the indigation and dismay of the Anglicans left them in little doubt.[4] Complaints arose on every side that waverers were forsaking the church for the meeting house.[5] On the first possible occasion, the defenders of the establishment would certainly clamour for the cancellation of privileges which so clearly operated to their disadvantage. But the Declaration of Indulgence provided an interval of security sufficient for the nonconformists to consolidate their life. They acquired a degree of confidence and strength which made it impossible subsequently to suppress them. There could no longer be any doubt that they would constitute a permanent element in the national life. For this reason Anglicans like Stillingfleet felt justified in dating the real beginnings of nonconformity from the year 1672.[6] The results of a decade of persecution had been inconclusive; the results of a few months of freedom were irrevocable.[7] In other respects also the Declaration of Indulgence marked a turning point in the history of Restoration nonconformity. One phase was clearly ending; another would soon begin.

The Dutch War proved as unpopular as it was unsuccessful. The king's financial needs compelled him to summon parliament, and his wiser counsellors realised that its members would assemble in no conciliatory mood. One of the first acts of the House of Commons was to protest vehemently against the Declaration of Indulgence; penal laws could be suspended only by parliamentary action, and the king had indubitably exceeded his rights.[1] Whatever the champions of the dispensing power might say, there was only one course open to the king. Charles was shrewd enough to see that capitulation was inevitable and he withdrew the Declaration of Indulgence.[2]

The House of Commons had protested against an unconstitutional action, not against the religious freedom which that action had conferred. The same ends could better be achieved in other ways, and the members had promised that as soon as the illegality was removed they would themselves provide relief for nonconformists. In due course the proposed measure was introduced; it commanded a large measure of assent, and was duly passed.[3] It was blocked, however, by the House of Lords. Before an agreement on the matter could be reached between the two Houses, the king adjourned parliament, and the bill automatically died.

The nonconformists now found themselves in an unenviable plight. The protection afforded by the king's Declaration had been cancelled; that promised by the House of Commons had not been conferred.[4] The course they ought to follow was far from clear. After some initial doubt, they decided to meet in public as before. They still held the licences issued by the king. These had not been recalled, even though the Indulgence which authorised them had been cancelled. Legally the licences had no validity, but the justices of the peace were undecided how to regard them, and for some time the nonconformists continued to enjoy a considerable measure of immunity.[5]

A change in the alignment of political forces was gradually creating a new situation. The results of his alliance with France had proved disappointing to the king. The Cabal and its policies were unpopular, and Charles found it expedient henceforth to rely on an alliance with parliament and the Anglican Church.

21

The minister selected to accomplish this change of policy was Sir Thomas Osborne, better known as the Earl of Danby.

Danby's accession to power roughly marks a watershed in the reign of Charles II. The king abandoned his efforts to save the nonconformists from the consequences of their convictions; in future any attempts to shield them from the persecuting acts would come from other quarters. New issues began to engage public attention, and a new pattern in public affairs began to emerge. In these developments, the nonconformists were intimately involved. They could not remain untouched by the fear of popery, and they were gradually implicated in the various expedients which that fear inspired. Political parties were in their infancy. As potential allies, the nonconformists were too important to be ignored, yet they were too inexperienced to save themselves from the worst consequences of their involvement.

For some years the fear of popery had been steadily gaining ground.[1] The public knew nothing of Charles's secret treaty with France, and consequently could not guess that he had promised both to become a Catholic himself and to promote in his kingdom the spread of that faith, but the suspicion was growing that some such project must be afoot. Alarm found evidence on which to feed, and when the Popish Plot was divulged the country was in no mood to examine with detachment the evidence produced. Something approaching national hysteria was the result, and it affected the nonconformists in a variety of ways. It deflected attention from them and focused it on the papists. Persecution throve on the cry of treason, and here were conspirators whose guilt the nation was not disposed to doubt. The preoccupation with the Popish Plot consequently afforded the Protestant dissenters a greater measure of freedom and security. At the same time it gave them a feeling that they were once more participating in the nation's life.[2] They shared to the full the traditional English dread of popery. Antipathy to Rome was one of the most vigorous strains in their tradition; any cry that Protestantism was endangered found a ready echo in their hearts.[3] But if Protestantism were truly in peril, it behoved its parties to draw more closely together; unity became an obvious measure of defence.

Both churchmen and dissenters appreciated this fact, and prominent Anglicans reopened negotiations with the leaders of the nonconformists. Proposals were advanced and alternative schemes were discussed. Bills to provide for the comprehension of dissenters were introduced more than once in the House of Lords. All such plans proved abortive, but discussions did not wholly cease until the fear that inspired them had subsided.[1]

The formation of political parties was one of the most characteristic features of a turbulent period of English domestic history. The atmosphere which prevailed gave to the struggle between the two factions a frenzied bitterness which finally proved disastrous to both. The excitement which the popish question engendered provided the setting within which this struggle developed and had fateful consequences for many of the participants. The Earl of Shaftesbury recognised the immense possibilities which lay in exploiting the prevailing fear of Rome. 'No Popery' provided a cry to which Englishmen were certain to respond. The exclusion of an unpopular heir to the throne afforded an immediate political objective. In the nonconformist groups Shaftesbury saw the means of consolidating a political body which would be able to challenge the king and his supporters.[2] By 1676 he had emerged as the leader of a party with a clearly defined policy. He advocated parliamentary restraints on arbitrary government, religious toleration (in a form as yet undefined) and freedom from dependence on France. Such a programme appealed strongly to the nonconformists. They had resisted royal absolutism; they had suffered from harsh laws designed to suppress their distinctive ways of worship, and they were fervently opposed to popery.

In the succeeding years they were drawn more and more closely into alliance with the Whigs.[3] When Shaftesbury selected Monmouth as his claimant to the throne, the nonconformists made him a kind of Protestant hero.[4] They used their influence to promote the election of Whig candidates.[5] They were more and more inclined to gauge the prospects of godliness by the fortunes of the Whig party.[6] In this they were affected by the fevered state of mind which had infected the whole of English political life. When Shaftesbury astutely turned the anti-popish frenzy to party purposes he carried with him the approbation of the non-conformists. When Charles dissolved the Long Parliament of the Restoration, the Whigs won three elections in rapid succession. The nonconformists were more than fascinated observers; so far as possible they were eager participants.[1] They felt that they were sharing in the victory of a party which was certain to give them the largest possible measure of relief. When parliament began to consider ways of improving the lot of dissenters, they believed that they were on the point of reaping the benefits of co-operation. They did not see that though they might share the successes of their friends they were also committed to their follies. A wild irresponsibility had infused itself into English public life.[2] The Whigs were apparently intent on using their advantage in ways that seemed destructive of national unity. A revulsion of public feeling took place. When the king dismissed his last parliament, he could strike at the Whigs with impunity because they had clearly alienated the goodwill of moderate men.

This did not mean that the Tories were likely to be wiser in their day of power than the Whigs had been. They, too, had been infected with the virus of irresponsibility and had prepared the way for their ultimate downfall. But with their enemies in full retreat they could turn to immediate advantage the opportunity they possessed. They enjoyed royal favour at a time when the king found that he could dispense with parliament. During the closing years of his reign he relied on French financial aid and on the support of Anglicans and Tories.[3] He was quite prepared to acquiesce in the consequences of his new alliance. He felt no desire, still less any obligation, to defend the nonconformists against persecution. By their recent behaviour they had forfeited his good will, and if his present friends wished to punish them, he had no wish to put obstacles in their way.[4]

The times were ripe for a new outbreak of persecution. The struggle over the Exclusion Bill had fanned the flames of royalist zeal. Enthusiasm for the legitimate heir had supplanted fear of popery, and the violence of political feeling commended extreme measures. Those who were eager to penalise the nonconformists were quick to detect that they need fear no hindrance from high quarters. Church authorities found that the courts showed a new readiness to co-operate in proceedings against dissenters. Informers saw unprecedented opportunities for pillaging their neighbours and hastened to make full use of their chance.[1]

A number of factors contributed to the vehemence of the Tory reaction; each of them intensified the unpopularity of the dissenters. The challenge to the principle of legitimacy had heightened royalist sentiment; the traditional enemies of the crown were the heirs of the Roundheads. Passive obedience was preached with new fervour; the Puritans supplied the arch example of the wickedness of resistance to constituted authority. The fear of political disorder had been revived by recent controversies; that fear had been firmly rooted in the consciousness of the English people by the Great Rebellion.

Once revived, the persecuting spirit was quick to seize on pretexts for yet severer courses. The corporate towns had been the strongholds of nonconformity. When Charles began to revoke and amend their charters, the dissenters joined heartily in the protest against this attack on ancient privileges. In this was detected the evidence of a subversive purpose. Repression always justified itself by an appeal to the danger of sedition, and rumours of nonconformist conspiracies began to fly. When the Rye House Plot was brought to light, the truth of the charges seemed to be fully established. The nonconformists denied their complicity, but there was no doubt that some of the minor conspirators had once moved in Cromwellian and Anabaptist circles, and public opinion required no further proof that the whole group was implicated.[2] The folklore peculiar to persecution was revived in its entirety: dissenters had always been traitors, and their existence was a menace to the state.

The nonconformists were suffering the penalty for their support of the Whig programme, and they were left to pay the price alone. The great magnates had retired to their estates; lesser political figures had capitulated and made their peace at Court.[3] For the nonconformists there was no protection. Magistrates proved their zeal by searching out meetings for worship and arresting those who were present. Fines of staggering magnitude were levied on the more prosperous nonconformists. Their houses were pillaged and their goods were seized. Even the humblest members found no immunity. Those who owned little lost it all; they were often driven from their employment, and in some places they were cut off from public assistance of any kind. Tradesmen were ruined. In some districts the dislocation of business was serious, and the cry was raised that the economic prosperity of the country was threatened. In the streets the nonconformists were exposed to such violent abuse that their leaders hesitated to venture abroad.[1] In their homes they were at the mercy of informers and of the turbulent rabble that followed at the heels of those harpies. Ever since the Restoration the nonconformists had intermittently been persecuted; never had their sufferings been so bitter or so prolonged.

Gradually meetings ceased to be held in public. The Quakers, it is true, formed a notable exception. When their places of worship were destroyed, they met amid the rubble. When the men and women were imprisoned, the children kept up the meeting in the streets.[2] Few of the nonconformists felt that they were called to maintain so uncompromising a witness. They met secretly at unaccustomed times and places. When they could no longer assemble with safety in the towns, they gathered in the fields or in the woods.[3] Before long the foundations of their corporate life seemed in danger of disintegrating, and still there was no prospect of relief. Then Charles II died.

The accession of James II promised no substantial improvement in the lot of the nonconformists. Neither their convictions nor their past associations were such as to commend them to the new king. As a fanatical Catholic he would have little sympathy with the Puritan aspirations, and he was not likely to have forgotten their share in the Exclusion agitation. At first there seemed no reason to expect that James would alter in any significant respect the pattern which had been established in the last years of his brother's reign. He assured the Anglicans that he would maintain their privileges, and his words afforded little hope to the nonconformists. The new parliament, strongly Tory and fervently

26

loyalist, petitioned the king for a stricter enforcement of the laws against dissenters, and there seemed little likelihood that he would disappoint them.[1]

The fate that individual nonconformists might expect was shown by Richard Baxter's trial before Chief Justice Jeffreys. The charges against the prisoner had singularly little plausibility, but under existing conditions even plausibility was not necessary in order to secure a conviction. The judge abandoned any pretence of impartiality. He abused the prisoner, berated the counsel for the defence, and intimidated the jury.[2] If a figure like Baxter, so eminent for his learning and so highly respected for his integrity, could be treated with such blatant brutality, humbler men had little prospect of securing justice. During the next few months the nonconformists had no protection against the worst vagaries of the judicial system. Persecution continued, severe and unabated.

While the new reign was still young, the Monmouth rebellion momentarily raised certain irresponsible hopes. In the south-western counties it laid an all-too-firm foundation for disaster. Monmouth posed as a Protestant champion, a deliverer from popery and persecution. Many nonconformists were willing to take him at his word.[3] Wiser men knew that he could never be the instrument of their deliverance, but in a time of crisis not everyone can be wise.[4] In their simplicity the weavers and yeomen of the south-west trooped to Monmouth's banner and were overwhelmed in his defeat. After the king's army had finished its work, Judge Jeffreys came through the districts affected on that tour of judicial murder long remembered as the 'Bloody Assize'. In retrospect Baxter claimed that the rebellion was not a rising of the nonconformists;[5] technically this is true, but the results for their congregations could scarcely have been more serious. Strong societies were almost obliterated; their records have vanished because their life was virtually stamped out.[6] The savagery with which the rising was suppressed sent a shudder of horror through the country. It prompted the first stirrings of that mood of angry disillusionment which finally proved so fatal to the king.

For nearly two years, persecution continued unabated. Then the requirements of royal policy caused a drastic change. James could suppress the nonconformists as long as he could count on Anglican support of his plans. To aggrandise the Catholics he needed the co-operation either of the churchmen or of the dissenters. Of late, however, events had made it clear that passive obedience, that cherished theory of the Church of England, would provide no dependable foundation for royal schemes. James had assumed that there could be no limits to the acquiescence of churchmen who made such emphatic protestations of submission to his will. He now began to learn that they had deceived him because they had first deceived themselves. James expected them to sacrifice the prerogatives of the Church of England in order to promote the growth of Roman Catholicism; they declined to play the role assigned them. When they disappointed him, James turned to the nonconformists instead. He knew that they had no cause to feel grateful to their persecutors; he assumed that they would welcome deliverance for themselves. With their assistance he would promote his purposes; as a first step he would attack the Church of England.[1]

In April 1687 James issued his first Declaration of Indulgence. The experience of four reigns, he said, proved the utter ineffectiveness of persecution. Uniformity in religion had been attempted; it had never been achieved. In the light of such a record of consistent failure only one course seemed feasible: all penal laws against all dissenters must be suspended. In spite of the apparent plausibility of the Declaration, its true purpose was apparent to all. No one believed that James II was genuinely concerned about religious liberty; he had adopted it as a temporary expedient for furthering the Roman Catholic cause, and he would abandon it as soon as it had served his immediate ends. For the nonconformists the Declaration created an uncomfortable dilemma. Emissaries from the king urged them to acknowledge his favours with addresses of thanks, and after considerable hesitation a few of them did so. Meanwhile prominent Anglicans warned them of the dangers so transparently present in the policy which James was pursuing. As Halifax pointed out, the king's determination to benefit the Catholics was incompatible with his promise to aid the nonconformists; his assurances would not survive the circumstances which gave them birth, and common prudence alone should warn the dissenters against placing any reliance on his word. And in the Church of England—so the same shrewd observer reminded them—they could look in future for a very different spirit from that which had prevailed in the past.

For the most part, the nonconformists decided that they could do no less than take advantage of the freedom offered them, and that they would refrain from any action which might suggest approval of the king's policy.[1] James was disappointed with their attitude, but he had plans to use them in other ways. He was systematically removing Anglicans from positions of trust, and he hoped to persuade the nonconformists to take their places.[2] They had no intention of yielding to his blandishments, and his efforts to enlist their support were a dismal failure.

Meanwhile the king had been systematically teaching his subjects that so long as he was on the throne all their rights and privileges were in jeopardy. By his second Declaration of Indulgence he brought matters to a head. He insisted that a document whose terms were abhorrent to Anglicans should be read in all parish churches. When the clergy with one accord refused to do so, seven of the bishops presented a petition defending their refusal. In his anger the king sent the bishops to the Tower and committed them for trial. In this crucial development, the nonconformists were not directly involved, but they made no secret of their sympathies. Their leaders visited the bishops in the Tower; when the king called them to task for supporting his opponents, they frankly stated their position and defended the stand they had taken.[3]

In other quarters their attitude was noted with grateful appreciation. The leaders of the Church of England were beginning to manifest the more cordial spirit which Halifax had predicted would henceforth govern their relations with dissenters. The popish peril had persuaded the Protestants of England that the beliefs on which they were agreed were vastly more important than the questions about which they were divided. Highly placed

Anglicans cautiously sought assurances that the nonconformists did not intend to profit by the difficulties of the Church of England, and they received a highly gratifying answer.[1] In due course Archbishop Sancroft took in hand the task of consolidating the good will which had been aroused. He initiated a revision of the liturgy, and began to work on a scheme which, by modifying ceremonial requirements, would make it easier for the dissenters to conform. In the articles which he distributed to the clergy of his province he directed them to treat the nonconformists with courtesy. A conciliatory spirit, he said, might win back to the church those who had left it; at least it would maintain that measure of unity which they had now achieved.[2] On all sides generous promises were freely made. No one questioned that toleration would be conceded. Many assumed that a scheme for comprehension would immediately be revived and would be carried to fulfilment without delay.

To the nonconformists such cordiality was almost bewildering. Only a few months previously they had been reviled and persecuted. For a generation their only respite from repression had been gained by the unpredictable requirements of political intrigue. With incredulity they observed the transformation which James II had achieved in the position of every major religious group in the country. So drastic a change could only be the evidence that a wise Providence was at work. With gratitude the nonconformists welcomed the relief that had been granted them, and with high expectation looked forward to a future that seemed bright with hope.[3]

CHAPTER II

THE PATTERN OF PERSECUTION

THE Restoration opened a period, lasting for a whole generation, in which persecution was the lot of English nonconformists. Admittedly the pressure was not consistently applied, nor was it uniformly severe. Even where the policy of repression was most relentlessly enforced, the sufferers felt that they could clearly distinguish the gusts in the gale which swept past them. By November 1681 a Bristol congregation that kept its records with some care had counted ten different persecutions, and much was still to come.[1] In some parts of the country the local authorities felt little enthusiasm for the official policy, and so showed little zeal in applying it. Some ministers were never arrested, and certain congregations were seldom disturbed. The sporadic character of the persecution must be borne in mind, but so must the fact that a single outbreak could cause untold suffering and ruin scores of inoffensive people.

When persecution overtook the Puritan, it came as an intensely personal experience, and naturally enough he described it in terms of what it meant to him. But even as he enumerated his sufferings—as he disclosed his fears or reaffirmed his faith—we can distinguish in the background the social, political and religious forces that inspired and sustained the policy of persecution from which he suffered.

The attempt to suppress religious dissent could claim a long ancestry and an impressive record of theoretical defence. It is true that in recent years the intellectual assumptions underlying a persecuting policy had been attacked with increasing zeal, but as yet a relatively small proportion of the population had been converted. Presbyterians as well as Anglicans had denounced toleration as a dangerous and subversive doctrine, and both sides appealed to political theories which were widely held. It was

31

generally believed that the life of a community was indivisible, and since the church was the religious expression of the corporate life, its unity was the condition of the nation's solidarity and strength. To allow cleavage in the church was to encourage weakness in the state. Religious disagreements had always been the pretext for, if not actually the cause of, civil wars, and 'the experience of all ages' proved that 'differences in religion always ended in blows'.[1] Consequently when a bishop was particularly harsh toward dissenters, his justification lay in his 'love to the repose and welfare of the government',[2] and a member of parliament could resist what promised to prove a conciliatory measure by asserting that he 'never knew a toleration which did not require an army to keep all quiet'.[3] This is, in its simplest form, the argument which was amplified and embellished in a hundred ways and which represented the core of the Anglican position. It justified the policy of persecution, though probably it was only in a minor degree responsible for it.

Even those who were familiar with the theory often acted from simpler but more forceful motives. Throughout the period, the parish priests of England played an important role in maintaining the pressure on the dissenters, but they seldom relied on the arguments so generally invoked in controversy. Sometimes they wanted to see the sects suppressed because the position of the church would then be relatively stronger,[4] and it may be that where the conventicles were full and the churches empty, a touch of jealousy prompted the priest to action.[5] A man who is suffering for his faith may find it hard to judge dispassionately the motives of his persecutor, but very often the parish rector used words or committed deeds which persuaded his victims that he was contending for his own interests rather than for the true faith.[6] And, indeed, he often believed that he was. Even from the accounts written by the sufferers, it is clear that the clergy saw in a purely legal light certain issues which to their critics involved a religious witness. To the Quakers, it was a matter of conscience to refuse the payment of tithes, whereas quite manifestly the rector regarded their claim to immunity as an impudent invasion of a right guaranteed by law.[7] The man who withheld tithes was

32

robbing the parson of what was his due; he was therefore as truly a thief as any pickpocket, and deserved the punishment which thieves received. This probably explains the extreme measures taken to recover trifling sums; on both sides it was a matter of conscience, but neither could understand the attitude of the other.

In many cases persecution was prompted by motives which were social and political rather than religious. The Restoration meant a dramatic reversal of fortunes. Men who for years had suffered severely suddenly found themselves in a position to repay their persecutors in kind. To forgive and forget might have been wiser, but that presupposed a measure of magnanimity which most Royalists could neither envisage nor command. Their plea might be for '*The Law of God* and *The Law of the King*', but it was clear that malice and revenge played a large part in prompting the clamour for the repression of dissent.[1] For twenty years, the vials of bitterness had been filling; now they poured out without restraint on any who could be held responsible for the indignities suffered in the past.[2] Moreover, the same turn of the wheel which gave former victims the power to persecute made it expedient for certain men to prove that, whatever the record might suggest, they were not to be identified with the recent régime. Sir Richard Browne, one of the most notorious of London persecutors, was a former Roundhead intent on showing that he was now a Royalist of unimpeachable zeal,[3] and many a lesser figure was equally busy working his passage home.

Certain people who had actually suffered little during the Interregnum had chafed a good deal under the restrictions incidental to the 'rule of the saints', and they welcomed the chance to throw off irksome restraints. There is no doubt that many Puritans had not hesitated to classify as 'godless' those who differed from them, and condemnation by the one side had awakened an answering contempt in the other. The ministers who had been most zealous in enforcing a strict system of outward piety were the first victims of the revulsion of public feeling. One type of person was reacting against the standards of another: while shaking off one kind of yoke, he was busy substituting another of his own devising. Differences in outlook tended to merge into distinctions of class, and that, in turn, was beginning to affect the cleavage between party and party. Before the period ended, this entailed serious results. In the first years of the Restoration, persecution was often prompted by nothing more than dislike of an uncongenial outlook; by 1680, denominations were becoming entangled in the strife of political parties. Because the churchman was so often a Tory, the dissenter was apt to become a Whig; when nonconformists used their influence to sway elections, their opponents invoked the penal laws to punish them.[1]

But in the intermediate period, before the lines were sharply drawn, a good deal of actual suffering was caused by what was little more than rowdyism and love of horse-play. With the more boisterous elements in the community, the Puritan had never been a popular figure, and the mob was all the more willing to vent on him the irrational cruelty which so often marks the reactions of a crowd. People who were ignorant of the law and indifferent to its actual intention would respond quickly enough when incited by those whose lead they normally followed; a word of encouragement from the magistrate or the clergyman sufficed, but what began in sport could not always be checked before it had ended in tragedy.

Among the discreditable motives that inspired persecution, the prospect of gain must count as one. The offer of a reward was enough to stir to action a constable who would otherwise have remained inert, and the evil crowd of informers hovered like a flock of harpies on the fringes of the dissenting groups. Many openly boasted that they would live in luxury on the spoils of nonconformists, and to see a Quaker riding a good horse or a Puritan harvesting a good crop was hailed as the foretaste of certain profit.[2]

In many cases the persecutor acted because he had no alternative. A magistrate reluctant to harry inoffensive folk might find that pressure from a fellow justice of the peace was compelling him to act. The character of the bishop was another factor which strongly affected the attitude of local authorities, and the non-conformists of Bristol noted that they suffered most when Guy

Carleton was pressing for their extirpation.[1] Frequently a clergy-man was busy stirring up the justices to act, and though sometimes he only gained contempt, often he achieved results. And for most of the period there lurked in the background the spectre of the insatiable informer, armed by the law with power to compel the magistrates to act and restrained by neither fear nor shame from using this advantage.

Among the varied influences responsible for persecution, fear probably held the most important place. The events of the Interregnum were very recent, and the Royalists were not likely to forget how often the Roundheads had routed them in battle. In every conventicle the authorities were apt to see a gathering of former Ironsides,[2] and in the early years of the Restoration one proclamation after another reflected the uneasiness of the government about the aims and activities of the disbanded soldiers of the Commonwealth. Chief Justice Bridgman defined a conventicle as 'a meeting together to plot against the King and state',[3] and there was at least some justification for his attitude. It was reported to the government that those who met at a con-venticle near London lamented the king's return and talked freely of the prospects of greater freedom, while an injudicious man let it be known that he kept a record of the acts of judges and magi-strates for use in the days when the tables would again be turned.[4] There is no doubt that some of the wilder sects needed to be watched, but there is also little question that the apprehensions of the rulers bore no relation to the extent of the actual danger. But unquestionably fear in high quarters produced greater vigilance at every level. Judges and magistrates felt they must watch for any suspicious signs, and at many points the peculiari-ties of nonconformists merely confirmed fears already aroused. Why should Quakers refuse to take the oath unless they had something to hide? 'The times being dangerous', remarked a judge to Francis Howgill in 1663, 'and things having now a worse appearance than at the last assizes, and people, under pre-tence of conscience, violating the laws and hatching treasons and rebellions, although I have nothing of that kind to charge against you, yet seeing you did refuse to take the oath of allegiance at the last assizes, the law doth presume such persons to be enemies to the King and government.'[1] The prevalence of such fears led magistrates to place a false construction on perfectly innocent acts. A letter arranging a meeting for worship might be interpreted as clear evidence of plotting, while the mere fact that those taken at a conventicle had come from widely separated districts was enough to arouse suspicion.[2] When sedition was such a common charge, it was necessary for nonconformists to defend themselves and to declare with some vigour that 'we are clear in the sight of God, angels and men from all hellish plots and traitorous conspiracies, and from all murderous designs and undertakings'.[3]

Whatever might be its cause, persecution began to cast its shadow across the life of the Puritan almost from the moment that the Restoration took place. Even those who rejoiced at the king's return noted anxiously the signs of approaching trouble. As they saw their opportunities of worship first restricted, then removed; as they noted that hostility was hardening into active opposition, and as they saw plans laid for their overthrow, they began to search their hearts in earnest. Had their past failures brought upon them present trials?—and, with worse in store, would they be strong enough to stand in the day of testing? If in God's providence trouble were to be their lot, would he permit anything amid which he would not also sustain them? Already the faint-hearted were beginning to falter. When Joseph Alleine appointed a day of humiliation, he was shocked that so few responded and he began to reason with the timorous one by one. Before long, those who feared persecution began to slip stealthily to their meetings in order to avoid detection. Many refused all such stratagems, and others did not need them. Some were safe for a time because the immunity of popish recusants made the justices hesitant to punish Protestants. Special reasons gave others a temporary respite, and even men so prominent as Giles Firmin and Richard Gilpin were undisturbed because their neighbours valued so highly their skill as physicians of the body that they were prepared to overlook their idiosyncracies as physicians of the soul.[4]

The storm of persecution did not break in its full force immediately, but premonitory gusts gave warning of its approach.

36

Before official action was taken, local hostility resulted in the outbreak of unorganised petty persecution. Individuals were harassed in minor but vexatious ways—though when a man's crops were destroyed his neighbours' antipathy might seem disastrous enough. Before long magistrates began to warn nonconformists of the consequences that would overtake those who persisted in dissent, and the sequel to such admonitions was usually the issuing of warrants for arrest. Even then, the blow might be temporarily parried. When friends warned you that a warrant had been granted for your arrest, you might successfully evade the officers of the law, and sympathisers might be glad to help you to do so. You might decide that it was expedient to stay at home or go abroad only in disguise; you might lock your door and submit to a virtual state of siege, rather than run the risk of enemies slipping in to apprehend you; you might choose to keep your shop shut on market day rather than open it and face the certainty that the constables would enter.[1]

This cat-and-mouse game could be played neither extensively nor for long. For some, the actual impact of persecution followed close upon the Restoration. Though the new laws had not yet been passed, there was old legislation which would serve the turn, and ill-wishers were quick to embarrass the Puritan preacher. As he mounted the pulpit, a minister would be tendered a Book of Common Prayer, and if he declined to use it, the magistrates were prompt to proceed against him. Persecution was often enthusiastic rather than skilfully devised, but though a man might escape punishment he was subject to serious inconvenience, and sometimes, even in the earliest days, he was handled with savage severity.[2]

A dissenter might be apprehended in the street or at his home, but the impact of persecution was most likely to strike him in his meeting house. Usually with violence, but often quietly and with consideration, the officers of the law would appear. The mayor and constables would enter, cry for silence, order the minister to desist, and command the people to disperse. Frequently the congregation would ignore them. Sometimes the minister would engage them in debate, and set against their appeal to royal authority the command of the King in whose

37

name the congregation had met. In either case the patience of the authorities was usually soon exhausted. By violence they tried to compel obedience. The commands of the officers would be drowned by the singing of the worshippers; attempts to disperse the congregation would be met with passive resistance, and in the face of stubborn non-co-operation tempers quickly flared. The constables, adding to the din with oaths, sweating as they pulled and shoved at the unyielding mass of worshippers, would begin to lay about them with sticks and staves or any improvised weapons that might come to hand.[1] And when the soldiery dispersed a meeting, violence broke out more quickly and with less restraint. To drive the worshippers into the street was merely the initial step, though often accomplished with so little ceremony that a dozen men and women would be dragged out to recover consciousness in the gutter. Once outside the meeting house, the soldiers would lay about them with pike-staffs and musket butts, and often men and women alike were so severely beaten that even the spectators cried out in protest. When mounted troops were used, the horsemen might attempt to ride down the dissenters; slashing at them with their scabbards, or even with their drawn swords, they pursued fugitives up alleys and struck at them as they cowered in doorways. So detailed and so circumstantial are the accounts that we are scarcely surprised to read that some of the victims died as a result of their treatment, while many others were maimed for life.[2]

A meeting for worship might be dispersed, but brave men would reassemble provided they had some place in which to meet. In due course, therefore, the attack was extended from the worshippers to the buildings where they gathered. The first step was to seize the meeting house, and so prevent dissenters from using it, but more drastic action was usually required, and in periods of intense persecution the damage done to nonconformist buildings was extremely heavy. In Bristol, George Hellier systematically wrecked five meeting houses, and left them in such utter ruin that hundreds of pounds were required for their repair.[3] His method—which was the same in every case—can be illustrated by his treatment of the Presbyterian place of worship.

First he pulled down the pulpit ('which he called the prattling-box'); then he demolished the pews; next he ordered the galleries to be broken down; and finally he tore out the doors, the windows and the floor. A rabble eager to share in the plunder quickly gathered, and till late at night they were smashing up and carting away anything that they could take as spoil. Often the work of destruction was less complete than this, but Puritans were little better pleased when soldiers or constables smashed down the doors, broke up the furniture for firewood, sent to the public house for beer, and jeered at the disconsolate owners even while they desecrated their house of worship.[1]

To destroy a building was easier than to disrupt a congregation. People could still gather amid the ruins; when this was forbidden they could meet in the street. The Quaker records abound in examples of the magnificent courage with which simple folk stood their ground in defence of their religious freedom. Drums could accomplish nothing since their worship was independent of the spoken word. Coaches driven up and down might part but could not scatter the meeting. Violence might harry them into prison, but not out of their composure, and when a justice had angrily thrown the benches out of a meeting-house he found the Quakers quietly taking possession of them in the street because, as one of them remarked, 'since they belong to us we might as well sit on them'.[2]

A congregation gathered in a public meeting place was inevitably vulnerable to attack, but as the pressure intensified the dissenters discovered that even the privacy of their own homes afforded them little protection.[3] When a small gathering of friends (just within the limits allowed by the law) was accidentally augmented by a little girl who fled in to escape from a dog's attacks, the informers and constables were in on her very heels. They forthwith levied twenty pounds on the minister for preaching and twenty pounds on his house for sheltering an unlawful conventicle, and then, having berated the gathering in the foulest language, they ransacked the house.[4] When three friends met to console a woman on the death of her only child, the husband incautiously led them in prayer, but a neighbour, who was

39

lurking at the door, overheard and reported this 'conventicle', with the result that a crushing though quite illegal fine was levied.[1] To see a dissenter entering another house (though merely to visit his sick cousin) might be enough to convince an eager informer that a meeting was in prospect, with the result that the place was ransacked from top to bottom.[2] Such search, by creating utter chaos in the house, might be highly inconvenient; it might equally involve complete disregard not only of elementary decencies but even of human safety. More common—and perhaps more justifiable—were the attacks on homes in which religious meetings were held. When the Broadmead Church gathered at the home of Edward Terrill at 6 a.m., the sheriff and a score of willing assistants besieged the house. Even with crowbars they could not force an entry either at the front door or at the back, and though they smashed through a shutter, they gained admission only when Terrill himself finally opened the door.[3]

To be harried in your meeting or at your home was one thing; to be arrested was another. This represented an intensification of the process of repression, and exposed the dissenter to the more drastic consequences of systematic persecution. The arrest might be made either by soldiers or by the civil officers of the law, but in either case the nature of the experience depended largely on the character of those who were responsible. Many constables were so reluctant to proceed against inoffensive neighbours that it was only with great difficulty that they could be compelled to act at all.[4] Some magistrates, though engaged in persecuting dissenters, were willing to treat individuals with humane consideration, and John Gratton mentions with gratitude a Lord Mayor of London who refused to arrest a man whose pregnant wife was taken with him.[5] Such cases at least show that the brutality which usually characterised persecution could be—and often was— modified by the decencies which grew out of life in the same community and possession of a common religious heritage. Even when soldiers were responsible for the arrest, they sometimes acted with restraint. It was a common thing, however, for them to seize their prisoners without showing any warrant. When challenged to produce one, they would clap their hands on their swords and swear that no other warrant was needed. Such indifference to legal forms encouraged an attitude which paid little regard to the rights of individuals. When a warrant was unnecessary, arrests might be wholesale and indiscriminate. Moreover, it is clear that the whole process was often strangely haphazard in character, and a dissenter might be arrested almost by accident. Some minor officer, in a fit of officiousness, might detain a stranger passing through the town, and then, suspecting he had made a mistake, could find no easy way of correcting it. And if his victim was as scrupulous as most Puritans were, it was useless to point to the open door and assure him that escape through the garden and across the fields was easy; a man seized by the law would wait to be cleared by the law, however embarrassing his presence might prove in the meantime.[1]

Conscience, though it might discourage escape, did not demand co-operation in effecting arrest. Passive resistance was the simplest method of frustrating the law and it unquestionably created problems for the magistrates and constables. The Broadmead congregation discovered that a congregation engaged in singing psalms could not easily be dealt with. The officers of the law could not make themselves heard, and though they might silence the members in their immediate vicinity, those at a distance, with their eyes fixed on their books, remained apparently impervious to what was happening, and so the volume of praise continued unabated. Temporarily the leaders of the congregation were invested with the anonymity that belongs to every member of a crowd, and magistrates looking for the minister or the officials were exasperated by a situation in which they could neither speak nor act.[2] This was a ruse that might be temporarily effective, but it might prevent the arrest of the leaders at the price of provoking the arrest of the whole church. Consequently most congregations devised some method by which their ministers were able to preach yet were assured assistance in evading capture.[3] In some cases a trapdoor opened into a lower chamber; in others a hatchway on the stairs could be shut at a moment's notice, and the preacher who had been using the lower part as a pulpit could escape to the upper floor and thus find refuge in a neighbouring house. Sometimes a curtain was hung across the room in such a way that on entering a stranger could not see who was preaching, and when the meeting was disturbed a cloak would be thrown over the minister's dark habit and he could make his escape amid the confusion that ensued. Narrow escapes were common, and often the magistrates missed almost by accident the victim they chiefly sought.

In the darkest days of all, when congregations met in the fields and the woods because they could no longer safely gather even in their homes, escape became more strenuous and more difficult. If warned in time, a congregation could disperse and most of its members could find a hiding-place. But often the notice was short, and the searchers many. A meeting, disturbed in one place, might scatter, reassemble in another, and resume their inter-rupted worship, even though the woods were full of foes. If suddenly surrounded by troops, the minister might have some chance of escaping on horseback—unless watchers posted at points of vantage could signal his route to the horse guards waiting in ambush. Occasionally, in seeking to preserve their liberty, worshippers lost their lives. When a congregation was disturbed in the woods near Bristol, some of the members quickly got to the river's edge and reached the other side in safety, but two men, who were hotly chased for half a mile, grew tired, and in a panic as they heard the eager shouts of their pursuers, thought they too might escape across the river. They were wrong: though one of them was rescued by the Kingswood miners, the other drowned.[1]

There was one point at which even ingenuity could not save dissenters from arrest. A funeral was particularly vulnerable; it could easily be identified, and common decency prevented flight. Though technically speaking it might not be a conventicle, it was a gathering of like-minded people for a religious purpose, and it often resulted in the arrest of the participants. This was a refine-ment of persecution particularly bitter to those who suffered from it.[2]

It was sometimes easier to arrest a dissenter than to find a satisfactory way of dealing with him. Often enough men were put in prison without appearing before a justice of the peace—for that matter without even seeing the warrant for their arrest—but this was vigorously denounced as a violation of the law, and even those who were responsible for it offered a very half-hearted defence.[1] But when no magistrate was available or when it was not feasible to lodge the prisoner forthwith in gaol, perforce some other arrangement had to be made. The dissenter might be placed under house arrest in his own home, and ordered to be ready on the morrow—or at the beginning of the next week. Sometimes he was released on parole and told to return at a specified time. Occasionally some house in the neighbourhood was pressed into service; or—as happened far more often—the prisoner was kept overnight at an alehouse or a tavern. As a preliminary to—or even as a substitute for—imprisonment a dissenter might be kept at the marshal's house, and there he would be lodged in comfort and treated with comparative consideration. But a favourite device was to lock the whole congregation in their meeting house, and, while subjecting them to ribald insult, to leave the mixed assembly there for hours on end.

An appearance before a magistrate was normally the first consequence of arrest. Its bearing on the fate of the dissenter could hardly be exaggerated. Often it initiated a course of events which involved not only imprisonment, but physical suffering, economic ruin and even death. This was particularly true of the Quakers. The oath alone might be sufficient to send a man to prison, and even if no case could be proved against him, he could be kept there indefinitely, merely by tendering the oath each time his case came up for consideration. Much, therefore, depended on the attitude of the justice before whom he first appeared. The magistrates, of course, were of all kinds. Many were sufficiently magnanimous to show a genuine desire to save him from the harsher consequences of his dissent. They might stubbornly resist attempts to coerce them into persecuting harmless folk. They could persistently ignore intimations that dissenters were meeting; they were willing on occasion to warn officers against going a single step beyond what the law allowed, and they could be openly contemptuous of the efforts of the clergy to stir up trouble for their neighbours. On the other hand, many of them nursed recent grievances and were predisposed to find fault. But even if the Interregnum had not been a bitter memory, some of their prisoners adopted an attitude certain to kindle their exasperation. The average country gentleman was quite incapable of appreciating the religious concern which lay behind many of the Quaker idiosyncrasies. 'Plain speech' and the withholding of 'hat honour' seemed gratuitous discourtesy. Annoyance at what appeared to be a studied insult quickly passed into unrestrained anger when the prisoner persisted in his attitude, and the fact that he would not take the oath seemed to prove his guilt as well as provide the pretext for his committal. But there is no escaping the fact that many of the persecuting justices were men in whom strong prejudices gave freer rein to violent tempers, and the dissenters who appeared before them had no chance of an unbiased hearing. They saw little reason to restrain their venom, and subsequently there were few enough opportunities to rectify their mistakes.

There was usually little formality about the prisoner's appearance before the magistrate. Whenever he was available and wherever he could be found, he examined the arrested dissenter. It might be in his back parlour or in the hall of his manor, but it might be at the local tavern; sometimes it was early in the morning but often late at night. Usually the justice was alone, but circumstances sometimes permitted—or even demanded—the presence of a colleague, and in addition curiosity might prompt neighbours or members of the household to attend. When Bunyan appeared before Francis Wingate, the vicar of the village ('an old enemy of the truth, Dr Lindale') hailed the occasion as an opportunity to put a journeyman-preacher in his proper place, but though he began by 'taunting [the prisoner] with many reviling phrases', he soon discovered that he was dealing with a tinker whom he could not easily subdue.[1] In most respects Bunyan's examination followed a pattern common enough throughout the period. There were the usual insinuations that the meeting at which the prisoner was arrested had actually met for subversive ends, the contemptuous references to the worship in conventicles, the fruitless arguments about sureties, and then at length the mittimus was drafted. Shortly afterwards, Bunyan's friends persuaded him to return to Wingate's house. Another justice had newly arrived upon the scene and they hoped that his presence might lead first to a reconsideration of the case and then to the prisoner's discharge. It was all to no avail. There was a long discussion of the subjects on which magistrates delighted to argue with dissenters—the right to worship at other times, in other places, or according to other forms than those authorised by law; the duty of following your own trade and not interfering in matters above your station and capacity; the place of scripture and its proper interpretation—but it all ended as before. If Bunyan would promise not to preach, he might be released; otherwise he must go to prison—and so to prison he went, 'with God's comfort in my poor soul'.[1]

Sureties, demanded in Bunyan's case and refused, were a constant source of trouble.[2] Bondsmen were usually forthcoming, but the implied conditions were such that no sincere dissenter could accept them. It would have been easy to guarantee to keep the peace, to appear in court when required, and to refrain from any kind of seditious action, and when sureties were given it was because this interpretation of their meaning was accepted by the authorities. But usually it was quite clear that the requirement was prompted by a different purpose. The magistrates obviously intended to use the provision of sureties as a means of preventing further meetings, and to escape imprisonment at the price of forfeiting effectiveness was something that few dissenters would do. But in some cases the demand was rejected on different grounds. The prisoners claimed that they were innocent men, and that to give a guarantee of good behaviour might be construed as an admission that it was just to treat them as potential offenders.[3]

The mittimus also created certain practical difficulties, though usually of a kind more likely to help than to hinder the dissenter's cause. Repeatedly when cases were brought to trial at sessions or assizes, the charges were dismissed because the mittimus was shown to be defective, and this happened so often that the reader is forced to conclude either that the procedure was gravely at fault or that the magistrates and their officials were not competent to handle it. And, indeed, a detailed account, which describes the clerk writing out one mittimus after another, only to have each found faulty when read, suggests that the resources of the average country house fell far short of the requirements of exact legal work.[1] The fact that so many elementary errors could be made—that dates could be wrong, that names and places could be incorrect, that inconsistencies and discrepancies could creep in— was fortunate for the man quick enough to see his chance and sufficiently intelligent to press home his advantage. But with the mittimus, as also with the indictment, it was often easier to point out defects than to use them as grounds for gaining one's discharge.

The opportunity to challenge the validity of the mittimus came later, but even at the preliminary examination a quick-witted dissenter could argue points of law with the magistrates. When a congregation was disturbed one day and its members did not appear till next day before the mayor, it was possible to demand 'proof of fact', and it was not easy for those who had arrested a score of people to prove that this or that individual had actually been present. And though the magistrates always felt entitled to debate the dissenter's right to meet for worship, the dissenter could sometimes turn the tables and challenge the magistrate's legal right to follow an intended course of action. But this was usually a fruitless procedure. Occasionally, without prompting, a magistrate would dismiss a case or quietly let it fall, but, failing such good fortune, the dissenter was almost certain to be sent to prison.[2]

For some offences a magistrate was authorised to impose a sentence, but usually he sent the offender to gaol to await trial at the quarter sessions or the next assizes. There was always a danger that the dissenter might fail to get his case brought to trial, in which event he was sent back to prison to draw such consolation as he could from the hope that next time he might prove more fortunate. He might merely discover, however, that his imprisonment was indefinitely extended, without his either facing trial or undergoing sentence, and he might even be detained for no more explicit reason than the surmise that he was a 'dangerous man'.

Trial in open court was the most formidable experience that the dissenter had yet faced. He had already confronted his opponents, of course, and often in ways sufficiently terrifying, but now he seemed completely in their power. The solemn incomprehensibilities of legal phraseology and procedure all heightened his sense of helplessness, and stamped the scene indelibly upon his memory.[1] As was true at every stage, a great deal depended on the attitude of the men whom he confronted. Sometimes justices or judges proved genuinely sympathetic. When they not only knew the prisoner but respected him, when they believed that he held his views with sincerity yet with moderation and advocated them without arrogance or fanaticism, they showed every consideration, and might even gather round to congratulate him when he was set free.[2] On the other hand, they might waste no good will on the dissenter, but they might be hesitant because uncertain exactly what to do. Official policy might have confused them, and they might fear rebukes from Whitehall;[3] possibly experience had shown that some judges were likely to dismiss a prisoner because of a faulty mittimus or free him for a trifling fine, and so the edge of enthusiasm had been blunted. Sometimes there was no unanimity on the bench, as when George Fox realised that he was facing judges divided among themselves. More often the attitude varied between contemptuous scorn and vindictive brutality. A justice, willing to relieve the tedium of the law by a practical joke, might clap a Quaker's hat on his head, and when the prisoner's conscience forbade its removal, punish him for contempt of court. A man more openly malicious would fill the hat with water before replacing it on the owner's head, while a man with still more venom and even less regard for the proprieties of the court room would heap it full of filth. And as he scoffed at the predicament of the prisoner, a justice might administer the oath to a Quaker who had been seized by virtue of an obsolete warrant.[4]

Frequently, because it was a court of law, the judge or the justices would debate the question at issue with the man in the dock. This was a natural, but a dangerous, practice. Though the prisoner faced a charge in law, he had been arrested for religious beliefs and practices. The discussion rapidly moved to an area where a knowledge of the law counted for little, but where familiarity with the Bible counted for much. Many a judge who had unwarily got entangled in a debate on scripture was glad to extricate himself with what grace he could by asserting that in a court of law such matters were irrelevant, and really should not be discussed. But even when experience had made him wary, he might find himself manœuvred into an awkward position, and to avoid a more embarrassing conclusion he might boldly stand to the view that by law a person was forbidden to worship as the Spirit of the Eternal God bade him.[1] The fact that law and religion intertwined at this point presented difficulties even for a judge anxious to prevent his own views from prejudicing the matter. He often found that prisoners would stubbornly refuse to answer according to the forms of law, but would argue endlessly the points about religion.[2] And sometimes the magnificent fortitude of the prisoner would become obscured by an exasperating tendency to lapse into figurative language of a barely intelligible kind. Straightforward questions would be answered by what seemed quibbling evasions, and it is remarkable that the judges were as patient as they were. A fragment of dialogue from one of Dewsbery's trials will serve as an example. '*Judge:* What is thy name? *W.D.:* Unknown to the world. *Judge:* Let us know what name that is, that the world knows not. *W.D.:* It is known in the light, and not any can know it but him that hath it; but the name the world knows me by is William Dewsbery. *Judge:* What countryman art thou? *W.D.:* Of the land of Canaan. *Judge:* That is afar off. *W.D.:* Nay, it is near, for all that dwell in God are in the holy city, Jerusalem,...where the soul is in rest, and enjoys the love of God in Jesus Christ, in whom the union is with the Father of light. *Judge:* That is true. But are you ashamed of your country? Is it a disparagement for you to be born in England?'[3]

As the period progressed, brutal intimidation of the prisoner increasingly supplanted willingness to consider his case. This coincided with the sharp deterioration in the character of the judges' bench which was so marked a feature of the decade before the Revolution. When men like Scroggs and Jeffreys held the highest posts in the judiciary, conscientious sufferers could look for slight consideration. And they got very little indeed. The ignorant distortions by which a judge could misrepresent the prisoners' convictions were matched by the truculence with which he launched into vindictive abuse of their attitude. The unrestrained violence with which Jeffreys insulted and berated Thomas Delaune was a fit prelude to his yet more shocking behaviour at the trial of Richard Baxter. Few scenes in the annals of injustice are better known, and in few are the elements of dramatic contrast so strongly present. Coarse intemperance on the bench confronted ascetic dignity in the dock in a way that emphasised the inherent quality of both, and contemporaries knew that dissent had never appeared in a more honourable light than when 'Baxter stood at bay, berogued, abused, despised; never more great than then'.[1] In this travesty of a trial, neither the prisoner nor his counsel was given a chance to present the defence which Baxter had so carefully prepared, while the judge apparently felt entitled not only to supplant the counsel for the prosecution but also to anticipate the verdict of the jury.[2]

A judge like Jeffreys might attempt to ignore the jury or intimidate it, but at least this period saw the first effective steps taken to establish the independent status of the jurors, and this crucial development arose directly out of the persecution of dissenters. It was still common practice for the bench to require a certain verdict, and to send the jurors back if they failed to find in the terms expected of them. If they stood by their verdict, an angry judge might commit them to answer for a misdemeanour, or he might fine them as much as a hundred marks apiece. No single incident did so much to settle the issue as the trial of William Penn and Matthew Mead. When the jury refused to find the prisoners guilty, the Recorder's anger knew no bounds, and he bluntly told the jurors that 'you shall not be dismissed till we have a verdict that the court will accept; and you shall be locked up, without meat, drink, fire, and tobacco;...we will have a verdict by the help of God or you shall starve for it'.[3] The jurors refused to be intimidated; they were heavily fined and imprisoned. Before the matter ended, it had become apparent to everyone that the constitutional importance of their case far exceeded that of the Quakers whom they had acquitted. When at length the whole body of judges gave it as their ruling that no jury could be fined because of its verdict, their contemporaries realised at once that a great bastion had been erected in defence of English liberty. Thenceforth a judge might still cajole or brow-beat the jury, but its members now had a new security as well as a greater confidence, and the results appear in the greater frequency with which dissenters were acquitted.

The Puritan who appeared in court usually suffered acutely from a sense of grievance. It is hard to be penalised for obedience to what you are convinced is the will of God, but it is specially bitter to feel that the law is being wrested from its true purpose in order to punish you. Many of the dissenters believed that they were most unjustly treated—and often they were—but frequently they misconceived the nature of their grievances. The Quakers, in particular, felt strongly that their treatment was a clear infringement of both the spirit and the letter of the law, and they often claimed that they suffered more greviously than the primitive Christians, since the Roman empire at least punished the martyrs according to the forms of law. The legal position, however, was by no means simple. Certain laws were aimed explicitly at nonconformity, but a number of older statutes could also be applied. Indeed, the situation was so complex and the possible punishments so various that it was actually difficult to imprison a Quaker illegally.[1] The term 'riot' was capable of such elastic interpretation that the laws which forbade tumultuous meetings were often invoked, and it was easier for the sufferers to feel aggrieved than to prove that the action was illegal. 'Seditious intent' was also vaguely defined, and in the apprehensive days which followed the Restoration was often the foundation of a charge.[2] The refusal to pay tithes left the objector open to action either in the ecclesiastical courts (under the provisions of 27 Henry VIII, c. 20) or in the civil courts. An action could be laid against a Quaker in the Exchequer Court, and then the law so operated that the defendant was often sentenced to an indefinite term of imprisonment. Moreover, the rules of this court compelled the defendant to employ counsel to sign his answer to the plaintiff's bill, and since this was a course which Quaker convictions usually forbade, a man became liable to punishment for contempt of court. The objection to oaths was a witness which would always serve to sentence a Quaker, and though the sufferer might know that the tendering of the oath was a malicious stratagem, it was perfectly legal for the court to do so. And not only the Quakers suffered on this score. Many of the Baptists also declined to take oaths, and paid the same penalty for their refusal. It was a statute of the reign of James I which made it mandatory to take an oath when required, and by its provisions a man who declined to swear could quickly be pressed to the point where he was subject to a sentence of praemunire: his goods were forfeited and he was imprisoned at the king's pleasure. Shortly after the Venner rising, the Quaker Act (12 and 13 Charles II, c. 1) provided an alternative series of punishments. Anyone who refused to take the oath when it was lawfully tendered, or who met with others as Quakers to the number of more than five, became subject to a fine of five pounds for the first offence and to one of ten pounds for the second. If his goods fell short in value of the amount levied, he could be imprisoned for three to six months; and on a third conviction he was to abjure the realm or be transported at the king's pleasure. This act did not replace the former one; it merely supplemented it. Sometimes one was used, sometimes the other; occasionally both were pressed into service. In other ways as well the inability to swear worked to the disadvantage of certain types of Puritans. It precluded them from giving evidence in court, and so from prosecuting those who infringed their rights, while in chancery cases a man who could not file an answer on oath faced the prospect of ruin.

Still another series of statutes was designed to compel attendance at church. In addition to imposing fines, these acts made the offender liable to arrest and to imprisonment (without bail) until he conformed, and after three months in gaol he was to abjure to the realm or incur the penalties of felony.

51

In many cases, the old laws which were invoked against the Puritans had originally been devised as weapons with which to attack the Papists. Their use against fellow-Protestants was an anomaly which caused deep resentment,[1] but it was not illegal. Even the highest authorities were sometimes surprised at the results. When twelve humble Baptists of Aylesbury were sentenced to death for their nonconformity, Charles II was amazed to discover that such a verdict could legally be given; as soon as Kiffin brought the matter to his attention, he promptly pardoned them all.[2] But this confusion arose because new laws overlaid the old, yet both could be used. From 1662 onwards, the courts had a series of measures specially designed to deal with nonconformity. The Act of Uniformity was aimed principally at ministers and teachers; the Five Mile Act also differentiated the leaders from the flock. But the Conventicle Acts of 1664 and 1670 were directed primarily at the people, and were largely responsible for the ruin and havoc which persecution spread among the nonconformists.

The sentences imposed on the Puritans could usually be defended in law; often the antecedent legal proceedings could not be defended at all. It was not merely that long imprisonment and crippling fines seemed heavy punishments to men who were suffering only for loyalty to their faith. The frustrating feature of the experience was the discovery that those who administered the laws apparently felt free to twist them in any way that the needs of the moment suggested. A prisoner might find that he had been condemned unheard; his commitment had been ordered before he was given any opportunity to speak in his own defence. The charges levelled at the nonconformists were often wildly irresponsible. Men would be charged with attendance at a meeting and convicted even though they could prove that, at the time, they were not even within the bounds of the county. A man who had actually been in prison on a given date was sentenced for an offence which he could not possibly have committed. A woman would be sent to prison in spite of the fact that neighbours could testify that she had given birth to a child early in the morning of the day when she was accused of attending a conventicle.

Evidence of the most supposititious character was accepted. 'He must have been; therefore he was' might not be a convincing argument, but it was often eagerly accepted by the courts. Because the nonconformists worshipped in houses, to see them emerging from a house was proof that they had met contrary to the law, and more than once a judge solemnly ruled that inference was sufficient evidence. Consequently the simple fact that a dissenter was seen in woods where it was believed conventicles had been held, was accepted as proof that he had attended a conventicle.[1] It was bad enough to be punished for supposed attendance at a meeting which had actually been held; it was far worse to be condemned because of a meeting which had never taken place but which it was assumed would have been held had circumstances allowed. Yet even this could happen.[2]

It was often difficult to secure a fair trial. Concerning this grievance complaints constantly recur. When party feeling ran high or personal animosity entered the picture, the rules of evidence were treated in the most cavalier fashion. It was no uncommon thing for a man to discover that his opponents, by intimidation or by inducements of reward, had secured false witnesses to testify against him, and consequently any semblance of fidelity to facts disappeared. He might be left in complete ignorance of what was happening; he might be convicted without being summoned; or fines might accumulate till they reached a figure he could never pay. He might find that he was denied any opportunity of facing his accuser or of answering the charge against him, while his protests against the illegality of proceedings fell on deaf or contemptuous ears. If he retained a lawyer, it was difficult for his counsel to gain a hearing; judges were often frankly partisan and the spectators violently hostile.[3]

As the period progressed, the Puritans became more and more firmly persuaded of the importance of legal assistance. Though the prisoner might still try to check arbitrary proceedings by an appeal to equity and justice, he relied increasingly on the means of self-defence which the law itself provided. Even a little legal knowledge often proved very useful, and it became clear that only systematic use of competent legal skill could protect the sufferers from cynical violations of the law. At one time, influential Quakers had argued that Friends should passively submit to persecution, but by 1668 the view was gaining ground that it was perfectly legitimate to seek redress of grievances. In 1675 Thomas Corbett, defending George Fox before Lord Chief Justice Hale, secured his release from a sentence of praemunire, and from then on the Quakers resolutely fought persecution with every weapon that the law afforded. As a result the Meeting for Sufferings emerged,[1] and its importance can hardly be exaggerated. Hundreds of humble people were rescued from their oppressors, and those who suffered were supported by the knowledge that their plight was not forgotten.[2] What the Quakers did systematically and on a national scale, the other groups of dissenters attempted in a more limited way. Individuals and congregations appealed to the law for protection against violations of the law. It was realised that simple folk were helpless in the hands of their adversaries, and because of ignorance would hopelessly incriminate themselves. Therefore the Baptists of Bristol were quick to recognise the value of first-class legal advice. Even with its help they did not always gain their point; when they prosecuted one of their most relentless persecutors, a conviction seemed certain— till the judge intervened to frustrate their expectations. Frequently it proved impossible to get justice against their oppressors; the same courts which broke the rules of proper procedure were not likely to reform themselves. Nevertheless, the benefits of retaining counsel appeared in case after case, and this was so generally recognised that on occasion all the Puritans would join in common action for their protection and defence.

Having learned the advantages of legal aid in the lower courts, the nonconformists began to appeal in cases in which gross errors in procedure aroused a hope that the original verdict might be reversed. It was, however, a slow and discouraging business. Often the appeal seemed hopeless in anticipation and proved so in the event. Sometimes it not only failed but involved the appellant in further penalties. Occasionally it was successful; then it not only rectified past injustices but served notice to all concerned that those who harried dissenters were not exempt from the further scrutiny of the law. A few convictions for perjury had a most wholesome effect in checking the arrogance and insatiable greed of the informer, but more important was the slow task of creating a public opinion ready to resent illegality even when its victims were unpopular people.

The trial usually ended in the sentence of the prisoner. Occasionally a case was dropped; sometimes the accused was acquitted, but in most instances he faced some form of punishment. This might involve imprisonment, either of an indefinite nature or for a fixed period; it might involve praemunire, banishment, or even death. The more extreme sentences were seldom imposed, perhaps because they were difficult to enforce. A callous judge might threaten the prisoner with death—and perhaps the prisoner expected it—but this was probably an attempt to intimidate humble people ignorant of legal practice. In all, a couple of hundred Quakers were sentenced to banishment, but the sentence proved so difficult to execute that relatively few were actually transported. The sheriffs had to find ships whose masters would agree to carry the prisoners, and many captains flatly refused to have any part in removing from their homeland people who were merely maintaining their faith. Even those who accepted prisoners found themselves so beset with misfortunes—contrary winds, disease, or unfavourable weather—that they were glad to disembark their passengers and sail without them.[1]

The consequences of imprisonment will be considered later. Meanwhile it is important to remember that the imposition of fines was an even more serious source of suffering. Most of the legislation which could be applied to dissenters contained clauses which provided for fines. The sums involved were sometimes small, but even the trivial amounts which could be levied for absence from the 'national worship' became threatening in their magnitude when they were retroactively assessed. Under the Conventicle Act of 1670, each person attending a nonconformist meeting was liable to a fine of five shillings, and the sum was doubled in the case of subsequent offences. The same act imposed a fine of twenty pounds on the minister who preached at a conventicle, while the person at whose house the service was held was answerable for a like amount. These sums could not only be increased when the offence was repeated; they could be distributed among others present if it proved impossible to collect the fine from those who were supposed to pay. Hence a worshipper might find that in addition to his fine of five or ten shillings he was assessed for the preacher or for the house up to a total of ten pounds per meeting. Moreover, if the person could not pay, there were provisions authorising the officers of the law to seize his goods and chattels to the requisite amount. For certain offences the Act of Uniformity and the first Conventicle Act imposed fines of one hundred pounds. In addition, that conveniently vague offence, a riot, involved a penalty of fifty pounds. And when the statutes failed of their effect, it was always possible to resort to the ecclesiastical courts. Moreover, a man might find himself involved in an exchequer process; the non-payment of tithes or the refusal to swear might bring him a fine in any one of the courts, or he might find himself facing the consequences of a writ of *de Excommunicato Capiendo*. The variety of alternative methods and the flexibility of the system itself explain the quite staggering sums which were imposed on individuals. A certain London minister was fined £840 for holding meetings during the five months from July to November 1682, and this was not unique.[1]

Sums of this magnitude could seldom be collected, and perhaps merely reflect the determination of the lower authorities to demonstrate their zeal. Far more disastrous was the cumulative effect of fines of intermediate size, especially when levied repeatedly on one man. After the Declaration of Indulgence in 1672 many ministers licensed their own houses as meeting places, and even when freedom of worship was cancelled, the congregation continued to gather in the same place. Consequently when a meeting was disturbed, the minister became liable to a fine of twenty pounds as the preacher and to another of twenty pounds as owner of the house in which the conventicle met. This might easily represent more than the value of everything he owned. If he had a modest estate, repeated penalties would ruin him; in despair he would sell his possessions and seek asylum elsewhere. Many of those fined were humble people, and they immediately found themselves reduced to destitution. It is impossible to assess the results of this persistent fining on the life of the dissenting communities, but the staggering totals so meticulously recorded by the Quakers give some indication of what the cumulative effect must have been.[1]

The man who had been fined seldom paid voluntarily—often because he could not pay at all. Even if he had the money, he usually disputed the justice of the penalty, and he was reluctant to do anything which might concede even by implication that to worship God as conscience commanded was to commit an offence which the law was entitled to punish. Failure to pay resulted in the far more serious consequences of distraint of goods. Armed with a warrant to seize whatever was necessary, the informers, goading the constables to action, would swoop down upon the houses of the Puritans. The greatest care and consideration could not have prevented hardship when articles of domestic use were seized to satisfy a monetary demand. Second-hand utensils might fetch very little when offered for sale, but their replacement value might be considerable. Usually, however, the distraints were made at the behest and under the supervision of informers, and in their rapacity they seized everything that was available. The disparity between the fine imposed and the value of the goods plundered shows that no attempt was made to equate what was seized with what could legitimately be demanded. In some instances dissenters, warned in time, could sell their merchandise or remove their household goods. Often there was no opportunity to do so; quite as often conscience made them hesitate. Philip Henry saw various ways in which he might have circumvented the efforts of those who came to seize the equipment and the produce of his farm, but he declined to act. There was no need to co-operate; it was legitimate to devise obstacles, and you might lock gates and barns when you suspected that the officers had come without a warrant to break down the doors, but further than that you would not go.[2] Usually the victim had no chance to decide what attitude he should adopt. Unexpectedly, and at the most inopportune times, a disorderly rabble would break into his house. After the fury of the initial plundering, the informers and their crew would settle down to an all-night orgy as they ate his food and drank his liquor. Then in the morning everything he had would be piled on wagons and driven away. The thoroughness of the process is emphasised by the care with which the articles taken are enumerated, and as a result we often get a most illuminating picture of the furnishings of a seventeenth-century home.[1] It was common for a family to lose all its beds, but it was felt to be a little heartless when a baby was left to lie on the ground because its crib had been distrained. Similarly, when a woman in childbed was turned out to lie on straw and saw all her bedding disappear as well as all her clothes, the victims were indignant.[2] But brutality and heartlessness were an inseparable part of the process. A widow, warming milk for her sick children, watched it thrown on the floor because the skillet was being seized. A man who had seen all his household goods removed was surprised when his coat was stripped from his back, and the departing officers assured him that the next time he would be left stark naked.[3] Often a workman's tools were seized—the nailer's hammer, the weaver's loom, the yeoman's plough—and so a man was left to face the future bereft of the means of support.[4] Merchants lost their stock, and ministers their books.[5] Farmers saw their cows and horses driven from their fields. Sometimes it was the magnitude of the loss that excited attention, as when a farmer lost sixty-three beasts worth £183; sometimes it was the disproportion between the seizure and the fine, as in the case of the widow who lost animals valued at twenty pounds in satisfaction of a fine of five pounds.[6] But when a justice seized a fat ox and killed it for his own table, the illegality of the act was so blatant that it could not be allowed to pass unchallenged, and George Fox took instant steps to secure redress.[7]

The authorities often found, however, that it was easier to seize goods than to sell them. When offered for sale, no decent person would buy them. For many people it became a matter of conscience not to share in the plunder of their neighbours, and often livestock, merchandise and household goods were hawked from one market to another without finding a single purchaser.

Even the very poor would have nothing to do with goods plundered from dissenters; when bread seized from a baker and cheese from a provision merchant were offered free to the destitute of the community they refused the bread and accepted the cheese only to return it to its rightful owner. But unfortunately this practical good will had its attendant drawbacks; what the upright would not buy, the unscrupulous could get for almost nothing. And though some justices grew weary of the whole business, others felt in honour bound to press forward all the more relentlessly. If the public refused to buy distrained bread, horses might have it, but at least the offending Puritans would not get it back, and if a cow would not fetch its proper price it would be sold for a shilling before the good work should languish.[1]

As a rule, however, this sordid business of plundering the defenceless and the poor continued only because greedy and unscrupulous men could compel the authorities to act. Many justices heartily detested the role they had to play. Neighbours refused to co-operate at any price, and constables and minor officers of the law often submitted to considerable fines rather than have any part in this detestable traffic. The good will manifest in these negative ways often took positive and constructive form. When a minister lost all his possessions, his friends refurnished the house.[2] If a man could not redeem his own goods, some neighbour paid the fine and brought them back. John Gratton's experience provides an excellent example of the lengths to which friendly people would go to shield a dissenter whom they had come to value and respect. As soon as it was known that a warrant was out for the seizure of his goods, neighbours came and removed all the best things for safe custody in their own homes. When the constable arrived he carefully pointed out the ways in which Gratton could circumvent him, and even encouraged him to lock the door in his face; a rebuff sufficient, he said, to make him throw over the case and desist from further efforts. He willingly agreed to take a list of what remained in the house, and publicly offer the goods for sale. When no one came forward to buy, he informed the justices that he had been unable to discharge his commission.[3]

Yet even when the best possible construction has been put on the case, it remains true that fines and the distresses made to collect them caused incalculable suffering to thousands of dissenters. They were stripped of all that they possessed; they saw their wives and children involved in the most acute hardships, and they watched their worldly affairs reduced to utter ruin.[1]

To a certain extent this misery was inseparable from the conditions—religious and political, social and psychological—which prevailed in the Restoration period. Those who had gained power were not willing to let those who had lost it dissent on easy or comfortable terms. A great deal of suffering, however, was either directly caused by informers or was aggravated by their activities, and any discussion of persecution which ignored their role would not be faithful to the facts.

The Conventicle Act of 1670 opened wide the door to the informer. It invested him with a definite legal status; it gave him the power to coerce magistrates and constables, and by offering him a fixed share of specified penalties it gave him all the inducement that he needed. Not all informers were men of doubtful character and broken fortunes. Hostility to the dissenters or enthusiasm for the Anglican cause might make a justice act as an informer; because of zeal a clergyman (or his wife) might undertake the task; perhaps officiousness turned a constable into an informer. When the bishop's servants assumed the role it was because they had been commanded to do so; and apparently they enjoyed the change from more monotonous duties. But as a rule the informers were men desperate alike in circumstances and in character. When need prompted them to plunder others, no scruples told them to desist. Many of them had ruined their fortunes by prodigality or drink, and now saw a quick and easy way to regain what they had lost. Some were thieves who had temporarily escaped hanging, but whom the gallows ultimately claimed. When a man had recklessly squandered money and landed in prison for debt, his wife might turn informer, and by shamelessly swearing to the truth of any imposture, look for whatever gain she could get. Even a demented old woman, roaming the countryside and blowing a battered old horn, might testify against dissenters.[2]

There was wide diversity in the motives which prompted men to become informers; there was almost perfect unanimity in the reaction they aroused. Only 'a man of a very wicked life', remarked Bunyan's Mr Wiseman, would become an informer. According to John Gratton all who practised that evil trade were 'dark, ignorant fellows'. John Howe described them as 'the worst and most infamous of men', while a mother, writing to dissuade her son from the course he had chosen, assured him that 'an informer is accounted the basest of men that are'. He is, said Pearse, 'the shame and scourge of his country'; of all who belong to that wicked tribe you can confidently declare that 'their morals are as bad as the very dregs of the age' because they are 'ignorant, infidel, voracious enemies to all religion'.[1]

Though everyone despised the informer, some people found it expedient to use him. 'After all,' said Archbishop Sancroft, 'you can't build a ship without using crooked timber',[2] and so clergy and magistrates alike were sometimes content to use bad men for what they believed to be good ends. Usually the informers needed no official encouragement; as we have seen, the terms of the second Conventicle Act not only provided all the incentive they needed, but placed reluctant magistrates completely in their power. The informer's task was not always simple, even when he undertook it with zeal. Persecution had made dissenters wary, and it was not easy to get the information you needed. Some depended on cunning to worm their way into meetings. Others resorted to hypocrisy; even though they had not gained admission to a service and none of the hearers would betray the preacher, by pretending a conviction of sin they might induce the unwary to reveal sufficient details about the sermon to provide evidence for prosecution. Sometimes it was possible to bribe small children to dog the steps of nonconformists, and report the houses where they met. By sneaking into a sick man's room on the heels of his friends, you could lurk in the background till he began to speak to them of the comfort of faith in the midst of suffering, and then you could swear that he had preached at a conventicle. Often such ruses were unnecessary. If the magistrates were at all complaisant, the informers would rely on the most reckless and extravagant charges, and nothing restrained them from venturing on flagrantly impudent falsehoods. In some cases this was due to the knowledge that the justices were ready to accept as true even the most preposterous story, but at times it sprang from a cynical belief that their victims would not take an oath and so could not challenge whatever they might choose to swear.[1] This irresponsibility in language was matched by a corresponding violence in action. It was safe to beat and bully Puritans, to knock them about, throw them down, fling them over stiles and fences, because no one would call you to account. Having attacked them in person, it was natural to plunder them of their substance, and often the practices of the informers could only be described as unrestrained and systematic pillage. In some places and at certain times they virtually usurped the right to control the legal system. They imprisoned men and released them; they altered warrants at will; they struck out whatever names they pleased and added others as they wished; they blackmailed the magistrates and made them the obedient instruments of their rapacity.

Such pretensions, however, did not pass unchallenged. Some magistrates refused to be intimidated, and threatened the informers with dire consequences if they transgressed in the slightest degree the letter of the law.[2] Since cowardice was as much a mark of the informer as arrogance, such warnings usually served their purpose. At times the populace intervened and declared their feelings in no uncertain way. When a London crowd discovered that the man responsible for Fox's arrest was a Papist, they tried to lynch him and he narrowly escaped with his life.[3] When a couple of Norfolk informers tried to ply their trade in Colchester 'the rabble stoned them so much that they desired to know of the mayor where they might lodge safe. He told them he knew nowhere safer than in the town gaol, so thither they went and got away very early in the morning.'[4] But the predatory ravagings of the informers could be restrained by other and less violent means. A constable, moved to pity at the plight of a poor man whose goods were being pillaged, gave the informers a bribe of twenty shillings and persuaded them to desist.[5] In-

creasingly the sufferers turned to the law to chasten these scoun-
drels who were perverting it into a mockery, and they quickly
proved that, for all the informers' arrogant bluster, they could
easily be cowed. Ellwood's notable success against that infamous
pair, Aris and Lacy, instantly checked the plundering of dissenters
in the home counties.[1] In due course it was possible to pass from
defence to attack, and when James II appointed commissioners to
investigate the activities of informers, George Whitehead produced so vast an array of incriminating evidence that the issue
was virtually settled at once.[2] But long before the courts curbed
this disastrous pillaging, the Puritans had found an alternative
source of comfort and encouragement. With care they noted the
fate which so often overtook the informer. They believed that
the wicked walk in slippery places, and to see an adversary fall was
a sure sign that God's hand was against him. Since informers
were usually men of dissolute life, they were often struck down
by misfortune or by sudden death, and the fact was always
solemnly recorded.

The informer was the cause of incalculable suffering; he was
also in part responsible for the dawning of a new day. In the
minds of all decent people he aroused such deep disgust that the
policy of which he was the instrument stood discredited and
condemned.[3] He served to crystallise a conviction that had been
slowly taking shape throughout the period; people had begun
to suspect that persecution was indefensible, and the informer
merely proved that they were right. Many different factors contributed to this willingness to abandon a policy of repression.
Everyone despised the informers, and few had much respect for
the persecuting magistrates. The justices who were most eager to
eradicate the dissenters were least likely to commend the rule of
law, and their unbridled violence, their intemperate language,
their arbitrary proceedings created the belief that a policy which
won such advocates had forfeited the support of reasonable men.
Could the church be strengthened by those whose only prayers
were oaths, and who observed no sacraments but the drinking of
healths?[4] A distaste for persecution was as strong as the dislike of
those who enforced it.[5] Gentlemen of the better kind, observing

what was required of a magistrate, were reluctant to undertake the duties of the office, while even constables and lesser officials became more and more unwilling to be the agents of repression. Complaints from bishops and clergy multiplied; it was increasingly difficult to persuade magistrates to act, and in face of their stubborn refusal to co-operate the whole programme of repression was in danger of collapse.[1] Time was healing former feuds. New relationships were growing up; personal kindnesses were blunting the edge of the persecuting spirit. The old caricature of the canting Puritan was being erased by the discovery that one's neighbours —people blameless in character and upright of life—were actually being punished for the virtues which made them useful members of the community. Men were beginning to 'believe their own senses; they had neither seen nor heard of any sedition or tumult or plot contrived among the Protestant dissenters. They know them to be men of abilities, piety, righteousness and peace, and have waded through the deep waters of many afflictions without sinking or drowning....'[2] In effecting this change there is no doubt that the bearing of dissenters under persecution played a large part. Their courage in facing suffering commanded the respect and won the sympathy of their contemporaries, while their constancy wore out the malice of their foes. In this heroic resistance to oppression the Quakers held a position particularly honourable, though not unique.

Gradually the temper of public life began to change. The vindictiveness which characterised the cavaliers on the morrow of the Restoration soon spent itself, and what survived, by being merged in party antagonisms, was at least subject to the restraints introduced by the system of checks and counter-checks which marks the political struggle. As time passed, even those who had actively participated in the policy of repression became reluctant to acknowledge the fact. In retrospect, persecution was hard to justify, and men began to feel that the whole process was indefensible.[3] This in turn was related to a change even wider in its scope and more extensive in its result. Persecution presupposes a temper which believes that because truth is indivisible, minorities cannot be endured. As the period progressed, the scepticisms of a new day began to corrode the fanatical certainties of the past. The rising authority of reason commended moderation and restraint, and the arguments in favour of toleration began to command an ever wider assent. Even the law of nature seemed to sanction diversity; could human society reasonably impose a uniformity conspicuously absent from the world which the new science was exploring with such success?[1]

Anglo-Saxons have always been quicker to concede the force of practical considerations than of theoretical arguments, and throughout the Restoration period Englishmen were becoming increasingly sensitive to the fact that persecution was bad for trade. To ruin industrious people contributed nothing to the prosperity of the nation, and Puritan apologists could multiply instances of upright men whom persecution had reduced to destitution. Was it wise to sacrifice solid advantages for the sake of a theory which had failed to demonstrate its worth?

In a variety of ways the eighteenth century was casting its shadow before it. In the cooler and calmer period that was dawning Englishmen would differ in politics without the violence of civil war, and in religion without the vindictiveness of persecution. Churchman and dissenter would still be separated: they would belong to different strata of society and to different parties in public life; they would worship in different places and according to different rites. The paper warfare would continue, and the controversialists of one side would challenge the champions of the other. Suspicion or even contempt would mark the relations of church and chapel. But gone forever were the days when fines and distraints, imprisonment and transportation were the means by which Englishmen conducted their religious disputes.

CHAPTER III

'PERSECUTED BUT NOT FORSAKEN'

PERSECUTION was a policy inspired by complex motives but directed toward simple and specific ends. Churchmen trusted that it would harry dissenters into meek conformity. Politicians hoped to find it a useful weapon against factions which they distrusted or disliked. Both alike were disappointed. Persecution suffered from certain ineradicable defects. It presupposed the full co-operation of all who administered the laws, but in many of the magistrates it aroused so little enthusiasm—or rather it awakened such pronounced antipathy—that it was never universally or systematically enforced. Only ruthless repression can succeed; unless it threatens its victims with annihilation it will merely confirm them in the convictions for which they suffer. By compelling them to re-examine their beliefs, it reveals to them forgotten depths of meaning and opens up neglected reservoirs of strength. For the Puritans persecution was essentially a spiritual experience. The courage with which they faced its threat and the comfort which they experienced amid its tribulations sprang wholly from their faith. Since persecution loomed so large in their lives it naturally occupied a corresponding place in their thought, and one of the characteristic features of Restoration Puritanism was its unremitting struggle to come to terms with the sufferings caused by persecution.

The actual experience of persecution might be postponed, but the prospect (as we have seen) was always close at hand. An interval of immunity might end at any moment, and suffering could appear even more alarming in anticipation than it often proved to be in fact. There is no question of the power of persecution to intimidate and terrify. Bunyan has described in memorable terms the way in which imagination dwelt upon and exaggerated the hazards which repression entailed.[1] Men looked ahead with apprehension and tried to assess not only the trials they would face, but the resources with which they could meet them. Such self-examination was in itself a protection against the dangers inherent in the situation. It was very easy to discover plausible reasons for avoiding dangerous duties. When ministers were tempted to give up preaching, they could find plenty of pretexts for doing so. And yet the religious need of the people was most desperate at precisely those times when the ministers were beset by subtle inducements to silence. How foolish to forget the benediction pronounced on those who suffer![1]

Was loyalty to the truth consistent with any latitude in interpreting its demands? Inevitably the period was marked by ceaseless debates on the subject. Were concessions permissible in times of persecution? Was it necessary to court disaster by flaunting your dissent in the face of the authorities? At what point did practical wisdom shade into weak expediency, or how could you distinguish common-sense from cowardice?

To such questions the Quakers returned an answer completely consistent with their literal interpretation of the injunctions of the Gospel. People who refused to compromise even with relatively innocuous forms of customary courtesy were not likely to heed prudential arguments counselling a measure of adjustment to the storm. The absolutism which marked their witness at every point forbade any concessions for the sake of safety, and the courage with which they faced the consequences of their testimony redeemed it from all taint of doctrinaire perversity. It sometimes exposed them, however, to the perils of spiritual pride. As they contrasted their own inflexible consistency with the more pliant policies of other nonconformists, they allowed a touch of complacency to creep into their denunciations of those less rigid than themselves.[2]

If other Puritans adopted a different attitude, it was not necessarily because of cowardice or the dictates of expediency. They were perfectly aware of the complexity of the problem; they realised that the man who rejects the absolutist answer is confronted with moral dilemmas very difficult to resolve. They knew how easy it is to find a plausible pretext for a discreditable attitude.

They started from the generally agreed position that danger does not absolve Christians from the duty of gathering together to worship God; even under persecution it is therefore right to meet. Consequently to seek safety by flight is to capitulate precisely at the point where constancy is demanded;[1] not by such expedients should persecution be avoided. A minister might protect himself against ominous peril by refraining from preaching, but he gained his immunity by implying an acquiescence in tyranny in church affairs.[2] And though it was easy to argue that silence protected others from the dangers of involvement in your own distinctive witness, it also barred them from bearing any part in your testimony to the truth and betrayed you and them into spiritual apostasy.[3]

But loyalty to the truth was not synonymous with a defiant courting of disaster. To invite needless trouble was utter folly. 'There is a mean, if we could always hit it, between fool-hardiness and faint-heartedness.'[4] 'Suffering for a truth', as Bunyan pointed out, 'ought to be cautiously taken in hand, and as warily performed....A man is not bound by the law of his Lord to put himself into the mouth of his enemy.'[5] This seemed in keeping with Christ's command to his own disciples to go into a hostile world armed with wisdom as well as innocency, and even a rigorously scrupulous man like Thomas Goodwin laid it down as a safe rule that suffering was to be avoided by every lawful means.[6] Nor was there any question that a man might legitimately take all possible steps to evade the temporal ruin which persecution so often entailed. To throw away the material things given to us in trust is the mark of careless stewardship, and we are entitled to keep them (and use them wisely) so long as we can do so without a self-condemning conscience.[7] If there is an open door of escape, we may be sure that God's mercy has provided it, and sullenly to insist on suffering is to slight His providence when we are most clearly called to trust it. Indeed, to ignore the means of safety and to run rashly into needless danger is so far from being a mark of virtue that it can safely be dismissed as the evidence of presumption and spiritual pride.

Consequently even during periods of persecution most Puritan groups continued to meet, but their modified practice clearly reflected their careful study of the issues at stake. If possible they would keep within the limits that the law imposed. When pressure became extreme they would use all permissible expedients to avoid drawing upon themselves the wrath of the authorities. They would meet at unusual times and in unaccustomed places, and they would employ every legitimate means of frustrating the efforts to stamp out their meetings and break their will to persist. It is true, of course, that certain congregations temporarily ceased to meet, and some gave up the struggle, disbanded and disappeared, but those who gave way before the storm clearly fell short of the standard which the great Puritans advocated in their writings and exemplified in their lives. In the experience of the persecuted there usually came a time when concessions were no longer possible, and then a man had to stand his ground and bravely accept whatever suffering the will of God might have in store for him. As soon as the attempt to avoid persecution imposed intolerable demands, a faithful man would have no doubt as to the course he must choose. When 'the voice of necessity' became 'a call to suffer for righteousness', the conscientious person would apply to his doubts about yielding the touchstone of a simple test. 'When, by my silence, the truth must fall to the ground; or when, by my shrinking, the souls of other men are in danger' was the moment when any evasion was treachery and cowardice.[1]

When persecution had such power to daunt the believer, it was important to see in true perspective the problems it created. The grounds on which a person suffered profoundly modified his reaction to the trials he underwent. The distinction between those who were punished as evil-doers and those who were persecuted for righteousness' sake must never be forgotten; to keep it clearly in mind was the condition of discovering the consolations reserved to those who suffer for the Gospel's sake.[2] Moreover, the Puritans believed that they were contending for a purer form of the Gospel than that generally received; that they stood in the tradition of the first Reformers, and were punished by men who refused to press on to the true goal.

They believed, moreover, that their spiritual ancestry extended back much further than the days when the power of popery was first challenged. Persecution was no new phenomenon. As soon as men began their struggle to appropriate the truth, they met the opposition of those who in their blindness relied on brute force in order to keep out the light. There have always been giants, as Bunyan tersely expressed it.[1] History shows that from the very beginning Christ's people have been a people under persecution; when they have been loyal to their Lord's commands they have incurred the contradiction of sinners and have drawn down upon themselves the wrath of evil men.[2] True worship, in particular, has always awakened the enmity of all who resent anything that disturbs their own lifeless conventionality,[3] and consequently those who serve God in simplicity and sincerity have been persecuted from the time of Haman to the days of Queen Mary.[4] Therefore sufferers could be sustained by the assurance that they stood in the authentic Christian tradition; they 'were built upon the foundation of the apostles and prophets, Jesus Christ himself being the chief corner-stone'. This awareness of their true lineage had the most practical and far-reaching results. Since God has sustained his people under past sufferings, they might rest assured that amid new persecutions they will never be forsaken. 'Oh, if we did remember his former goodness, we should not be so ready to doubt his future care.'[5]

The Puritan felt that it was necessary to recognise the lineage of persecution; he knew that it was even more important to understand its nature. Because it manifested itself in a number of different spheres, it operated at a variety of levels. It could be regarded as a natural evil, the product of the forces which were at work in the world as man knows it. It was part of the political pattern, and those who so lightly invoked its aid should have realised the consequences it has always brought in its train. It was actually the enemy of the person and government of the king. It robbed him of the love of many of his subjects. It caused strife and aggravated bitterness among his people. It weakened the hands of just and sober men, while it encouraged the violent, the careless and the profane. It brought discredit on the processes of government and made the authorities obnoxious to the righteous God as well as to all good men.[1] Its evil character was reflected in the evil consequences which followed whenever it was applied.[2]

Though experience showed how disastrous persecution must always be when used as a political weapon, it was in the moral and spiritual realm that its nature was most fully disclosed. Because of its repressive effects, because it rooted out, tore down and destroyed, it could be regarded only as a Babylonian activity, working untold havoc in the house of God. It was a direct result of the malice of Satan; it was his chosen instrument for achieving his wicked ends.[3] Seldom did the devil directly assault the people of God, and even when he appeared to launch a violent attack he actually worked his will by subtle stratagems, and hid both from the persecutors and from their victims the true nature of what they did or suffered.[4] When seen in this light, persecution became not an isolated episode but one phase of an eternal process. In a sense it was inevitable; it was caught up in the unceasing struggle between good and evil. The children of darkness had always opposed the children of light; there had been unceasing enmity between 'the two seeds', and at a given moment the sufferer was merely bearing his part in this ancient and unending contest between righteousness and iniquity.[5] Persecution could best be understood as a manifestation of that hostility which, as Christ foretold, the world would always show to his disciples; therefore it was something which could be expected and it should not surprise the Christian when it comes. Since Christ himself 'endured such contradiction of sinners', those who in a heartless world would be his followers must expect no less. The Christian could not hope and should not try to avoid the Cross; it was enough for the disciple to be like his Master and the servant like his Lord.[6] This was not only a prognostication of the fate of Christ's people, it was a test of their loyalty. Though godliness might expose Christians to reproach in the world, they could take comfort from the fact that their very sufferings proved that 'the persecuted precisians' were in reality the people of God.[7] And yet it would have been naïve on their part if they had expected to be permitted to suffer avowedly for their faith. The primitive Christians were persecuted only when their detractors had fixed on them the odium of unmentionable deeds. As then, so ever since; ostensibly the Puritans were not attacked because of their faith. Only when groundless charges of sedition had been invented against them were they persecuted.[1]

In the last resort, the true character of persecution became intelligible only to those who tried to see it as God sees it. Darker spirits have always been tempted to regard it as a clear mark of divine displeasure. God had a controversy with his people, they said; consequently he visited them with the tokens of his wrath. But this was a dangerous approach, and often led to morose repinings. Nevertheless, the Puritans were persuaded that we dare not forget that in God's sight we always deserve persecution. Neither our character nor our achievements entitle us to stand complacently in God's presence and claim his approbation.[2] We need to realise that when persecution appears, sin is present—our sin no less than the sin of others. The violence which breaks out in human life is a symptom of the evil in which we all participate, so that none of us can contract out of the responsibility or re-pudiate his share of the blame. When we have declared the whole truth concerning the part played by 'wicked men', it remains a fact that 'our own selves are the deserving and procuring cause of all our woes'.[3] How carefully, therefore, must we search our own hearts to discover the ways in which we ourselves have contributed to the evils which we so vociferously deplore! How necessary, too, to realise that the sufferings by which we are engulfed are sent to compel us to search out in our hearts the roots of sin in order that by repentance we may eradicate them.[4]

And so, although persecution overwhelms the church 'in great distress, when there is no prospect of relief, no beam of light', we may well discover that periods of affliction are actually less dangerous than times of freedom.[5] But it is not enough merely to accept suffering as a means by which our sinful hearts are discip-lined. In the life of the Christian, persecution plays a constructive as well as a chastening role. To the sufferers it proved to be a part of God's providential ordering of man's existence; in it they could detect his mercy, even when they experienced the wrath of men. He permitted it because it provided one of the few infallible means of distinguishing hypocrites from true believers; insincerity could never abide its searching test. In history as well as beyond it, he set the sheep on one side and the goats on the other. But he did more than separate the one kind from the other; he constantly used the disciplines of suffering in order to bring his own people to the knowledge of himself. Those in whom faith had been awakened found that their insights were deepened and their loyalty strengthened.[1] Oppression served to establish them in the truths for which they suffered; persecution clarified their convictions and confirmed them.[2] Even their afflictions taught them to throw themselves with more complete abandon upon the mercies which could not fail; God was able to bless them according to his good purpose simply because they were ready to receive what he is always waiting to give.[3] The good, as they were made better, were also rendered more fruitful. Persecution was a process of pruning; as needless and irrelevant things were stripped away, the full energies of faith were so directed as to achieve their due and rightful end.[4] When such benefits accrued from the afflictions of the faithful, was it not reasonable to trace even in their sufferings the hand of God? He granted them a season in which to grow in grace, a day wherein they could improve their interest in the things that issue in abundant life.[5] There was not a virtue they possessed, not an attribute they might acquire, but it was strengthened through the disciplines of persecution. Patience was taught to endure and love to abound, while faith learned to appropriate that strength which made them 'more than conquerors through him that loved us'.[6] The whole religious life was rendered vital and active to achieve, in the present, the purposes of faith; but it also learned to relate immediate experience both to the past and to the future, to the days in which God first declared his power and to those in which he would finally vindicate his purpose. Hence the Puritans were bold to claim that even amid afflictions God was opening a way by which his followers could manifest their faithfulness to, and their affection for, him. Moreover, because persecution is always one of God's instruments for

73

delivering his people from the power of sin and breaking the bondage within which it has held them, they could not rightly regard it as the problem which it was often represented to be. Could they legitimately quarrel with the method by which God chose to bring them such incalculable blessings? If he was willing to lead them into the glorious liberty of his children, could they complain at the blows which struck the shackles from their feet?[1] If they could be made perfect only through sufferings, let them gladly admit the values that attach to persecution, and praise God that he had brought them thus early into his school.[2]

It seemed clear that the ineffectiveness which distinguished so many Christians sprang from their failure to allow their professed standards to control their common attitudes. In theory they asserted values which in practice they were reluctant to translate into conduct. At this point persecution played a most valuable role. When they had become obsessed with mundane interests, it broke the grip of material things. The hold which worldly possessions had gained upon their hearts was loosened when affliction robbed them of the things which once they had held so dear. For the first time, it might be, they were provided with a simple test to reveal whether their minds were fixed on the outward things with which God had blessed them, or on the Lord who gave them.[3] This was a discipline so necessary to Christians that they could hardly hope to escape it, but when once they submitted to it they discovered that in fundamental and far-reaching ways their attitudes were altered. As their preoccupation with material things decreased, they found themselves more fully and naturally the citizens of an eternal order. Earth might be their dwelling-place, but they discovered that heaven was actually their home.[4] Not only did their attitude to possessions alter, but gradually they were brought to a truer estimation of themselves.[5] They were taught, too, the methods by which a sane valuation of life's elements could be sustained: God 'sharpens our faith and quickens our prayers; he brings us into the secret chamber of our own heart, which we had little mind before to visit by a self-examination'.[6] In the process, their physical nature proved less turbulent and recalcitrant than it had been, and they learned the

74

secret of governing the flesh. The tyranny of convention, the lifeless grip of formalism, the dependence upon externals—these things forfeited their importance, and as they were relegated to their proper status, the earnest inquirer discovered that a true estimation of life's essentials produced a surer mastery of life's details.[1]

The drift of the argument is obvious. If persecution was within God's providence and was controlled by it, it was more likely to reveal his nature than to deny it. When the Puritans penetrated beneath the surface, when they probed the significance of the sufferings which persecution brought, they discovered that even their afflictions were the expositors of God's love.[2] He appointed them of his grace, and he used them for the good of his children. Though persecution seemed to threaten the destruction of the church, God in his loving wisdom ordered it otherwise, so that seeming disasters were the means by which his greatest mercies were disclosed. 'God many times saves his people by sufferings, and brings them to shore upon the planks of a broken ship.'[3] Persecution was thus a kind of spiritual surgery; when the gathering was lanced, the poison drained away, and the sufferer was restored to health. So far from weakening the church, oppression issued in its increase. Those who were members of the Christian fellowship were driven back to the true sources of their strength, and even the catastrophes which scattered its members awakened them to their duty and increased their opportunities of serving God. Experience proved conclusively that when persecution came, 'goodness in God [was] the principal cause and orderer of the affliction'.[4]

Persecution was not a phenomenon divorced from personal considerations. It was a manifestation of the failure of men to achieve right relationships among themselves. The sufferings it occasioned were due to the actions of their fellow men, and these in turn rested upon deliberate choices. Prejudices and resentments played their part and helped to create a situation in which good will was seriously endangered. A true understanding of what persecution meant could not be divorced from a realistic evaluation of those who enforced it. The character of the oppressor affected the nature of the experience, and it was necessary to examine him as objectively as possible. The harshness so invariably associated with repression was the quality which first commanded attention, for the persecutor was 'always a hunter without pity'.[1] He was the successor of all the evil men who have held down the truth in violence. Like all wicked men who have gained power, he was very fierce in his wrath.[2] Pride also was responsible; the oppressor had yielded to that 'confident insulting genius, which makes a man think himself competent to be a standard to mankind', so that when he could not persuade his opponents by reason he resorted without hesitation to 'club or faggot arguments'.[3] What, then, was the right attitude to adopt toward Christians who, instead of bearing the cross themselves, delighted to lay it upon others? Could such men really claim to be of the household of faith? Was there any alternative to the conclusion that the persecutor was really not a Christian at all?[4] And yet this was a view which might easily prove dangerous to the person who held it. Only ceaseless vigilance could protect him against the perils of embittering of his inward life by nursing secret grievances against his foes. 'Take heed of hurting yourself by passion or sin, because others hurt you by slanders or persecutions. Keep you in the way of your duty, and leave your names and your lives to God.'[5]

But though the Puritan knew that he would be wise neither to reproach his persecutors nor condemn them, he was at liberty to note the fate that usually overtook such men. However their worldly interests might fare, he could observe that they were seldom without fear. Indeed, the policy on which they relied was itself a confession of their weakness, an acknowledgement that the true faith was not in them.[6] Consequently they seldom achieved results that bore any reasonable proportion to the efforts they had put forth; but need this occasion wonder? Could it be otherwise when the hand of God was so manifestly against them?[7] Even their victories were fleeting and ephemeral; a momentary triumph could not save them from the overthrow which, in a moral universe, was their inevitable fate.[8] The judgement which overtook evil men was simply a means of advancing the purposes

of God's sovereign rule and of promoting the glory and dignity
of his government.[1] When God brought low the persecutor, he
did it to encourage and confirm his people; this was one of the
surest ways of pressing home 'the lessons of extremity and
deliverance'.[2]

The attitude of the Puritans to their oppressors was the fruit
of much reflection on the message of the Old Testament prophets.
They believed that because God's judgements are abroad in the
earth, retribution finally overtakes the evil man. There is a causal
sequence in the moral world; though the proud may flourish for
a season, their downfall is predetermined. Their character and
their actions contain within them the seeds of their overthrow.
It was this approach which gave its distinctive note to the Puritan
custom of observing the disasters of their foes. Admittedly it was
easy to conclude that you were specially favoured of God and
that your oppressors were the children of wrath, but it was impossible to fall into the vindictive malice which delighted in the
disasters of others. The death of persecutors might occasion a
respite, all the more appreciated, because of the remorseless pressure which had preceded it, but much more important was the
conviction that the righteous were beholding 'the great deliverance of our God'. They were spectators of, indeed they were
participants in, the vindication of the moral principles on which
the universe itself must rest. From this sprang the particular
solemnity with which the destruction of evil men must be observed. At their fall, remarked John Whiting, 'I never rejoiced,
or desired that the evil day should hasten to come upon them.'[3]
Nevertheless, he carefully recorded the fate which overtook
notorious persecutors. The annals of the sufferers abound in
references to the miserable death of those who had been conspicuous oppressors. A particularly harsh gaoler died in horrible
agony of mind and spirit. A justice who had sworn not to spare
his dissenting neighbours was involved in a duel and was killed
before he could carry out his threats. A justice, riding home from
the tavern, tumbled from his horse, and was drowned in the ditch.
A priest, fresh from harrying dissenters, fell downstairs and broke
his neck. Cases of strange diseases, painful and lingering, were

common, and on his deathbed many a persecutor, tortured by the pangs of conscience, bewailed the cruelty he had shown to harmless people. So striking was the retribution visited upon the heartless that even those not directly concerned took note, and these instances of 'just judgements' became the means by which others were taught to take heed and fear God.[1] But, however the worldly might react, the righteous could improve to their own advantage the fate which overtook the wicked.[2] Humbly to confess their sins, gratefully to admire God's power, willingly to submit to his will—these were the proper uses of the awful spectacle of the punishment of the ungodly.

It was important to see persecution in its true character and in proper perspective, but by itself this brought no immunity from the problems it created. No intelligent person would minimise their seriousness, but only someone disciplined by experience could appreciate their full range. One of the simplest difficulties —yet one of the hardest to meet—sprang from the reluctance of wife or family to share in the sufferings which a man's convictions entailed. Courage, even when fortified by the encouragement of others, found it hard to face persecution without flinching; what could be expected when the voices of those nearest and dearest whispered counsels of conformity? Moreover, every man found within himself the advocate of a less uncompromising attitude. 'The flesh' has its own forms of persuasion, and it was no mean psychologist who remarked 'skin for skin, yea, all that a man hath will he give for his life'. When the pressure became too remorseless, it was natural to look longingly at less arduous paths, and when faced with the prospect of ruin a man might chose an easier way. So John Gratton noted the Presbyterians who fell away through fear of heavy fines, and John Owen pointed out that persecution always tempts men to forsake the truth of God because it so obviously attacks 'their secular interest in this world'.[3] As a result the backslider became not only a source of discouragement but an occasion of temptation, a clear example of the feasibility of a less exacting course. But even when a man stood firm, his attention might be so completely absorbed by the sufferings of body and the misfortunes of estate which he endured, that he had little time for more important matters. Just when he found himself 'in greatest need of strength' he might discover that he had been betrayed into spiritual negligence. Indeed, there was always the danger that amid afflictions men, forgetting God and despising his help, would grow faint and so would sink beneath the waters of despair.[1]

Persecution was unquestionably a disaster, but not one about which it was permissible to complain.[2] Only those who misconceived its nature would yield to the ever-present temptation to rail against the providence of God or to question the justice of his decrees. How arrogant was anything which suggested 'a presuming to instruct God', yet how easy! 'All murmuring [was] a fastening error upon unerring wisdom',[3] and therein blasphemy and folly combined. But this attitude reflected only one of the many forms of frustration which persecution bred. It was a constant struggle to prevent the soul from sinking into bitterness, and charity was often the first casualty in the contest between those who should be brothers.[4] Natural instinct was always prompting the desire to return upon your oppressors what you suffered at their hands. 'Take heed', warned Baxter, 'of giving way to secret wishes of hurt to your adversaries, or of reproachful words against them; take heed of hurting yourselves by passion or sin, because others hurt you by slanders or persecutions.'[5]

Repression, when prolonged, created in its victims a restiveness as difficult to discipline as it was impossible to avoid. When every manifestation in which the religious impulse normally found expression was denied, the Puritan felt that he was being driven relentlessly into an all-embracing experience of frustration.[6] He was debarred from worshipping according to the forms which he believed were right and from witnessing to his faith in the way he considered his duty. Everything he esteemed most highly was made the subject of reproach.[7] The feeling of exasperated impotence was heightened by the kind of abuse to which he found himself exposed. Official policy prevented him from stating his case, yet he was reviled because of his silence.[8] The licensing laws made it hazardous to justify his views in print, and

79

he was not allowed to defend his position by speech. First he was gagged; then he was ridiculed because he had nothing to say. All the while, the very clergy who urged the magistrates to extirpate dissent were commending to dissenters the virtue of resignation.[1] This was a real trial to the sufferer's patience, and deepened his feeling of helplessness and frustration.

However the Puritan might react, he was certain to face major spiritual problems. He might be needlessly depressed, or he might be foolishly elated, and it was difficult to say which state was more dangerous. As he faced the dark forces which the persecuting spirit had released into the world, he might be weighed down with oppression of spirit. It was 'a cruel, bloody, persecuting time'; it required all a man's faith to see that 'the Lord's power went over all'.[2] As he studied the world in which he was set to give his testimony, he might find it hard to discern the pattern that the hand of God was tracing; he needed to be reminded that the study of providence was more difficult now than in former ages, 'because God seems to manage things in the church more by his wisdom than power, which is not so intelligible to man as the sensible effects of his strength'.[3] He saw the godly punished, and the ancient problem of the severity of God's hand upon his people assumed a new relevance. On the other hand, he faced the perils of spiritual pride. It was easy to be lulled into the false confidence which believed that persecution earned special spiritual rewards and entitled the sufferer to distinctive privileges. Once a man was lifted up in spirit, he might unwittingly contribute, by his pride, to the destruction of the unity of the household of faith.[4]

One further problem remained. The man who approached the ordeal of repression in the wrong spirit was certain to forfeit the blessings which it could bring. Even though he were susceptible to its teachings at the time, he would find that as soon as freedom brought relief it would be perilously easy to forget the lessons he had learned. Careful self-discipline was consequently the price of real improvement.[5]

So fierce were the fires of persecution that only the person who was prepared and fully fortified could hope to emerge unscathed from the ordeal. It therefore became a matter of paramount importance to teach men and women how to turn affliction into spiritual gain. One by one the great virtues of the faith were invoked and the particular contribution of each was assessed. But in so earnest a struggle none but the superficial looked for quick deliverance or an easy victory. After all, it is God's chosen method to leave his people to endure extremity before affording help; he 'lets the concerns of his church go backward, that he may bring them on with glory to himself and satisfaction to his creature'.[1] It would seem, indeed, that the people of God have always been a suffering people; their faithfulness is purchased at a price, and they cannot expect to pay it without preparation. Before anticipated sufferings are actually upon them, they must fit themselves to endure whatever the day of trial may bring.[2] Yet it is not by taking anxious thought about the future that men make ready to abide afflictions. They must commit their souls to God. Because the issues of time and eternity are in his care, there is no need to fear, but on any other basis the outcome is so uncertain that any kind of confidence reflects presumptuous pride. The acquiescent spirit, however, is never passive. The man who yields his soul to God's guidance becomes a partner in an ever-expanding enterprise, and discovers the secret of true freedom. He gains the liberty which makes it possible to endure persecution gladly and with confidence; the voluntary acceptance of suffering removes the problems which normally make it so bitter an experience. Instead of the poisons of frustration he receives the strength and assurance of which the Scriptures are the distinctive channel. Inner peace becomes the choice of the sufferer; the spirit which he learns to cultivate—the spirit of love and joy and peace—is the guarantee that he will first win the victory within.[3]

No one who knew anything about persecution questioned its power to intimidate and terrify; to meet and overcome its threats represented a personal triumph of a very high order. And though the victory was won within, it was never won alone. The sufferer knew that he belonged to a community of faith and love, and the prayers of his fellows constantly sustained him. The support of fellow-believers was a factor of inestimable importance in breaking the power of persecution. Only because the Puritans believed that the mercy of God had united them in the family of his love could they endure the trials to which they were exposed. To an amazing degree they were willing to share one another's sufferings; they constantly visited the prisoners, they helped those whose goods had been plundered, and they unremittingly pressed upon the authorities the hardships which their fellows were called on to endure. The same unity which enabled the victim to receive, helped him also to give. He knew that he suffered as a member of a community and his witness was to a corporate faith. His constancy and courage contributed to the spiritual resources of the church; they strengthened and confirmed his fellow-members. But he also offered a testimony before the whole world, and he knew that persecution must be so endured that righteousness would thereby be commended. Even in the most difficult times the Christian bears the responsibility of so conducting himself that the cause of God will be advanced.[1]

Though supported by others, the sufferer had to discover how best to appropriate the resources he could claim. He had to learn the importance of concentrating his thoughts on Christ. The example of his Master would in itself accomplish wonders in steeling the wavering will, but it was to a present Lord, not to a remote exemplar, that he was commended. With undaunted confidence he must invoke the aid of him who is 'the same yesterday, to-day and forever', and he must do so in the conviction that those who ask will receive. He should remember that his belief in the Holy Spirit proclaims the intimate presence of that God who had revealed himself in Christ; then he would realise that 'affliction is part of the provision that God hath made in his house for his children'. Moreover, he could draw reassurance from the constancy of those who, in situations like his own, were made strong to endure. Instinctively the sufferer's thoughts turned to Daniel—to his courage when threatened, to his reliance on the efficacy of prayer, and to his experience of the power of God to deliver his people.[2]

Patience, though apparently an elementary virtue, was at once difficult to acquire and supremely necessary to possess. The man who chafed at his lot or fretted over the sufferings that befell him had already been defeated in his soul. It was easy to concede that patience was desirable, but hard not to grow restive under the hand of wicked men. To cease to worry about the fate of Cain, to remember that such matters are in God's hands, not in ours— even this often seemed a counsel of perfection.[1] To master this elusive grace, the sufferer had to forget both his persecutors and himself. He had to begin with God; recognise his sovereignty, and his own problems would begin to fall into their proper place. The magnitude of man's ignorance should have made him slow to censure the incomprehensible mysteries of God. 'We have sense to feel the effects, but not heads to understand the reasons and methods of God's government.' Where we cannot see, his utter holiness should teach us due submission, for 'he is righteous in his darkness, wise in his cloudiness'.[2] Even the thought of the unchanging constancy of God emphasised the wisdom of patience, since 'to murmur is to contend with God'.[3] But those who also believed in the goodness of God had more winning persuasives to teach them humble silence; though they could not understand, they knew that they could trust. A calm serenity was consequently the mark of those who had really come to terms with their fate; they had ceased to struggle because they had learned to acquiesce.[4]

When once the springs of comfort were opened a man discovered how copious and inexhaustible was their flow. The thought of God in any form was a means by which peace and power could come to those who were afflicted. Let a man contemplate the power of God, and he would realise that 'our evils can never be so great to oppress us as his power is greater to deliver us. The same power that brought a world out of chaos, and constituted and hath hitherto preserved the regular motion of the stars, can bring order out of our confusions and light out of our darkness....From this attribute of the infinite power of God we have a ground of comfort in the lowest estate of the church. Let the state of the church be never so deplorable, that power that created the world, and shall raise the bodies of men, can create a happy state for the church, and raise her from an overwhelming grave.'[1] Or think of the goodness of God; have we anything to 'fear from the conduct of infinite goodness?'[2] Or again consider God's universal domination. 'As a sovereign he can be the remover of [our sufferings]; he can command the waters of affliction to go so far and no farther....The consideration of the divine sovereignty may arm us against the threatenings of mighty ones and the menaces of persecutors.'[3] How great is the comfort which springs from the assurance that whatever happens to us is governed by God's will and lies within the orbit of his order and design! When we are under his rule we are within his care; in this confidence the Puritan could fearlessly face the unknown future and find that he was upheld in difficult duties, amid harassing fears, and in the most terrifying extremities.[4] The consideration of God's attributes led naturally to the experience of God's presence. The sense of God's nearness was a support in 'opposing tribunals' or in prisons; there was no affliction that need shake the firm assurance that God was near at hand.[5] When face to face with his foes, the Puritan found that 'omnipresence' was not a term lifted from theological text-books but a sober fact which proved its reality in the comfort it afforded. It was the means by which a man could calmly face long years of persecution and imprisonment, and affirm, with Ambrose Rigge, that through it all 'the Lord carried me with cheerfulness and contendedness, without the least murmuring'.[6] In one area after another, as experience confirmed the truths which faith affirmed, the believer found new sources of encouragement. And in quite ordinary ways the disciplines of daily life ministered comfort to the sufferer. The accustomed forms of worship revealed an unsuspected power of sustaining hard-pressed believers; 'whatever their outward, distressed condition' might be, they found 'order, beauty and glory in the worship of God, above all that the world can pretend to'.[7] They discovered a way of accepting and bearing 'crosses' that made even grievous ones seem light, and when they were tempted to murmur they were reassured and sobered by the elementary fact that though the Lord had taken away some of their 'ease, liberty, health and estates', he might justifiably have swept them away entirely.[8]

Though it was important to acquire patience and to experience comfort, more positive qualities were needed before the problem posed by persecution could successfully be mastered. There was no prospect of true victory unless a man had gained the courage which could make him unafraid in the face of anything his enemies might do.[1] Some men are brave through ignorance, some because of an excess of natural spirits, but the courage demanded by persecution (as the Puritans well knew) was of a different order. Calmly to assess the situation, and, with full awareness of the facts, to adhere to your position, presupposed fortitude of a kind that comes only from the conscious possession of adequate spiritual resources.[2] Only those who rightly grasped the relationship between human endurance and divine power could achieve this highest form of fearlessness. To rely upon God was not merely a sure defence against discouragement and repression, it was the only way of banishing the fear of man. Let a man 'look up to the all-sufficiency of God'; let him stay his mind on God and walk before Him in all humility, and he would then find that all terrors disappeared.[3] What was more, he would discover that, amid all afflictions, his courage was renewed and his joys immeasurably increased. This accounts for the strong note of praise which runs through the literature inspired by persecution. Sufferings proved to be blessings; they were an occasion for gratitude, and the ways in which thanksgiving could be duly cultivated and expressed were clearly indicated.[4]

Courage of this kind was one aspect of a settled confidence which looked with calm assurance on the whole of life. Uprightness and integrity might help to confirm it, but the Puritan knew that its true foundations lay much deeper than that. It rested on the fact that the truth outlasts all things, but 'truth' itself was merely an abstract term unless the steady contemplation of God filled it with meaning.[5] The literature of the Puritans vibrates with the unshakable conviction that God's power is over all; endlessly, irresistibly, it streams forth to accomplish its beneficent and holy ends. Only blindness could ignore it, and trust was merely the grateful commitment of our life to an unfailing power of wisdom and love. And since God rules in the affairs of men, we can calmly and confidently wait for his deliverance. The lesson of trust, once learned, helps us to submit to the discipline of events; persecuted Christians find that even when they are thrown into the lion's den, 'into places where no eye can see them, no hand relieve them, where no one knows whether they are among the living or the dead', even then God is their rock.[1] This assurance becomes solid fact only through the believer's faith in Christ, and its natural fruit is a hope which is satisfied that ultimately Providence cannot 'miss of its aim'. Men may ignore or even oppose the divine purpose; when faced with their anger the upright may be tempted to fear, but his unfailing assurance is grounded in the wisdom which orders all things well. God permits as much suffering as is good for the church; just 'as the physician weighs out as much as may curb the disease, not kill the patient',[2] so God uses afflictions to achieve his holy ends.

The Puritan met persecution assured that in due course God would certainly bring deliverance. But this was not a facile faith. Escape might only come through death; it would be into fuller life, but it might be after grievous suffering. Nevertheless, in life or by death, to those who persevered the issue would finally be certain victory. To keep inviolate the citadel of your soul; to hold firmly to great convictions and to bear faithful testimony to their truth; to meet danger without flinching and to endure suffering without complaint—this was a real measure of triumph. The Puritan humbly believed that it was 'the victory that overcometh the world'. Beyond the sufferings which he experienced in this world, he saw the incomparable compensations of the future; he knew that 'the happiness of his glorified estate' would infinitely outweigh 'the misery of his present afflictions'.[3] Though Faithful died at the hands of his enemies, his friends were satisfied that the fiery chariot had been waiting to snatch him off to his reward, and to the attentive ear there came, far-off and faint but unmistakable and clear, the trumpet notes which sounded from 'the other side'.

The Puritan prepared for persecution by understanding the true nature of the experience he had to undergo; he supported himself under the ordeal by laying hold of the full range of spiritual resources open to him; he also attempted realistically to estimate the results which followed from his sufferings. He noted the heightened sense of unity within the persecuted group, and the practical spirit of brotherhood which it created. He observed that his own experience duplicated that of the earliest Christians; persecution might break up a worshipping community, but in so doing it merely scattered the seed.[1] A few might fall; here and there a congregation might disappear, but essentially the churches gained more than they lost. The fires of adversity refined but did not consume. 'God lets the concerns of his church go backward, that he may bring them on with more glory to himself and satisfaction to his creature.'[2] The corporate experience was reflected in the life of the individual. If a man had any faith at all, adversity merely confirmed his convictions. It was impossible to drive from his position a man who had suffered persecution for it.[3] As a consequence, Puritanism became, for a whole generation, more a matter of life and less a subject of theological debate than it had ever been before. With humble amazement, the greatest spokesmen of the persecuted groups noted that their sufferings had led to fuller life and to incalculable spiritual benefits. When the Lord had already spread a table for them in the presence of their enemies, they could gratefully rest in the conviction that goodness and mercy would follow them all the days of their life.

CHAPTER IV

'SHADES OF THE PRISON HOUSE'

THE processes of law were sometimes swift and arbitrary, sometimes tedious and slow. The Puritan, faced with persecution, might find himself adequately fortified against it or he might discover that his spiritual resources were painfully insufficient for the ordeal. In any case, the course of justice often brought him to the gaol. This was the scene of his most searching trial; frequently it was the setting for his most convincing triumph.

Even the journey to prison might prove a harrowing experience. Often the distance was considerable; the brutality of the guards might make it seem immeasurably greater. Thomas Horrockes, with a sergeant riding on either side of him, was treated with a degree of ignominy which his friends thought fitting only for a criminal.[1] Henry Parsons, when taken from Taunton to Ilchester, was forced to dismount from his horse, and mile after mile the troopers whipped him through the mire of the rough and heavy roads. A Quaker, similarly driven on foot before mounted guards, was run up hill and down dale, beaten and clubbed if he so much as flagged, and he died in prison from the hardships he suffered in getting there. But this was not the invariable pattern. A prisoner might be treated with consideration and even with respect. Oliver Heywood was committed to the care of his own son, who was charged to deliver his father to the gaoler, and as the two men rode toward York, they had an opportunity for religious fellowship which both found very precious. In the same way, Joseph Alleine, with his mittimus in his own pocket, started out surrounded by friends, and his journey to prison was almost like a triumphal progress. When he reached Ilchester, he found the gaol locked and the keeper absent. A crowd of people, prompted by curiosity, began to gather, and Alleine seized the chance to preach another sermon—

thus repeating, on the very threshhold of the prison, the offence for which he had been sent there.[1]

Once the prison door had closed behind him, the prisoner found himself amid conditions which varied all the way from comparative comfort to indescribable squalor. Some men were well satisfied with their treatment, and felt that they had little cause to complain. Richard Baxter's first imprisonment caused no serious hardships, and in retrospect he could even regard it with pleasure. Prison life, of course, inevitably involved some drawbacks. At night the noise disturbed him; during the summer he suffered from the heat. Kind friends who came to see him consumed too much of his time. He had no chance to go abroad, and to be cut off from public worship was a serious hardship. On the other hand, he had a considerate gaoler; he was able to bring his own bed from home; he had liberty to walk in a pleasant garden, and he never lacked for company. His wife stayed with him, and 'she was never so cheerful a companion to me as in prison'. They were able to establish satisfactory housekeeping arrangements, and Baxter remarked that the whole experience was not unlike securing lodgings in London for six months.[2]

Two other distinguished nonconformists, both among the best known preachers of this period, were equally fortunate. Oliver Heywood was so considerately treated at York Castle that he felt that he could have fared little better if he had been staying with friends. He had a room to himself, the benefit of a considerate gaoler, and the company of his ever-faithful wife. In addition, he added: 'I have spiritual liberties, privileges, secret opportunities of communion with my God, liberty of studying and writing as if I had my own house, the sweet company of Mr Whitaker and his wife, that are in the next room to me, many precious servants of God out of the city to visit me, to pray and discourse with me.'[3] Philip Henry, writing from Chester Castle, remarked that he and his fellow-prisoners were 'better accommodated...than we could have expected', but he adds, significantly enough, 'we must pay for it'.[4]

In many cases prison life was what you were able to make it, and some men have little skill in making themselves comfortable.

The presence or absence of a wife was apt to be decisive. Both Baxter and Heywood received in prison the same care they received at home, and unquestionably this coloured their accounts of prison life. William Dewsbery, the Quaker, was in Warwick gaol for nineteen years, and when his little granddaughter came to stay with him, her presence brought into that dark place a light which gladdened the old man's heart.[1]

Yet even with a wife, a man might be only moderately comfortable. At Ilchester, Alleine found himself thrust into a room crowded almost beyond endurance. Among his fellow-prisoners he mentions fifty Quakers, seventeen Baptists, and thirteen ministers, as well as many others who lent themselves readily to religious classification. With these people he spent the next four months, with few breaks of any kind. This suggests a life so constantly exposed both to the scrutiny of others and to the pressures of proximity and noise as to be scarcely tolerable. Yet Alleine was able to secure himself a tiny island of privacy in this sea of humanity. He was even able to curtain it off, introduce his own bed, and bring in his wife—to add perhaps to the congestion, but certainly to help him to cope with it.

Crowded conditions were common; the power to mitigate them was rare. Even by seventeenth-century standards, prison accommodation was hardly equal to the normal demands upon it, but in periods of intense religious persecution the gaols were suddenly expected to receive hundreds of people who would normally never see the inside of a prison. The available space was wholly inadequate when, in addition to the criminal element of the population, it had to accommodate large numbers of the most conscientious members of the community. The figures for arrests give some idea of the magnitude of the problem thus created, and afford an explanation of the appalling conditions which prevailed. In February and March 1660/1, 229 Quakers were imprisoned in the West Riding of Yorkshire, and 129 in the North Riding. The number of Quakers in the various prisons of the county rose during these months to 535, and a large proportion of them were in York Castle. During the same period, the aftermath of the Fifth-Monarchy scare brought Somerset

Quakers to Ilchester gaol in droves, and by the beginning of the new year 212 prisoners had been added to the numbers usually accommodated. By March 1661 there were 270 Quakers in Lancaster gaol. A couple of years later, the weekly totals sent to Newgate from the Quaker meetings in London tell the same story. For a five-week period in 1664, the figures are 200, 40, 150, 175, 232, and few of these could expect early release.[1]

Terrible congestion was the inevitable result. Into a small room which would normally accommodate a single person, thirteen prisoners would be thrust. Beds might be available for some, but many had to lie on the floor, and when even that proved impossible, they had to sit up day and night. In the Bridewell prison at Bristol, fifty women shared four beds among them, which left more than thirty to lie on the filthy boards— and presumably left little space in any of the beds. A complaint from the prisoners in Newgate, in the same city, describes in greater detail the problems created by lack of space. In one room there were nine beds; in another, thirteen feet square, there were seven. Usually three or four men slept in each bed, and the rest sat up. But the beds, though utterly insufficient at night, were exceedingly inconvenient by day. They reduced living space to a minimum. There was no room to move about, no chance to work, no decent opportunity of meeting the barest needs of physical existence.[2]

Even this suggests a higher standard than frequently prevailed. When the crowding became really desperate, there were people in hammocks, tier above tier, people lying on tables, people sleeping in kennels under the table, people lying all over the floor, people for whom there was no room to lie down at all, and who leaned against the walls, or sat propped against the table legs.[3] At the height of the Venner scare, one hundred people were crowded into a single room in Newgate prison in London; no one could lie down, few could even sit, and standing room was so limited that it was scarcely possible to move one's arms and legs. In mild weather, as many as could safely do so slept outside on the 'leads of the roof', and though their bed was neither soft nor safe, at least they escaped the horrible stench which filled the overcrowded and ill-ventilated rooms inside. Three hundred years ago people who lived in cities had been trained not to be unduly squeamish about smells, but even they could not face with equanimity the overpowering odours of a congested prison. When such crowded conditions prevailed, any attempt to segregate men and women was abandoned; scores, even hundreds, of people were herded together in a stinking, sweating mass of humanity.[1]

When the air was foul, both heat and cold caused untold misery. Summer weather made the congestion almost unbearable. In a large crowded room directly under the roof, lack of air in combination with the high temperature was insufferable, and the prisoners found relief only by stripping off some of the tiles. Those within the gaol might dread the warm weather because of the discomfort it caused, but those outside thought with apprehension of the threat to public health which lurked in such conditions. Cold weather might be less dangerous, but on the whole it caused even greater misery. Many prisons were like Bunyan's gaol at Bedford: they had no fireplaces, and consequently no means of keeping the prisoners warm.[2] Where it was possible to have a fire, it was often impossible to obtain fuel. In bitter winter weather, prisoners at Lynn were left to lie on the bare floors in unheated rooms, and when they finally secured straw to sleep on, it was promptly seized and given to the felons in the common gaol.[3] At Maidstone, during the winter months, Samuel French found that he could get neither fuel for warmth nor candles for light, and every evening he sat in the dark and the cold.[4] Sometimes, when a fire could be obtained, the chimney proved so defective that the room was filled with clouds of smoke. The prisoners in Launceston gaol reported that 'they were much nipped with the asperity of the weather and cold situation of the place and though fuel be pretty plenty, yet dear, and smokiness of the chimneys make our fires less serviceable unto us'—yet in spite of the physical miseries which the place entailed they enjoyed such spiritual comforts that the prison seemed 'like a palace or a place of pleasure'.[5] Worse still was the plight of those who, with no fire themselves, were suffocated by the smoke which seeped into their rooms from the imperfect chimneys. George Fox tells of sitting, cold and wet, in a cell in Lancaster Castle where the smoke was so dense that even when he lit a candle he could scarcely see its flame. Often, with no warmth inside, there was no way of keeping out the wind and the rain. At Lancaster, Margaret Fell was imprisoned in a room so exposed to the elements that every storm made it almost uninhabitable. George Fox a man of iron constitution, had his health broken by the miseries he suffered in cells that were both damp and cold. At Lancaster, the winds drove the rain into the room, and since the ceiling leaked, both his clothes and his bedding were often wet for days on end. When moved to Scarborough Castle, he was lodged on the seaward side of the building, and his room afforded scant protection against the storms which swept in from the North Sea. 'The wind', he says, 'drove in the rain forcibly, so that the water came over my bed, and ran about the room, that I was fain to skim it up with a platter. And when my clothes were wet, I had no fire to dry them; so that my body was benumbed with cold, and my fingers swelled, that one was grown as big as two.' Neither ingenuity nor expense—and he tried both—could secure him protection against the weather, and the winter was a protracted ordeal of unmitigated misery.[1]

Usually there was no remedy for such conditions, and consequently no respite for the prisoners who endured them. But occasionally an opportunity arose to lodge a protest, and at Lancaster assizes, in August 1664, Margaret Fell boldly remonstrated with the judge. '*Judge:* Mrs Fell, you wrote to me concerning the badness of your prisons, that it rains in, and they are not fit for people to lie in. *M.F.:* The sheriff knows, and has been told of it several times, and now it is raining if you will send, you may see whether they be fit for people to lie in.' When Colonel Kirby, a local justice of the peace, rose to defend the sheriff and justify the treatment accorded to the prisoners, Margaret Fell fearlessly charged him with thoughtless cruelty in putting people 'in a cold room where there was nothing but bare boards to lie on', and many of them, she added, were ill and old, but of unquestioned integrity. Moreover, she added, 'when William

Kirby was asked, Why they might not have liberty to shift for themselves for beds? he answered, They were to commit them to prison, but not provide prisons for them.' Even the judge was touched and sobered by this recital of prison hardships. It was not right, he said; 'they ought to have prisons fit for men'.[1]

Whatever a humane judge might feel, many of the prisons were fit only for beasts. Sanitation, even at the best, was extremely rudimentary, and often it did not exist at all. The sudden arrest of a group of worshippers might fill to overflowing a room which, because no one had bothered to clean it out, was already deep in filth and crawling with vermin. At the whim of a gaoler, scores of prisoners might be kept locked in their room for many hours—even for days—with no chance of leaving it and with results which can more easily be imagined than described. The discomfort caused by the filth and the stench of the gaols might afflict even moderately fortunate prisoners, but possibilities yet more horrible were close at hand. Conditions might be nauseating in the better parts of a prison, but in the common gaol they were infinitely worse. The felons, existing in a miasma of filth and brutality, were never far away, and often made their presence disagreeably insistent. All day long, the prisoners in the upper rooms listened to the rattle of the chains of the condemned men; they were constantly conscious of the blasphemous violence with which the felons wrangled among themselves, and often they lay sleepless throughout the night while the noisy songs from the common prison made the Puritans tremble with thoughts of final judgement and the punishments of Hell.[2]

In theory the felons were segregated from the other prisoners, but the lines of division were often blurred. Sometimes they all shared 'the house of office', with results revolting in every respect. Sometimes, the only yard where you could walk was common ground, and you got fresh air at the price of submitting to the ribald jests of the felons. Alleine, possessing his serious soul in patience, remarked that it was not merely the coarse language which was offensive; he shuddered as he watched the vermin crawling over the clothes which the felons hung out in the yard,

94

and, as always, his heart was stirred at the sight of destitution and abject spiritual want. All too often, every distinction between prisoners disappeared, and those who suffered for conscience' sake were thrust in among those who were punished for crime. This was sometimes done at the bidding of the authorities; magistrates grew impatient, and in exasperation consigned to the common gaol men and women whom they regarded as stubborn and perverse. Often it was an arbitrary action of the gaoler himself. Sometimes (one suspects) it was because there was no room anywhere else. Once there, the nonconformists often found that there was no place to sit or lie except on the floor, and only utter exhaustion could compel decent people to subside on the inexpressibly filthy straw. Moreover, the felons and the women who lay among them, being more aggressive and much less squeamish, managed to appropriate the less revolting sections of the room, and the new arrivals were driven, when weariness compelled them to capitulate, to sit down in places which their accustomed usage had rendered unspeakably foul.[1]

Many prisoners had to submit for a time to a fate even worse than confinement among the felons in the common gaol. In most prisons there was a dark filthy dungeon, reserved for the utterly recalcitrant or for desperate criminals on the eve of execution. For a variety of reasons, but usually with little warning, a nonconformist might find himself violently thrust into one of these hideous dens, and there he might be left for many hours, or even days. At Totnes, prisoners so infuriated the mayor by commending their faith to those who passed outside the grated windows of their gaol, that with every refinement of violence and arbitrary ignominy he thrust them into the 'Dark House', and shut two doors upon them. 'One of their persecutors said, They would soon be smothered there, for the place was so close and dark they could scarcely see one another at noon, and the excrements of other people had been emptied there, which caused a grievous stink....' A large company of Norwich Quakers were confined in a dark dungeon twenty-seven steps below ground, and though they could hear the footsteps of people walking at liberty in the streets above, little light and less air struggled through the tiny grating which opened upward toward the world of day. At Launceston, George Fox and his companion were consigned to a dungeon called Doomsdale, 'a nasty stinking place where...the excrements of the prisoners... had not been carried out...for many years, so that it was like mire, and in some parts up to the tops of the shoes in ordure and urine. Here they were forced to stand up all night, for they could not lie down by reason of the filth....' In Chester Castle there was a 'hole hewed out in the rock' called Little Ease, a place unbelievably restricted for the accommodation of a human being, and into which Richard Sale, a corpulent man, was thrust and the heavy door slammed upon him; he was so badly crushed that the blood gushed from his nose and mouth. At Leominster, prisoners were crowded in such numbers into 'a close nasty hole' that they could not all lie down at once. Since they were not allowed out for any cause, and since the dungeon was never cleaned, it became 'so loathsome that those who came to speak to them through the hole of the door could hardly endure the stench for a few minutes'.[1]

One further penalty remained. A prisoner, in additon to being consigned to the dungeon, might be clapped into irons. A minister whose service was broken up might easily find himself in chains, with no prospect of relief save through the importunity of friends. In many instances, a gaoler, exasperated that his prisoners should persist in holding services of worship, would seize the moving spirits, and, casting them headlong down the stairs, would put them in fetters. As an added humiliation he might from time to time parade them through the streets in their chains, to the scandal of all who had known them as upright and God-fearing men. Because petulance usually prompted this kind of punishment, relief came when anger had subsided, but occasionally a prisoner was left to suffer for weeks on end. John Whiting was shackled by 'hand-bolts' to one of his companions, and the two men remained manacled to each other for almost a month and a half. They could not change their clothes nor even take them off, and throughout the whole period neither could make the slightest movement without involving the other in discomfort. When at length the fetters were removed, the prisoners' wrists had been rubbed completely raw.[1]

It is clear that there was little uniformity in seventeenth-century gaols, and no consistency in the way they were administered. Conditions varied widely, and a prisoner's treatment was often determined in the most arbitrary way by the character and disposition of the men into whose hands he happened to fall. The administration of justice was so largely a local matter that the attitudes of the magistrates and the temper of the gaoler might determine not only whether a prisoner was comfortable or wretched, but even whether he lived or died. Records were carelessly kept, and it was no uncommon thing for troopers to hint that a man need not go to prison at all; a small bribe would settle the matter with the officers who had seized him. There is abundant evidence to prove that a prisoner's fate might be decisively affected, either for good or ill, by the intervention of the justices of the peace. A man of venomous spirit might pursue a victim even within the prison walls; he could insist on close confinement, he could instigate the gaoler to practise minor cruelties to which the man might be prone enough already, he could demand the cancellation of any liberties which good will had suggested or laxity had allowed. Sometimes the harshest forms of prison suffering were blamed on this kind of unrelenting animosity on the part of an embittered magistrate. But we hear just as often of cases where the lesser officials were restrained by the humanity or the good sense of those who possessed greater authority. A prisoner might be completely at the mercy of a brutal gaoler, and might suffer horrible discomforts until the sheriff or one of the justices intervened. When the gaoler took off the shackles or opened the dungeon door, it was often because he had been ordered to do so. And occasionally a word spoken by someone highly placed could considerably moderate the hardships that the prisoner had to suffer. Jeffreys, who could be cruel enough to nonconformists when he chose, was sometimes unexpectedly lenient. Toward Philip Henry he adopted an attitude which certainly saved that good man from serious trouble.[2] When the quarter sessions at Chichester had sent a number of

Quakers to prison, he made it clear to those most likely to listen to a royal favourite that he wished the prisoners 'to have all the lawful favour that could be shewed'.[1] This was in 1682, at a time when dissenters were mercilessly harried, and when they could normally expect no protection against the full rigours of the law.

In prison as well as out of it human relationships largely affected the character of a person's life. When good, they could help to mitigate the worst conditions; when bad, they could make life almost unbearable. In the little world of the prison house, the gaoler's power was paramount, and the way in which he chose to use it was an important factor in determining a prisoner's fate. The peculiar nature of his office explains the way in which he often discharged it. Three hundred years ago a gaoler was no doubt a civil servant (of a kind), but in actual practice he was likely to regard himself as the keeper of a distinctive type of lodging-house. His tenants came to him against their will and with no freedom to choose alternative quarters; and their times of arrival and departure were beyond their own control. But if they wanted decent accommodation, they must be prepared to pay for it. To the gaoler himself, his office was as much a position of profit as a post of trust, and his conduct was largely determined by this simple fact. Oliver Heywood remarked that 'the main thing those men look at' was the advantage they gained from keeping prisoners.[2] A prisoner was within his rights if he insisted on having free accommodation, but such a demand robbed the gaoler of what he regarded as his rightful expectation of gain. In exasperation he usually retaliated by putting the offender in the filthiest quarters the prison afforded. When George Whitehead was doing his utmost to secure the release of his fellow-Quakers who were confined in the dungeon of the Norwich prison, a judge with whom he discussed the case told him that one reason for their harsh treatment was that 'they would not pay for convenient rooms and chose free prison'. This was a matter of which Whitehead had first-hand knowledge; he himself had once been imprisoned in Norwich, and because he would not comply with the gaoler's 'extravagant demands for lodging', he was forced to sleep in his clothes on the bare floor.[3] Twopence a night, though a large sum for a poor man, was a modest charge for a prison bed. Francis Smith, who published Bunyan's early works, tells us that he was locked up in a bare room and charged ten shillings a week. 'Before I had been there three nights', he adds, '£7. 15s. was demanded for present fees. That is to say, £5 to excuse me for wearing irons, ten shillings for my entrance week lodging, five shillings for sheets, five shillings for garnish money, and the rest for turnkey's fees.'[1] Often these charges, so frankly exorbitant, bore no relation to the ability of the prisoners to pay them; when George Fox the younger was imprisoned with a number of companions at Harwich, 'the sergeant-at-arms sent his clerk to demand fees and chamber rent of the prisoners, asking fifty pounds for fees and ten shillings a week for chamber rent'. Even if injured innocence had consented to such terms, poverty would have made them impossible. Instead, the prisoners made a counter-offer of their own; they would pay two shillings and sixpence—though they did so with a keen awareness that the windows of their room had been devoid of glass till glazed by the prisoners themselves.[2] In addition to renting rooms, the gaoler had other means of augmenting his income. Sometimes he furnished food, and often he sold drink. It was a personal grievance when prisoners refused to buy his liquor, and he usually resented it if they arranged to have their meals sent in from outside. We read of one case where the gaoler demanded sixpence for a penny loaf, the same amount for a quart of milk, and threepence for a quart of water, and placed a strict embargo on food from outside.

The restraints upon a gaoler's powers were few, intermittent and ineffective. If he translated his exasperation into violence, there was little likelihood of his being checked in its exercise or called to account for its results. He was often a man of explosive temper, with little ability to restrain his anger and even less desire to do so. It was no uncommon thing for him to knock his prisoners about, to throw them down flights of stone steps, to kick and beat them without compunction, and to swear at them without restraint. An earnest Puritan might easily feel that conscience required him to reprove such conduct—especially to

7-2

rebuke the horrid sin of blasphemy—and by doing so he usually opened wide the flood-gates of wrath. But the gaoler had other ways of expressing his resentment. When violence palled, he could embark on a policy of petty pinpricks. Visitors from a distance would not be admitted to the prison, the flow of supplies would be interrupted, and minor concessions would be revoked. He might encourage his underlings to be high-handed and tyrannical, and he might devise ways of annoying the prisoners and disturbing their peace. When George Fox was in a filthy dungeon at Carlisle, the gaoler brought a fiddler to play outside the door; 'and when he played', wrote Fox, 'I was moved in the everlasting power of the Lord God to sing; and my voice drowned them and struck them and confounded them, that made them give over fiddling and go their ways'. In the same way and for the same purpose, the gaoler at Gloucester castle, always watching for ways of irritating John Roberts and his companions, 'hired a tinker to trouble them in the night by playing on his hautboy'. Fox had a resonant voice and a personality which awed even the most frivolous minds, yet Roberts finally gained an equally marked ascendancy over his keeper through the persuasiveness of a singularly winsome nature.[1]

The gaoler, though often a sinister figure, sometimes proved himself a friend in need. In a rough age, rough men were likely to hold the office, and only too often their treatment of others alternated between brutal violence and petty persecution. But there was another side to the picture; decent instincts often lurked beneath an uncouth manner, and the records of the time abound in references to considerate gaolers. Though a direct rebuke from a prisoner usually invited retaliation, patience often called forth an answering good will. John Gratton, though harshly treated by the Derby gaoler, always met abuse with courtesy, and finally elicited a corresponding response.[2] In describing a period of relatively easy imprisonment, John Bunyan implies that he had a lenient gaoler,[3] and there is no doubt that the rigours of prison life could be considerably mitigated when once the keeper's co-operation had been won. Special favours could be granted, and a flexible system could be allowed to operate to the prisoner's benefit. A gaoler might help to provide evidence likely to gain release; he might forgo his right to customary fees; he might even seriously endanger his own position for the benefit of those under his care. It was usually a gentle and forgiving spirit that penetrated the brutality so characteristic of gaolers; it gave a man's fundamental decency (the decency obscured but not obliterated by a coarse life) the encouragement it needed to break through the crust of hostility and restore dignity to human relationships. An inflexible integrity, though less winsome than unassuming humility, could achieve comparable results. By the time George Fox left Scarborough Castle, he had not only gained the good will of the governor but had won the reluctant respect of the soldiers who guarded him. 'He is as stiff as a tree', they said, 'and as pure as a bell; for we could never stir him.'[1] And it is reassuring to observe that an unbending man like Fox could not only awaken respect in others, but could acknowledge the good will they showed him. Under pressure he would never yield an inch, and he would resist to the uttermost every exorbitant exaction or unjust charge, but he was willing to tip a man who had been courteous to him in gaol. In Sarah Fell's *Account Book*, there is an entry which informs us that Fox gave half-a-crown to Thomas Benson, 'for his civility to me being a prisoner'.[2]

Within the prison the gaoler was supreme, but those subject to his power had relations with each other as well as with him. Often enough his own attitude determined the behaviour of the prisoners to one another. A drunken keeper, who made boon companions of the felons, would do nothing to check the fury with which dissenters were often harried in the common gaol. A defenceless newcomer was an open invitation to men who had been sent to prison for theft; the felons would immediately rifle his pockets, and appropriate anything that took their fancy. Though a man might have no money in his purse, he still had a coat on his back and a hat on his head, and if the felons hesitated to seize them, the gaoler often gave them all the encouragement they needed.

A seventeenth-century prison was normally divided into two sections, one for the felons, the other for debtors and prisoners of a less criminal type. In times of persecution, the latter part of the prison was crowded with nonconformists. Though they suffered for the same cause, they did not necessarily find themselves of one mind. At Ilchester gaol, the Independents, Baptists and Presbyterians felt that the Quakers were deliberately disrupting the fellowship of their little community. 'The Quakers', said Mrs Alleine, 'would molest them by their cavils in the time of their preaching, praying and singing, and would come and work in their callings just by them, while they were in duties.'[1]   At Lancaster there were long discussions between the Quakers and the other nonconformist prisoners, and one particularly heated argument with a Baptist called John Higgins resulted in the rash of pamphlets so characteristic of seventeenth-century controversy. Usually, however, relations were close and cordial. The prison literature of the period abounds in references to the warm fellowship which bound together those who were united in affliction. Their sufferings grew out of witness to a common faith, and the convictions which had caused their arrest upheld them in the day of trouble, and were in turn sustained by common worship in the prison house. Experience repeatedly proved the power of this kind of fellowship to overcome suspicion. When Richard Davies found himself a prisoner among Independents and Presbyterians, they looked askance at him as a member of the turbulent and troublesome sect of Quakers, but hostility rapidly yielded to the persuasions of good will.[2] When once a group had discovered the spiritual benefits which prison fellowship could confer, they feared few things more than a return to the comparative apathy with which they had previously been content.[3]

The prisoner, though cut off in varying measure from the outer world, had numerous contacts with the community beyond the prison walls. Those who shared the faith for which he suffered did not forget him, and most prisoners speak gratefully of the companionship of friends. In smaller centres the public was inquisitive but usually friendly, and in remote places the curious might be disappointed to discover that dissenters were ordinary people—'Christians, like ourselves'.[4] Often strangers sought out a prisoner in the conviction that a man so steadfast and sincere could speak to their spiritual needs. Thus a woman, perturbed in conscience because she had robbed her employer, came to John Bunyan to ask his help in dealing with her difficulties.[1] And not least in importance was the power of patient courage to reach even the person responsible for the imprisonment, and so to create a new bond between the persecutor and his victim.

When conditions were tolerable, the prisoners soon adapted themselves to their new life, and developed a routine suited to their circumstances. The Puritans took very seriously their duty to use time wisely, and this was both a defence against boredom and an incentive to find useful employment. A man might bring to the prison not only his normal interests but also his accustomed work. A minister might not be able to travel, but he could write to those whom he could no longer visit. He could always preach to the prison community, and he could occupy himself with prayer and study. When Thomas Lower shared George Fox's imprisonment at Worcester, he reported that they were busy from morning to night. Fox was sleeping well, eating heartily and steadily improving in health. Friends came to enjoy the company of their great leader or to seek his advice; there was a good deal of writing to be done; in addition, other kinds of work required attention, and by the time it was all finished, few moments remained unfilled.[2] Joseph Alleine discovered that each day was far too short for him to accomplish all that he felt it his duty to attempt. He rose at four in the morning; the quiet hours before the rest of the prisoners were awake proved best for private prayer and meditation, and at the other end of the day, when all his companions had gone to bed, he often prolonged his devotions throughout the night. When he could find a quiet corner in the prison, he set aside a part of each day for study; reading and meditation filled all the moments he could save for himself. The rest of his time was occupied with manifold activity. There were meetings of all kinds. He held solemn fast days, he organised seasons of humiliation, he had regular services for prayer and the preaching of the Word. He held conferences with friends who came to visit him from outside the prison, he cate-chised the young, he taught those of any age who were willing to

learn, and he often officially deputised for the prison chaplain.[1]
In his *Diary*, Oliver Heywood gives an even more detailed
picture of the way in which a Puritan minister filled his prison
days. 'After our rising, we kneeled down and I went to prayer
with my wife.—She in her closet, and I in the chamber went to
secret prayer alone.—Then I read a chapter in the Greek Testament while I took a pipe.—Then a chapter in the Old Testament
with Poole's Annotations.—Then wrote a little here [i.e. in his
Diary] or elsewhere.—At ten o'clock, I read a chapter and went
to prayer with my wife as family prayer.—Then wrote in some
book or treatise I was composing till dinner.—After dinner, Mr
Whitaker and I read in turn for an hour in Foxe's *Acts and Monuments of the Martyrs*, Latin edition. Then went to my chamber;
if my wife were absent, I spent an hour in secret prayer, and God
helped usually.—After supper, we read in the *Book of Martyrs*,
studied, went to prayer, read in Baxter's *Paraphrase on the New
Testament*.'[2]

How to maintain yourself in prison was a more pressing
question than how to spend your time while there. The state
imprisoned you, but it accepted little responsibility for your
support. The gaoler, as we have seen, expected to rent you rooms,
and he hoped to sell you food and drink as well. When imprisonment might easily last for months or even years, it was necessary
to find means of self-support. Friends could help, and often did.
On behalf of a minister beloved by his people they might organise
a collection, and the proceeds would suffice to cover his expenses
for some time. Wherever possible, however, it was desirable for
a prisoner to earn his own keep. The more fortunate found that
they could continue in prison the work which they normally did
outside. Others were compelled to master some simple craft.
John Bunyan made laces. In one of the earliest accounts of his
life, written by an anonymous friend, we are told that while in
prison Bunyan did not 'spend his time in supine and careless
manner, nor eat the bread of idleness, for I have been witness that
his own hands have ministered to his and his family's necessities,
making many hundred gross of long tagged laces to fill up the
vacancies of his time, which he had learned for that purpose since

he had been in prison'. Making laces was an occupation which required little training; it was within the compass of most prisoners, and it is not surprising that we find frequent references to it in the records of the period. In due course, when the Quakers began seriously to study the problem of helping prisoners to achieve self-support, they turned immediately to such simple crafts as making laces or cobbler's pegs; it was the natural point of departure. Various kinds of handicraft could be practised in prison—tailoring, basketry, leatherwork, or the simpler forms of weaving—and as long as a man had any skills or was willing to acquire them, there was no excuse for idleness. The fact that the common chamber was workroom as well as bedroom often created problems. In times of overcrowding, space in which to work might be sacrificed to meet the need for room in which to sleep. The activities of one group of prisoners might conflict with the interests of another; when those who wanted to work interrupted those who wished to pray, two characteristic Puritan emphases came into collision. Sometimes, when an angry gaoler expropriated the prisoners' tools, work might temporarily cease, but under normal circumstances a man might hope to fill a good deal of his time with activities which were both useful and remunerative.

At best, however, imprisonment was likely to prove an economic disaster. Work in the prison might mitigate its hardships, but a man's dependants were certain to suffer. Anxiety about those left at home was therefore a shadow which deepened the prison gloom.[1] The victim might hear of misfortunes which he was powerless to avert, or reverses from which he could never hope to recover. A letter of Bridget Fell gives a graphic picture of the problems created by imprisonment. At Swarthmore money was scarce and prices of agricultural commodities very low. There were no men to carry corn to market, but unless produce could be sold, there would be no possibility of paying wages. With seed-time approaching, the men ought to be tilling the fields; if they were kept in prison, matters would deteriorate still further, and the problem of providing for their maintenance would become acute.[2] There are innumerable tales of the frantic efforts of a prisoner's dependants to keep the family fortunes from utter ruin. Occasionally the nature of a man's business and the exceptional capacity of his wife combined to stave off disaster, but in most cases when he was sent to prison he knew that the collapse of his worldly affairs would be the inevitable consequence and would bring his family to destitution. It was therefore a matter of real importance to devise some way of maintaining the dependants of conscientious sufferers, and the practical genius of the Society of Friends appeared in their grasp of the fact that encouragement for the prisoner would be effective only when combined with measures for the support of his family.

Man does not live by bread alone, but when the frontiers of his life have shrunk to the compass of the prison walls, his meals assume a disproportionate importance. Prison fare was unusually bad. It was uncertain in quantity and deplorable in quality. Careless cooking robbed it of its flavour, and it was doubly unappetising because it was usually cold long before it reached the prisoners. As a result digestion suffered and health began to deteriorate. When Sarah Fell was imprisoned at Dalton, she had to buy a pint of stomach water (price eightpence),[1] but many who might have benefited from medical care could not afford it. A simpler remedy was to improve the food itself. Friends often arranged to send in supplies, and under favourable conditions it was possible to set up reasonably satisfactory housekeeping arrangements inside the prison itself. When there was no chance to cook your own food, you could arrange with a sympathiser in the neighbourhood to buy your provisions, prepare them in her kitchen, and bring them hot to the prison at meal-times.[2] This method had certain practical advantages; it had the serious defect that its interruption provided a peevish gaoler with a perfect way of penalising his prisoners.[3] The determining factor in the situation was whether the good will of friends would be allowed free course. In speaking of her husband and his companions, Mrs Alleine assures us that 'their diet was very good and sufficient, and sometimes abundant....Their friends were exceedingly kind to them, endeavouring by their frequent visits, and provisions for diet, and supplies of money, to make their prison sweet to them.'[1] To a greater extent than most of his fellow-sufferers, Philip Henry gives us explicit information about his prison fare. He exercised great care about his diet, lest the change from an active to a sedentary life should jeopardise his health. He noted that he had had no butter on his bread since leaving home, and as a typical dinner he mentions that 'we had beans and bacon, salmon, etc.'. An admirer had sent him a bottle of wine; he shared it, like all other special delicacies, with his fellow-prisoners.[2]

Given good health, a man could cope successfully with most of the problems which imprisonment created. Illness spelled disaster. It sapped his vitality, and left him unable to cope with the hardships inseparable from his lot. It broke his confidence, and thus robbed him of the resiliency of spirit which he needed in order to keep discouragement at bay. Bad food often began the process; it weakened the prisoner and made him an easy prey to the diseases which lurked in seventeenth-century gaols. 'The fever' was endemic. Even in John Howard's time, it swept through the crowded prisons and carried off the inmates by the score.[3] What it meant to be striken with this malady appears from the account of Edward Burrough's last illness and death. He lay on a narrow pallet bed, thrown down on the mouldering straw which covered the stone floor of the common prison. Close by ran the open drain, and the filth from it saturated the straw and even the mattress itself. Yells and curses, wails and jests filled the crowded room. Two friends, crouching on either side of him, tried to protect him from the jostling of those who would have carelessly trampled upon him. Alternating fits of burning and shivering seized him, and from time to time his companions moistened his brow or his lips with water—a commodity hard to obtain in that filthy place. His fevered mind wandered to the hills and fells of the Lakeland where he had grown to manhood, but before he died, during an interval of perfect mental clarity, he declared in deeply moving terms the marvel of God's love as it reaches, even in dens and prisons, the people who suffer for his sake.[4]

More serious than the threat of fever was the menace of small-pox or the plague. There was no system of segregating those who were infected; both the necessary knowledge and the requisite facilities were lacking. When a group of Quakers found themselves crowded in a tiny room and learned that smallpox was raging among the felons just below them, they might be alarmed but no preventive measures were within their reach. They could only wait for the infection to reach them. During outbreaks of the plague, the incidence of the disease was specially high in the prisons. When the weather grew warm, men with an elementary knowledge of public health became apprehensive as they thought of the overcrowding and the filth in the nearby prisons, but any suggestions for improvement were blocked by the inertia of officialdom.[1] Those who had their liberty could fly to the country when the plague broke out, but the prisoners could only wait and die. And die they did in great numbers. It was difficult for their friends to escape the angry bitterness which unnecessary suffering always excites. During the terrible outbreak in London, Richard Flavel and his wife were arrested for attending a religious meeting and were sent to gaol. Though promptly granted bail, they had been imprisoned with victims of the plague, and as a result both of them died.[2] For those who had been long in gaol, however, deliverance by death might seem a merciful release from their miseries, but it was natural that minds with an apocalyptic bent should see the terrible mortality in which the capital was involved a sure sign of divine judgement. Had not George Bishop of Bristol prophesied in explicit terms what would happen to a persecuting nation, and had not his forecasts been fulfilled to the minutest detail?[3] All the greater was the gratitude of those who had come through the visitation and been spared. 'Through the great love of my God', wrote Morgan Watkins, 'I am wonderfully preserved to the praise of his name...the day was dreadful to all flesh, and few were able to abide it and stand in the judgement; but the Lord was very merciful to the remnant of his people....'[4] The miseries of illness in prisons are underlined by the broken health of those who recovered. After repeated illnesses William Dewsbery found that even in the course of a short walk he had to pause frequently to rest.[5] When George Fox was released from Scarborough Castle his physical condition was deplorable. 'I was so weak with lying about three years in cruel and hard imprisonments, my joints and my body was so benumbed, that I could hardly get on my horse; neither could I well bend my knees nor hardly endure fire nor warm meat, I had so long been kept from it.'[1]

Whether in sickness or in health, worship provided the greatest source of consolation open to the Puritan prisoner. Each day brought its opportunity for united prayer and witness. In the fellowship of men and women of like spirit, all of them suffering in a common cause, hope was re-established, constancy and courage were confirmed. Alleine's days at Ilchester were punctuated by innumerable services of every kind, and his *Christian Letters* repeatedly refer to the comfort and strength which prisoners drew from their worship together. Margaret Fell describes the meetings which the Quakers held each day in a large room at Lancaster Castle, and in London the comment was freely made that Newgate had become a house of prayer instead of a den of thieves. Dewsbery reports from York: 'We have liberty to meet together in the prison every day, and the presence of the Lord crowns our meetings to our great comfort and the astonishment of his enemies.'[2] Opponents might be amazed, but they certainly were not silenced. A hostile magistrate or a surly gaoler was likely to regard these prison conventicles as a challenge to authority, and he found in them an excellent pretext for venting his exasperation. When a group of justices, playing bowls in the neighbourhood of the prison, overheard the preaching and the prayers of the prisoners, they intervened and clapped the offenders into irons. It was not easy, of course, to devise a punishment for people already in gaol. The gaoler might knock them down the stairs or encourage others to beat them; he might put them in fetters or clap them in the dungeon, but there was little satisfaction in such measures. The victims too obviously felt that victory rested with them. 'The ministers of the gospel may be shut up in gaols for the Testimony's sake,' remarked Gratton, 'yet the word of God cannot be bound, for then it had free course and was glorified.'[3]

Preaching had an important place in all Puritan worship. In

prison that place was certainly not diminished. The special services—of humiliation, confession, thanksgiving—all left room for exhortation. In addition to the need of improving each occasion and of forcing home the lessons of adversity, there had to be a place for the systematic exposition of the scriptures. 'By these things men live', and in prison their need of that diet became all the more insistent. But in addition to the community within the prison walls there was the public outside. The ministers in Ilchester gaol made it their practice to preach at least once a day and if possible twice to the crowds that gathered beneath the prison window.[1] Some might listen simply because curiosity prompted them to pause, but the devout Puritan held it a privilege to wait on such a ministry. Adversaries, of course, objected. The crowds were often menaced and dispersed, and sometimes the preacher himself was threatened. Ministers were even shot at as they preached through the gratings of their prison window.[2] Certain themes came naturally to mind, and we read of exhortations to constancy, of encouragement to face risks, together with much emphasis on the comfort which springs from true faith.[3] For sermons on such subjects there was no need to search either for material or for illustrations, and example proved (as always) the best expositor of truth. The conscientious preacher, however, would not presume on such advantages; a good sermon still required careful study and earnest prayer, and there was no skimping of preparation, even though the necessary time had to be snatched from the hours of sleep.

The Puritans lacked neither convictions nor the will to express them. Usually their faith found utterance in speech; imprisonment forced them to seek an outlet in writing. However unfavourable conditions might be in some respects, the prisoner had a certain amount of leisure on his hands, and the duty of stewardship (especially of time) turned his thoughts to composition. Bunyan had started to write before he went to prison, but he fully mastered the craft in Bedford gaol. Sometimes his books grew naturally from the sermons he preached to his fellow-prisoners. 'Upon a certain first day,' he tells us, 'I being together with my brethren in our prison chamber, they expected that according to our custom, something should be spoken out of the Word to our mutual edification.' At first he felt himself so dead and barren in spirit that he seemed to have nothing to offer his expectant hearers, but in a moment of inspiration the description of the new Jerusalem, open before him in the Bible, glowed with an intensity of meaning he had never found there before. Pausing just long enough to dart heavenward a prayer for blessing, he began to expound the truths that unfolded as he read. The new splendour with which the passage had become invested subsequently grew upon his mind, and his book on *The Holy City* was the result.[1] Often his writing was closely related to the subjects which were naturally uppermost in his mind. *Praying in the Spirit* supplied him with an opportunity to state his views concerning imposed liturgies—one of the grounds of the nonconformity for which he suffered. In *Grace Abounding* he describes his past experience, but he also gives us a memorable glimpse of the apprehensions of a man facing persecution and of the anxieties which haunted him in prison. With Bunyan it was the power of imagination which made it impossible for the prison walls to hem him in. 'As I walked through the wilderness of this world, I lighted upon a certain place where was a den, and laid me down in that place to sleep: and, as I slept, I dreamed a dream.' And as he dreamed he saw the familiar landscape invested with new meaning; local landmarks became milestones in the pilgrimage of the soul, and as the outline of the Berkshire hills took on the new dignity of the Delectable Mountains, he saw rising beyond them the battlements and pinnacles of the Celestial City. This was a power which transformed the world of common things. When he had heard the songs of praise with which the hosts of the redeemed swept onward through the everlasting doors, he might well feel a wave of nostalgia surge over him, but he had found the most effective antidote to the depression of the prison house. Like Christian, Bunyan had discovered in his breast a key which opened the dungeon of Doubting Castle and delivered him from the power of Giant Despair.

Few men saw such visions or dreamed such dreams as Bunyan, but most of the Puritan leaders found that writing provided a link with the wider world from which they had been temporarily cut off. By means of books and letters they were able to maintain the pastoral care which imprisonment threatened to interrupt. Joseph Alleine was determined to keep in touch by letter with all the communities which he normally visited in person.[1] Through the written word he hoped to offer the same kind of encouragement and maintain the same kind of supervision as had marked his ministry among his people. He knew that his fellow-ministers would also need to have their faith confirmed if they were to persevere in the face of persecution; for them he wrote *A Call to Archippus*—a book that became one of the most popular of Puritan devotional manuals. From each of the gaols in which he was imprisoned, William Dewsbery sent forth letters to confirm Quakers in their faith and to encourage them amid their sufferings. George Fox not only wrote to his followers, but undertook to defend them, both against their persecutors and before the world at large. Consequently the literature inspired by pastoral concern rapidly expanded into the detailed record of sufferings, and to this fact we are indebted for a vast amount of information regarding every aspect of persecution in the Restoration era.

Imprisonment in the seventeenth century differed widely from its modern counterpart. For one thing, the sentence was much less exactly prescribed. For certain offences a man might be sent to gaol with no knowledge of when he could expect release. Refusal to take the oath resulted in a kind of indeterminate sentence which might be ended by proclamation of an indulgence or by the intervention of the higher authorities, but which might equally drag on indefinitely. Praemunire also left a man's future dependent on the king's will—or whim. Failure to pay tithe involved a sentence which nothing but payment of arrears could terminate; since this presupposed a radical change of outlook, a man with conscientious scruples could only hope that his persecutor would relent or that a general pardon would set him free. These facts explain the long terms which many of the Quakers served. William Dewsbery, who had been imprisoned at Northampton, York and London, was nineteen years in Warwick gaol. George Fox, who himself had wide experience of indeterminate sentences, wrote feelingly of 'the sore tedious imprisonment' of his friend Thomas Taylor.[1] Ambrose Rigge was in Horsham gaol for more than a decade, and John Gratton was imprisoned for five and a half years before James II granted him his discharge.[2]

The latitude allowed a prisoner varied as widely as the conditions under which he was detained. To an extent difficult for us to understand, the prison door was often left ajar. Imprisonment might involve close confinement, but this was not certain nor even likely. To be kept strictly within the prison might be one of the consequences of praemunire; it might be a further indication that a man had forfeited his normal civil rights. Sometimes it was a result of official alarm—as in so many centres immediately after the Venner scare. Often it was the result of hostility on the part of the magistrates or the gaoler. Close confinement meant that the prisoner lost all freedom of movement and was kept strictly within the limits of the gaol. He was often cut off from the visits of friends; normal supplies were interrupted; and if he fell ill he could not leave the prison to recover. The latter point was particularly serious. When epidemics were so common and conditions so injurious to health, close confinement often proved the equivalent of a sentence of death.

Normally, however, prison life permitted a degree of latitude to which modern conditions provide no parallel. Permission to walk in the prison yard was the most elementary concession and was regarded almost as a right. In many cases the prisoner was allowed to go out into the town, and he might even be able to walk daily in the surrounding countryside. 'And after I had the liberty of the town', writes John Whiting, 'I used often and delighted much to walk in the fields, which I never knew the comfort of so much before (not having been debar'd the liberty of them) to read and meditate some hours together.'[3] Liberty to go abroad was often as much a matter of usage as of right. John Gratton describes the long and fruitless arguments by which he tried to persuade the gaoler to allow him some measure of freedom. He never won his point; the gaoler declined to rescind his refusal, but he finally showed him where he kept the key, with the hint that Gratton might use it as he wished.[1] Once the door had been opened, a prisoner could employ his liberty in a wide variety of ways. If he lived in the neighbourhood he would certainly go home, and it might be possible so to arrange matters that he spent only his nights in prison. Jasper Batt, in a letter to George Fox, describes the way in which his son-in-law ('who is also a prisoner, but pretty much at liberty at home') had sent a bed to the prison for Batt and his wife, who accordingly slept there, but otherwise spent most of their time in their own house.[2]

During her imprisonment at Lancaster, Margaret Fell went home at least once in order to supervise domestic affairs at Swarthmore Hall, and on another occasion she was allowed to join George Fox at a meeting in Cheshire. To go home was the first use a prisoner made of his greater freedom, but it was not difficult to extract further concessions. A man's poverty might so stir the pity of the gaoler (or his wife) that he would be allowed to go out to work in the town, and thus earn some money for his own support. If it were important to attend a particular fair, or if a journey seemed necessary for business reasons, the requisite arrangements could often be made.

In so flexible a system, the concessions granted by the gaoler were the measure of the liberty allowed. He could—and sometimes did—take it upon himself to parole a prisoner. If he did not give formal permission, he at least connived at what was done. Usually we discover that a concession has been made only because we learn that it has been revoked. Though the gaoler might be willing that his prisoners should go abroad, the justice of the peace who sent them there might take a very different attitude. He might not only insist that the prisoners be denied freedom of egress, but he might also take punitive measures against the gaoler himself. It is clear, however, that the sufferers felt it a genuine grievance when their liberties were curtailed, and their attitude suggests that such concessions were considered almost as a right. When a prisoner's wife, burdened by anxieties and the weight of domestic cares, 'became distracted', it was regarded as a serious hardship if the husband were refused permission to go home. If a man took ill, it was assumed that he ought to be able to leave prison and recover in his own house— possibly because it was also assumed that in prison a sick man was certain to die.

So long as the authorities did not intervene, the latitude allowed to prisoners could be steadily enlarged. Sometimes the gaoler came to trust the prisoner's judgement as much as his own. Though in the first instance Gratton's keeper allowed him out only with the greatest reluctance, he finally decided that he could safely let him do as he pleased. Having gone to a wedding, a premonition warned Gratton that he should return to prison sooner than he had promised; he did so, and had no more than arrived when a justice, furious because of a rumour that Gratton was at large, came storming up to the door to investigate. The gaoler's reaction is interesting. He concluded, not that concessions to Gratton were dangerous, but that a man with so sure an intuition of when he ought to be in prison could be allowed to come and go as he wished.[1]

Experience taught gaolers that religious prisoners could be treated in a variety of unconventional ways. When the assizes were held in other towns, there was no need to provide a guard to conduct dissenters thither; they could be trusted to go by themselves, and even when a cavalcade of two hundred Quakers set out, you could be sure that the correct number would appear in court.[2] If the prison were overcrowded, those who were newly arrested could be sent to find lodgings for themselves in the town, or the gaoler himself might accommodate them in a private house. In either event, they were likely to be left largely to their own devices. They could come in and go out as they wished, and in their own interests they might find it desirable as well as expedient to establish some system of self-supervision.[3] In one respect, however, the nonconformists were unable to gain their point: they could never establish the right to substitute one man for another. They contended that when certain convictions were common to a society, it was usually an accident that this person rather than the next was seized. When illness combined with long imprisonment to jeopardise a man's health, or when

8-2

his domestic affairs urgently required his presence, there were companions ready to take his place in prison. The Quakers often attempted to gain this kind of relief for one or other of their members, but even in the case of George Fox they always failed. The authorities would not concede that one prisoner—any prisoner—met the requirements of the law. On demand they must be able to produce not merely a religious sufferer of a certain type, but a particular man who had been arrested at a specific time and place and for a designated cause. Prison administration might be flexible, but there was a point beyond which concessions could not be stretched.

Imprisonment involved the nonconformist in physical hardships, in social disability and in economic disaster. It might undermine his health and jeopardise his life. It remained, however, primarily a spiritual experience. Whether or not he could overcome the problems he confronted depended largely on the inner resources which he possessed. The dignity, even the grandeur, which marks the records springs from the fact that in accepting and enduring the hardships of imprisonment the sufferer was bearing witness to spiritual convictions. A slight compromise, a small adjustment of his views or practices, and he could completely escape the perils and discomforts of the prison house. Some who had once shared his views had sought and found such safety; this only made the temptation the more acute. In deciding whether he must be loyal to his convictions, he had to reckon with his ability to abide the searching test to which they would be subjected.[1] As the imminence of imprisonment increased, every earnest Puritan found his thoughts reverting more and more constantly to the ordeal he realised he must undergo. 'Before I came to prison', writes Bunyan, 'I saw what was acoming, and had specially two considerations warm upon my heart; the first was how to be able to endure, should my imprisonment be long and tedious; the second was how to be able to encounter death, should that be here my portion....'[2] As always, Scripture proved his comfort, and supported him to meet the coming trial. In the early days of the Restoration, Heywood found in every spiritual blessing a means of support against the day of trouble. Surely, he says, such mercies are worth a prison; if God gives us such gifts in the way, can we protest if the end of the journey is a gaol?[1] Under some circumstances it is clearly better for a man to be in prison than have his freedom—'Free communion with God', wrote George Hughes, 'is worth a thousand liberties, gained with the loss of liberty of spirit. The Lord keep us his free men.'[2] At the very outset, almost before the prison gates had closed behind him, a man might discover that an experience which he had dreaded would prove a blessing in disguise.[3] The prophet was right: the Valley of Achor could become a door of hope.

Spiritual resources were necessary in order to meet the spiritual problems that immediately arose. A man could be miserably lonely even though deprived of privacy and constantly surrounded by crowds. The difficulties created for his family and the ruin in which he was involving them caused anxieties which preyed continually on his mind. 'The parting with my wife and poor children', wrote Bunyan, 'hath often been to me in this place as the pulling of the flesh from my bones, and that not only because I am somewhat too fond of those great mercies, but also because I should have often brought to my mind the many hardships, miseries and wants that my poor family was like to meet with, should I be taken from them, especially my poor blind child, who lay nearer my heart than all I had besides. ... Oh, I saw in this condition I was a man who was pulling down his house upon the head of his wife and children; yet thought I, I must do it, I must do it.'[4] Bitterness was as great a problem as anxiety. The dissenter insisted that he was a loyal subject and a law-abiding citizen, but it was difficult not to resent the attitude as well as the actions of the government. To suffer for your faith was hard enough; it was doubly bitter to be branded as a rebel and to have your religious gatherings derided as seditious meetings. To refrain from reflections on rulers was as difficult as it was necessary. 'Take heed in laying the cause of your troubles in the badness of temper of governors.'[5] A more immediate temptation was to blame the men who were directly responsible for persecution. It was easy to brood on the vindictive attitude of those who should have been able to recognise your honesty and sincerity, but to let bitterness creep in was to suffer defeat in your own soul. If your witness was a testimony to spiritual truth, and you permitted your spirit to be darkened with anger, your adversary had conquered you and demonstrated the falsity of your claim. The nature of the times laid a special duty upon dissenters —that of loving and forgiving their enemies.[1] If they failed at that point, their imprisonment was sure to be a disaster as well as a misery; if they succeeded, it could be the first step toward a greater measure of inner peace and spiritual victory.

Comparisons may be odious, but it is often difficult to avoid them. The prisoner noted those who had lost their liberty and those who kept it, and he found it hard to believe that essential justice was being maintained. Those who had most of the spirit of prayer, remarked Bunyan, were all to be found in gaol, and those who had most zeal for the form of prayer were all to be found at the alehouse.[2] Both Thomas Taylor and William Dewsbery, in letters written to Charles II, pointed out that while the righteous were imprisoned, gamesters, actors and morris dancers had every encouragement that liberty could give.[3] 'Drunkards and swearers, fighters and such as are subject to vice' enjoyed their freedom; so did those who 'go after mountebanks and stage-plays, or run a-hunting', yet all the while upright men lay in prison for no other offence than loyalty to conscience.[4] This contrast underlined an ancient perplexity that has always troubled thoughtful men. Why do the ungodly flourish while the righteous suffer? When you go into the sanctuary, you see the problem in true perspective; when you go into the prison, it is much harder to preserve the insight which is the guardian of inner peace. 'The severity of the hand of God towards his children, with his forbearance towards his enemies'[5] proves particularly difficult when you are the child that endures chastisement. When righteous Mordecai finds his own life threatened, he sees in the power of haughty Haman a direct challenge to his faith.

A prisoner for conscience' sake might take comfort from the fact that his opponents often relied upon carnal weapons. Defoe could speak contemptuously of 'the knocking-down arguments of a gaol and fine'; he knew that retort by imprisonment represented an acknowledgement of weakness by the other side, but Defoe was a born controversialist, and was not in gaol.[1] But the man who, like Thomas Delaune, found his 'sober arguments' answered with 'sour coercives' was bound to feel the injustice of his treatment. He expected reasonable discussion; he was met with brute force. Convincing arguments might have changed his outlook; bolts and bars would not. 'Debate by the prison and not by the pen' was unlikely to convince him, though it would probably bring him to his death. Delaune correctly predicted his own fate; he also accurately reflected the deep frustration which oppressed his spirit as he looked beyond the prison to the grave.[2]

It was worse to be forgotten than to be aggrieved. Even the attention which sprang from malicious spite paid the prisoner the compliment of taking seriously his claim to consideration. But as the months passed, it was easy to feel that he had dropped into oblivion. His case seemed to have faded from the minds of men. Those responsible for his imprisonment were utterly unconcerned about his sufferings; apparently they did not care about any aspect of his life. Then the sense of grievance tempted the prisoner to complain. But in his wiser moments he knew that the embittered spirit was more than a symptom of weakness; it was also a sign of defeat. If the inner citadel of his soul yielded to anger or self-pity, then he had both undermined his witness and endangered his own soul. Earnestness is not by itself a sufficient safeguard against the subtle deception of sin. 'Alas! our ignorance of these things is manifest in our unwillingness to abide affliction, by our secret murmuring under the hand of God; by our wondering why we are so chastised as we are, by our thinking long that the affliction is no sooner removed.'[3]

The spiritual problems created by imprisonment were many and severe; the spiritual resources available in imprisonment proved to be greater, alike in number and in scope. In moments of despair a man might feel forgotten, but as a rule, he discovered that the fellowship of a religious community was a continual support.[4] Brotherhood became a reality, and he began to understand how strong were the bonds which united him with his fellow-believers. Imprisonment was not so much a misfortune for certain individuals as a challenge to the whole religious society. Fellow-prisoners found themselves united in a fellowship far more intense than they had ever known before, and the faith of each became part of the spiritual resources of all. To share in the sufferings of the prisoners was a privilege for those outside as well as a necessity for those within the gaol. Those within reach came regularly to visit, and we have abundant evidence to prove the importance of such calls in maintaining the morale of the prisoners. In the moment of his trial, a minister found himself surrounded and upheld by the love of his people; the gratitude which they had always felt, but which they had lacked the opportunity to show, they could now express in a most convincing fashion. When distance cut off personal contact, letters maintained unbroken the bond of fellowship. 'The life of the righteous was much cherished' by a message of good will,[1] and often a group of sufferers in one gaol would send a word of encouragement to prisoners in another. 'Companions in tribulation, fellow-sufferers for the testimony of Jesus and prisoners for the hope of Israel, which never makes ashamed; we your fellow-servants and members of the body which edifyeth itself in love, and counted worthy to be sufferers with you in bonds for the Testimony, do in the singleness of our hearts and fervency of love, yea in the fellowship of his suffering, who is our life, and also in the unity of the one spirit, hereby salute and embrace you.'[2]

Support from others was invaluable, but ultimately the victory had to be won within. The prisoner had to reconcile himself to his lot; when he silenced the murmurs of resentment and indignation in his own heart, he could expect to appropriate the blessings of inner peace. Admittedly it was not always easy. He would probably need help if he were to master that hard, hard lesson of facing without bitterness the scorn and contempt which adversaries heap on their victims when misfortunes have overwhelmed them. A man would have to lay hold of the covenant mercies which the Scriptures promise and test them in the school of bitter experience.[3] The beginning of a new confidence was the discovery that the prisoner had 'a gospel worth suffering for'—and one which repaid its adherents a hundred-fold. 'Rejoice with trembling in your prison comforts', wrote Alleine; '...who can tell the mercies that you have received here?'[1] As one by one the great phrases of the faith were filled with new meaning, the sufferer realised that he had found in prison a means by which he could be more nearly conformed to his Master. It was an honour, not an indignity, to be in gaol. It was natural, therefore, that the songs of the prison house should be hymns of thanksgiving. 'Indeed, God hath been so good to us, and still is so, that it doth overbalance all these light afflictions....He hath given content, comfort, unity, peace and love amongst us greatly; and by his fatherly care hath so provided always for us, that we have had no want. For all which mercies we desire you with us to praise the Lord, and to pray unto him for us here, that God would for ever keep us in faithfulness to him, that we may become even as monuments of his mercy, that he who alone is worthy, who is all and doth all, may have all the honour, praise and renown, now, henceforth and for evermore.'[2]

It is a spiritual triumph of the first order for a prisoner to write from a seventeenth-century gaol that 'this is a place of joy indeed, and eternally doth my soul rejoice in the Lord',[3] and it was only the vivid sense of God's presence which made it possible. The knowledge of the divine was both more intense and more authentic because it had come out of the midst of sorrow and affliction. To talk about the Cross was no longer to use the hackneyed phraseology of conventional piety. Those who 'have not begun at Christ's Cross' are not likely to find the secret of that courage which fears God and nothing else. But even those who have embarked on the right journey are far from the true goal. Hence the constant warnings against complacency. Prison life could be a blessing, but the benefits it offered were for use and not merely for enjoyment. Sufferings should lead to careful self-examination—for example, what are the inward failings which have brought upon us these outward afflictions?—but the immediate result should be a thorough reform; this would lead to a deepened faith, and in due course its natural consequence would be a more complete obedience in every department of our life. If prison was the school where men learned the lessons of faith, the wider world was the sphere where they must apply them; the mercies received in gaol must inspire greater service abroad. One of the first fruits of prison life should be a desire to maintain and extend the spirit of brotherhood so marvellously fashioned in adversity: 'the bonds of affliction' must strengthen 'the bonds of affection'. To be released from prison is not to be relieved of responsibilities, and to meet the new demands which come from fresh mercies a man must realistically assess his position. In material things, imprisonment has caused him heavy losses; have his spiritual gains been proportionately great? Has he learned to subdue resentment and to repress spiritual pride? Has he discovered the secret of inner peace, and learned to keep the soul untouched by the evils which afflict the body? Has he learned to trust completely in the providence of God, and to rely continually on the support of His presence? If not, he will fail to improve the opportunities which release will bring; if so, he will be able to meet the requirements of ordinary life, and to rise triumphantly above the further hardships which the future doubtless holds in store. And if liberty is delayed, and he remains in prison, he can do so with the proud assurance that he 'rests a freeman of the Lord Jesus Christ'.[1]

The prisoner who remained Christ's freeman had scored a notable triumph, but he had not achieved his end. It was not his aim to remain in gaol; so long as the law kept him there, he might learn to draw the sting from a necessary evil, but it was always his purpose to obtain release. The first step was to appeal to the men responsible for imposing the sentence. Sometimes a friend would approach the justice who had sent a nonconformist to prison, and might persuade him to quash proceedings. If there were no friends to intervene, a man's wife could undertake the tedious and often thankless task of inducing the authorities to relent. This might involve the kind of ordeal so memorably described by Bunyan. When his wife's initial efforts to secure his release had failed, she went to see the judges in a large room where they were gathered with the justices and the gentry of the county. For a simple woman to intrude on such company was in itself a terrifying prospect, and she came 'into the chamber with abashed face

and a trembling heart'. Though inwardly fearful, she was out-
wardly bold. With magnificent courage she stated her husband's
case; in face of hostility and abuse she maintained his innocence,
and with moving simplicity touched on the privations which she
and her children had had to bear. Nor would she concede for a
moment that her husband's religious activity had been anything
except a pure and peaceable ministry of the Word of God. "'He
preach the Word of God!" said [Judge] Twisdon; and withal
she thought he would have struck her; "he runneth up and down
and doth harm." "No, my Lord," said she, "it is not so; God
hath owned him and done much good by him." "God!" said
he; "his doctrine is the doctrine of the devil." "My Lord," said
she, "when the righteous Judge shall appear, it will be known
that his doctrine is not the doctrine of the devil."' Sir Matthew
Hale was sympathetic and considerate, but the most he could do
was to advise her what further steps to take. An uneducated
woman, arguing an unpopular cause before a group so distinguished and so hostile, might well give way before the end, but
even her confession of failure is couched in terms that suggest the
secret of Puritan strength. 'Only this I remember,' she told her
husband, 'that though I was somewhat timorous at my first
entrance into the chamber, yet before I went out, I could not but
break forth into tears, not so much because they were so hard-
hearted against me and my husband but to think what a sad
account such poor creatures will have to give at the coming of the
Lord....'[1]

Though others might intercede, the prisoner himself was not
necessarily silent. He might not be able to speak, but at least he
could write, and the Quakers in particular developed the letter of
protest to a high degree of effectiveness. It was Fox himself who
set the pattern. Whenever he was sent to prison, he wrote to the
authorities responsible, affirming his own innocence, pointing out
the ways in which they had strayed from the paths of justice, and
urging on them the duty of speedy reformation. These were
not conciliatory letters; they were much more likely to infuriate
than to mollify, but their uncompromising honesty, together
with the invariable appeal to Christian standards which everyone

acknowledged, must have made them subtly disturbing to their recipients. Other Quakers were quick to follow his example. From the prisons of England there issued a voluminous correspondence which set forth in the plainest terms the reasons for release. Magistrates were shown the contrast between their own conduct and their obligation to dispense even-handed justice; bishops were reminded of the way Christ's law of love condemned their harsh vindictiveness; members of parliament were assured that they were not doing their duty if they acquiesced in conditions which disgraced their constituencies with continued injustice. As you read these letters it is hard to believe that they really promoted their ostensible purpose.[1] Certainly they seldom gained immediate release for those who wrote them, but at least they made it impossible to forget the authors' plight, and probably they did a good deal to undermine the spirit which sustained a policy of persecution. You might not comply with the advice of such letters, but you did not enjoy receiving them.

In the administration of justice, local factors played an important part, and the man who had influential friends was likely to obtain early release. When prominent people came forward to defend a popular minister, those responsible for taking action against him found it discreet to drop the case. Sometimes the justices of the peace, out of respect for the prisoner, reversed the action previously taken by one of their number, and occasionally those who held the highest places in the land intervened to secure a minister's release. Where there was a desire to be lenient, local authorities did not hesitate to act, but if mercy seemed likely to arouse criticism, they remembered that mercy was the prerogative of the king. Consequently appeals to the throne became an important part of the effort to gain release. From prison, men like Fox and Dewsbery wrote to urge Charles II not to lay intolerable burdens on the consciences of his people nor to allow just men to suffer for their faith.[2] Personal intervention was more likely to succeed, and from few sources do we get so graphic a picture of the king as from the accounts written by the Friends who went to intercede on behalf of fellow-Quakers. The king was surprisingly easy of access. Throughout a period of six weeks, Margaret Fell saw him at least once a week, and often two or three times. She found him kindly and considerate, but she began to realise how great were the obstacles in the way of securing the prisoners' release. Men of influence blocked any move to give effect to his promises of greater liberty of conscience.[1] It became increasingly clear that many things besides the king's own wishes determined his conduct. 'The man', she wrote, 'is moderate and I do believe hath an intent in his mind and a desire to do for Friends if he knew how and not to endanger his own safety. He is dark and ignorant of God, and so everything fears him.'[2] His apprehensions were by no means the only factors which checked his generous impulses. When the soldiers were brutally attacking Quaker meetings in the city, Charles pointed out that they were not his troops, but those answerable to the Lord Mayor of London.[3] As his own extravagance made him more and more dependent on parliament, he became increasingly cautious. When Thomas Moore interceded for Fox, the king (alarmed at the indignation which his Declaration of Indulgence had aroused) 'was very timorous (it being just at the pinch of the parliament's coming on) of doing anything to displease them, his occasions being so great for money...'. He promised to do what he could, 'but not of himself, for he said the burnt child dreaded the fire'.[4] But when the pressure of necessity relaxed, Charles showed that he could do a good deal for the relief of prisoners. With good temper and forbearance, and often in a quizzical and slightly bantering tone, he discussed with the Quakers their characteristic views, and usually he promised to bring the case of the prisoners before his Council or to speak to the judges before they set out on circuit. But the fact that the respite he could grant was often so limited, alike in scope and duration, was merely an indication of the weakened constitutional position of the Crown.

An order for release was no guarantee that the prisoner would either go free or remain so. Even when the law was satisfied, the gaoler might still have his demands. A man of scrupulous conscience, feeling that the keeper's charges were exorbitant, might decline to pay them, and so might be kept in prison until he changed his mind. Often, however, the gaoler himself relented and, through generosity or weariness, abandoned his claims. So the prisoner came forth, and immediately discovered that the freedom he had recovered was beset with dangers both old and new. Having secured the king's pardon, he might at once come under the bishop's condemnation; having just been liberated from the sentence of one kind of court, he might be sent back to prison by another. If he had hitherto been leniently treated, a vindictive justice might issue a new mittimus, and contrive to send him to a gaol where conditions were notoriously bad. Though the influence of friends might gain release, the malice of opponents was usually sufficient to end the freedom which it had cost so much time and effort to win.

As soon as he was released, the devout nonconformist at once organised a day of thanksgiving. He called together his relatives and friends; gathered in the family circle, they praised God for the providence which had preserved the prisoner amid the dangers and discomforts of the gaol, and for the mercy which had restored him again to his accustomed place. He had been sent to prison for worshipping as his conscience commanded; his first act on gaining his release exposed him to renewed attacks. Again and again, the authorities offered to release prisoners who would promise not to preach. They threatened them with severe penalties if they persisted; they pointed out how much they prolonged their captivity and how greatly they jeopardised their freedom by not giving the assurances which were required. To suffer for your convictions makes you prize them all the more, and the disciplines of adversity sent the prisoner out more eager than ever to serve a Master who in the time of need had so marvellously sustained him. 'If I were out of prison to-day,' said Bunyan, 'I would preach the gospel again to-morrow, by the help of God.'[1] This was no idle boast; as soon as the opportunity came he proved as much, and scores of others did the same.

For many there was no release—except by death. And after weary months in prison, even death wore a gentle aspect and seemed a friend. Men recognised, of course, its loneliness and poignancy when its victim had been cut off by close confinement from all his friends, but they knew that it was merciful and realised that in its own way it represented a spiritual triumph of the highest order. It was a victory—but often it was not without concomitants of shame. A man who died in Leominster prison was kept several days in the hope that his family would pay the coroner's fees, and then was buried with savage indignity. The coffin was tied by the hangman to a ladder and carried by four felons, with the hangman himself walking ahead and the keeper of the prison following. 'When they put him into the grave the hangman said, He died like a hog, and should be buried like a dog, adding that had not the weather been wet, they should have made a grave under the gallows and buried him there.'[1] The grotesque brutality of that committal does not rob of its dignity a life laid down for conscience' sake. It merely underlines the elements constantly present when men suffered for their faith. The shades of the prison house were scattered by 'the light which was shining in the darkness', and even the most gloomy corners were made bright. When you are persuaded that you stand upon the testimony of the gospel, 'then may you look on your sufferings, not as your shame, but your glory and honour;...not as a forerunner of your future misery, but as a pledge of your future glory. For if you suffer with Christ, you shall reign with him.'[2] Confidence increased as persecution grew more severe, and even the prospect of death held no terrors. 'The cup of afflictions for the gospel is the sweeter the deeper,' wrote Thomas Browning, 'a stronger cordial the nearer the bottom: I mean death itself.... I tell you, if you knew what Christ's prisoners...enjoyed in their jails, you would not fear their condition but long for it....Come, the worst is death, and that is the best of all. What! do we stick at dying for him who stuck not at it for us?...There is no shadow like the shadow of God's wings; therefore keep close to God.'[3]

CHAPTER V

PURITAN WAYS: THE INDIVIDUAL
AND HIS EXPERIENCE

AN accident of genius made the story of a man's pilgrimage from this world to the next the best known of all Puritan works. This was profoundly appropriate; indeed, it was almost inevitable. No other theme gave comparable scope to the spiritual insight and the imaginative power of the greatest Puritans. Bunyan wrote many allegories, but none of them—not *Mr Badman*, nor *The Holy War* nor *The Heavenly Footman*—has the sure touch and the sustained power of *The Pilgrim's Progress*. The subject was old, yet ever fresh. It concerned a journey on which many had embarked, but on which each man must set out for himself. The objectives and the demands of that journey shaped the character of the Puritan's life and gave to his days their distinctive quality. He shared his pilgrimage with others; friends provided company, companions gave encouragement and support. Yet it was an intensely personal experience throughout, and at many of its most solemn moments he stood alone with God. The life he lived in the religious community to which he belonged was thus balanced and completed by the more intimate fellowship into which he was drawn by his relationships with his friends, with his family and especially with his God.

The pattern of his personal experience was affected by many factors over which he had no control. Great national events caught him up in their train. Little though he might understand their causes or their character, they swept him along through a turmoil of upheaval and suffering toward a future whose outlines he could not even foresee. For the most part, however, his days were shaped by the simple regularities which grew from his view of life and from the relationships which he was able to create. He believed that all events afforded opportunities for spiritual training and self-improvement; it was his duty to make the most of all of them. It was a mistake to regard religion merely as 'a set of opinions'; it was 'a divine discipline to reform the heart and life'.[1]

Week by week, the return of Sunday reminded the Puritan of the simplest yet most fundamental element in the structure of his life. The day was God's gift; it reflected his gracious purposes and so it must be used to promote them. 'Man's chief end is to glorify God and to enjoy him forever'; what fitter day for this duty than 'the Sabbath of the Lord your God'? So the Puritan was immediately involved in that unrelenting sequence of services which consumed so many of the hours of the day of rest. Sunday opened with religious exercises in the home; the morning service led, after a short break, to the afternoon diet of worship. Often the interval was improved, as the congregation sat waiting in the chapel, by one of the members 'repeating' a sermon, and thus every possible moment was conserved for the necessary task of edifying the people of God. In the afternoon there would also be catechising of the younger members of the flock. At night there might be a 'lecture', but in every earnest home there would certainly be 'repetition'. When faced with so uncompromising a programme, the faint-hearted might quail, but human frailty could expect few concessions. To the question, 'Should the whole day be spent in holy exercises?' Baxter gave an unhesitating reply. There are five unanswerable reasons, he said, why 'a holy, thankful Christian, if he have but leave to spend all day for the good of his soul and those about him'—in 'reading and meditating on the word of God, and praying and praising him, and instructing his family'— will rest content.[2] 'The religion of England', said John Evelyn, 'is preaching and sitting still on Sundays.'[3] Apparently it was.

It was an austere regimen, and one not easily maintained. When Ralph Thoresby visited Holland, he was shocked at the casual character of 'the continental Sunday', but his diary gives ample evidence of the difficulties that even a conscientious Puritan encountered in 'remember[ing] the Sabbath day to keep it holy'. It is true that when he was in London, he spent his Sundays as a well-brought-up young man should do, in eager pilgrimage from one place of worship to the next. He heard the most celebrated preachers, and made careful notes of what they said. When his journey northward involved him in Sunday travelling, he was deeply distressed, but once at home in Leeds he found that temptations beset the path even of an earnest seeker after godliness. Visits to friends might seem harmless enough, but they consumed far too much time, and might easily lead to frivolous conversation. It was dangerous to dine out; in more ways than one the tongue, that most unruly member, might offend. It was not even permissible to show inquirers his coin collection, though his vanity was flattered by their request to see it.[1] The worship of the Lord's day not only fed men's minds and spirits, but kept their feet from straying where they should not go. Heywood noted that when there was no afternoon sermon at the parish church the people soon fell into evil habits; they went visiting in one another's homes, they walked abroad to inspect cattle and discuss the crops, they even turned to the tavern and ended the day in a riot of unseemly mirth.[2] How fortunate, then, that God so clearly displayed his wrath against those who transgressed his commandment and desecrated his holy day! A man who neglected worship, and rode off to do business in a neighbouring community, sat too long at the ale-house, and on his way home fell from his horse and was drowned in the river. When a man went on Sunday to cut down a maypole and fetch it home, he brought disaster upon himself, and the escapade cost him his life. The judgements of the Most High were abroad in the earth, and discretion as well as the thirst for righteousness helped to keep the discreet Puritan in the straight and narrow path of strict observance. Yet it must not be thought that the obligation seemed heavy. The delights of the Sabbath appeared no less real because they were neither 'meretricious nor gaudy'. It was a woman of serious outlook but not of Puritan loyalties who remarked on the calming effect that Sunday had on people, and who sagely observed that it was consequently a good day for breaking bad news.[3]

Sunday had its distinctive duties, but so had every other day of the week. It was important to know your obligations in detail; then you could discharge them as you should, and everything would fall into its proper place. The regulating of each day began before it had actually broken; the Puritan went to bed persuaded that he must 'proportion the time of [his] sleep aright', lest he waste his 'precious morning hours sluggishly in [his] bed'. Six hours sleep, added Baxter, was enough for any healthy person. Holy duties began as soon as he was awake. Attire must be simple, lest time be wasted in the unprofitable necessity of dressing. If your station warranted it, 'you [might] employ a child or servant to read a chapter in the Bible while you [are] dressing you and eating your breakfast (if you eat any)'. There followed the prescribed routine of prayers, both private and family, and then the Puritan was ready to face the world. He would not go forth, however, without consciously recalling his ultimate end; at the beginning of his day's work he would remember that all he did must be part of his service of God. What could not so be offered had better never be undertaken. Then, having thus prepared himself, he would 'follow the labours of [his] calling painfully and diligently', watching against temptations as well as seizing opportunities, till the approach of nightfall closed the day with prayer and praise.[1]

Life, however, did not always follow the pattern that the moralists prescribed. Daily work, though undertaken as a vocation, had a disconcerting way of becoming an all-engrossing secular preoccupation. More than once Elias Pledger acknowledged with contrition the spiritual barrenness which resulted from too complete preoccupation with his business, but it was easier to confess his failures to his diary than to break the hold which worldly pursuits had established on his heart.[2] Ralph Josselin, a Puritan minister who escaped ejection simply because no one disturbed him, and who conformed by imperceptible degrees, became increasingly absorbed in husbanding his material resources. Perhaps business helped him to disregard the unwelcome whisperings of conscience; perhaps time was dulling the perceptions that had once been so keen. Whatever the cause, a man who began with a high sense of his responsibility for material things ended with an unedifying desire to multiply his worldly possessions.[3]

And in any case life was seldom as serious as the moralists supposed. The undeviating earnestness which they commended was broken by many a lighter moment. Often we hear about these only because they had multiplied to the point where an uneasy conscience has felt that protests were required. Cards were dangerous, not because they were necessarily wrong in themselves, but because of their fatal power to consume time. One hand led to the next, and the next, and in melancholy retrospect the Puritan confessed that he had wasted far too much of the day. Dining out was a necessary as well as a pleasant part of life's pattern, but it easily led to intemperance, and was beset with pitfalls.[1] Shuffle board, which might seem a harmless sport,[2] could awaken fierce delights, and Henry Newcome, having sadly noted that he had allowed himself 'too great latitude in mirth' and spent far too much time at play, firmly resolved that henceforth he would never take part in a game till he had a worthy day's work already behind him. He was perfectly ready, however, to join with others in a celebration at the ale-house, and in retrospect he did not feel that the party had been unduly gay. About some things he clearly had scruples; when a fellow-minister suggested that they go to see a performing horse he refused—why, he does not say, but he felt that the decision was worth recording in his diary. And he sorely rebuked himself when he lingered too long in watching 'the dancers on the rope'.[3]

In many popular recreations of the time the Puritan felt that he could have no part. It was the concomitants inseparable from bear-baiting and cock-fighting, rather than their inherent character, that made them seem so evil. Betting and gambling flourished on an extravagant scale; poor men wagered (and often lost) sums that left their families impoverished and in need.[4] Races were suspect for the same reason. Such gatherings were marked by a vast amount of drinking, and often they were organised by men who were far more interested in their own aggrandisement than they were in sport. Even the maypole, which to later times has seemed the charming symbol of the gaiety of a carefree age, appeared in a very different light to many contemporaries. They knew that the festivities which began so innocently on the village green were often prolonged into an orgy of drunkenness and vice. With horror the Puritan contemplated the degradation of life which resulted, and he knew that he could not countenance such activities nor have any part in them. It was wise, therefore, to specify the bounds of innocent recreation. With great care Baxter enumerated the eighteen distinguishing marks of legitimate recreation, and showed conclusively that 'stage-plays, gaming, cards, dice, etc.' did not fall within its bounds.[1] Robert Barclay, the Quaker, firmly ruled that sports and games were inconsistent with the gospel. The character of the Restoration stage naturally confirmed the belief that plays 'are a studied complex of idle lying words'. The best recreation in the world, he concluded (though not very specifically), is the fear of the Lord.[2] William Perkins was slightly more lenient as well as more precise. 'Recreation', he said, 'is an exercise joined with the fear of God, conversant with things indifferent, for the preservation of bodily strength and the confirmation of the mind in holiness. To this end hath the Word of God permitted shooting (2 Sam. i. 18); musical consort (Neh. vii. 67); putting forth riddles (Judges xiv. 12); hunting of wild beasts (Cant. ii. 15); searching out or the contemplation of the works of God (I Kings iv. 33).' Unfortunately these scriptural suggestions did not prove very helpful; neither 'putting forth riddles' nor 'hunting of wild beasts' held a prominent place among contemporary pastimes.

Permissible pleasures were simple and sober. Many of them were associated with the life of the congregation. Others grew naturally from the social situation in which the Puritan found himself. An ejected minister would look forward to visits from his brethren similarly placed, but the pleasure he found in their company was tinged with melancholy. When three ministers called on Philip Henry, the four went to visit a fifth, and they were acutely conscious of the vocation which they had accepted but which they were forbidden to exercise. They were all of them merely 'candles under a bushel'.[3] When Adam Martindale came to see Henry Newcome, they went together to service in the parish church, but they were oppressed by the thought that, though they had been called to preach, they were both condemned to silence; 'we went', said Newcome, 'with the rebuke of God upon us.'[1] When a country minister found himself in London he eagerly seized the opportunity of meeting the great figures who were the ornaments of nonconformity. He could see and hear the men whose books he had read in the seclusion of his own study; he might even be called to conference with them. In times of intense persecution, the privilege might be attended with dangers. When Heywood was in the capital, he saw Nathaniel Vincent often and preached for him just before and just after Vincent's arrest. Only good fortune, he felt, had saved him from a similar fate, but he neither refused the next invitation to preach, nor hesitated to visit the imprisoned minister in gaol. Nevertheless he was profoundly relieved to find himself once more safely home.[2] Such experiences, with the solemn overtones which danger gave them, were common enough in the Restoration period, and they played a large part in the life of many of the Puritans. In a time of persecution, personal contacts resulted in fellowship of a distinctive and intimate type, more often marked by gravity than by gaiety.

The brevity of life, no less than the imminence of danger, was responsible for the earnestness so characteristic of the Puritan. Day and night there hung over his spirit an urgent sense of the incomparable value of time. 'Keep a high esteem of time', wrote Baxter, 'and be every day more careful that you lose none of your time than you are that you lose none of your gold or silver. ...And for the redeeming of time, especially see, not only that you be never idle, but also that you be doing the greatest good that you can do, and prefer not a less before a greater.'[3] Human life was bounded by an eternity that was pressing in upon it; the issues involved were as momentous as the permitted span was brief. The last words a dying man could gasp to those who stood around his bed were an exhortation 'to improve time before we launch into eternity'.[4] 'Time is running into eternity,' cried Henry, 'O, what wisdom it is to redeem it, and how much am I wanting in that wisdom.'[5] Any event might come as a rebuke for wasting this incomparably precious commodity, time. To hear a young man preaching with power was enough to move the listener to shame that he had used his own opportunities so poorly: he could not even practise what the preacher could so skilfully commend. Amusements were treacherous: time flew past so quickly that a man learned too late how much he had lost. Company was dangerous: he lingered too long in unprofitable conversation. Sleep, in particular, presented temptations against which a man needed to be ceaselessly on guard. 'For some time past', Pledger confesses, 'I have indulged myself in unnecessary ease and sleep in the morning....Lord, strengthen me against this, and I desire to improve that strength thou has given me already against it....We lose much time and many choice opportunities for God's service by our slothfulness....Oh that I might be more careful in the improvement of my time than formerly.'[1] Thoresby, though so ill he could neither eat nor drink, was bitterly rebuked by his conscience when he allowed himself a little extra latitude in the morning.[2] Heywood noted that the old Adam in him fought a stubborn rearguard action against grace—and wanted to fight it mainly in bed. To help in the task of 'redeeming the time', numerous expedients were commended. Rebukes might have some value, and on no subject did Baxter find stern warnings more needful.[3] A diary might prove helpful; its pages gave a picture of the use to which time had been turned, and a yearly review of the record would rebuke for past failures and incite to future diligence.[4] Various activities might be combined; as Fox demonstrated to his friends, a man who had to travel could learn to read or write on horseback. Conversations could so be regulated as to lead naturally to profitable themes, and in the house or by the way men might thus improve the passing moments. Over every aspect of life there brooded a firm conviction from which in turn there crystallised an unfaltering desire: 'Time is precious; Lord give me skill and wisdom to redeem it.'[5]

It was equally important that the inner meaning of each experience should be recognised and turned to the soul's advantage. Every ounce of spiritual profit must be squeezed from the events which each day brought. To observe the stocks in the marketplace could remind a man of the penalties of sin, God's grace in delivering him from a life of outward wickedness, the magnitude of his own undetected sins, and his constant need of God's forgiveness. The fate of a spendthrift, finally arrested for debt, reminded the Puritan of the extent to which we are always under obligation to God and cannot hope to wipe out the score. When a young girl was drowned in the river, the mishap was a proof that 'to God the Lord belong the issues of death, and from death; he alone kills and he makes alive'. The purchase of a new suit was an occasion for meditating on the need of being reclothed in righteousness. A fall from a horse or a tumble on an icy patch of the road recalled God's providential care of his people, but also the undeniable fact that their feet are set in slippery places. When the thatch of the roof caught fire it was a humbling reminder of temptation's power to kindle the flames of sin in man's heart; when the fire was put out it was proof that grace can extinguish all the fiery darts of the devil. Much of this was merely the expression, in the idiom of the seventeenth century, of the religious man's conviction that his true life belongs to an order of mercy and truth; whichever way he may turn, his insight will detect the signs of providential care where the secular mind will see merely the evidence of good fortune or bad luck. Associated with this attitude was a firm belief that natural phenomena had a spiritual significance. Comets blazing across the night sky or stars falling from their places in the heavens were accepted as the appropriate counterparts of human joys or sorrows. When ministers were ejected, when religious liberty was revoked, when national fortunes seemed desperate or when evil was signally triumphant it was to be expected that the heavenly bodies would be touched with pity for our human plight. A natural portent was usually forthcoming; it was always recorded with wondering solemnity.

Holiness was to be commended by a life commensurate with its demands; its nature was to be demonstrated in the heart and before the world, but also within the family circle.[1] Each household was to be in miniature a church of the living God. The New Testament greeting to the church which is in this house or that was to be applied (with a slight variation) to every family, and in days when persecution prevented public meetings, the Puritan recalled with gratitude the fact that 'every home was a Bethel'.

Even that centre of worship might be disturbed and disrupted; men driven from their houses, sent abroad to wander as strangers in unknown places, found that all the customary supports of domestic holiness were broken down. To maintain them in normal times and to repair them speedily when damaged became an inseparable part of the Puritan's ideal. The household, of course, included servants in addition to members of the family. They were to share in the life of worship as well as in the routine of work. Their well-being was to be carefully considered, and they were to be built up in sober godliness and in Christian under-standing. When one of the servants yielded to temptation and fell, his shame was shared by all the members of the family, and they joined him in seeking forgiveness at the throne of grace.[1] Often the servants became in the truest sense members of the inner circle. They shared in all the joys and sorrows of the family; they joined in the solemn fasts and in the days of thanksgiving. Hey-wood's maid was largely responsible for bringing up his mother-less children; when, after sixteen years in his family, she left to be married, Heywood remarked that he could not have felt her departure more keenly if she had been his own daughter.[2] Apprentices, too, were often brought into the same kind of re-lationship. It was a matter for profound gratitude when a young man found himself apprenticed to a genuinely godly master. His parents were deeply relieved, and he himself thankfully acknowledged the benefits he enjoyed. This concern for the wel-fare of apprentices, so characteristic of most Puritans, was made a matter of corporate responsibility among the Quakers; the whole fellowship had a duty toward the young, to see that they were well placed and wisely guided toward a useful life.

Guests also were brought within the orbit of the church-in-the-home. When they arrived, prayer together was the seal of inti-macy; when they departed, it was the final expression of good will and concern. There are few glimpses of Puritan friendship more charming than Newcome's account of his reception when he went to visit Thomas Leadbeater. 'I remember the good man said upon his kissing me when I came in, that Moses and Aaron were glad to see one another in their heart when they met near the mount of God. We went to prayer as soon as we came in.'[1] When Heywood's sons visited their father, the old man's favourite way of passing the time was to summon them to join him in prayer. And no matter who the guest might be, he did not leave the house till the family had committed him to God's care and sought the divine blessing upon his journey.

Within the household, parental concern watched every opportunity of improving events to the advantage of each member. It was particularly necessary to see that children grew up to recognise God's hand in all things. A thunderstorm, therefore, formed a useful pretext for inculcating the fear of God; and when there could be added to the impression created by natural phenomena a cautionary tale about children who had been struck by lightning when playing on the Sabbath day, we may be sure that the admonition was not without effect.

The organisation of family life to promote the godliness of all concerned could not be left on an accidental or haphazard basis. Simple expedients might be used, for anything that would keep fresh in mind the claims of a holy life was important. In many humble homes it was customary to paste on the walls handbills explaining the duties of the believer. Puritan authors of great eminence provided such broadsheets for the instruction of the earnest seeker. Joseph Caryl issued *Plain Directions for the More Profitable Hearing of the Word*. Joseph Alleine wrote *Directions for Covenanting with God: also Rules for a Christian's Daily Self-Examination*. Bunyan wrote *Of the Trinity and a Christian, Of the Law and a Christian*, and *A Map of Salvation*. Baxter, in enumerating his works, mentioned a number of sheets which he published as a means of training simple souls. Books might also play their part. Thoresby was careful to read to his family works that would promote piety. In many homes there would be few books, but in a great many there would be one or two, and Puritan philanthropists were eager to increase their number. Lord Wharton, for example, devoted much time and money to the distribution of Bibles and devotional manuals among the poor, and Puritan ministers were his chosen agents.

Unforeseen events might be turned to good account, but what

was needed was a carefully regulated pattern of communal experience. Within it, four principal activities normally had a place: household catechising, family prayer, the repetition of sermons and the singing of psalms.[1]

Systematic instruction of the family was one of the chief means by which the Puritans hoped to combat religious illiteracy. At hand to help them was the Assembly's Catechism, and all possible means were taken to encourage its use. On Sunday, of course, it formed the basis of the public instruction of the young, but this was obviously insufficient. To supplement such use, conscientious ministers began a house-to-house visitation of their flock. They called the family together and examined the members one by one in the truths of religion. This accomplished much, but if the head of the household could be persuaded to exercise his true responsibilities, the whole situation could be transformed. The minister's role would be to correct (if necessary), to encourage and confirm, while the basic instruction became a means by which the proper character of the home was further established.[2]

The repetition of sermons was also a method of religious education by which the Puritans set great store. It presupposed, of course, close attention to the sermon while it was being preached. It usually relied, too, on some system of taking notes, and the more conscientious members of the congregation, having pondered the theme as they walked home, would then write out the sermon in full. Some became amazingly proficient at this exercise; even without relying on notes they could repeat a sermon almost verbatim. On Sunday night, when the family was assembled after the evening meal, one or other of its members would be assigned the task of repeating a sermon (it might be either the morning or the afternoon discourse), and the listeners would supply any omissions. Nor was it safe to forget, even at this point. In many homes there would be repetition during the family preparation for the following Sabbath day. There was the added hazard that at any time the minister might call; having required one person to repeat the sermon, he would examine the others on its meaning.

The singing of psalms likewise played an important role in the religious life of Puritan families. It had scriptural sanction and apostolic authority. It impressed the truths of religion on the people's minds even while it gave expression to the emotions in their hearts. In a country where music was still a living part of the people's heritage it was easy and natural for them to sing. They needed encouragement, however, and it was a sign both that the gospel was being diligently preached and that the people were giving faithful heed to it when they improved their leisure by singing psalms at home. In describing the effect of his ministry at Kidderminster, Baxter tells us that there was no disorder in the streets on the Lord's day, 'but you might hear a hundred families singing psalms or repeating sermons as you passed through them'.[1]

Family prayer, however, occupied the largest place in the discipline of the Puritan household. It was a duty constantly advocated by the most influential leaders, and was faithfully practised in many of the ordinary homes. Indeed, it was assumed that the development of praying families was the true gauge of effective ministerial work in a community; when there was prayer in the homes there was vitality in the church. Great care was taken to encourage the diffident and train the backward.[2] A minister might decide that when he prayed with his wife, kneeling with her night and morning by the bedside, it would be well for her to pray aloud; then, in his absence from home, she would have greater confidence in conducting family worship. The duty, of course, rested primarily on the head of the household. It was his priestly responsibility to minister to and intercede for the souls whom God had committed to his care, but he could sometimes delegate his authority.[3]

In any well-ordered household, said Baxter, family prayers should be held twice a day. Plausible arguments on behalf of such a routine could be strengthened with cogent scriptural proofs.[4] Morning prayers, at least, were very common. When the family met for breakfast—or more probably when the meal was finished—the entire household gathered; then a psalm was sung, the Bible was read, and prayer was poured forth. It was not a perfunctory performance. Earnestly, seriously and at great length the Puritan thanked God for his goodness, prostrated himself before the divine majesty, and besought help and guidance during the coming day. Matthew Henry gives us a detailed account of family worship as his father conducted it. It was never omitted and it always had priority over every kind of worldly business; when there were no family prayers within the house, he said, you could safely paint the plague warning on the door. He began with a short but very solemn prayer, in which he asked God to vouchsafe his presence, and by his spirit bless the Word to the hearers. This prayer always ended with a doxology. Then the family sang a psalm, systematically working their way through the psalter. Then he read a passage from the Bible: we speak to God in prayer, he said; it is right that we should let him speak to us in his Word. He did not select a chapter at random, but steadily read through the Bible. Nor did he leave the words to make their own impression; carefully, and in language suited to his hearers' needs, he expounded what he read, and this was prompted by a desire both to clarify the meaning of the passage and to kindle the devotion of his family. To remove any possibility that the chapter might still be unintelligible, he called on the children to give its sense in their own words. Then the family knelt for prayer, and Henry, drawing on the psalm they had sung or the chapter they had read, implored God's aid and blessing on the family. It was a prayer freely composed and adapted to the needs of the household as they were seen in the light of scripture. He was always 'most full in giving thanks for family mercies, confessing family sins, and begging family blessings'. He always concluded worship with a solemn benediction. In conclusion, the children knelt one by one before their parents and asked a blessing; it was given with all possible solemnity. Occasionally some part of the proceedings might be curtailed, but nothing was ever omitted, and on Sunday everything was done on twice the normal scale. Daily prayer, added Matthew Henry, was a joy to the children and the servants, not a burden; it never seemed unduly long.[1]

Every morning brought its season of prayer; so, theoretically, did every evening, but sometimes the opportunity was put aside and the duty neglected. When Heywood, acknowledging in his diary the failings that disfigured his days, noted sadly that he often skimped evening prayers, he introduced an element of human frailty to counteract the exacting austerity of Puritan precept. When tired after the day's work or when preoccupied with worldly concerns, it was easy to curtail devotions or postpone them altogether. Conscience, however, was uneasy, and registered its protest.[1]

Special occasions required special observances. Even Saturday night, because it was a time of preparation for the Sabbath day, received particular attention. One evening, breaking off his work on the morrow's sermons, Heywood spent the period from 6 to 9 p.m. in prayer with his wife and his sons. 'Oh what an evening it was of pleadings, groans, tears!'[2] In some households a family conference was held every Saturday night, and questions were propounded for discussion by all present. They certainly did not waste their precious time considering trivialities. What are good arguments against sin? What are the common hindrances to man's salvation? What are the ingredients of true repentance? What does it mean to believe in Jesus Christ for salvation? What are the evidences of love to God? How can we best express our love for our neighbours? These were questions actually propounded in Henry's household. Six or eight points were advanced in answer to each question, and every contribution had to be supported by an appropriate text from scripture. At the end Henry himself always closed the discussion with a 'use'—a practical application of the doctrine to the needs of daily life.[3] This doubtless represented an ideal not often attained; if it were in any degree typical, it is not surprising that so many of the Puritans were firmly grounded in the Bible and thoroughly conversant with theological issues.

At times a whole day would be set aside for special prayers, and the entire family would participate. As in duty bound, the head of the household would initiate proceedings. 'I spoke something', said Heywood, 'of family concernments that might affect our hearts, and my son Eliezer began, prayed sweetly, sensibly, though but short; wept much, did well. But John was both a good while, and prayed to my admiration, pleading with God, and using such expostulations as I wondered at, together with lively affections, many tears. Then Martha (the maid), then my wife, then myself....Blessed be God for the gift and spirit of prayer.'[1] Joys and sorrows provided the pretext for special family exercises; they were the occasion for days of thanksgiving or for solemn fasts.[2] When a new house was occupied for the first time, it was necessary to dedicate it to God, and to pledge the members of the household to his service. When a member returned from a journey, when good news from an absent son ended an anxious interval of silence, when someone had recovered from a serious illness, even when death had made a gap in the family circle, the right thing was to gather in God's presence, return thanks to him (if only for the life that had been taken) and ask his blessing and his help.

The corporate devotions of the family were only one phase of a life carefully regulated and severely disciplined throughout. The ties of mutual obligation bound together all the members of the household. Masters had certain responsibilities toward their servants; the servants, in turn, had distinctive duties which they owed their masters. Parents were expected to guide and discipline their children; but they were not to exercise negative or repressive supervision; with all care they were to deflect the young from evil ways in order to bring them up to know God and do his will.[3] Children in turn should respond in obedience and helpfulness. Husbands and wives were joined in a relationship of delicately balanced privileges and obligations. It was an exacting programme, and the Puritans were expected to develop the qualities which would fit them for their task. They were to be 'a watchful, painful, industrious, sober, meek, merciful, patient people'.[4] When engaged in such rigorous duties, strictness of life was the mark of elementary wisdom. The runner could not win without undergoing training; the Christian could not persevere without submitting to stringent discipline.[5] 'The slovenly sort of professors' could hardly fail to 'fall short of eternal life'.[6] With grave demeanour, with conversation free from flippancy or loquacity, the Christian would earnestly go forward on life's

143

way. A devout seriousness became the distinguishing mark of family life among the Puritans. They themselves did not feel, however, that they had thereby been condemned to a morose or sullen existence. After describing the work of his distinguished fellow-Quaker, Thomas Story, John Whiting remarked that his daily life had indeed been distinguished by sobriety, but equally by mercy, hospitality and a readiness to entertain.[1] And from their records, we know that in their homes the Puritans often found deep and abiding satisfactions. Baxter's life of his wife is one of the most patently sincere tributes to a happy marriage ever written. Philip Henry, returning from a journey, observed that 'home is home indeed to me, blessed be God. My wife is my helper, present, absent, and my heart doth safely trust in her, the Lord's most holy name be blessed and praised.'[2] Equally moving is Kiffin's tribute to his wife. 'Her tenderness to me and faithfulness to God, were such as cannot by me be expressed. She sympathised with me in all my afflictions, and I can truly say I never heard her utter the least discontent under all the various providences that attended myself or her, but, owning the hand of God in them, she was a constant encourager of me in the ways of God. Her death was to me the greatest sorrow I ever met with in this world.'[3] 'When there is peace in the heart', says the Chinese proverb, 'there is happiness in the home.'

The intimacy which marked the life of a happy home was at once reflected in and confirmed by the relationships built up between members of the family circle. The partnership of husband and wife was founded on a common understanding of the purpose of life. Because they were agreed in their interpretation of the ultimate mysteries of human existence they could co-operate with a greater measure of unanimity in dealing with the details of ordinary experience. In a pious Puritan household, husband and wife knelt together first thing in the morning and last thing at night. In other ways, too, they tried to place daily relationships in a setting profound enough to invest them with true significance. Step by step an earnest minister would lead his wife into a deeper understanding of the truths that meant so much to him. Sometimes her reticence might baffle him; sometimes his own negligence would fill him with shame; nevertheless, there would be sure signs of progress and a corresponding encouragement. He could note greater confidence on her part in speaking of religious subjects, a greater ease and naturalness in prayer, an increasing readiness to find in her devotions an aid in perplexity and a comfort in trouble. Heywood, who watched so carefully for these signs of growth in his wife, records that in due course she was as ready as he to find in prayer an unfailing support in every crisis. If warning came of an intended raid on their meeting for worship, and for the moment duty and discretion seemed in conflict; or if he were called to accept some distateful task, or had to face the consequences of a bitter feud, she would join him and together they would 'go to prayer'.

The way, however, was not always smooth. Occasionally differences arose between them, and then prayer was more necessary than ever. Once, when Heywood had just embarked on a private session of prayer, she unwittingly disturbed him. It was an exasperating interruption; his 'soul was warm and working busily at it', and he knew full well that the mood would be dissipated. So he was irritated, 'chid her and gave her sharp words', though, as he ruefully acknowledged, she could not have guessed what he was doing. At all events there was little peace in the household that day, nor much rest during the ensuing night. In the grey light of dawn they candidly discussed the matter. 'I confessed my fault and folly in my passionate finding fault with her, and vain-glory in discovering what I was doing. We knelt down by the bedside, I prayed, we both wept, and were comfortably closed.' Or, again, there was the time when he unwarily invited a houseful of guests without consulting her, and discovered that she had made other and quite different plans. Heywood quickly read the danger signals, and offered to write at once and cancel the suggested visit. They spent a troubled day, followed by a restless night. After tossing and turning till 2 a.m., she rose; when he followed her, he found her with her Bible open before her. He suggested that they might pray; she demurred, but he ventured to begin, found the right words and plenteous 'openings of heart', and they were reconciled. With gratitude, he recorded in his diary that prayer was always his sovereign remedy, an aid that never failed—but next morning he wrote to cancel the arrangements he had so rashly made. The small disputes which at the moment seem so large are a variant of an old, old, story; it was a typically Puritan solution of a perennial problem that Heywood applied to the differences involved in family life.[1]

At no point does the true quality of the Puritan home appear more clearly than in the records of bereavements. With pathos yet with dignity, in sorrow but with hope, the story of the end is told. In spite of faith, the parting was not always easy. When Mrs Stockton's eldest child was seriously ill, 'I found a great lothness', she reports, 'to part with such a dear and desirable child, having also buried four before, and having but one more, and that a very weakly child also.' With earnestness edged by despair she prayed for her daughter's life, but as the illness increased its hold, the comfort that came to her was in the all-embracing assurance of God's inscrutable purpose and his unfailing love.[2] However great the sorrow might be, it, no less than the joy which preceded it, was encompassed by the covenant into which God brings his people. While meditating on death in the loneliness of his stricken home, Elias Pledger remembered that he had given his children as well as himself to God; in return he had received the assurance that God would be not only his God, but the God of his seed also; and though we may imperfectly fulfil our pledge God will ever be mindful of his covenant. Even when he strikes us with his rod, he merely chastises us in order to bring us back to dependence on his grace.[3] When Baxter lost his wife, he placed on record his unfaltering conviction that God had 'called away to his blest rest and glory the spirit of the most dear companion of these last nineteen years of my life'.[4] Heywood, who was deeply persuaded of the value of recording the last moments of sincere Christians, left a profoundly moving account of the death of his first wife. As her bodily strength slowly ebbed away, the strong confidence of her faith blazed forth with astonishing vitality. She was going into 'the world of light'; and though her husband knew that death would be swallowed up in victory, that did not mitigate the burden of his grief. For weeks his life seemed lost in

146

an abyss of loneliness and sorrow. Whichever way he turned, he was conscious only of his loss. 'I want her', he cried, 'at every turn, in every place, and in every affair; methinks I am but half myself without her.'[1]

The life of the individual, though related in so many ways to other people, was continually renewed and sustained in secret. In the discipline of his own soul must be found the key to the character of the Puritan. The record of each day was firmly bound between two simple acts of recollection and commitment. First thing in the morning and last thing at night he recalled God's presence and yielded his life to his guidance and care. 'Let God have your first waking thoughts,' said Baxter; 'lift up your hearts to him reverently and thankfully for the rest of the night past, and briefly cast yourself upon him for the following day; and use yourselves so constantly to this, that your conscience may check you, when common thoughts shall first intrude.'[2] These waking thoughts, as we have seen, were likely to come early in the morning; nothing filled the Puritan with such horror, and against nothing was he so ceaselessly on guard, as the sloth which lies late abed. It was Joseph Alleine's custom to rise not later than 4 a.m., 'and he would be much troubled', reports his wife, 'if he heard any smiths or shoemakers or such tradesmen at work at their trades before he was at his duties with God: saying to me often, "How this noise shames me! Doth not *my* Master deserve more than *theirs*?"'[3] Not many were so Spartan in their discipline, but the constant confessions of tardiness in rising show that this was a point concerning which the Puritan conscience was particularly sensitive.

Behind this unrelenting discipline lay a motive clearly defined in each person's mind, and strong enough to mould his entire life. All his religious activities were to serve one all-important end. 'I will set myself', said Heywood, 'to pray oftener and better in my family society, and closet, to get my thoughts and my affections more entirely fixed on God. I will meditate, walk close with God, and perform every duty with a design to meet with God and engage my heart to approach to him and endeavour to get daily influences from him.'[4]

In helping the Puritan to fulfil this aim, the reading of the Bible naturally held a pre-eminent place. No book, said Baxter, has 'so much power and fitness to convey the Spirit and make us spiritual, by imprinting itself upon our hearts. As there is more of God in it, so it will acquaint us more with God, and bring us nearer him, and make the reader more reverent, serious, and divine.'[1] It would naturally prove its efficacy in every area of life. It was the surest weapon with which to beat off the assaults of temptation.[2] When the pressures of persecution were severe and the courage of believers wavered, they turned to the Bible and found their faith confirmed.[3] When problems of any kind arose, it was to the Bible that men and women looked for light and guidance. If they were puzzled about their spiritual condition, wondering whether they were in a state of grace or had fallen into sin, a verse such as Job xxxiii. 27 helped them to overcome their doubts. The evidences of saving faith were made clear when reading I Peter ii. 7, while John xi. 40 and Psalm cxix. 49 brought comfort when the fear of bereavement was strong.[4] Such passages were not merely read with joy, but were carefully copied out, and kept at hand for easy reference.

Other books, though occupying an inferior status, might also help the seeker forward on his way. Romances, of course, were barred from the homes of the godly, and so were stage-plays, while controversial works were a hazard to all but mature and stable Christians. Sermons and devotional works, on the other hand, could play a very useful role. 'The writings of divines are nothing else but a preaching the gospel to the eye, as the voice preacheth it to the ear.' The advantages of sermons when preached were carefully weighed against the merits of the same sermons when printed. Reading had less power to stir the emotions, but a good book was always at hand; it could not be forgotten (as even the most moving sermon might be) and it could neither be silenced by the civil powers nor banished from the land. A book brought the words of the greatest preachers into the parlour of the humblest home: 'so that good books are a very great mercy to the world.'[5] A 'sound catechism' would stand beside the Bible on the bookshelf, and then a good concordance. To these indispensable volumes could be added the writings of the great Puritans of the previous generation: the letters of Samuel Rutherford, and the sermons of Perkins, Preston, Sibbes, Hildersham and half a dozen other worthies. Admonitions to value good books and read them were certainly not wasted. Ralph Thoresby not only read Manton's works, but helped to secure subscriptions to the volumes as they appeared; he studied Charnock's 'incomparable' discourses; he read Baxter's *Dying Thoughts*, and the works of Diodati, Poole, Alsop, Wilkins and Hall. He followed the debates between conformists and nonconformists; he verified the accuracy of the statements in *The Conformist's Plea for the Nonconformist*, noted the soundness of Rogers's *Persuasion to a Friendly Correspondence*, and remarked on the moderate spirit of Calamy's *Abridgment*. He even read the *Journal* of George Fox. Thoresby was a cultivated man with historical and antiquarian interests, yet almost all his reading was devotional or theological in character. Mrs Stockton remarked that sentences gleaned from her reading reproved her fears of falling from grace, and among books she had found helpful she mentioned Mr Caryl on Job, Mr Crow on the Lord's Supper, *The Christian's Daily Walk* and *The Spirit's Office Toward Believers*.[1] Devotional books like Baxter's *Saint's Everlasting Rest* and *Call to the Unconverted* circulated very widely, while Bunyan's works—exegetical no less than allegorical—appealed to an extensive public composed in very large part of humble Puritan folk.

Reading proved its value as soon as a man turned to another necessary discipline: meditation. The poverty and emptiness of his own mind drove him to draw upon the insights of others. The Bible, of course, was an incomparable aid in guiding one's thoughts into profitable channels, but it was foolish to neglect the help that could come from other sources. Joseph Alleine regularly used books like Baxter's *Saint's Everlasting Rest* as an aid to profitable reflection, and what he practised himself he commended to others.

From meditation it was a short step to self-examination. Having contemplated things divine, the Puritan turned to consider that most human object, his own heart. Daily, weekly, monthly, yearly, he scrutinised the record, and considered the progress he had made. He counted up his blessings, he assessed the use he had made of his opportunities, he examined the way he had discharged his responsibilities. Usually he found himself examining a strangely mixed account—of good things received and defective ones returned. 'As I have cause of gratitude,' observed Heywood, 'so of humiliation.' He had not sufficiently studied God's mind in the scriptures, had been careless in the guard he had kept over his lips, had yielded to envy and discontent, had seized too readily on excuses for postponing evening prayer, had been negligent in performing religious duties in the home, had not been faithful in discussing 'soul-matters' with his wife, had not turned to profitable use the hours he had spent in travelling. Sometimes, overwhelmed by the bleakness of the record, he doggedly set himself to catalogue the temptations he had faced. He had been too prone to dwell on 'the conveniency of his worldly accommodation'; pride had made him quick to detect slights even where none had been intended; he had jealously watched to see if people flocked as eagerly to his preaching as to that of neighbouring ministers; he had been angry when, being placed last in a service, he discovered that others had left him insufficient time, and his intended discourse had perforce been sadly mutilated. Most humiliating of all was the memory of the Sunday when he had received the quarterly collection, and could not resist the temptation to take it up to his study and count it—even though at the very time he had had to choke the rebuking whisper which told him he was desecrating the Sabbath day. With dogged honesty the melancholy facts were faced; then, having spread out the bitter truth before a God who was able as well as willing to forgive, the Puritan found peace.[1]

Meditation not only convicted of past faults; it helped to guard against future sins. Few tasks were more urgent than 'laying in store against temptation'. At this point meditation passed into that sovereign answer to every spiritual need—the practice of private prayer. This was the duty that should come first each morning. Before a man faced the world he must find in the fellowship of the Father Almighty the strength and wisdom he would need. All wise counsellors told the Puritan that this obligation took precedence of all others; his own experience taught him the sad results of postponing it. He might neglect his prayers, and go in haste into the world where men conducted their affairs; if so, he went with a troubled conscience, and any misadventure seemed a providential chastisement from God.[1] The price of procrastination was always an impaired religious effectiveness. It was the more needful, therefore, to give earnest heed to those who could instruct him in this most necessary duty. Since it was a private matter, it must be done in a private place; since it was a personal encounter, let it be done naturally and easily; since it went to the root of all spiritual affairs, let it take account of every urgent difficulty and of every elusive problem which beset the soul, but failed to find adequate consideration in more public worship. The seeker must avoid carelessness on the one hand and the loss of spontaneity on the other, and he must govern his devotions with a wise flexibility which would save him both from the tyranny of custom and from the artificiality of undeviating rules.[2]

It was surely a melancholy symptom of the deceitfulness of the human heart that so sovereign a remedy was so sparingly used. The Puritans conceded the supreme importance of private prayer, and then sadly confessed that they often neglected it. They rushed into the world without renewing their strength in God's presence, and they accepted any plausible excuse for cutting short the time they should assign to prayer. It was a disconcerting fact, remarked Philip Henry, that even serious illness did not make him more earnest in private prayer; it was disturbing to observe how seldom he found real satisfaction 'in secret duties'.[3] Sometimes private prayer proved a dull and lifeless routine, though the Puritan knew it ought to be fresh and vital. Strenuous efforts were necessary to offset the lethargy of the soul: 'I tugged hard at it', noted Heywood in describing his devotions on a day when his spirit seemed dead.[4]

Where duty was clear yet failure frequent, every available means was taken to fortify the wavering will. A method which was considered particularly effective—and one which was consequently commonly employed—was the renewing of solemn covenants. The Bible had taught the Puritans to regard themselves as people who were bound, individually as well as collectively, to God; it showed them, too, the spectacle of a chosen race who by their disobedience broke these solemn ties, and yet were taught to believe in a new covenant, written inwardly on men's hearts. When patriarchs and prophets made covenants with God, and renewed them from time to time, should not lesser men be even more scrupulous in doing likewise? 'Upon such considerations as these', said Heywood, 'I have formerly entered a solemn promise, covenant and protestation to devote, dedicate and make over myself to the Lord; and I have abundant ground, reason and necessity now more than ever to renew my covenant, but also I have broken covenants formerly made.' So, after due meditation on the omniscience and omnipresence of God, and having humbly confessed his sins, he pledged himself anew to God. Then, in his own handwriting, he inscribed the deed of gift: 'Dreadful Jehovah, I thy poor creature and grievous sinner, a transgressor from the womb, and a wanderer all my days to this moment....' So the covenant was sealed anew, and buttressed with pious resolutions. 'Covenants renewed in these particulars', noted Henry on New Year's Day: '1. By the Lord's help and purpose to be more substantial in secret worship. 2. More sparing of precious time. 3. More constant in reading the Scriptures alone and meditating in them. 4. More careful to improve all opportunities of doing good to souls.... 5. Less fearful about events, when in a way of duty, in all which I have lately missed it, but the Lord has pardoned me in Christ Jesus.' This is the recurrent note. 'The poor gifts I have', said Heywood, 'I do resolve to improve and lay out for thee, since all is thine own.'[1]

Private prayer, as a regular feature of the Puritan's life, conformed to no prescribed pattern. Heywood tells us that it was his regular custom to turn up the hour glass, read a couple of chapters of the Bible as an incentive, then embark on confession, praise and intercession. Baxter, having commended flexibility, left the form, and all the details, of private prayer to the judgement of the individual. Beyond the customary occasions, however, there were special days, and then private prayer could claim a vastly expanded scope and a proportionately extended time. When Henry was leaving his former home to take up the management of the lands which had come to his wife by inheritance, he appointed a 'secret day of prayer' to seek God's help and to ask for wisdom and diligence. At least once a month Thomas Jolly 'retired' for a day. He did not merely observe a season of more intensive prayer; he selected some special pretext of justification in order to provide firmer direction for his thoughts. He concentrated on some fault in himself or some situation in the community; he took account of developments in the national life, and dwelt on some cause of hope or fear. Sometimes it was a domestic anxiety that served to give his prayers greater definiteness and urgency. His purpose, quite obviously, was to prevent his devotions from subsiding into a lifeless routine. At regular intervals, but for varied causes, he would pray with particular earnestness for special objectives. A development of this practice was the custom, which was widely current among nonconformists, of setting apart an agreed hour each week for intercessions on behalf of the nation. The habit arose during one of the periods of crisis that so frequently agitated the country during the rule of the later Stuarts, and what began as an emergency measure continued as a regular feature of nonconformist practice. Every Tuesday morning, from 8 to 9 o'clock, devout men all over the country joined in prayer for the rulers of the land.

At times special days of prayer arose merely from a man's craving for greater intensity in his own religious experience and for fuller surrender in his service of God. In Heywood's diaries, at once so expansive yet so intimate, we have a singularly detailed picture of the devotional life of one of the later Puritans. Toward the end of the century (and the close of his life) Heywood records in detail a day of special prayer. 'After I had read my chapters in Ezra 3, 4, in the house, I went up to my chamber, having a fire, it being darkish. I fell on my knees, was assisted about half an hour confessing sins, pleading for mercy, God was with me till about 8 o'clock. Then I went down, washed me, ate my breakfast, went to family prayer, came up again at nine o'clock, set myself to my work. Read Psalm 73, meditated on it, then fell on my knees, pleaded with God, was moved to fall down on my face, so continued till 10, was greatly enlarged in confession, supplication. Then rose up, read Psalm 72, fell on my knees again, pleaded for my wife, my son John, his wife, children. God helped me. Then for my son El(iezer) and for his settlement....Then I pleaded for my servant S.T., for a saving work of grace; then for my neighbours and people, many of them by name...then about 11 o'clock I rose up, read the 74th Psalm, descanted upon it with reference to the Church, fell down again upon my knees, began to plead for Zion which I did for a season.' Consistently he worked his way through the Psalm, applying it in detail to the situation of 'the godly people, who formerly were called Puritans, then Roundheads, whom Christ redeemed with his blood'. Throughout the course of twenty subdivisions he expatiated on their needs and problems: the famine of the Word which they suffered, the persecution they had endured, the revilings they faced, the anxieties they had endured, the witness they had borne to scriptural standards of simplicity of worship and righteousness of life. To conclude his special prayers, there were intercessions for the nation.[1] Then, aglow with exhilaration, he rejoined the family for dinner. A typical comment epitomises his reaction to such a programme: 'Oh, what a sweet heart-melting forenoon was it! Blessed be God!'

The Puritan minister was more vocal than his people. He left a far fuller record of his days than they did. Yet in one respect they fulfilled more completely than he could hope to do a particular aspect of the Puritan ideal: they exercised the vocation of a Christian amid the activities of the world. Serving the needs of society was the means whereby they also served God. They found it more difficult, however, to save for the cultivation of their souls the time and care that this necessary discipline required. In the life of the minister, therefore, the ideal of constant prayer found fuller expression. It issued in a life which commanded the devoted respect of the people, and which brought to the minister himself deep and abiding satisfaction. Of that life and of its joys, Heywood again provides us with one of our fullest and most intimate accounts. Each returning day, he informs us, has been crowned with blessings. 'I have risen out of my bed, fallen down on my knees by my bed-side with my wife, thanked God for that night's mercies, had nothing to do but go to my chamber, read my chapter, sometimes a comment thereon (Calvin on Harm. of Luke, John, Acts, I read over within the year 1692) fell down on my knees, prayed, went down, made ready, had breakfast, family-prayer, went to my study (except I had some whither to go). There I studied, read, writ till noon, dined, walked to some neighbour's an hour after dinner, came home, took my pipe (in doing which I read in some book, read over many thus doing) went to my study, continued till 4, then read my Scripture comment, prayed, went down, we had supper, prayed, went again to my study till 8 or 9 o'clock, read some good book to my family till bed-time, then upon our knees put ourselves into the hands of God. Ordinarily slept comfortably. This is my manner of life. None visit us but Christian friends, in whom is my delight; I go not to dinners or feasts, nor do I visit any but such as are sick or upon spiritual accounts. Lord's days are the sweetest in the week, fast-days are my feast-days, studying and preaching sermons is my recreation, young men's conferences my delight.'[1]

'I will sing praise to my God while I have my being', said the Psalmist. To repeat these words, and with increasing sincerity to make them his own, was the ambition, usually unavowed but always unmistakable, of the earnest Puritan. At every point that ambition moulded to its own pattern the form of his personal life.

CHAPTER VI

THE CORPORATE LIFE OF THE PURITAN PEOPLE

THE Puritan was convinced that God had called him. He was subject to a claim to which the only possible response was un-faltering obedience. He was faced with a responsibility which his whole life was insufficient to discharge. But he knew that it was no solitary quest to which he had been called. The pilgrim bound for the heavenly city had companions on the way, and even when he seemed most completely alone he was encouraged by the voices of those who journeyed with him. This sense of solidarity with others—expressed in a great variety of ways— was as much the mark of the Puritans' faith as was their belief in God's personal dealing with their souls. They belonged to a people whom God had brought into a covenant relationship with himself. They were 'a chosen race, a royal priesthood, a peculiar people'. The life of faith might begin in the lonely anguish in which a soul, convicted of sin and weary of wandering, 'closed with the promise of forgiveness' and entered into the experience of God's saving mercy. The discovery to which it led was so intensely personal that no formal phrases could describe it and no conventional routine could satisfy its claims. But it always ended in membership in some society of like-minded persons. Critics who lay exaggerated emphasis on the individualism of the Puritan misinterpret the nature of his experience. His life was not a circle with one centre but an ellipse with two foci; he was a personal follower of Christ, but he was always a member of the church of the living God. The one issued in the other; it was no accident that the man called of God usually found himself a member of a gathered church.

His relationships with others profoundly affected the nature of his life. As persecution widened the gulf between the Puritan and the rest of the community, it made him increasingly dependent on the religious society to which he had chosen to belong. The pattern of its life determined the character of his experience. If it brought him into danger, it supported him with sympathy in it. It provided him with interests to fill his leisure moments; it gave him companionship and activity, standards by which to govern his conduct and a sense of significance that lent dignity and meaning to his days.

The church, so often uppermost in his thought, was always central in his experience. Corresponding to the place it held in his prayers was the part it played in his life. Leisure was limited in the seventeenth century; the hours conceded to the demands of the religious community accounted for most of the time a man could spare from his daily work. When he gathered with others, it was in a great variety of places; in times of persecution, it might be at almost any hour of the day or night. In some centres, where chapels of ease lay outside episcopal jurisdiction, the nonconformists continued to use the buildings in which they had met before the great ejection. When local circumstances allowed—when it was considered injudicious to interfere with a highly respected minister, or when the bishop 'looked through his fingers'[1]—the congregation of dissenters might still use a building around which gathered the hallowed associations of long years of worship, but this was rare. Usually the minister and his people met in a house —his own house as a rule. In the early days, when he had just been silenced, when his former pulpit was closed to him and as yet no definitely organised group had taken shape, he gathered his family about him for prayer and the exposition of the scriptures, and at such times friends and neighbours joined the circle.[2] This was usually at an hour which would not conflict with public worship, and any one who cared to come might do so. As persecution sharpened the lines of division in a community, the members of the congregation still met in the minister's house. It was the natural place, and the safest one available. The penal legislation made any alternative impossible. The Conventicle Act forbade more than four to join in worship with the members of a family, but at least that number could claim the sanction of the law. In the days when repression was severe, a man might divide his congregation into groups of four, and at great cost in time and effort repeat his sermon to tiny gatherings throughout the day.[1] Under extreme pressure, a church might devise an elaborate schedule of small gatherings, meeting Sunday by Sunday in various houses, so that every member could attend worship without incurring the penalties of breaking the law.[2] But prudence was usually dispelled by zeal—and zeal, of course, was confirmed by long intervals of relative immunity—and then the people flocked to the minister's home. After his ejection, Heywood's church at Coley always met in his largest room, but there were many other homes as well in which he preached. Often only a part of his congregation could find a place within doors. Even in the depths of winter, or when the rain was pouring down, eager hearers gathered outside the open windows, and only those entirely out of earshot grew discouraged and went home.[3]

Though a house was the natural substitute for a church, any kind of building might be pressed into service and adapted to the needs of a congregation. In Bristol, the Broadmead congregation, which had ample experience of meeting furtively in homes, ultimately secured a hall formed by removing the partitions of a house and throwing four rooms into one.[4] It might still be necessary, of course, to meet in lanes or fields, or in the woods beyond the river, but these were emergency measures to which they were driven by violent persecution. Exceptional circumstances of this kind often compelled dissenters to meet in quarries or chalk pits, in remote valleys or in deep woods, but they were more likely to meet in barns, in malt-kilns, in oast houses, or in any kind of building which could accommodate the people who assembled for worship. The owners who made such premises available ran serious risks in doing so, and the congregation not only gladly acknowledged the conspicuous service they rendered the cause, but gratefully noted instances where the possible penalties of their actions were not visited upon them. Courage of this kind was often, but not invariably, displayed. In some places, and at times of exceptional danger, no one might be willing to receive the church, and this was widely regarded as a proof that prudence, being destitute of faith, had degenerated into cowardice.[5]

Sometimes the congregation gathered spontaneously and without previous appointment. A minister, not expecting that his people would brave the dangers of forbidden worship, might be surprised, but greatly heartened, to find them coming in twos and threes to his door. Then, of course, he had no alternative but to gather them together to hear God's Word; his own wife might tremble when she thought of the impending danger, but a minister cannot deny his calling or ignore the people's cry for help, but when the gathering had safely dispersed he humbly thanked God for deliverance.[1] The worshippers themselves might encounter dangers as they assembled. The vicar, noticing the road dotted with people who were manifestly not bound for his church, might ride off in a rage to invoke against them the rigours of the law. When the gates of a city were watched and those seized whose destination was suspected to be a conventicle, the members of a congregation might make their way in disguise to the appointed rendezvous. With none of the customary marks of the Puritan bound for church they would converge by separate routes upon the agreed place of worship. At times, however, all discretion was cast aside. In Newcastle, when the nonconformists met in hundreds, the bishop was horrified at the reports of the psalms of seditious intent which they had sung and at the unabashed confidence which they had shown.[2]

There was little uniformity in the gatherings of which the Puritan, having braved the perils of the way, might find himself a member. When danger was particularly great the meeting would unquestionably be relatively small. It was a common ground of complaint that the faint-hearted so quickly fell by the way.[3] But even under the most favourable circumstances it might still be a very humble gathering. Richard Adams, we are told, ministered to 'a poor and small people' in Southwark;[4] Owen remarked that worshippers 'are for the most part poor and contemptible in the world'.[5] The Puritan often had occasion to ponder the scripture which assured him 'that not many wise men after the flesh, not many mighty, not many noble are called'. Even when we allow for the natural prejudice of the witnesses and the avowedly partisan purpose for which they gathered their facts, it is significant that in the episcopal returns the recurrent refrain is 'small, . . . mean, . . .not many. . .few. . .of the lowest quality'.[1] The preacher, noting the poverty of those to whom he was sent and ruminating on the absence of financial reward, could at least take comfort from remembering that these were lost sheep for whom no one else seemed to care, and that the shepherd of souls was sent to gather the lost. Of course there were always exceptions. The episcopal returns, with no motive for exaggeration, often referred to congregations in which the worshippers numbered several hundred.[2] Heywood frequently noted that he had large gatherings: 'very full', 'multitudes', 'hundreds'. Excited informers sometimes reported enormous congregations, and even allowing for the fantasies of fear or greed, there is no doubt that some of the churches, especially in London, were very strong.

Nor did their strength lie only in their numbers. The Presbyterians, in particular, still included among their members some prominent and influential people. The nominal adherents and all the time-servers had quickly found strong inducements to conformity, and the pressures of the age—legal, social, intellectual—made it harder every year for the nonconformists to hold the loyalty of the titled or the rich. But throughout the period there were many who still put their convictions before their interests, and remained loyal members of the dissenting congregations. Dr Manton numbered several eminent people among his flock. Dr Owen, though his church was very small, ministered to a group which included several persons of rank, and many who had rendered conspicuous public service. In Yorkshire the dissenting interest was strong, and an itinerant preacher like Heywood frequently found the homes of the gentry open to him. The serious worshipper might find, of course, that places were empty and the numbers few for other reasons than fear or danger. 'Are not you absent,' asked Clarkson, as he pondered the problem of thin congregations, 'are not you absent upon small occasions? A little rain, cold season, small employments, prejudice against God's messengers, keep you at home.'[3] Even in Puritan circles, the corrosives of indifference were fortified by the temper of the Restoration period.

As a rule the church met for worship on the Lord's day both in the morning and in the afternoon. Normally times varied slightly from place to place, but during periods of intense persecution the overruling consideration was to find an hour as well as a place which might promise some measure of immunity. Congregations gathered early in the morning or very late at night. They might worship from 4 a.m. to 8 a.m.; perhaps from 6 a.m. to 10 a.m., or even from 2 a.m. to sunrise.[1] Any hour except the accustomed one would possibly procure deliverance. But whatever the time, the service was seldom hurried and was never brief. The normal length was about three hours, but four was common, and even five was not exceptional. When a minister was unusually 'exercised in soul' a long service was likely to result, but a simple miscalculation of the time could have the same effect; having lost count by a whole hour, the minister would ruefully confess to his diary, 'I preached too long to-day'.[2] On special occasions, two or three ministers took part, and though the last to preach might feel that he was stinted of his proper share of time, he was certainly not likely on that account to cut proceedings short. From ten till six the earnest-minded Puritan would implore God to pity or to heed the exhortations of his servants. It would have been a gruelling ordeal both for ministers and people had it not also been their chief delight. When Howe described to his young friend Edmund Calamy the kind of public fasts he used to hold, 'he told me', says Calamy, 'it was upon those occasions his common way to begin about nine in the morning with a prayer for about a quarter of an hour in which he begged a blessing on the work of the day; and afterwards read and expounded a chapter or psalm, in which he spent three-quarters of an hour, then prayed for about an hour, preached for another hour, and prayed for about half an hour. After this he retired and took some little refreshment for about a quarter of an hour more (the people singing all the while) and then came again into the pulpit, and prayed for another hour, and gave them another sermon of about an hour's length; and so concluded the service of the day, at about four of the clock in the evening, with about half an hour or more in prayer.'[3] Even Calamy felt that this was a bit excessive.

In the Restoration period circumstances often deprived the minister of the dangerous privilege of expansiveness on such a scale. When he had just embarked on his prayer of confession or had begun to pour out his soul in 'the pleasing task of giving thanks', a whispered interruption would warn him of the approach of constables, and, concluding his prayer in shortened form, he would dismiss the people before danger was actually upon them. He might, of course, spurn prudential counsels and continue till the officers of the law burst in upon them. In many cases the worshippers had no warning, and consequently did not have the alternatives of scattering to safety or of continuing steadfast in prayer. But to guard against such dangers the congregation often devised elaborate precautions. They set guards to give warning of the approach of suspicious strangers; they filled the entries and the stairs with women so tightly wedged together that a surprise attack was impossible; they had trapdoors through which the minister could escape; stairs by which he could retreat to an upper story and so across the roofs to another house; lofts in which he or they could hide. Sometimes curtains cut the room into two so that those who entered could not see who was preaching; often disguises were available, so that in an ordinary cloak the minister might mingle with the people and so escape detection. Sometimes an aperture was cut from one house to the next so that the minister literally preached from next door; he and his people could not be apprehended together, and his hearers could truthfully swear that there was no preacher among them. Such expedients unquestionably complicated the task of the constables, but provided no certainty of deliverance for the worshippers.

For all its perils and excitements, the faithful Puritan never questioned the supreme value of the kind of service he preferred. Though the world might scoff, he was satisfied that he had participated in 'true Gospel worship'. Everything he did was sanctioned by the precept or example of scripture; having resolutely put aside the liturgy—'that nurse of formality and chain of security'—he was content with the stark simplicity of prayer, preaching, the reading of the scriptures and the singing of the psalms. In some quarters there was disagreement about the way the psalms should be sung and even about the version that should be used, and hymns, as mere human 'conceptions', were still widely suspect. Though congregational singing was in its infancy, the church member had other avenues of participation in the worship. Emotion played an important part in Puritan services; preachers recognised its force as a motive power in human life, and they tried both to arouse and to direct it. If the people were not stirred, they believed that a service had seriously failed to achieve its appointed result. And when the hearers were moved, why should their emotions be denied an outlet? So there were floods of tears, and groans abounded.

Worship was of one general type, but the occasions on which it could be practised were various. The Puritans never questioned the value of instruction and admonition, but this did not blind them to the importance of fellowship in the Christian community, and many of the week-day services provided opportunities of strengthening it. Lectures, it is true, were more austere and more demanding than the services of the Sabbath, and formed a course of adult education of a most exacting kind; those who attended, however, were inspired and sustained by a firm belief in the value of an instructed membership, and the people's eagerness to learn usually matched the minister's zeal to teach.[1] Prayer meetings and fasts were much more intimate in character. On all special occasions, public or personal, the nonconformists met together to implore God's blessing or to acknowledge his mercy. Observing fasts was, as Owen remarked, a distinctively Puritan activity.[2] If public affairs assumed a threatening guise—if plague was rampant in the capital, if the nation was on the brink of war, if parliament seemed likely to initiate harsher measures against dissenters, or if popery appeared particularly menacing—the members of the church would gather at a stated time and earnestly and at great length they would pour out their souls before God, imploring him that his people might 'be borne up under all afflictions, or delivered from the hands of our enemies'.[3] Times of rejoicing were similarly observed, but whether it was because they lived in a time when dangers came oftener than joys or because of the

11-2

temptation to dwell upon the gloomy aspect of affairs, fasts usually far outnumbered days of thanksgiving.[1] Private fasts were commoner than public ones. A child was taken seriously ill; a pregnant woman approached the time of her delivery; a family was moving to new quarters; a new venture was to be undertaken; young men were leaving to pursue their education—whatever the occasion, two or three ministers and a score of friends would gather, and hour after hour the work would be 'carried on'. The individual was never left to bear the burdens of perplexity and grief alone. When he was oppressed by sorrow, friends came to share it; when he was uncertain what course to follow, they joined in prayer that a straight way would open before him. What, then, could be more natural than that they should also participate in his joys? When his wife had survived the ordeal of childbirth, when he had received good news from his sons, when his ventures had prospered, or even when the event had proved that his fears were liars, friends came to celebrate these evidences of the goodness and mercy of God.

There were other types of service which the Puritan also attended. Nonconformist groups of all kind—in loyalty to their common Calvinistic background—held a preparatory service on the Friday evening before the celebration of the Lord's Supper. Groups within a church might covenant to meet regularly in one another's houses for the purpose of engaging in prayer. Great importance was attached to conferences of young men. These were primarily gatherings for prayer, and were seen as a special defence against the perils to which faith and morals were exposed in a licentious age. But they also offered opportunities to discuss common problems and to share spiritual resources. How can we know when afflictions are sent by God? What are the means by which we can resist temptation? How may we place our delight in God? How are we to behave ourselves in a time of the church's adversity? Questions like these were earnestly debated, and serious young men would jot down in their diaries the suggested answers. As much as six hours might be spent in prayer and fellowship, and before dispersing the members would be assigned a subject to revolve in their own minds during the interval before their next meeting. If one of their members grew lax —worse still, if he showed signs of falling into sin—a letter of earnest expostulation would attempt to bring him to a due sense of the error of his ways.[1] Lest Puritan life seem unduly dour, it is important to realise that on these special occasions prayers and preaching were varied with other things besides tears and groans. After entreating the Lord for a couple of hours, all present would adjourn to the dining room, and a man whose heart had been 'marvellously drawn forth in prayer' could note with satisfaction that his wife had prepared for the company a goodly feast. Then, refreshed, they would return to their religious exercises. Good fellowship, in fact, had an important part in the good life, and it was not on special occasions only that worshippers interrupted their devotions with a common meal. Some members of a congregation came from too great a distance for them to return home between morning and afternoon services of the Sabbath day, so the minister's table was spread to entertain his people. When a dozen sat down with him, and as many more were served elsewhere, weekly hospitality became a burden—carefully noted, but apparently not begrudged.[2]

Even the very godly live in a world where mundane matters claim attention, and in a basically democratic society like a gathered church the temporal responsibilities of the congregation became the concern of all the members. The church meeting for business inevitably played an important part in the life of non-conformist societies. Questions of all kinds required consideration. In groups where the ministry was largely voluntary, the congregation would decide when and where worship would be held, and which 'gifted brethren' would preach in which place, and usually a date was appointed for the next business meeting.[3] Financial matters were also settled; appeals were authorised for needy brethren or deserving causes, collectors were appointed to receive the free-will offerings of the people, and the payment of necessary expenses was authorised. Normally it was the task of the congregation to provide a place of worship. Amid the uncertainties which persecution created, they might be content to meet wherever possible, but ultimately the question of a permanent meeting house arose. If the congregation seemed apathetic, the minister himself might provide it[1]—sometimes with a certain sense of grievance—but it was rightly the responsibility of the people and usually they were eager to accept it. Again, when death or removal had created a vacancy, there was the necessity of calling a minister, and the privilege was undertaken with the utmost solemnity. Having met for prayer, the members would conclude that the minister under consideration should be called, and they would all signify their consent by 'lifting up their right hands unto the Lord'—'and so the room being thronged, as it were a cloud of naked hands were erected toward the ceiling of the room'.[2] Then, having drawn up the call in sonorous scriptural phraseology, all the members of the church would sign it. The minister, of course, had to be paid, and there would be further meetings to discuss the question of his support. And if he died in prison (as he easily might in those perilous days), the congregation would consider how best to fulfil its duty to his widow and their children.[3]

The maintenance of the congregation in full strength and vitality was another task which required the attention of the members. In some churches those who joined were received by the minister himself or on his recommendation. In others, 'constant hearers' were accepted as members during the indeterminate period when many nonconformists hesitated to act as though the ejection from the national church was final, but when circumstances gave the congregation a firmer basis, minister and people, by formal covenant, pledged themselves each to the other, and 'set to their names' in token of their acceptance of the obligations which full membership entailed. In congregations where the 'gathered church' tradition was particularly strong, the reception of new members was a matter in which all the congregation had a part. Evidently it was not an easy matter to gain full admission. In all nonconformist groups, it was customary for a person who desired to share fully in the life of the church to 'declare the work of grace in his soul', and by an account of his religious experience, to prove that he was qualified to receive the special blessings and discharge the responsibilities which membership entailed. But in many congregations reception was neither prompt nor automatic. Each case was carefully examined. Was the applicant really sound in the faith, or did he incline to Arminian errors? Though a young man seemed eager to join, had he had time to be sure of his experience? When two young lawyers presented themselves, their reception was postponed; even after they had described God's dealing with their souls, they were still delayed; finally, when in the presence of the whole congregation the elders had impressed upon them their duty to God, to the church, to the world, and admonished them appropriately, they were received.[1] Delay was customary, and careful scrutiny of each case the rule.[2]

Once admitted, the new member was expected to walk before the world in a way befitting his profession. When fellowship was strong and a sense of responsibility for others real, the conduct of each member was subject to constant and careful examination. This was not due to curiosity nor to the idle impulse to pry into other people's private affairs. It corresponded to the firm conviction—so characteristic of the Puritans—that discipline was one of the marks of the true church and consequently its inescapable duty.[3] Among their complaints against the Church of England (and hence a justification of their dissent from it) was the laxity which so largely neglected discipline. Even dignitaries of the established church admitted the need of stricter regulation, and emphasised the magnitude of the problem. The Puritans were not content to deplore the difficulties; they set out to enforce the remedy.

The application of discipline rested on an appropriate theory, and the theory—so the Puritan contended—rested on the authority of scriptural command. Certainly they regarded discipline as an unquestioned part of the gospel dispensation. They believed that it was 'the due exercise of that authority which the Lord Christ, in and by his Word, hath granted unto the church for its continuance, increase and preservation in purity, order and holiness, according to his appointment'.[4] Naturally, therefore, it concerned itself with 'the qualifications and duties of those who are to be admitted into the church, their deportment in it, their removal from it'.[5] 'In particular', added Owen, 'it is ordained that those who are unruly and disorderly, who walk contrary unto the rules and ways of holiness prescribed unto the church, shall be rebuked, admonished, instructed; and if, after all means used for their amendment they abide in impenitency, that they be ejected out of communion. For the church, as visible, is a society gathered and erected to express and declare the holiness of Christ, and the power of his grace in his person and doctrine; and where this is not done, no church is of any advantage unto the interests of his glory in this world. The preservation, therefore, of holiness in them whereof the discipline mentioned is an effectual means, is as necessary and of the same importance with the preservation of their being.'[1] To exercise discipline carelessly was as serious as to neglect it altogether, and a great deal of thought was given to the proper method of enforcing it.[2]

The relevance of discipline became apparent as soon as a congregation began to celebrate the sacrament of the Lord's Supper. Holiness of life was essential to church communion.[3] In the New Testament, the Puritans read words of solemn warning addressed to those who partook unworthily, and they regarded the desecration of the ordinance with the same seriousness as the imperilling of the individual's soul. They could not leave the matter to each person's discretion, content that 'every man should so examine himself, and so let him eat of that bread and drink of that wine...'. Unless the table were 'fenced' against unworthy communicants, the sacrament would be brought into disrepute, righteousness would be jeopardised, the distinction between right and wrong obliterated, and all order in the church destroyed.[4] 'It hath always been my principle', remarked Heywood, 'that the grossly ignorant and scandalous are to be debarred from that sealing ordinance.'[5] When an unworthy person presented herself at the Sacrament, Philip Henry passed her by without comment, and was evidently relieved that she, too, was content that there should be no explanation. When a man who was a member of another church appeared at the Lord's Supper without previously coming to the minister to make known his mind in the matter, Henry allowed him to partake, but was evidently unhappy in his mind about the matter.[6]

The result of this power to admit to the Lord's Table or to debar from it was a particularly close connection between discipline and the sacrament, but the scrutiny of the members' conduct did not cease at this point. It ranged over every aspect of their lives. The Christian stands before the world as a witness, and the church as a whole is answerable for the testimony he gives.[1] Unless men who profess and practise 'the form and order of Christ's doctrine, shall also beautify the same with a holy and wise conversation, in all godliness and honesty, the profession of the visible form will be rendered to them of no effect, for "without holiness no man shall see the Lord"'.[2] Consequently the nonconformists noted with the deepest concern any conduct that might reflect unfavourably upon the Gospel, and bring the cause of Christ into ill repute. It was a sin when a girl murdered her illegitimate baby; it was a matter of added regret that it should happen in the home of a professor.[3] The fact that evil could invade the household of faith was a further argument for relentless vigilance lest occasions of sin should arise. Because the contamination of evil could spread so fast, it was the part of wisdom to cut yourself off from the openly profane, and to separate yourself from the world and its ways.[4] It was necessary to begin by keeping a careful watch over the faith professed by the members; those who held false doctrines would be sure to fall into wicked ways. But the main emphasis always fell on the discipline of conduct; indeed, it was a part of the Puritan's boast that he transferred to the realm of deeds a scrutiny which everyone advocated in the more nebulous region of opinions.[5]

Supervision of the lives of others was a prerogative easy to claim but hard to exercise. The aim of the Puritans was positive; their purpose was to help men and women to 'walk in uprightness of life'. Originally the spirit was charitable; you were to help those who fell, knowing that you also were likely to fall. But it was perilously easy for the result to be negative and for the prevailing attitude to be censorious and harsh.[6] It is all the more important to realise that in the seventeenth century the oversight of other people's lives was often exercised with both wisdom and forbearance. Among the Quakers the closest kind of supervision was maintained over all the members of the society, but the spirit was seldom inquisitorial. The care with which newly married couples were guided and helped reflects the ideal of a sober, watchful, industrious integrity rooted in a home which was itself a centre of worship. And in most of the records of groups which seriously exercised discipline the desire to reclaim is more apparent than the impulse to condemn.[1]

Everyone was agreed that discipline must be exercised with the greatest care. It was therefore important to adopt a method likely to minimise the dangers of misuse. Those who had fallen from grace were not likely to be present when their case was first discussed, so individual members were delegated to lay before them privately the nature of their fault and to urge them to repent. When this was not enough, two or three were sent to reason with the offender; if this proved ineffectual, he would be summoned to appear at a church meeting at a certain date; if he still remained impenitent he would be commanded to answer the charges against him on pain of immediate expulsion. When the culprit appeared at the meeting, proceedings usually opened with an exposition by an elder of an appropriate passage of scripture (Leviticus xiii was regarded as an excellent warrant for the exercise of discipline), and then the members proceeded to consider the case before them. The offender was told to stand forth; one by one his faults were enumerated and exactly specified. The meeting would not accept vague rumour or popular report: there must be detailed information, supported at every stage by the testimony of reliable witnesses. The culprit was certain to acknowledge his guilt—the obdurate would not appear at all, and so his very presence was a token of repentance. The members of the congregation were then asked if it was their will to lay upon him their solemn admonition, 'to the end that he might be thoroughly convinced of his sin and reclaimed from it, which is the end of Christ's command for dealing'. When they had signified their consent, the pastor laboured to demonstrate to the offender 'the evil nature, danger and consequence of his sin'. Then the minister proceeded to pronounce sentence 'in the names of our Lord Jesus Christ and this congregation', and when he began to repeat the solemn words, 'all the sisters stood up' and 'all the brethren put off their hats'. Reproof, however, was not the final word; after the pastor had admonished him to turn from his sin, the offender usually declared his repentance, his sorrow for what was past, and his hope that he would be granted time for amendment of life. Whereupon one of the elders, in the name of all, would assure him that he was not cast out of the church, but only lay under its admonition till such time as the tenor of his life proved that he had profited by correction and was ready to resume his place.[1]

Unfortunately matters did not always conform to this desired pattern. Often the man at fault refused to receive the representatives of the congregation, or listened unmoved to their entreaties and rebukes. Even when different messengers were appointed, they reported similar lack of success. And so, since impenitence had obviously confirmed the sinner in those faults which destroy church fellowship and bring discredit on the profession of the faith, the congregation voted 'to withdraw from him'—which meant that temporarily he had ceased to be a member of the church and had forfeited his place at the Lord's Table. Even when a man had accepted admonition, had professed repentance and had asked the prayers of the people as he embarked on a new attempt to walk in the accepted way, he might forget his good intentions and might relapse into sin. With regret the congregation would note that he had been absent from his place; with sorrow they would receive well-authenticated evidence that he had been drunk and disorderly, and so with all solemnity they would declare that he had forfeited his part in the fellowship of Christ's people.[2]

Lapses of two types made a member subject to the discipline of the congregation: he might have been remiss in the performance of his church duties, or he might have broken the moral standards which the Puritans accepted. Irresponsibility might hardly seem as serious as grave lapses in conduct, but since it disrupted the effective functioning of the congregation, it was visited with disciplinary severity. Perhaps a member had slept in church, 'to the grieving of the others present', both minister and people, and this was certainly an evil example which could not pass unchecked.[1] Possibly someone did not contribute to a particular cause even when the congregation had laid it on the consciences of the members as an obligation. Then the recalcitrant brother might be ordered to 'give account why he refuses to subscribe'; when there were several defaulters they would be warned to answer at the next stated meeting, or an individual might be reminded that his failure in the duty of charity caused serious scandal in the eyes of the world.[2] Of grave concern to the congregation were those who fell away in times of persecution and either sought safety in absence or weakly conformed to the established church. Such cases were common; they could not be ignored, but they were not easy to reclaim.[3] Much less serious but even more common were those guilty of 'neglecting ordinances'. It was disturbing to note that a member was absent because engaged in secular pursuits, and the backsliders were exhorted to repent and 'make good their places'. The congregation might go further and appoint certain members to keep a close watch on the truants and report regularly to the elders. But the problem of the member who will not faithfully attend his church was neither new nor novel, and the nonconformists were no more successful in finding an answer than other earnest people have been in other ages.

One further failure in connection with church duty demands notice; the 'sin of mixt marriage' was a problem chiefly to the Quakers and the Baptists, and in both groups it claimed a great deal of time and attention. The closed fellowship faced many problems, but few were so difficult to control as those created by the troublesome fact that young Baptists would fall in love with those who were not Baptists, and young Quakers would do the same. Marriage with an unbeliever was regarded as a transgression of the law of God, and consequently for those so married to live together was sin. So the General Assembly of the General Baptists ruled, but they found themselves in difficulties at once. The offence was unquestionably a sin, but it was not fornication; rather it should 'be called a marrying out of the Lord or out of the Church', and ought to be visited with excommunication. But what should then be done? It was not safe to separate such persons, so the Church must either accept the unfeigned repentance of the guilty party or proceed to excommunication, and since neither course was free from danger it seemed better to be merciful than severe. What the Assembly did not clarify is how a person really repents of a sin in which he intends to persist, and in none of the records is there a satisfactory recognition that the marriage is a partnership; the other party to the sin is frigidly ignored. The rule, because so difficult to apply, caused infinite trouble. The local congregation would faithfully rebuke, admonish and withdraw from those guilty of this sin, and then, on acknowledgement of their fault, would receive them back again. But the frequent appeals to the Assembly for clarification of the rule indicate the exasperation which it aroused, while the answers of the Assembly reflect the perplexity which always follows when sincere conviction refuses to conform to the elementary facts of social life. But when, thirty-six years after committing this offence, a member repents and is restored, the reader notes that this dear sin could be persisted in for many years, and he also wonders what had finally happened in that home.[1]

Society at large was indifferent to the observance of the rules by which a dissenting group might organise its life, but it was quick to observe breaches of the generally accepted moral code. It was a matter of comment when the strict and godly were overtaken in the very faults for which they were so ready to rebuke others. The contrast between profession and practice is always painful. Partly because of their stark incongruity, partly because of the discredit it brought on religion in general and on the dissenting community in particular, moral failings occupied a large place in the discipline which the nonconformist churches exercised. Almost any fault to which frail human nature is subject was considered a suitable pretext for admonishing a member and exhorting him to walk more worthily. Strong or violent passions, backbiting or railing, anger ('without provocation'), a peevish and contentious spirit, dishonesty, idleness, association with 'profane persons', insubordination, borrowing and not repaying, harsh treatment of fellow-members—these and many other offences were listed as just grounds for discipline.[2]

Some offences demanded attention more constantly than others. It was a dangerous thing to keep bad company, unfitting in itself and often the prelude to more serious faults. A spinster who went out with 'light' young men needed more than a gentle warning; before long she would be playing cards, or dancing, or committing unmentionable sins—and perhaps aggravating the fault by transgressing on the Sabbath day. If a brother sat loitering in the tavern when the church had met for prayer, he deserved a rebuke even if his worldly friends had not also led him into intemperance. So often evil communications corrupted good manners! Those who listened to oaths would presently begin to swear; those whose friends frequented town feasts would be drawn thither themselves. It could be assumed, in fact, that a man who kept questionable company would soon be guilty of a conversation which fell far short of Christian standards.

A quarrel of any kind, as a breach of the cardinal Christian obligation of love, required the mediation of the other members of the church, and sometimes demanded severe measures. Gossip and the spreading of rumour, as causes contributing to division, were to be checked at all cost. When anger broke out and hot words were exchanged, it was the duty of the church to exercise its reconciling function, and restore the unity which had been broken. Quarrels between fellow-members were serious enough —since the world always took note and ridiculed the faithful— but quarrels within families were worse. Mediation was the first step, but in the background there was always the threat of discipline against those who proved recalcitrant in their wrath. If an agreement had previously been sealed, had the parties faithfully fulfilled its terms? Had those charged with faults given a satisfactory answer in the spirit of charity? When a protracted dispute had caused widespread scandal, one of the parties to the quarrel might be sternly admonished to go to the other 'and agree with him speedily or else appear at the next church meeting'.[1]

Drunkenness caused constant trouble.[2] It was an occasion of scandal in itself, and it led to innumerable other offences. Because of the nature of his fault the same delinquent figured repeatedly

in the accounts of church meetings for discipline. He appeared and was admonished; he fell and was reproved by a couple of the brethren; he fell again and was earnestly exhorted to do better. After another stern admonition in public, the church appointed a solemn day of prayer and fasting for him in particular, 'if it might be the Lord would be entreated to cast out the drunken devil out of him, which did overcome him and carry him captive at his will'. So the church met at his house. A brother prayed; then the pastor laid open the serious nature of his sin. They asked him what demonstration he would give of his willingness to reform, and he countered with a question as to what was required of him. The decision, they pointed out, rested with him, but they reminded him of the example of the Rechabites, and commended to him the vow they had taken. So, 'after great wrestling he concluded and said he would refrain and abstain from wine and strong liquors for a year'. Four months later, he asked to be readmitted to his place in the church. The congregation promised to give special consideration to the case before the next day of prayer, and meanwhile he was publicly to declare to the church 'how the Lord turned him to leave his sin of drunkenness'. Unfortunately, this is not the last we hear of this particular offender. Once more he fell from grace and remained impervious to the pleas and threats of his brethren. So finally there came expulsion. When he neither returned to the congregation nor repented of his sins, the members unanimously agreed that sentence must be duly passed. Because of his failure to turn, he 'was from henceforth to be no longer a member of this congregation, but was cast out into the world, and no longer to be partaker with us in the holy mysteries of the Lord, nor fellowship with us, nor to enjoy the privileges of God's house;—and the Lord have mercy upon his soul.' The final comment on the case is particularly illuminating as to the aims of church discipline and the spirit in which it was exercised. It was with 'lamentation and sore trouble', they recorded, 'that we were forced, for the preservation of the glory of God and the church's purity, thus to proceed to our duty, as the last means of his recovery. First,...
Brother Terrill showed his crime and the evidence that it was

true and obvious. Secondly, that this crime was a sin that who-soever should live and die in it without repentance should not inherit the Kingdom of God; as 1 Cor. vi. 10. Therefore those that should continue in such sins should not be continued in the church. For what Christ will judge hereafter, his people should judge here, and have no fellowship with such works of darkness.' With these solemn words Brother Jeremy Courtney disappears from the record, but it is encouraging to note that in other cases the 'drunken devil' was successfully exorcised, and the culprits reclaimed to a life of sobriety and industry.[1]

During the years which followed the Restoration, the standards of sexual morality which prevailed in the community at large were seriously relaxed. The Court gave an example which many were content to follow even though they might be eager to criticise. The records of petty sessions and of archdeacons' courts recur, with melancholy reiteration, to bastardy and its attendant problems. Oliver Heywood noted that illegitimacy had been commoner in Halifax parish than at any time in living memory, and reported that the vicar of the parish had prepared a list of over thirty cases currently under consideration.[2] An infection so widespread was not likely to leave the Puritan societies entirely untouched. Richard Baxter, it is true, suggests that in most non-conformist congregations the problem never arose. During fifty-six years of intimate contact with such groups he had heard of only one instance of fornication; the offender had been instantly disciplined, and after years of penitence had not as yet been re-stored to fellowship in the church.[3] How different a standard, as Baxter hinted, from that of many who delighted to vilify the Puritans! But unquestionably the problem existed. An instance of fornication caused the Broadmead congregation a great deal of trouble. A member of the church was with child by her master, and he refused to marry her. The first step was to express the concern and disapprobation of the congregation. After service, when all 'hearers' had been put forth, Edward Terrill, as one of the leading elders, expounded the views of the congregation. The basis on which judgement must rest was set forth, under seven heads, with considerable moral realism but also with charity and the promise of mercy. Some offences, it was pointed out, ran so directly counter to the essential principles of the Christian life that the church could not countenance them without ceasing to be herself; moreover, the power of discipline was used with apparent severity but wholly in order to reclaim a soul in danger, and when there was good evidence of repentance unto life the offender would be welcomed back into the church. The next step was to deal sternly with a fellow-member who might have helped her fallen sister but had failed to do so—and who had not been too faithful in her own attendance at worship. The real problem, however, was posed by the attitude of the girl's master. The congregation decided that until he yielded, two men would be sent each day to reason with him. The first two pairs were completely unsuccessful. When Terrill and a companion inter-viewed him, they pressed upon him (with detailed application of Exodus xxii. 16 and Deut. xxii. 28) the obligations of God's holy law and his duty to marry the girl. Finally, the man capitulated; then, without a moment's delay, they scoured the district to find a clergyman to perform the ceremony before second thoughts might again harden the offender's heart.[1]

Relationships within the nonconformist group largely moulded the social life of the members. The dissenters formed a group slightly apart from the rest of the community. Their stricter standards and their distinctive ways created barriers which per-secution strengthened, and in the background, to impede free intercourse with others, there were always the repeated warnings about the danger of associating with the world. Contacts with members of the immediate congregation were supplemented by the wider relations within the whole body of nonconformity.

The minister of a dissenting congregation stood in a distinctive relationship to his people. His office set him slightly apart, but his daily work brought him into the closest contact with the members of his flock. To the sincere Puritan, no dignity could be greater than that with which the man of God was invested. In speaking of his mother, Heywood remarked that 'she entirely loved all godly ministers'; it was her chief joy to hear them preach, and her highest honour to entertain them in her home. She was constantly overwhelmed by the thought that two of her sons had been called to this holy office. 'Oh, where shall I put my head', she asked, 'when my sons go up into the pulpit to preach? How unworthy am I of this high honour!' And when Heywood's own sons chose the ministry as their calling, he declared that he would rather see them faithful in that task than have them princes or nobles in the land.[1] Though the dignity of his office elevated the minister to a special place in the eyes of his people, his work brought him into close and constant contact with every aspect of their lives. The diaries of nonconformist ministers—Heywood and Henry, Newcome and Martindale—show how intimate were their relations with their people. At birth, at death, and at every time of joy or sorrow between, the minister was in the homes of his people. The Puritan ideal gave that oversight a systematic regularity which meant that no detail escaped the watchful concern of the pastor. In *Gildas Salvianus*, Baxter had offered his brethren a detailed outline of the way in which, from house to house, a minister should examine and catechise his people, and the influence of the book was widespread. After reading it Heywood was convinced that he had fallen short of his duty and must set up a course of instruction in the home. One day a week (or perhaps two half-days) must be reserved for this purpose, and he was pleasantly surprised both at the cordiality with which the innovation was welcomed and at the knowledge which his flock displayed.[2] Martindale was less encouraged; his people were loath to submit to the teaching he was so anxious to give, and their evasions and excuses made it difficult to establish the desired system of training.[3] But in less formal ways, the minister was always among his people to admonish the backsliders, encourage the diffident and comfort the sad.

The duties of the ministers to their people were defined (by the minister themselves) with some care, and on the whole were performed with exemplary devotion. The corresponding obligations of the people to the minister were less exactly indicated and often less scrupulously discharged. It was usually assumed that the support of the minister was the responsibility of the people, but even here there were exceptions. The Quakers, of course, with their strong antipathy to a 'hireling ministry', stood by the principle of voluntary leadership. The General Baptists also expected the minister to earn his own livelihood. This exposed the denomination to the weaknesses incidental to a ministry ill-educated and preoccupied with other tasks, and the General Assembly frequently urged the congregations to accept the obligation of ministerial support.[1] The Broadmead Church offers an excellent example of a high sense of responsibility toward their minister. After they had called Mr Hardcastle, but before he arrived, the members seriously discussed their duty toward him, 'not only for their good to call him, but to take care that he may have a comfortable subsistence yearly coming in for the maintenance of him and his family'. They decided that not less than eighty pounds a year would be necessary to free him from financial worries, 'and that it lay upon the church to take care about those carnal things, and he about spiritual things'. None of the members challenged the principle of adequate support, but there was some disagreement as to the best method of providing it. Some proposed that the matter be left entirely to the conscience of the individual; each person would contribute when and how he chose. 'But the rest of the members were otherwise minded, and they judged the gospel way was a way of regularity, as well as of liberty;—which could not be to leave a minister's mind in bondage, every now and then, not knowing where to have food. Therefore, they said, it was rational and scriptural for everyone to engage what they would do freely and yearly, that so we might know our duty in some measure was performed, that he had so much as reasonably might support him.' The conclusion at which they finally arrived was that this matter of regular ministerial support was as much an ordinance of God as any other, and that consequently each member should be as scrupulous in observing it as he was in any other part of God's worship and service. So they set down the scriptural authorities for their attitude (especially Gal. vi. 6 and Neh. x. 32) and drew up an agreement by which members were to pledge what they could and agreed to pay their contributions quarterly. One of the elders, assisted by a grave and senior member, retired with the written agreement to an adjoining room; then another elder called out the names of the members and one by one they went in to sign the document and pledge the amounts they could give. Eighty pounds was a large sum for a small group of humble people; by sacrificial giving they raised the whole amount.[1]

In many congregations the question of the minister's support was treated with far less conscientious care. At first, as friends gathered in the ejected man's parlour, little thought was given to replacing the tithes which he had lost. As he preached here and there, some of his hearers would press into his hand a sixpence as they left, and often he received nothing at all for his pains. Gradually a system of congregational support grew up. When the Declaration of Indulgence strengthened the corporate life of the nonconformists, their affairs tended to be regulated with greater care, and then quarterly payments to the support of the minister became more common. Heywood, who considered himself the poorest paid of all the ministers in his neighbourhood, received about twenty pounds a year from his people. This was not very much. In 1660 the authorities of the Church of England indicated that the desirable minimum was a stipend of eighty to one hundred pounds; admittedly this was little more than a pious ideal, but at least it indicated the figure below which a clergyman would encounter some degree of hardship. Judged by this standard, many nonconformists received pitifully small amounts, even when we allow for the fact that some Puritans sincerely believed that a ministry supported in comfort was exposed to dangerous temptations. For the latter part of the period, thanks to the records of the funds which were set up to aid the needy ministers, we know in some detail what the different congregations paid, and sums below twenty pounds were common.[2] Sometimes, of course, a man received a providential windfall. Wealthy nonconformists like Lord Wharton or Lady Hewley gave annual grants to poor ministers. In the early days of ejection, merchants in London contributed to the needs of impoverished ministers in the provinces, and occasionally the nonconformists benefited from a bequest left by someone who remembered their ministries with gratitude.

The relationship of one member to another was apt to be decisive in determining the character of a congregation. By inference we can surmise that contacts were usually close and relations cordial, but such things are seldom recorded. They must be deduced. Both in the records of congregations and in the diaries of individuals we can trace, through casual references, innumerable acts of kindness and generosity. Members in financial straits were helped with seasonable loans; those in sorrow were surrounded with sympathy; those in difficulty or temptation were supported not only by prayer but by such acts of practical helpfulness as good will suggested. This was natural in tightly knit societies where contacts were close. It was also natural, since these congregations were composed of human beings as yet imperfectly redeemed, that the very intimacy of the fellowship should sometimes create friction. It would be wrong to assume that disputes were the distinguishing mark of the life of nonconformist churches. Simply because contention was exceptional it was faithfully recorded. The gathered church is constantly reminded that it should be a community of love; when signs of hatred appear they are recognised as a challenge to the true nature of the fellowship and a threat to its very life. Disagreements were not necessarily about serious things, though doubtless disputants could always convince themselves that they were contending for essentials. Sometimes the trouble arose from financial dealings between two members; sometimes it was the result of misrepresentation or gossip.[1] It might be that one person felt that another had been disloyal to nonconformity or had betrayed its standards—as happened in Newcastle when a quarrel broke out because one of the members had attended conformist churches when visiting London.[2] Or again an individual might have contravened the commonly accepted principles of the group— as when a Baptist prayed with those who had not received believers' baptism, and had asked them in turn to pray.[3] Some quarrels related to matters of belief. All congregations were vigilant in safeguarding soundness of doctrine, and any lapses from the true faith were quickly detected and forcefully denounced. Calvinism, though commonly the creed of Puritans, had its opponents, and differences regarding the person of Christ—a foretaste of greater troubles yet to come—were already disturbing the life of churches.[1] Members might also disagree as to the proper ordering of the congregation's affairs or the most profitable use of the minister's time. When they were seeking a new minister, they might be divided not only about the right man to choose but also about the best method of calling him. Whatever the cause, a quarrel was hard to heal. Sometimes the intervention of the minister or of some respected elder was enough to compose the ruffled spirits and bring peace, but often a congregation was split from top to bottom and innumerable meetings were necessary before peace was finally restored. And such meetings were not always a credit to the congregation or to the wider cause of nonconformity. Ambrose Barnes ruefully noted that quarrels always generated bitter party feeling, and the good name of religion was thereby disgraced.[2] At Ford, a church meeting reached so abusive a pitch of turbulence, that one member roundly declared that it 'was like a Billingsgate and he would come no more among them'.[3]

The intense preoccupation of the Puritans with religion combined with the narrow orbit within which they lived to make their quarrels dangerously bitter. That is why nonconformity was so easily and so often rent by divisions. The effect of this fissiparous tendency was actually reduced by the persecution which in most cases had already destroyed denominational unity, and reduced even those who believed in organisation to a practical congregationalism. Nevertheless, the relations between one group of nonconformists and another played an important part in their corporate life. Though many congregations had perforce been driven to a practical independency, they were affected by their contacts one with another. In some respects, tensions were less acute than they had been during the Interregnum. A common danger emphasised their essential unity, and lesser grounds of division were allowed to fall into the background. Presbyterian and Independent let their older controversies die, and the lines of division gradually became confused. Often congregations of differing strains agreed to unite, and apparently their common dissent was a bond too strong to be jeopardised by their theories about church order. In some districts Baptists and Congregationalists were so closely associated that the denominational loyalty of a particular church might not be clear. One of the most remarkable examples of united action for common (though limited) ends was provided by the Baptists, Presbyterians and Congregationalists of Bristol. There was no question of their sacrificing anything of their independence or autonomy, but in the face of a threat to their very existence they concerted plans to frustrate the expectations of their foes. As a first step, the four dissenting congregations chose two men from each, and the committee of eight so formed became responsible for initiating such action as would be most likely to protect the dissenters from the worst ravages of persecution. They held a watching brief to see that no legal safeguards were neglected. For some time they forestalled the arrest of the ministers, and when all of them were finally imprisoned they met to consider how the life of congregations might best be maintained. As a first step they devised a system by which at least token services could be held—the members would meet, one of the brethren would pray and read a chapter, then after singing a psalm, another brother would pray and the meeting would disperse. Matters were so arranged that there would be one week-day service daily but no duplication, but finally, since greater numbers complicated the task of the adversary, they suggested that there should be one large weekly lecture. This presupposed a greater measure of actual union than anything yet considered. The basic principle underlying this step was accepted without serious difficulty, but on certain specific problems agreement was harder to achieve. Four points in particular required careful study: the duty of praying for magistrates, the corporate singing of psalms, the place of the ministry and the nature of baptism. Three of the congregations finally accepted the formula of compromise that was proposed, but the proposal collapsed when the Presbyterians refused to concur. Even so, joint days of prayer were held each quarter; fast days were observed whenever one of the congregations requested or the committee suggested; and an agreed procedure was devised for meeting the attacks of informers on joint gatherings. Arrangements were made to keep exact records of who was injured and by whom. At certain points, however, tension became acute and the scheme finally fell into disuse, but it shows how closely congregations could cooperate, and it provided a specific example of that unity among nonconformists for which men like Bunyan so fervently appealed.[1]

Unfortunately, the record was not always so happy. A congregation might show resentment because a visiting minister appointed a special day in its area at a time which conflicted with its regular meeting. Sometimes a church felt that its neighbour was acting in a way that imperilled its own well-being. Occasionally disputes arose about letters of transfer: a member who had moved to a different place wanted to unite with another congregation, but the home church (in what often appears a factious spirit) refused on some technical ground. When one congregation wished to call a minister, the church with which he was associated might refuse to part with him, even if they were not making regular use of his gifts. In some cases the attitude adopted toward all other churches was so narrow and intolerant that reasonably charitable relations were hindered from the very start. In addition there were the grounds on which the different Puritan groups conscientiously differed, and from the discussion of which persecution itself could not deflect them. The Seventh Day Baptists quarrelled with their brethren regarding Sabbath observance, and all Baptists differed from other groups about the nature and meaning of the sacrament of baptism. The Quakers were suspect to almost everybody else. It was easy to classify them 'with all other wicked sects';[2] Owen specifically associates together the pernicious errors of popery and Quakerism.[3] The Presbyterians and even the Independents had little sympathy with the more extreme Puritan groups (among whom they included the Quakers), but one of the bitterest disputes within nonconformity was between the Quakers and the Baptists.[4] In certain respects they were much alike; in the eyes of the community at large they seemed, for identical reasons, to be equally dangerous; but there is no doubt that nothing divides so effectively as common convictions held with a difference.

Controversies between churches affected the life of the dissenters; so did disputes between their leaders. In times of persecution, the opinions of one man could have far-reaching repercussions on the fate of others. Injudiciously to advocate a certain view might gravely embarrass hundreds in maintaining a witness to which they were conscientiously committed. Men as eminent as Richard Baxter and John Owen doubtless differed on many points, but when they disagreed as to the lawfulness of attending service in the established church their debates immediately became of interest both to churchman and dissenter. When it was learned that Baxter intended to reply to a book of Owen (then dead), a friend of both wrote urgently to dissuade him. In a letter, outspoken in its expostulations but closely reasoned in its arguments, this anonymous correspondent pointed out the serious harm that disputes among leading dissenters could cause. They would weaken and divide those who needed all their unity and strength. If there were differences among nonconformists, at least they should not so be handled as to aggravate the problems of any of the persecuted groups. Baxter kept the letter; apparently he heeded its plea.[1] It was always easy to be suspicious of the motives of those who were more conciliatory and accommodating than their stiffer brethren, but the writer was pleading for the recognition of a truth that all the Puritans admitted when not immediately involved in a dispute: disagreement destroyed the unity of those who were witnesses to truths held in common, and by accentuating divisions weakened the effectiveness of all they did. So serious were the consequences of such controversies that by the end of the century nonconformists were ruefully remembering Stillingfleet's prophecy; let the dissenters alone for twenty years and they will destroy themselves.[2]

The Act of Uniformity ejected the Puritans from the national church; it also excluded them from the universities. Not only were their representatives debarred from places of influence and advantage—no longer could they aspire to be fellows and tutors, professors and heads of houses—but the sons of Puritans could not even enter in order to pursue their education. A strong and distinguished tradition, which had made Cambridge in particular a Puritan citadel, was to be irrevocably broken. Men who had been great luminaries of former days—Perkins and Preston, Bolton and Sibbes—were to have no successors in the remodelled universities, and Emmanuel was no longer to be a nursery of Puritans. In addition, of course, the Act threatened to make the nonconformists an ignorant as well as an ostracised element in the nation. It would deprive them both of leaders and of status. In spite of the restrictions, some dissenters tried to send their sons to Oxford or to Cambridge, but the experience of young Martindale showed that they were so beset with inhibitions and incapacities that the attempt was not worth making.[1] Some turned to Scotland, others to Switzerland or Holland, and in the universities of those Calvinistic countries they found unhindered access and a sound education.[2] But such provision, because remote, was insufficient. A three-fold need remained to be filled. Young people who frequented nonconformist places of worship were likely to find themselves expelled from the schools they were attending, and so facilities for secondary education were needed. Many, in the Church of England as well as without it, were alarmed at the tide of debauchery which had engulfed the older universities, and wanted some place to which they could send their sons without danger of their being corrupted. The problem of providing a succession of competent ministers required the establishment of centres in which young men could be trained in sacred learning, and so fitted for the calling which they had chosen.

The dissenting academies arose to meet these needs. Some of them were, quite frankly, little more than schools. Elias Pledger describes his experiences at more than one of these institutions and what he chiefly stressed was the emphatically religious atmosphere which pervaded them. Every Saturday the state of the pupils' souls was rigorously examined. In his study the master wrestled with them, one by one, in prayer, and strove to bring them to a keen awareness of their sins. He used to 'examine us seriously what we thought of our state and what we thought of ourselves if we died in our sins,... which brought tears from our eyes, many and free....But this was no sooner done but the impression soon wore off, and we returned to our old course as mad as ever.' Special visitors urged them to a life of piety, and week by week the Sunday services added their influence to the forces already at work. Quickened to a sense of need, some of the scholars might join in special sessions of prayer in their rooms, but such fervent resolutions usually proved short-lived, and the picture that emerges is of normal schoolboys not very different from their counterparts in any other age.[1]

Many of these schools were very small; some were doubtless mediocre, since parents who made no complaint about the godliness of the master often transferred their sons to another institution. The better academies were undoubtedly very good. The public schools and the universities of the time gave an education which was extremely restricted in scope, and in comparison a good academy offered a curriculum much more comprehensive as well as much more advanced. The school conducted by the Rev. Charles Morton of Newington Green was progressive both in the measure of self-government it allowed the pupils and in the subjects which it taught. French, mathematics and science—disciplines almost universally neglected at that time—were included in the course. The school even had a laboratory of sorts, 'and some not inconsiderable rarities, with air-pumps, thermometers, and all sorts of mathematical instruments'.[2] The teaching was in English; the principal, who wrote an excellent English style, tried to teach his pupils to do the same. Morton was admittedly an unusual man, open-minded, widely read, pious in spirit but urbane in outlook, and when he emigrated to New England he became vice-president of Harvard. It is not surprising that to such schools others besides dissenters sent their children, and that men prominent in the life of the next generation (like Bishop Butler, Archbishop Secker, and the Earl of Oxford) were educated in them.[3] But, for all their excellence, even the best of the academies suffered from a serious defect. They were small, and failed to give their pupils the advantage of mingling with boys from varying types of background. Defoe contended that they did not provide the free intercourse of mind with mind which fitted a lad, when he left school, to move freely among men of all kinds and discourse naturally with them on any topic which might arise.[1] The restricted and ingrown character which marked the nonconformist congregations became characteristic also of the nonconformist schools.

The academies were a natural development of the circumstances which the ejection of 1662 created. A large number of the nonconformists were highly educated men, and had held teaching positions in one or other of the universities. The Act of Uniformity cut them off from further public usefulness either in the pulpit or the classroom. In spite of the threats which hung over their heads, they naturally turned to teaching. In it they could find employment, a chance to use their gifts and an opportunity of earning a living. But the circumstances which explain the rise of the academies account for their ephemeral character. Admittedly their size and their simple organisation made it easy for them to move from place to place when persecution compelled them to migrate, but also made their continuance wholly dependent on one man. The school he founded disappeared when he died.

Much more significant, both in intention and in influence, were those academies whose purpose was to provide an education comparable to that which the universities offered. As centres of higher learning they fulfilled a very useful function, and the dissenters were not the only ones who benefited from the general training they provided. Primarily, however, these academies were founded and maintained as training grounds for future nonconformist leaders. To the smaller sects—those who disapproved of a ministry specially trained and set apart for their work—the succession of educated preachers was not a problem; any 'gifted brother' who emerged from the life of congregation could be chosen to meet its religious needs. But to the Independents, and even more to the Presbyterians, it was a matter of supreme importance. They might note with satisfaction the high gifts of mind and spirit of the 'Bartholomeans', but what would happen when they died? The answer was found in such academies as that conducted by the Rev. Richard Frankland.

It was no easy task which he had undertaken. He had some assistance, but for the most part it was a single-handed venture which he conducted. This was its weakness as well as its strength. He got to know his students intimately, and clearly he set the imprint of his personality strongly on them all, but inevitably the training was narrower as a consequence. Being an able and learned man, he was able to cover with remarkable success the curriculum which was considered necessary. As an earnest Puritan, he transmitted to his pupils something of the emotional atmosphere as well as of the theological standpoint of the previous generation. What was natural and spontaneous to the fathers was derivative in the sons, but it was not Frankland's fault that the great leaders of Puritanism were succeeded by lesser men. 'The wind bloweth where it listeth', and the wind which stirred the souls of Baxter and Bunyan was not blowing through the halls of Frankland's academy. Nevertheless, the detailed list of his graduates which is preserved in Heywood's *Diary* proves conclusively the immeasurable extent to which he placed non-conformity in his debt.[1] In the years during which he conducted his academy he educated 303 young men; 110 of them became ministers. There were scores who could report, with the Rev. Joseph Boyse, that they had not been trained at either of 'the public universities', but had been 'under Mr Frankland's care'.[2]

The difficulties of conducting a university and a theological college combined were great enough in themselves, but they were enormously aggravated by the circumstances of the time. It was contrary to the law for a nonconformist to teach—there was no doubt on that score—and Frankland was repeatedly forced to move. His friends were in constant apprehension, and on one occasion noted as a great mercy that the justices had given him permission to remain where he was till the end of the year, and had sanctioned a proposed move that would not too seriously disrupt his work. Only an institution such as his could be transplanted from place to place without disastrous results, but the persecution unquestionably caused him great trouble and inconvenience. Archbishop Sharp of York at the outset adopted an overbearing attitude, and told Frankland that on no account would he permit him to educate persons for the nonconformist ministry within the bounds of his province. Frankland, however, was not the man to be intimidated by threats. 'I resolved to abate him nothing', he reports; 'I told him there was other work much more proper for him and of far greater importance, to be done by him. He asked me what it was. I told him, that as to the exercise of severity, he should begin at home, with those of his own clergy, many of whom were scandalous, a great reproach to religion, and stood in need to be reformed. And for other work, I told him, I judged it much more suitable for him to endeavour union and agreement amongst good men, though differing somewhat in their notions, than to cause rents in the church about such poor and trivial things as ceremonies.' Sharp conceded both points, and 'after became very moderate'. In a second interview, he discussed at length with Frankland the problem of providing proper training for confirmation candidates. He also showed him a petition which many of the clergy had drawn up against the academy, but seemed chiefly interested in learning about the character of the petitioners, and remarked that Frankland had 'great friends at London'.[1] Indeed, Sharp was sufficiently puzzled by the problem of how best to deal with Frankland that he consulted the Archbishop of Canterbury. Tillotson advised him to ignore the fact that the man was a dissenter; concentrate instead, he suggested, on the oath which as a graduate he had taken not to teach university subjects outside the bounds of a university, and stress the fact that any conformist would be equally subject to discipline for the same offence.[2]

Though the best way of dealing with Frankland might not be clear, many of the local authorities devised rough and ready ways of hindering his work. Many of the other ministers who kept academies also found their efforts obstructed at every turn.[3] Under the circumstances it was perhaps more remarkable that these institutions managed to survive than that many of them were small and some of them of doubtful standing. The first generation after ejectment saw no fewer than 150 ministers turn to teaching, and not all of them were of the quality of Frankland or Morton, Doolittle or Gale. By the end of the century, when many of the academies were already extinct, a heated controversy as to their value broke out. What Samuel Wesley attacked, Samuel

Palmer defended.[1] Defoe, writing to Harley in 1714, suggested that the academies had not really strengthened nonconformity, but had burdened it with a miscellaneous assortment of ineffective ministers.[2] Unquestionably far too many men undertook to train their own successors, and did so with insufficient means, without reference to agreed standards, and without co-operative oversight of any kind. And yet when all is said, the academies were not merely a striking feature of the life of nonconformity in the latter part of the seventeenth century; they pointed to a need which other schools were failing to meet; they reflected a high degree of education among the ejected ministers and a considerable zeal for learning among the people. And though much of their activity was ephemeral, this was not wholly the case. The Quaker concern for education—to take one example alone—has been a continuing witness which has borne very worthy fruit.

Once men were prepared for the ministry, they usually embarked on a probationary period, but after they had gained some experience and proved their fitness, they were solemnly ordained. So seriously were the obligations of the ministry regarded that neither candidates nor congregations were hasty in pressing for ordination. At Broadmead Chapel, a minister, duly called, served for three years before he was formally set apart, and apparently many of the young men ordained to Presbyterian or Congregational churches had already been preaching for some time. Indeed, some took so grave a view of the matter that they proposed to do the work of a minister while postponing their ordination indefinitely—a view which Frankland condemned in no uncertain terms.[3] And yet for a number of years after the ejection even the nonconformist leaders had been reluctant to ordain young men. The Presbyterians believed in a national church, and as long as comprehension remained an open question, they did nothing that would complicate negotiations or suggest that they were committed to the principle of separation. After 1672, however, the situation gradually changed. Talk about comprehension had raised false hopes too often to be seriously regarded. The Declaration of Indulgence seemed to promise a new era of effective service. Moreover, death and the passage of time were causing so many gaps in the ranks of the ministers that the issue could no longer be postponed. 'Some provision', it was felt, must 'be made for a succession of fit persons in God's way to do God's work in after-times (since so many were dying).'[1]

The ordination itself was one of the most solemn of all the occasions in the life of the nonconformist congregations. Proceedings began in private on the day before the service itself. The candidates were carefully examined regarding their educational qualifications; in addition to giving evidence of due familiarity with the major disciplines of theological learning, each man had to defend a thesis which was assigned to him by the presiding examiner. He was also required to give an account of his faith, and to preach a sermon. Even if only one candidate presented himself, this procedure could easily occupy an entire day. Early next morning the ministers and people reassembled. After two of the ministers had prayed earnestly for God's blessing on the occasion, the moderator (as chosen for the occasion) propounded to the candidate the appointed questions, to which he returned the appropriate answers. Then one of the ministers 'gave up' the candidate to God in prayer; and the moderator, by prayer and the laying on of hands, ordained him.[2] There followed a sermon, a solemn acceptance of their new minister by the congregation or its representatives and a charge to the minister and people. This was no formal or perfunctory part of the proceedings. When Timothy Jolly was ordained, his father, a highly respected Bartholomean, enumerated 'thirty or forty appellations given to ministers in scripture, applying them distinctly and very usefully'. The ordinand closed the proceedings with prayer, 'and the whole company was then dismissed, we having continued in the Lord's work from eight o'clock in the morning till eight at night, except about half an hour's intermission between four and five o'clock'.[3]

The corporate life of the Puritans may appear to have been restricted in scope and monotonous in character. To them it did not seem so. Life in all classes was much simpler then than now. Interests were fewer, and in many of the diversions of the community the Puritan could not join. Racing—whether of horses on the moors or of men on the common—entailed drunkenness and gambling;

cock-fighting meant heavy wagers and considerable violence; the theatre of the Restoration era (where it existed) was ruled by standards which would have filled the godly with shame and horror. But they were content with a simple life. Persecution, social pressure and the inducements of advantage were steadily robbing the nonconformists of their rich and prominent members. Those who could not be moved, whose loyalty was proof against the threat of imprisonment and the danger of ruin, were simple people, occupying humble places in society and of little account in the eyes of the great. A study of marriage returns in the Society of Friends proves that most of the London Quakers came predominantly of the yeoman class.[1] The members of Bunyan's congregation were people similar in origin to himself.[2] The demands of earning a livelihood consumed most of their time; the wider life in which they shared gave them standards by which they could be ruled in all their affairs, a sense of dignity in this life, and an unquenchable hope for the life to come. In prayer and praise they found deep emotional satisfaction. While listening to a sermon they were sharing in what was still one of the chief intellectual interests open to Englishmen at large. Their books, so far as they possessed any, were few in number; but there was always the Bible to shape their thought and mould their speech, and a people could be accounted fortunate for whom Baxter wrote works of practical guidance and Bunyan dreamed his immortal dreams. The monotony of their lives was tempered by high ideals and dignified with glorious hopes. In conducting the affairs of their congregations they might sometimes lapse into pettiness or manifest an unforgiving spite, but at least they were sharing in a democratic process of self-government beyond anything that most of their neighbours knew. And wherever they went and in all that they did they were constantly strengthened and encouraged by the belief that 'the grace of God that bringeth salvation hath appeared to all men, teaching us that, denying ungodliness and worldly lusts, we should live soberly, righteously and godly in this present world'.

CHAPTER VII

'BY PRAYER AND THE PREACHING OF THE WORD'

WORSHIP held a central place in the experience of the Puritans. It was not a marginal interest; it was at once a pre-eminent privilege and an obligation with which they were continuously preoccupied. This was natural. Though many people regarded them as the advocates of a particularly austere view of life, their distinguishing mark as an ecclesiastical party was their desire to carry forward the work of reformation in the church.[1] On the whole they set less store by changes in polity than by the purification of ways of worship, and when they were compelled to choose between conformity and ejection, liturgical questions played an important part in determining their course of action. Nonconformity, indeed, was the final result of a long and hitherto indecisive struggle about the true nature of the church and the proper character of its worship. In loyalty to their convictions the Puritans were willing to forego advantage, preferment and the prospects of advancement. When they were prepared to sacrifice so much, it is not surprising that they found in their chosen ways of worship a comfort proportionate to the hardships they so willingly endured.

Their type of worship was one of the characteristic features of dissenting societies, but it was not for this reason that the Puritans valued it so highly. They were satisfied, of course, that their ways were right and they were consequently ready to defend them at any price; but they also knew that worship was necessarily one of the primary obligations of any church. To forget to worship was to ignore the creaturely character of human life; it was to claim an illusory autonomy at which man's sinful pride might snatch, but which lay forever beyond his reach. When a man responded to God, when he confessed his own need and implored the divine mercy, he discovered that his experience of forgiveness and grace was intensified and marvellously enlarged by fellowship with others. As an individual he might know much; as a member of a fellowship he would know infinitely more.[1] He learned that when he identified himself with a church he entered a community whose inheritance was the glorious promises of God, and he was persuaded that these promises rested firmly upon the divine constancy and power.[2] God had chosen for himself 'an holy people, an hearing people, a praying people, a zealous people'[3]— which merely declared that when a man was drawn out of the loneliness of a selfish life into the companionship of the redeemed community he found that he was partaking in the experience of a worshipping fellowship. He discovered, too, that he was faced with responsibilities which could be discharged only by those who turned to God for strength. It ought to be a simple matter to distinguish the people of God from the children of this world— '"be ye holy, as I am holy", saith the Lord'—and worship was both the measure of that difference and the means by which it was preserved.

The Puritans worshipped because God demanded that they should. It was his command, but it was also their proper, indeed their instinctive, response. As God was the object of their worship, so his nature provided 'the foundation of all true religion and holy religious worship in the world. The great end for which we were made, for which we were brought forth by the power of God into this world, is to worship him and to give glory to him...whence it is holy and religious, as the nature and being of God himself. There are, indeed, many parts or acts of religious worship which immediately respect (as their reason and motive) what God is unto us, or what he hath done or doth for us; but the principal and adequate reason for all divine worship is what God is in himself.'[4] Consequently the full sweep of the Puritan's conception of God became immediately relevant to the kind of worship in which he participated. The earnest solemnity, the profound reverence, the awestruck wonder of his self-prostration before the Almighty were all due to his persuasion that majesty and holiness are the marks of the Most High. Though in his grace God might bid his children come to him, it was intolerable that they should approach that splendour with anything suggestive of presumptuous familiarity. The austere restraint which marked Puritan worship sprang directly from much humble meditation on the inexpressible glory of God's being. Those who ponder such matters are of necessity constrained to speak of God with honour and respect, and even their praises are likely to be solemn and serious.[1] Contemplate God's unsearchable wisdom: is it possible to respond except in awe? 'If God be infinitely wise, it shows us the necessity of our addresses to, and invocation of, his name'; even our ignorance should teach us to turn to him who is 'perfect in counsel'.[2] The holiness of God likewise compelled men to approach him with reverence, and Baxter tells us that he had known many Puritans whose casual gestures suggested that awe had become a constant element in their outlook on life.[3] So one by one the attributes of God were invoked as reasons for worship, and as his providence, his immutability, his omniscience were extolled the most inattentive hearer could understand why the Puritans regarded it as an exceptionally solemn activity to come into God's presence. Worship, at all times and in every aspect, was surrounded by and suffused with a sense of the greatness of God.

The Puritans firmly believed that within evangelical Protestantism men were most likely to appropriate the 'privileges of the excellent, glorious, spiritual worship of God in Christ, revealed and required in the Gospel'.[4] In part this was the result of serious preoccupation with a worthy conception of God, but it was due in equal measure to a constant emphasis on reconciliation, on justification by faith, on sanctification, and on adoption. These were the great evangelical tenets; they all declared and offered a new relationship with God. Those who dwelt much on the way in which men have peace with God were likely to find that they had passed beyond the enunciation of old truths into the appropriation of a grace which was ever new. Worship was merely the outward expression of this experience, and the Puritans believed that worship corresponded to its perfect norm when it translated into outward forms the eternal truths which the Gospel declared. It would be direct and intimate; the believer could come to God immediately, without the need of priestly mediation. It would be simple, because dignity does not depend upon elaboration. It would be in the name of Christ, since it appeals to his true nature and relies upon his completed work. Consequently it would inevitably be both to the glory of God and the edification of his people.[1]

Though evangelical worship would never strive for effect, it would nevertheless achieve beauty of a high and distinctive order. This followed inevitably from the way in which God works; he had ingrafted in men's minds, as a natural principle, the conviction that his worship 'ought to be orderly, comely, beautiful and glorious'.[2] Though the careless might confuse beauty with gaudiness, the two qualities were quite separate and distinct; the beauty of 'that spiritual gospel worship' would consequently consist 'in its own naked simplicity, without any other external adventitious helper or countenance'. Nor were men left, in this uncertain area, to find the true criterion of themselves; of beauty, as of everything else, 'the Holy Ghost in the Scripture was the judge'.[3]

Such worship might be simple; it was not therefore easily performed. All external aids having been stripped away, a man had to rely upon the light and leading which the Holy Spirit always gives to genuinely expectant minds. For the right performance of Gospel worship three things were necessary: there must be light and knowledge in the mind, grace in the heart, and adequate ability to use these gifts which God has granted. But even conspicuous capacities had to be improved, and the Puritans never fell into the delusion that free worship dispensed with the drudgery of preparation. A man who conducted worship knew that he must come prepared in mind and spirit. The most earnest diligence was necessary; otherwise worship would subside into inert conventionality or slovenly unseemliness.[4]

The minister who embarked upon this high duty was satisfied that he possessed guidance sufficient for his needs. The things to be done in worship had been prescribed by God. Scripture provided the rule; it laid down the standard from which men dared not deviate.[1] When God had revealed the proper pattern, 'his wisdom (was) affronted and invaded by introducing new rules and modes of worship, different from divine institutions'. Many, with a high regard for Scripture, had argued that what was not expressly forbidden in its pages might legitimately be used. The Puritans, with the rigorous logic so characteristic of them, contended that anything not explicitly commanded must be wrong. The Bible was God's Word; everything else was man's invention. Any element in worship that was of human devising could be regarded only as a blasphemous intrusion on the divine prerogatives, and stern judgement would inevitably follow. 'How slight will that excuse be, "God hath not forbidden this or that", when God shall silence men with the question, "where, or when, did I command this or that?"'[2]

The Puritans assumed that worship which followed the divine pattern would fulfil the divine purpose: it would be worship in spirit and in truth. When carried to extremes, emphasis on spiritual worship was responsible for the strange and bizarre phenomena which sometimes appeared—'breathings' and ecstasies and inspirations—but it also created a keen sense of the reality of the eternal world and a strong persuasion of the relevance of its values to the problems of daily life. It naturally led to a grave suspicion of all reliance on externals. A religion which trusts in things seen or handled 'will never save any man. A person may be a wicked man, and liable to be turned into hell, notwithstanding any religion that lies in mere outside shew.'[3] Formal worship was beset with pitfalls, and wisdom alone should prompt a man to fear and avoid it. From this it naturally followed that the Puritans regarded liturgical worship with grave distrust. They did not repudiate set forms completely—after all they had their Directory, and there was that remarkable *tour de force*, the complete liturgy which Baxter produced in fourteen days[4]—but they believed that elaborate ceremonial distracted the mind from the proper consideration of God's glory. Moreover, it was an invasion of the divine prerogative. 'When God had by his sovereign order framed a religion for the heart, men are ready to usurp an authority to frame one for the sense, to dress the ordinances of God in new and gaudy habits, to take the eye by a vain pomp.'[1] Vestments and ceremonies not only endangered the true simplicity of spiritual worship, but also corrupted the hearts of those who trusted in them. History suggested that when the Church became 'lost in carnality, not content with itself, and its own native comeliness, but affected to shine in borrowed lustre and ornature, when (as harlots are wont) it began to paint, to be fond of gay attire, and devise things for deckings to itself most alien from its original state and constitution'—then these extraneous matters became the subject of bitter contention and were made the pretext for cruel persecutions.[2]

Free worship, guided by the Spirit, confirmed one of the convictions for which Puritans contended most strongly: that it was their right to frame their own prayers as God should give them utterance. Some of the Puritans were suspicious of set prayers as such; dependence on a form of words would so lull Christians into acquiescence with the words of others that they would lose the power to pray themselves. 'Those who will never enter the water but with flags or bladders under them, will scarce ever learn to swim. And it cannot be denied that the constant and unvaried use of set forms of prayer may become a great occasion of quenching the Spirit, and hindering all progress or growth in gifts or graces.'[3] Even the Puritans who were willing to use liturgies insisted that there must be some place for free prayer. Baxter felt that it was as necessary at times for the minister to find his own words in prayer as it was right for him always to express his own thoughts in preaching, and he was satisfied that when everything had been conceded to liturgical forms it remained true that a congregation was more truly edified by free than by set prayers. Simple people, if encouraged to use them, might assume that forms were obligatory; by falling into the mistaken view that God could be worshipped in no other way, they would seriously impoverish their own religious experience. Moreover, set forms could never achieve the directness, the particularity, the immediate relevance to specific circumstances, that belonged to free prayer.[4]

It was fully realised, of course, that extempore prayer has its dangers. Both Bunyan and Baxter were quite aware of them, and warned others against them.[1] It was too easy to be verbose and undisciplined. It was possible unintentionally to impose on others the moods to which the minister was subject. Through laziness or lack of care, a man might fall into habits so pronounced that his own prayers had all the defects of a liturgy without any of the compensating advantages. As the Restoration period progressed, two developments marked the worship of the non-conformist communities. Free prayer, even among the more moderate groups, prevailed as the virtually universal pattern; experience emphasised the need of discipline in preparation. Seemliness was valued as highly as suitability.[2] Nonconformists were urged to 'observe a decorum' in their words, 'that they be well-chosen, well-weighed, well-placed'; as Matthew Henry remarked, the use of 'some proper method' would ensure 'that we offer not anything to the glorious majesty of heaven and earth which is confused, impertinent and indigested'. But 'a gift in prayer' remained a quality highly prized. Fluency was of little value without fervency, and though the dawn of the eighteenth century ushered in a more formal spirit, most nonconformists would still have agreed that it was a mark of real grace for a man to be able to pray for two or three hours without being guilty of repetition.

The Puritans were satisfied that the experience of God's presence in their gatherings justified their theory and practice of worship. What God had owned, could not be wholly wrong; it could not even be so far astray that their critics were entitled to crush them. 'God hath encouraged us in our work', wrote Baxter, 'by his undeniable blessing on many souls. If you take it for nothing for men to be turned from ignorance, worldliness, deceiving, lying, sensuality, and fleshly lusts, to the serious belief of a life to come, and to love of God and man, and to the joyful hopes of glory, and the obedience of Christ, and confidence in his salvation; we take this to be worth our labour and our lives.'[3] All this was the consequence of their worship; should not their own gratitude be matched by forbearance in others? They found the vindication of their approach to God in the kind of life he enabled them to live to his praise; and ultimately, as Howe realised, it is not arguments that silence an antagonist, but the witness of character and conduct—'the sobriety and consistency of their discourse', 'the unaffected simplicity, humility, and heavenliness of their conversation'.[1]

Worship was founded on scripture, but the meaning of scripture was unfolded in preaching. Men deeply persuaded of the incomparable importance of the Bible naturally assigned in their worship a large place to the preaching of the Word. They knew that they faced an inescapable obligation; because of the nature of the Gospel they had to undertake the task of preaching it to any who were willing to hear. It was a high and exacting duty which they had to discharge as best they could. They did not preach in order to parade their learning or to express their personal opinions; they were messengers and heralds, sent by the Most High to proclaim to his people his demand for repentance and his assurance of pardon. They were to 'turn...the disobedient to the wisdom of the just; to make ready a people prepared for the Lord'. They were sent upon a warfare in which their chief weapon was to be the preaching of the Word. They were persuaded that it was 'the main instrument to advance Christ in the world, by casting out Satan, and by beating down sin, and promoting holiness'.[2]

In the first instance, preaching was addressed to man's actual situation. It began by taking account of the plight in which he found himself. Man must be taught to realise his need; he must be made to feel acutely the misery and the peril of his position.[3] At this point, therefore, the preacher could begin. He would excite the minds of his hearers to heed the danger of sin, and he could do so with confidence and courage, because there is no more effective means of creating a sense of sin and need than the preaching of the Word. Hence the vehemence with which the Puritan preacher dwelt also on the dissuasives from sin; and hence too the earnestness with which he pressed upon his hearers the encouragements to diligence. He was not concerned merely to diagnose the disease; it was his duty to effect a cure. So the preacher began with the task both of creating an awareness of need and of building upon it; 'he was very pertinent in the application, insomuch that he made poor Mansoul tremble. For this sermon...wrought upon the hearts of the men of Mansoul; yea, it greatly helped to keep awake those that were aroused by the preaching that went before.'[1]

The preacher knew, however, that deliverance could never be secured so long as men trusted in false methods. The Puritans had many failings, but a lack of psychological insight was not one of them. They recognised the discrepancies in which human nature and human conduct abound; they realised how readily man deludes himself with false hopes, how constantly he relies on the little expedients he can devise by himself.[2] Many of them had tried to silence the clamours of an awakened conscience by the merit earned by a legalistic righteousness. They had trembled beneath the mountain that blazed with fire; they knew the impossible nature of the demands put forward by the law, and they had sensed the inexorable sentence of damnation which it imposed. There was no alternative save to raze man's life to the foundations. The superstructure of dead works must be cleared away, and a wholly new start be made.[3]

The desperateness of man's situation—whether enmeshed in sin or beguiled by confidence in his own resources—gave to Puritan preaching its distinctive note of urgency. These men were not engaged in some academic exercise; they were striking for a verdict in their hearers' hearts. They believed that they had been sent to labour diligently for the conversion of souls. They were 'to turn the carnal and worldly from the love of sin to the love of holiness; from the love of earth to the love of heaven'.[4] The highest tribute that could be paid to an earnest Puritan preacher was to declare that 'he was infinitely and insatiably greedy of the conversion of souls',[5] and the thought that some who heard had not turned from their ways always haunted a man, even though he had tried to do his best.[6] The converse of this sense of mission was the drastic claims which the Puritan preacher placed on the attention of his hearers. Each sermon was regarded as a kind of moral crisis; it was potentially a watershed in the listener's life. The life of the spirit was a matter of the utmost importance; delay or procrastination might be disastrous, and the preacher's voice was an admonition to the careless to give heed. Every sermon heard should be like a judge's warning before the opening of the assizes, commanding men to obey the laws of the king. If thereafter they disobey, they are like rebels stripped of the last shreds of justification.[1]

To convict of sin was only one part—and by no means the most important part—of evangelical preaching. It was not enough 'to snatch men from Satan'; the preacher's task was 'to bring them to God'.[2] How could men attain to faith unless they were confronted with its claims? And how could they 'close with Christ' if he were not presented to them in his winsomeness and grace?[3] The preacher's distinctive task, therefore, was 'to bring sinners to the knowledge of Christ, to open their eyes that they [might] see him, to unveil Christ that they [might] behold him with open face'.[4] And so, as the nonconformist sought out a preacher under whom he could enjoy 'a searching, convincing, and lively ministry',[5] he did not look merely for denunciations of sin and warnings of judgement. If fortunate, he would find a pastor convinced that his essential work, in the pulpit and out of it, was feeding the flock; and he would 'sit under' a man who knew that the mark of a true preacher was his ability to keep alive in people's hearts the truths of the gospel, and who found his greatest reward in persuading men to love God.[6] Early in the next century Dr Calamy epitomised the ideal which had governed the preaching of considerably more than a generation when he urged young nonconformist ministers to 'preach to your people the Christ whom St Paul adored, the grace which he taught, the faith, the life, the spirit, the hope, the love, the Sacraments and other services which he recommended, open to those that sit under your ministry the foundation of all religion, the divinity of the Scriptures, and their sufficiency, the covenant of grace, and the terms of acceptance with God, and the suitableness of the mediator provided for lapsed creatures, the riches and fulness of the divine promises, the odiousness and malignity of sin, the nature, necessity and excellence of holiness; and the certainty and importance of things immortal.'[7]

It is obvious again that the orbit in which Puritan preaching moved was not a circle with one centre but an ellipse with two foci. There was the preoccupation with sin, involving the threat of damnation, and there was the offer of forgiveness and the assurance of God's grace. Man's plight and God's succour—these were the two great themes with which the Puritans were preoccupied. But they did not always deal with them simultaneously, nor did they always treat them with equal emphasis. And certainly it was not the iniquity of sin nor the terrors of hell that were slighted. In some cases this was due to limitations of experience, in others to deficiencies of temperament. In Bunyan's case, the emphasis changed from one to another as he learned more fully the meaning of the gospel. A mere beginner could denounce sin, but it required deeper insight to expound the mysteries of divine love. So Bunyan started with the condemnation of the flesh and all its works; the note he struck was that of terror;[1] in due course he learned the equally necessary art of ministering comfort. The mark of all his mature preaching was the ability to hold the two in equipoise; but his vivid account of his development in *Grace Abounding* makes it clear that he grew from the one to the other.[2] What was an epitome of his spiritual history became his settled method of appealing to men; but in its use he was certainly not alone. The sermon which played so large a role in Martindale's conversion began with threats and ended with promises; it 'proved like a sharp needle, drawing after a silken thread of comfort in due season'.[3] And when Owen, one of the greatest of Puritan preachers, defined the ends which all preaching ought to serve, he merely reduced to systematic form the principles which governed the practice of his brethren. There are three purposes, he said, which preaching should promote. The first is 'the conversion of the souls of men unto God'; they are to be warned of the perils of sin and persuaded to turn to God. The second object is 'the edification of them that are converted unto God and do believe'; as Christ commanded us, we are to feed the sheep and lambs of his flock. The third purpose is to 'promote the growth of light, knowledge, godliness, strictness, and fruitfulness of conversation' in the members of the household of faith.[4]

The aim of Puritan preaching naturally affected the content of Puritan sermons. As we would expect, the grievous character of sin occupied a large place, and no matter what the ostensible subject might be, some preachers twisted the sermon into a dissertation on sin. There was a constant undertone of horror at the inexpressible nature and incalculable consequences of ungodliness. The reality of judgement and the terrors of God's final tribunal were vividly portrayed, and men were earnestly called to act at once, 'to embrace Christ' while yet there was time.[1] But the more positive aspect of the preacher's task was to commend divine grace and to build up in his hearers a knowledge of God's nature and his ways. Hence we have those majestic series of sermons on which the Puritan preachers embarked with such undaunted courage—and to which the Puritan congregations submitted with such unmurmuring fortitude. George Trosse spent several years preaching steadily through the attributes of God; so did Samuel Charnock, but he defined his task on a scale so comprehensive that though his sermons fill five large volumes, they are only a tiny fragment of the projected whole. Manton followed the same method, but was more apt to expound passages of scripture than doctrines of the creed. When Howe unfolded 'the Principles of the Oracles of God', he steadily worked his way, unhasting and unflagging, through the tremendous topics of God's nature and his ways with man. These great subjects, he remarked, must be taught; and that not once, but repeatedly. They must be 'taught over and over, for these are things that we cannot too thoroughly have learned, or be too much versed in'.[2] In the hands of lesser men the continued treatment of a single theme could become tedious and absurd, and when a congregation, having listened for four months to an exposition of Joseph's coat of many colours, nicknamed their minister 'Eternal Bragge', we can surely catch an echo of their weariness. And it is also true that even able men created for themselves problems of considerable magnitude. The Puritans were not likely to swerve from their course because a topic proved hard, but though they tackled difficult questions with exemplary courage, they did not always find convincing answers. When Charnock wrestled with the causes of human inequalities he was driven to rely on arguments that are of doubtful cogency, to say the least—for example, that 'it is not well with bad men here', or that no good man would exchange his afflictions for the blessings of the unjust.[1]

There is no question, however, that the boldness with which the Puritans embarked upon the greatest of all themes gave to their preaching, at its best, a dignity and power seldom equalled. Through their pages there still thrills the eagerness with which they approached the incomparable splendours of divine grace. 'How should we endeavour after the enjoyment of God as good!' cried Charnock, 'how earnestly should we desire him!'[2] The note of 'reverence and veneration of the divine majesty' sounds clearly even through the intricacies of the most elaborate argument; the grandeur of the subject and the conviction that the overruling power of God can turn all things to his praise, light up the heavy and abstruse paragraphs.[3] The consciousness of unplumbed depths and unscaled heights in the providential ordering of the universe delivered Puritan preaching from any taint of triviality, and gave it the awestruck wonder which so deeply moved those who listened. To these men preaching was a tremendous commission. They received it from God; in discharging it they were supported by his grace; and they believed that their faithful efforts would bring to their people the knowledge which would make them wise unto salvation.

Such a ministry could be sustained only by study. If a man were to teach, he had first to earn the right to do so, and the Puritans set high store by a learned ministry. They were aware of the insufficiency of human knowledge. Unless the Lord gave wisdom, preoccupation with books merely produced a pedant—perhaps a fool. But even the Spirit of light and truth demanded the co-operation of the man himself, and the Puritans were satisfied that 'faith does not abolish but improve reason'.[4] So the conscientious minister gave himself to study with a kind of maniacal zeal, and considered it a sacrifice when matrimony reduced his daily span of work from fourteen hours to eight or nine.[5] Charnock devoted almost all his time to study; his library was his 'workshop', and his friends solemnly observed that 'had he been less in his study, he would have been less liked in the pulpit'. Even when he walked abroad, his thoughts still ran on his studies, and he would pause to jot down ideas that might be useful in his sermons.[1] During his ministry at Kidderminster, Baxter lived a life of many-sided and incessant toil, but in his study he accomplished prodigious feats of work—as his innumerable books so eloquently testify. Puritan preaching was marked by those qualities which much study is likely to produce. In his funeral sermon on John Howe, John Spademan pointed out that the characteristics which distinguished Howe's preaching were his ability, his copiousness, his piety, his great learning and his marvellous knowledge of the Bible,[2] and the original editors of Charnock claimed that the qualities which a preacher should bring to his work were 'solid judgement, weighty thoughts, extensive learning, cultivated imagination'.[3] It is perhaps permissible to wonder whether the congregations really esteemed learning as highly as the preachers thought. Sometimes, surely, they got a little suffocated by so much erudition, and the mind goes back to Mr Pepys, as he abandoned the attempt to follow the sermon and turned in his Bible to the Book of Tobit. But though the Puritans may have overvalued learning and overestimated the amount that the average hearer could absorb, they had a method in their madness. They had little of the pedant's love of parading knowledge. The close reasoning, the tight logic, the massive array of arguments and texts were designed to meet a specific need. People were ignorant and must be taught, and the preachers honestly believed that the method they adopted was suited to the nature of their material, as well as to the needs and capacities of their people. And, as we shall presently see, they could count on certain aids which the modern preacher wholly lacks.

The structure of the Puritan sermon was determined by two facts: the intellectual background of the preacher and the cumbersome mass of material which he poured forth. Strict order was the only alternative to utter chaos, and the scholastic logic in which all the great Puritan preachers had been trained made exact division of the subject a congenial exercise. At the very outset the massive structure of the sermon was fully exposed to view. In the opening sentences the preacher declared his theme and enumerated the subheadings. In dealing with Psalm ix. 17, Howe immediately laid bare his subject: 'There are two observations that offer themselves to our view from this scripture. First, that it is the property of the wicked man to forget God. And, secondly, that it shall be the portion of wicked men, who forget God, to be turned into hell. These two I intend to handle together in this order. I. I shall shew you what we are here to understand by the wicked. II. What by forgetting God. And then, III. I shall evince unto you, that they are wicked persons who do forget God. And then, IV. That such wicked persons shall be turned into hell. And so, V. Make use and application of the whole together.'[1] Here was the main skeleton of the sermon; from the outset the listeners knew what to expect. But the work of reducing the subject-matter to its constituent elements had only begun. Many preachers opened with a detailed exposition of the Biblical context of the passage they had chosen.[2] Exactness of exegesis thus became a preliminary to meticulous subdivision of the material itself. With almost artificial precision a subject was unfolded, and its negative and positive implications indicated; distinctions were carefully noted and clearly defined. The process was subtle, but seldom unintelligibly so, and was usually more apt to clarify the issue than confuse it.

Both in their own day and since, Puritan preachers have been ridiculed for the mania which pushed subdivision to such extremes. South, eager for any stick with which to beat them, treated it as a mark of the Puritans alone.[3] It was actually a characteristic of all who had shared the same type of training. After all, Charles II chided Isaac Barrow with being an unfair preacher; he dealt with any subject he treated so exhaustively that he left nothing for anybody else to say—and to read Barrow's works is to appreciate the king's complaint. The method itself had a long history; it had descended in unbroken succession from medieval times. It had been devised as a necessary instrument of exact thought; it was perpetuated because it enabled preachers to deal with complex subjects without creating utter confusion in their hearers' minds. Exactness in exegesis and the use of formal logical distinctions were thus among the indispensable weapons in the armoury of the Puritan preacher.

The preacher did not subdivide his subject for nothing, nor was this the only evidence of his intensely practical purpose. Both ministers and people knew the value of sermons that were direct in character and immediately relevant to the situation of the hearers. Consequently the subjects chosen were by no means always abstruse and theological. When Howe dealt with the sin of quarrelling—the Carnality of Contention, as he called it—his meaning was unmistakably clear.[1] The desire to preach to the actual problems which people were facing appears in the kind of text chosen during periods of persecution, and because the minister himself shared in all the afflictions of his people he often found for his purpose words of startling relevance.[2] It was the aim of the preacher to meet his people where they were, to help them understand their problems, to afford the strength they needed to overcome temptations, and to cultivate those qualities of life and conduct which should characterise those who live under a sense of God's overruling providence.[3] The aim of the preacher was to make his hearers better Christians. So the truths of the Gospel had to be applied to the problems which they faced, and often the advice given was remarkably concrete and constructive. The pastoral purpose of the speaker was seldom in doubt, and many of the sermons of the period revealed a remarkable measure of profound psychological insight. The nature of evil, the deceptive plausibilities of sin, the character of our response to its seductions, the measures necessary to fortify our resistance—subjects like these were handled with penetrating skill. Often both the perception of need and the ability to meet it were due to the fact that the sermon sprang straight out of the preacher's own experience. 'I preached what I felt,' says Bunyan, 'what I smartingly did feel.' Out of an agonised concern for others a man drew upon the things he had learned in life; and, since he knew at first hand the subtlety of Satan, he dared not set forth his sermon without desperate cries to God 'that He would make the Word effectual to the salvation of the soul'.[4]

The practical aim of the preacher determined even the structure of his sermon. There were usually three main divisions: the doctrine, the reason, the use—or, to express it otherwise, the declaration, the explanation, and the application of the Christian faith.[1] No sermon, however involved, was complete without the 'uses'. Nothing was too abstruse, nothing was too commonplace, to be improved to the congregation's benefit. Whether it was the most secret counsel of God or the simplest matter of daily experience, it had its 'use'. Nor was it enough merely to enumerate 'Help one' or 'Counsel two'; in order that the last drop of improvement might be wrung from the subject the 'uses' were classified—some for instruction, others for comfort, still others for exhortation.[2]

It is easier to state an ideal than it is to achieve it, and the reader sometimes wonders why the Puritans, with so practical an aim before them, preached sermons so tediously involved. Surely many besides Pepys found 'the Presbyterian manner' dull. Sometimes the preacher may have been self-deceived; he may have believed that truths obvious to him would be equally clear to others—as when Howe emerges from an intricate theological discussion of very abstruse matters and blandly assures us that he is only treating of simple and practical affairs.[3] Sometimes, no doubt, the method suitable to the 'lecture' carried over into the 'sermon'. The lecture was more specifically and avowedly a teaching medium; the preacher believed that he could claim closer attention, for a longer time, and could legitimately deal with more technical subjects. Many of the Puritan sermons which survive are really lectures. The place where they were given was the same; the general method was the same; but the audience would consist of the Puritan elect—those who delighted in such disquisitions, and came on weekdays to supplement the simpler fare of the Sabbath. But unquestionably the distinction between lecture and sermon was often blurred; what the preacher intended to be the one, the bewildered hearers regarded as the other. There were always kindly critics to enter a plea for simplicity in the interest of the congregation; 'I prevailed with him', said Martindale of a fellow minister, to preach 'plainly to the edification of the people.'[4]

When preaching, the Puritan did not strive for literary effect, but he evolved a style which was suitable to his purposes and reasonably successful in achieving his ends. Though his pages might be 'gray with argument', he did not complicate matters by using an ambitious or complicated style. There is little to suggest the intricacies of Andrewes, the quaint conceits of Donne, or the iridescent splendours of Jeremy Taylor. This was deliberate and intentional. Baxter tells us that he carefully resisted the temptation to aim at a polished literary style; life was too brief and too serious to waste its moments playing with words. It was his aim to set down his thoughts as quickly and forcefully as he could; he accepted the words that came, and wasted no time straining after elegance or effect.[1] Simplicity and directness were the qualities suitable in a man's speech when he commended the things of God; his words were to be decent but not theatrical. Indeed, any other qualities would have been glaringly inappropriate in view of the desperate earnestness of the responsiblity he had assumed. With the slightly defiant attitude which often marks the self-educated man of letters, Bunyan remarked that he could 'have stepped into a style much higher than this...but I dare not. God did not play in convincing of me, the devil did not play in tempting of me, neither did I play when I sunk as into a bottomless pit, when the pangs of hell caught hold upon me; wherefore I will not play in my relating of them, but be plain and simple, and lay down the thing as it was.'[2] The temptation might occur 'to study and speak handsome words' when you found yourself facing a congregation of genteel folk, but it was a temptation resolutely resisted. The same principle governed the use of quotations. A man who, like David Clarkson, had been a college tutor for years might occasionally slip in a Latin, Greek or Hebrew phrase, but most preachers studiously avoided them, while some, like Bunyan, rather truculently asserted that their spiritual authority derived from sources other than the books of men long dead.[3]

This did not mean that the Puritan sermon was devoid of all graces. Sentences tended to be relatively short, often with a strong sense of balance and an effective use of contrast. Sometimes

14-2

the speaker achieved a terse and epigrammatic quality which he had doubtless learned from the Book of Proverbs: 'as the image on the seal is stamped upon wax, so the thoughts of the heart are printed upon the actions.'[1] Long and unintelligible words were usually avoided, and there was a serious attempt to keep within the range of the hearers' comprehension. Sentences were often given a graphic twist, and metaphors, frequently chosen with great skill, abounded. There was a notable freedom from play on words, from unnatural similes and verbal conceits. Illustrations were usually taken from common life, and some, like Howe's story of the man who tried to pass off a corpse as a living person, were startling in their vividness. Striking and graphic touches were common, as when Bunyan dwelt upon the folly of procrastination: 'this is the man that hangeth tilting over the mouth of hell, while death is cutting the thread of his life.'[2] A great deal of the power of Puritan preaching came from its reliance on graphic imagery; no one who has read it is likely to forget the man who is eager to gallop, but whose horse will do no more than trot, or the person summoned to court who elbows his way through the crowd of idlers at the gate in order to get there.[3] Because imagery is always beset with dangers, it occasionally got out of hand, with grotesque results. To illustrate the truth that 'God is righteous without being cruel, and merciful without being unjust', Charnock declared that 'the bowels of mercy are wound round the flaming sword of justice, and the sword of justice protects and secures the bowels of mercy'.[4] But the lapses were relatively rare, and page after page displayed the preacher's loyalty to the qualities which he considered of paramount importance; in discharging 'a lively, godly ministry' a man was wise to rely on 'a clear, masculine style, a spiritual judicious discourse'.[5]

It was a common gibe that the Puritan, in his earnestness, developed ludicrous idiosyncracies of speech and manner. The 'pulpit voice' has never been the prerogative of any single group, but certainly their critics felt that the Puritans developed a particularly disagreeable variant of the sanctimonious whine. In the questionnaire which Walker circulated while gathering material for his *Sufferings of the Clergy*, he included an inquiry concerning Puritan ministers: 'What accounts', he asked, 'are there among you of. . . their ridiculous praying or preaching, canting?'[1] South never let slip an opportunity of mocking at their mannerisms.[2] When voices have long been silent, such things are hard to judge. It was not a complaint levelled against the greatest Puritan preachers, probably because their complete absorption in a task of transcendent importance delivered them from the perils which beset the zeal of lesser men. And as regards gestures, it was recognised that no rules can really be laid down without reducing the preacher to the level of the rhetorician. What is extreme and affected in one man is, as Bunyan pointed out, natural and effective in another.[3] But it could emphatically be said that 'we are against all indecent expressions in praying or preaching, and all indecent habits, gestures or actions'.[4] Regarding one matter, however, we have the testimony of the Puritans themselves. In their preaching they commonly moved not only others, but also themselves, to tears. Emotions were deeply felt and freely expressed. We read of one minister who rarely left the pulpit without weeping copiously, while Oliver Heywood, a singularly virile and robust man, seems to have carried on his ministry amid floods of tears. 'I found extraordinary enlargement in prayer and praise', he writes, in recording a service held at a time of great danger, 'and oh! what floods of tears were poured forth!'[5] After he had been preaching for many years, Thomas Jolly noticed that his eyesight had deteriorated, and he attributed this to much weeping in the pulpit. Never had he failed to drench at least two handkerchiefs during every service he held.[6]

The length of Puritan sermons was likewise a cause of complaint, though apparently those who read them are more likely to be oppressed than those who heard. The seventeenth century was an age of long sermons. Howe, when Cromwell assigned him a text at the last moment, expounded it for two hours, and showed no signs of intending to stop, but Isaac Barrow, who was not a Puritan, could, and did, preach for three and a half hours. On one celebrated occasion the vergers of Westminster Abbey persuaded the organist to 'blow the organs', because they saw no other way of curbing this inexhaustible divine.[1] The sermon, of course, was one of the great sources of interest and instruction open to men and women in that age, and a popular preacher had a following of hearers eager to listen for far more than one hour. When Burnet, noticing that the sands had run out in the pulpit hour-glass, held it aloft and dramatically turned it up to indicate that he was going on for another hour, the congregation broke out into delighted applause.[2] So the Puritan, with his usual standard of one hour, was certainly not transgressing the accepted norm. Admittedly he was doing nothing to establish a new one, and there were signs that a new day was dawning. At the end of the period, the same Burnet who had confidently preached for two hours, was recommending his clergy to be content with a quarter of that time.[3] The Puritan, however, held his ground; the sermon was too important to suffer such curtailment. 'Mr Sharp', remarked Ralph Thoresby of his minister at Leeds, made a most incomparable discourse, both learned and long (not tedious) for he preached two hours and a half.'[4] As the time could not be curtailed, neither should the opportunities be restricted. At baptisms, at betrothals, at weddings, at funerals, as well as at times of thanksgiving or of crisis or of sorrow, in the home or the church or the community or the nation—a sermon always seemed appropriate and so a sermon was always forth-coming.

In this great task of commending God to men, the Puritans knew that they were beset with difficulties and problems. Some lay within, some without. There was the peril of spiritual pride; the subtle whisperings of self-content assured a man that he had preached with great distinction. So he would find himself puffed up in spirit, and because he took credit to himself when all the glory belonged to God, he would become a castaway. Few things were so perilous to a man's soul as the adulation of admiring devotees. The promptings of sin could make a minister preach in the wrong spirit and for utterly inappropriate ends: they would 'make a man preach for a place and praise rather than to glorify God and save souls'; they would 'put a man upon talking that he may be commended'.[5] In what he doubtless considered righteous zeal, a minister might use his sermon for controversial purposes, and discover, when it was too late, how futile preaching could be when directed to contentious ends.[1] There was the constant danger—so easily forgotten by the preacher, so deeply frustrating to the congregation—of unintelligiblity. In a letter describing a Presbyterian meeting held in Oxford after the Declaration of Indulgence, a writer tells his correspondent that Dr Langley, formerly master of Pembroke College, preached for two hours on the Holy Spirit (on which he had preached for two years 'in the late times') 'and they say he was all the while so unintelligible that from that time to this nobody could tell whence the sound thereof came or whither 'tis going'.[2] In meeting the charge that Charnock was 'too high for the vulgar hearers', his friends conceded that perhaps his preaching was better suited to the capacities of 'the more intelligent sort of Christian'—a reasonably explicit acknowledgement that many people found him hard to understand. 'I find', confessed Clarkson, 'I am apt to be mistaken, and such constructions put upon my words as the expressions will not bear, and my thoughts were never guilty of.' But there was also the danger that the hearer would choose to understand no more than would comfortably accord with his own wishes, and to believe he had grasped the real meaning of the sermon when he was actually intent on deflecting its point from his favourite faults. Those who seriously tried to pay attention did not always find it easy. If sermons were always long; sometimes they were abstruse as well. A very simple service would last two or three hours, and on special occasions almost the whole day would be consumed in prayer and praise and preaching. The eager no doubt made a serious effort to participate throughout, but the less devout apparently made no effort at all. So there were 'many who talk[ed] away sermons'; and those whom good taste restrained from such irreverence found themselves much troubled with wandering thoughts—a failing which robbed them of almost all the advantage which the sermon ought to yield.[3] Some of the hearers, it is sad to relate, fell asleep. Whether this was a rare occurrence or a common one we do not know, but Increase Mather found it necessary to deal explicitly with the offence.[1] All the while, both within and without, the preacher knew that he faced the opposition of Satan; the devil's frustrating stratagems were the chief obstacles to good hearing, and this was perhaps inevitable, since the prince of evil understood that preaching was 'the principal means of salvation'.[2]

The task was urgent and the obstacles were great. It was therefore vitally important to train people to listen with profit. When preaching required such earnest effort on the preacher's part, it was right to require of the hearer a proportionate attempt to benefit from the sermon. Unfortunately good hearers were rare: 'the most part that hear', remarked Clarkson sadly, 'perish'.[3] Too many were altogether careless; instead of giving earnest heed, they merely ridiculed serious preachers.[4] Just as error assumes many guises, so the unsatisfactory hearer appeared in many forms, and Howe distinguished no fewer than eleven different types of listeners whose response to preaching must be condemned.[5] The first requisite was a due sense of responsibility, a proper awareness of the consequences which would follow for those who were remiss in hearing the word of life. 'Hearing is the provision made for the soul's eternal well-being...; if you fail here, you perish without remedy; at the day of judgement an account of every sermon will be required...the books will be opened, all the sermons mentioned which you have heard, and a particular account required.'[6] But though the message might come as stern judgement, it could prove a great mercy; it could be a blessing no less than a curse. It was necessary, therefore, to break loose from the preoccupations in which the world ensnared the unwary, and give undivided attention to the things that belong to man's true welfare. For the beginner there was no safer rule than to 'keep close to the best preachers', to 'cleave to a sound ministry'. He must come with eager anticipation, 'as expecting God to speak'. In addition to this prior preparation, there must be concentration during the sermon, with 'a settled design to learn something in order to apply it'. It was important to grasp the intent of the preacher; it was much more vital through it to understand something of the mind of God. Here discrimination was needed, but it achieved little unless reverence were added to judgement, and without diligence all good qualities would be of no avail. Above all, the hearer must be watchful for truths that applied directly to his own situation, and, having given faithful attention during the sermon, he must go forth resolved not to fall into the self-deception of those who are hearers of the word only and not doers.[1]

Fortunately the poor listener, trembling at the thought that a special doom awaited those who gave unworthy heed, was not left to his own resources. The preacher, accepting his share of responsibility, did his best to help. Though the vast quantities of material he poured forth might seem to doom to failure all efforts to remember anything, the care with which the sermon was sub-divided was intended as an aid to the memory. Not only were points clearly indicated and distinctly labelled, but they were numbered, and each might be provided with a key word which could readily be recalled. Baxter recommended the practice of giving each division a title beginning with the same letter.[2] But even this was not enough, and the Puritan method of preaching becomes defensible as well as intelligible when we remember that many of the members of the congregation took notes. Ralph Thoresby made it a regular practice to write down as much of the sermon as possible, and he was greatly distressed when he found himself so wedged in among the members of a vast congregation that he could not possibly take notes. His fears were justified; he subsequently discovered that he could remember only a small part of what he had heard. Nor was he an isolated case. Many of the sermons of the great Puritan preachers were published not from the author's manuscript but from the notebooks of various listeners. When he got home, the conscientious hearer would follow Thoresby's method, and transcribe what he had taken down in church. But the less methodical were also taught simple ways of remembering. They were to hold at bay the world's distractions till they had a chance to fix the sermon clearly in their minds. As they walked home they were to recapitulate the points, and to give a few minutes' careful thought to each. Perhaps most important of all was the Puritan habit of repeating sermons. On Sunday evenings, but also at other times, those gathered in the family circle carefully reviewed the last discourse they had heard. The minister, if he happened to be present, might undertake this 'duty' himself, but it might fall equally to any member of the family circle, and if the minister called during the week he would certainly catechise the members of the household, and examine them on what he had said. The likelihood that you would be called so promptly to give an account of the things you had heard was a powerful inducement to pay attention to the sermon while it was being preached.[1]

The care with which every possible precaution was taken against failure reflects the Puritan conviction that preaching was a supremely important task, but one which abounded in difficulties. The Puritans themselves realised how great were the obstacles in their way and how often they failed to surmount them; they needed neither the criticisms of their contemporaries nor the confident superiority of those who have followed to convince them that they were unprofitable servants. They took their standards from a source transcending all human wisdom, and their awareness of the tremendous responsibilities they had undertaken meant that they were always acutely conscious that they had come short—far short—of the glory of God. They believed that theirs was a task which they could worthily discharge only if they possessed spiritual wisdom, the authority which comes from personal experience, skill to divide the Word aright, knowledge of the condition of their people, zeal for the glory of God and compassion for the souls of men—but who is ever equal to these things? Yet the greatness of their undertaking gave them also that dignity which even the limitations of a vanished age cannot hide. And it gave them, too, that sense of urgency which made them yearn to communicate to others the things that they themselves had learned. In all his preaching, Bunyan tells us, he was driven on by the desire that others should see, as he saw, what sin and death and hell and the curse of God mean, but also that they should discover, as he had discovered, what grace and mercy and forgiveness and the love of God can do for men. In preaching upon the cardinal truths of the Gospel it had seemed to him 'as if an angel of God had stood at my back to encourage me. Oh it hath been with such power and heavenly evidence upon my own soul, while I have been labouring to unfold it, to demonstrate it, and to fasten it upon the consciences of others, that I could not be contented with saying, I believe, and am sure; methought I was more than sure, if it be lawful so to express myself, that those things which then I asserted were true.'[1] In that apologia lies the secret of the greatness of the Puritans and the explanation of their power, not wholly lost, to hold the hearts of those who read them.

CHAPTER VIII

THE CLASH OF IDEAS

RELIGIOUS debate was the chief intellectual preoccupation of the seventeenth-century Englishman. Other interests competed for his attention, of course; in science and philosophy great names represented revolutionary advances, and literature, both in poetry and prose, could point to important developments. Yet the stationers' lists show that theological works outnumbered all others. Differences in doctrine and discipline, controversies concerning ways of worship and forms of church government were eagerly canvassed and fiercely debated. A turgid stream of pamphlets poured endlessly from the presses. Badly arranged, abominably printed, graceless in style and dreary in atmosphere, these ephemeral works are themselves the most convincing testimony to the Englishman's insatiable passion for theological controversy. Page after page, one author refutes another, dissecting, sentence by sentence, his opponent's work and attacking his argument phrase by phrase. Ponderous logic which no longer carries conviction alternates with vicious sarcasm which has lost all power to amuse, while often the torrent of abuse flows on unchecked by any of the courtesies of debate. Since the great figures sometimes entered the lists, able works alternate with dreary fulminations of lesser men. But Bunyan and Baxter are not remembered for their tracts, and even Marvell's irony is often pedestrian enough. Brilliant pamphlets like Halifax's *Letter to a Dissenter* are so rare that the reader of this transient literature of controversy is left with the conviction that only a public avidly interested in theological debate would have purchased such works in such volume.

Even those who took part in this venomous wrangle often deplored the spirit which it engendered. Edward Fowler, whose views on justification seemed so semi-pagan to John Bunyan, and who in reply showed himself so competent a master of foul abuse, could nevertheless write to Baxter of his deep desire 'that all Christians would at length be so convicted of the amiableness and necessity of a meek forbearing and charitable temper as to endeavour to demonstrate the truth of their Christianity by nothing more'. Only so would 'those deadly feuds and animosities that this worst of ages abounds with' be finally subdued.[1] Baxter noted with dismay that religious contention set neighbours at enmity one with another, 'like Guelphs and Gibelines ...by talk, press and pulpit quenching brotherly love'.[2] Charles Hatton deplored the 'scurrilous satyrical' insolence of Marvell's attacks on Turner.[3] Even so cool a partisan as Pepys could relish the anti-Presbyterian diatribes of a contemporary pamphlet— 'very witty' to him, though dull enough to a modern reader.[4] Yet, even in that age, when courtesy imposed no limitations, abusiveness was not allowed to degenerate into blasphemy, and the Anglican rector who wrote *The Presbyterian's Pater Noster, Creed, and Ten Commandments* was compelled to make a public recantation.[5]

And yet as the religious cleavage in English life took permanent form it was through the press that the issues at stake were discussed. Admittedly the press was by no means an ideal medium of debate. For considerable parts of this period, the licensing laws denied its use to the dissenters. Churchmen abused them for their errors, and then taunted them on account of their silence, but there was no possibility of offering a reply.[6] Nevertheless, most of the basic subjects which account for the emergence of nonconformity were thoroughly canvassed in the pamphlet literature of the time. Why Puritanism ceased to be a party within the Church of England and became instead a distinct body outside it becomes intelligible to the reader who will stir the ashes of these ancient fires. He will be amazed at the fierceness with which they once burned, and he will find abundant evidence to prove that the public that bought these works followed the struggle with breathless eagerness.

When reduced to its simplest terms, the controversy resolved itself into a debate as to whether sufficient grounds for a cleavage actually existed. Many Anglican writers insisted that nonconformity was not rooted in principle at all; it was born of stubbornness and pride, and men who could not really justify their dissent were hiding behind specious pretexts which they forced to do service as arguments. To the nonconformists, such insinuations seemed unfair as well as unconvincing. Surely an argument made absurd demands upon credulity when it suggested that vanity or an obsession with party slogans could make men impervious to every claim either of moral integrity or of material advantage.[1] To suggest, as was often done, that the nonconformists objected to impositions simply because these were imposed was to be guilty of the very perversity of which the dissenters were so freely accused,[2] while to assert that the issues involved were marginal and indifferent overlooked the true nature of the dispute. Many Anglicans were prepared to regard them as such, but the nonconformists could not agree. They felt that it was unreasonable for the state to compel, as a condition of membership, unequivocal acceptance of matters which Anglicans admitted were indifferent, but which many nonconformists considered sinful.[3] Some of the points might be of relatively minor importance, and a great many dissenters would have been perfectly willing to remain as members of a church in which these things were customary but not compulsory. To this question, the debate repeatedly recurred. 'Why', asked the nonconformists, 'do you impose things which you yourselves confess to be indifferent but which we find to be an occasion of offence?' From first to last the Anglicans pointed to the necessity of uniformity. There could be no divergence from the required norm. For some to add to, and others to detract from, the rites and ceremonies of the church would have dangerous consequences far beyond the church itself. In addition to the necessary things fixed by our Saviour, there must, said Hoadly, be ecclesiastical regulation in things indifferent, and it must be so imposed that no man can be a member of the church without complying. On the contrary, replied Calamy; though Christ has left the necessary circumstances of his worship to be determined by human prudence, yet he gives no one a mandate to rule his church despotically and close the doors to those who have conscientious scruples.[1]

The nonconformists felt that at least they should be given credit for refusing to adopt a lax or careless attitude. They noted that many a conformist professed his adherence to things which thereupon he proceeded to ignore, and for an unscrupulous person this was unquestionably a simple as well as a highly satisfactory solution of the problem. To many nonconformists it seemed 'more honest either to refuse to take (an oath), or to act according to the sense of the imposers'.[2] The crux of the matter was the problem of sin. The source of impositions was immaterial, but their moral and spiritual consequences were not. You cannot blindly believe what you are told to accept merely because you are commanded to do so; such an attitude would make the law of God of no effect, and would excuse men from the exacting and often painful duty of deciding what was right.[3] Because a man's life is governed by moral considerations, and since these rest on a divine mandate, the final authority in each person's life must be God's will as he understands it. Consequently, if even a single requirement imposed on ministers seemed to them to be a sin, they had no alternative but to refuse it. To separate from the church or to sin against conscience was an agonising alternative; even unsympathetic critics should realise that the choice would be made only after prolonged and earnest searching of heart. 'We nonconformists', said Baxter, 'offer our solemn oaths that we have by prayer and earnest search and study laboured to know the truth herein. And as our worldly interest would persuade us to conform, so we would readily do it, did we not believe that it is a sin against God.'[4]

Of necessity the nonconformists were driven to ask, what can be considered obligatory in the ordering of the Church's life and worship? They concluded that nothing except the law of God is really mandatory, and what that law is we can know only through revelation. The right procedure was to establish what things could claim a man's unquestioning consent because it had been proved that they represent the divine purpose. These would determine the nature of our worship in 'the primary and eminent sense';

questions of 'secondary diminutive' importance ('as being un-covered, bowing, standing, kneeling, the words of prayer and praise, etc.') could be left as matter for agreement among men who were taught to realise that in some areas we lack the right to coerce the consciences of other people. The imposition of doubtful requirements could not strengthen the churches; at best it would fill them with hypocrites of hardened conscience. Nor would it ever create 'the full and desirable unity' among the Christian Protestants of England which was ostensibly the goal of every party.[1]

When they protested against the required uniformity, the non-conformists knew that the onus was upon them to indicate the kind of church in which they would be glad to find a place. Apart from the conscientious separatists and the members of the smaller sects, most of the Puritans earnestly desired to be in-cluded in the establishment. The Presbyterians (loosely so-called) represented the majority of the nonconformists, and from the early days of the Reformation they had been actively engaged in propounding solutions. John Corbet pointed out that the sup-pression of the Presbyterians would not really strengthen the country or the church; it would not even satisfy the demands of justice. The Episcopal party would not suffer if the church were comprehensive enough to include the 'sober Puritans', and 'a just and equal accommodation' of the two parties was more desirable in itself and more likely to advance the cause of Christ than 'the absolute exalting' of one group or the other.[2] The fertile mind of Baxter was ceaselessly engaged in devising ways and means by which the establishment might be modified and the 'mere nonconformists' incorporated in it. He was certain that this would satisfy the great body of moderate evangelicals who could not accept the Laudianism of the re-established church; he also believed that it would greatly strengthen the church itself.

All these proposals had one thing in common: they presup-posed that the reformation of the church was not only an incident in the past but an ideal which might influence the future. The nonconformists knew that ever since the reign of Henry VIII there had been a party in the church devoted to the ideal of bring-

ing its organisation and its worship into closer conformity with
the pattern which they discerned in scripture.[1] With these reformers, the nonconformists knew that their affinities were very
close. They had been included in the established church; was it
unreasonable to hope that their successors might also have a place
within it?[2] Was the voice of reform to be stilled for ever? Was
the church now so perfect that it would henceforth be sacrilege to
suggest any changes? In asking such questions, the nonconformists were ignoring the use that the Laudian leaders intended to
make of the victory which they had won. There was something
naïve as well as unrealistic about the way in which some of the
Presbyterians embarked upon the discussions of the new reign.
In 1660 Cornelius Burgess published a book[3] in which he assumed
that the church's life stood in need of reform at almost every
point. Doctrine as well as discipline, worship as well as order
must be re-examined—with the assumption that if found defective
they would be changed. Charles II was annoyed; the church's
doctrine, as he pointed out, had not been called in question, and
such statements were not the way to confirm him in his generous
endeavours. Most of the Puritans were a great deal more moderate, but all of them belonged to the party that believed in change.
They grew weary of reiterating the fact that their desire was a
modified but not a mutilated establishment. They did not object
to episcopacy but to prelacy; they would accept bishops, but
they criticised the pride and power of lord bishops. They were
prepared to use a liturgy, but they hoped that certain features
would be reformed or at least left optional. They knew that a
church must have rites and ceremonies, but they trusted that some
of them might be regarded as permissive.[4] They wished to continue from within the church the movement for reform which
had been a feature of the religious life of England for more than a
century. From the Anglican side there came, in reply, the emphatic declaration that those days had gone for ever.

The search for a satisfactory settlement of the religious issue
was infinitely complicated by the oaths and counter-oaths which
each party had tried to lay upon the other. The seventeenth century believed in the value of compulsory vows; few of those in

which it trusted had a more stormy history than the Solemn League and Covenant. The enthusiasm it aroused among its advocates was fully matched by the bitterness it created among its foes. Since the one side had applied it as a test of loyalty, the other side insisted that it be regarded as a mark of treason. Under certain conditions it is useful to possess an infallible Shibboleth; it helps both to identify opponents and to punish them. The demand that the Covenant be explicitly repudiated was a natural move on the part of the Royalists; it was the symbol of the exactions under which they had smarted and it provided an opportunity for revenge which it was difficult to resist. And yet the requirement that it should be repudiated was more than pure vindictiveness. It may not have been wise, but it was not utterly perverse. Many of the Presbyterians were claiming that the Covenant of necessity would modify the terms of the impending settlement. They were appealing to inferences which might be drawn from its clauses, and insisting that any episcopacy that might be reintroduced must conform to its requirements. To ignore that kind of challenge presupposed a degree of magnanimity which few of the Restoration era Cavaliers even wanted to possess. Moreover, the revived emphasis on unquestioning obedience, fortified by the new cult of the royal martyr, branded the Covenant as the symbol of all the traitorous instincts so freely attributed to Puritanism.

Inevitably, therefore, the Covenant became one of the subjects most fiercely debated in the early days of the Restoration. It was a binding oath, said Zachary Crofton; it was free of the kind of ambiguities and contradictions with which it was charged. The requirements it imposed were just and lawful, and, since its obligations were public as well as personal, it should be maintained.[1] The reply from the episcopal side was issued by John Gauden, an ecclesiastic eager both to atone for his ambiguous attitude during the Interregnum and to establish his claim to high promotion under the monarchy. Gauden claimed that the Covenant had become an object of superstitious veneration and was serving to aggravate a spurious tenderness of conscience. He proved that it was defective in point of law and limited in the authority it could claim; it could validly appeal neither to the Old Testament nor to the New. It was originally designed as a means of reforming episcopacy, not as an instrument for extirpating it, and should be regarded as a step toward re-establishing the historic forms of church government. With great ingenuity, he proved that a very small part of the nation had taken the oath at all, a still smaller number had taken it willingly, and no one was actually bound by its terms.[1]

The debate thus begun raged for many months. White Kennett noted that in the course of the year 1660, Gauden wrote nine works against the Covenant, and Croften never let his attacks go unanswered. Others also joined freely in the debate, and inevitably its bounds were extended to include various related subjects which were simultaneously under discussion. It is not in such works, however, that either the Anglican or the nonconformist position is best exemplified. Gauden, who did not yet foresee the extent of the victory his side would win, was willing to regard the Covenant as a step toward modified episcopacy, but the dominant party in the Church of England made it mandatory that the Covenant should be explicitly and unequivocally repudiated. Crofton, on the other hand, represented an attitude much more self-assured than subsequent events could justify.

By stipulating that all ministers of the Church of England must disavow the Covenant, the Anglican authorities made certain that it would constitute one of the causes of nonconformity. Under ordinary circumstances it would soon have dropped into oblivion; instead, it acquired lasting significance as an important factor in determining the scale of the cleavage which divided English life. More than forty years later, Calamy could point to the Solemn League and Covenant as one of the reasons for the existence of dissent.[2] Baxter, it is true, insisted that there had always been other and far more important reasons why so many ministers had refused to conform. He agreed that the Covenant was unquestionably one cause among others, but it was absurd to suggest that anybody had chosen nonconformity simply because he was required to repudiate the Covenant.[3] Moreover, subsequent legislation raised to the status of distinct issues many of the elements implicit in the Covenant, and its indirect influence can

15-2

be detected in many other areas. To acquiesce in forms and ceremonies, said Clarkson, would be 'perfidiousness toward God';
had they not repudiated all dependence on outward aids when
they took the Covenant?[1] But to the Puritans the seriousness of
the required repudiation lay in the moral implications of the act.
The accredited representatives of the nation, as well as thousands
of individuals, had solemnly taken an oath before God. To say
that the contents of that oath were ill-advised did not remove the
obligations incurred by those who took it. Every reader of the
Bible knew that godly men had always felt themselves most
solemnly bound by any vow which had invoked the name of God.
Nor did the plea that the oath had been reluctantly taken render
its obligations null and void. The Covenant was 'an antecedent
obligation to God' laid upon the nation,[2] and anyone reputably
conversant with seventeenth-century systems of morality knew
that if there was anything lawful in any vow unlawfully imposed,
that lawful part remained in effect. Lightly to repudiate what you
had most solemnly sworn was perjury—in this case perjury against
Almighty God. Could a nation claim divine approval if it began
a new chapter of its history with a deliberate and calculated act of
apostasy? To the Puritans the answer seemed transparently clear.
Consequently many men who had never taken the Covenant and
who had always criticised its terms were deeply shocked at the
demand that it should be repudiated. Often their objection had
very little to do with the contents of the document, and they
were deeply pained when controversialists on the other side
suggested that they clung to it merely because their disloyal
hearts were wedded to its traitorous doctrines. An oath—even
a bad oath—could not lightly be dismissed; to postulate the
contrary was to endanger all the foundations of sound national
morality.

Puritanism was a religious movement which had recently
produced astonishing political results; it was inevitable that nonconformity should be branded with the consequences of past
association. Many an Anglican pamphleteer felt that treason and
disloyalty were the charges that could most convincingly be
levelled against dissenters.[3] Were they not indistinguishable from

their predecessors of 1642? Had they not brought the king to execution, and defiled the land with sacred blood? Those who had once overturned the monarchy would unquestionably attempt to do so again, and the fact that they scrupled at the honoured pattern of church government meant that they must be disaffected to the political forms associated with it. The Puritan's incurable propensity to rebellion was proved by the plots for which (so it was assumed) he was primarily to blame. By an easy progression, many Anglican publicists proceeded from an assumed proof of guilt to a vociferous appeal for punishment; they warned the magistrates of the political perils latent in dissent, and urged that the full penalties of the law be unleashed against all who held such pernicious views. With indignation the nonconformists repudiated these accusations; to do so was the obvious and necessary preliminary to a fuller defence. 'I have been charged', said Matthew Meade, 'with faction and sedition, nay that I preached rebellion and treason is charged upon this sermon, merely because I spoke of sinful compliance with the ceremonies against conscience, though I mentioned not either the King or his government.'[1] Even before the Restoration, the Presbyterians had explicitly repudiated responsibility for the execution of King Charles, and indeed for much else that had been done during the Interregnum. They knew that they had played a large part (a decisive part, as they believed) in paving the way for the king's return. To confuse them with republicans was pushing carelessness to the point of wanton irresponsibility. They knew that the moderates were far the largest single group among the nonconformists. Consequently on every possible occasion they repudiated as a malicious calumny the accusations of treason. They had not murdered the late king; they were not responsible for the plots which were so unduly magnified by rumour; they were completely free from any seditious designs. As Lord Delamere pointed out, the attempts to fasten the execution of King Charles on the nonconformists had never been supported by anything remotely resembling proof; even if convincing evidence had been forthcoming it would have been irrelevant, since the Act of Oblivion had swept away all occasion for such debates.[2]

Yet simple denial of disloyalty was obviously not sufficient. It was necessary to prove that the nonconformist could be (and usually was) as faithful a citizen as any churchman in the land.[1] But this involved a careful definition of terms. Though the political overtones of the Act of Uniformity made it unacceptable, and though the Oxford oath was one which many Puritans could not take, they nevertheless had a political theory which they felt was entirely compatible with good citizenship and which they were perfectly prepared to defend. It was quite true that they refused to accept the sweeping definition of the powers of the magistrate which high-flying Tory churchmen advanced. When Samuel Parker, in his *Discourse Concerning Ecclesiastical Polity*, exalted the king's authority above that of conscience, and made the temporal ruler the final arbiter of all moral issues, the nonconformists immediately protested.[2] There are, they pointed out, crown rights of the Redeemer as well as of the prince. This did not prevent them from professing their fervent loyalty to the king, and in this respect most of them felt that they went as far as (indeed, a good deal farther than) many exponents of Anglican doctrine. But they believed that the power which kings possess is derived entirely from their status. Earthly rulers are officers of God the Creator; from him comes their authority, and to him they are subordinate. As they have no power save from him, they can use what is committed to them only to promote his ends. Most moderate nonconformists repudiated any theory which assumed that power resided in the people. It is God's will, they said, that men should live in an ordered society, and sovereignty and obedience, which are both derivative from that fact, have consequently the authority which belongs to a law of nature.[3]

This does not mean that royal power is absolute. It may not be subject to any higher human authority, but it is always subordinate to the commands of God, and it may be modified by a contractual agreement with the people. In so far as either of these serves as a restriction on the king, it is in the interest of the subject's freedom. Good government promotes the well-being of the people, and liberty is an essential part of the properly ordered life of society.[1] Tyranny on the part of the ruler is as great an evil as insubordination on the part of the citizen.

The nonconformists rejected the demand for unquestioning submission to every requirement of the king's; with equal emphasis they repudiated the caricature which accused them of exalting any whim of conscience above the royal commands. Here, as elsewhere, you could only expect the right answer if you asked the proper question, and the proper question 'must be this, whether the conscience or apprehension of our duty to God, and of his commands, or of the king's commands, should be most prevalent with us for our obedience'. When the king demands obedience, you must ask yourself whether God antecedently commands you to do otherwise. If so, you are to obey God, not the king; if not, you must obey the king. It is an invalid objection to claim that we may be mistaken about God's will; we must do what we believe God demands, and always strive to be delivered from the errors which mislead us. From this it follows that more perfect obedience waits upon constant education of our powers of judgement, and fortunately God had appointed the means whereby we may be trained in understanding. We are to 'hear, read, meditate, pray, forbear the sin that grieveth our guide; cast out corrupt affections, passions and lusts, and lay by carnal interests that would prevent the judgement'. Though slow, progress will be sure, and the humble seeker will learn even the hard lesson of bearing himself wisely when his conscience constrains him to disobey his king.[2]

Such a defence left all zealous Tory partisans completely dissatisfied. They were not impressed when they were reminded that the extreme Erastianism which gave the head of the state unquestioned power over the consciences of men left Christians at the mercy of changes in the religious convictions of their governors, but time brought its own revenges. Belief in passive obedience had been hailed as the characteristic mark of the loyal Anglican and the peculiar glory of his church. When the events of the reign of James II touched that theory with the cold hand of reality, it collapsed, at once and completely. A few rigorous extremists defended, even in exile, the claims of unquestioning obedience, but most Anglicans quietly discarded the whole elaborate system of the divine right of kings. But nonconformist writers were not willing to forget it so fast. For a whole generation they had been abused and reviled because they did not accept it. The pulpits throughout the land had rung with denunciations of their treason because they reserved the right to bring the commands of the king to the bar of conscience. When events had so signally confounded their opponents, it was hard to resist the temptation to point the moral.[1] On the whole it is surprising that they made such restrained use of their opportunity. The political predicament of the Anglicans does not figure very prominently in post-Revolutionary controversy. The new régime, to which the nonconformists were so enthusiastically committed, had been a national not a party achievement; perhaps men felt that it should not be used for partisan purposes. Moreover, the interest of the controversialists rapidly shifted to other subjects, and on the whole the nonconformists were content to make the most of the toleration they had won. But the past was not completely ignored. When the old charges were revived against the nonconformists, they were quick to point out how mistaken in conception and how disastrous in application the cherished Anglican theory had been. When even the apologists of the church produced such lame excuses for their former devotion to passive obedience, surely the worn-out accusations of treason could rest.[2]

The nonconformists might not be seditious, but to many Anglicans they were certainly schismatical. Treason was a cry which any writer could raise; to lay a charge of separation from the true church presupposed far greater learning, and the controversy on this point reached a far higher level. The issue, though always present after 1660, did not immediately attain major proportions. In 1679 Henry Dodwell published a massive volume which proved that *Separation of Churches from Episcopal Government as Practised by the present Nonconformists* was clearly *Schismatical*, but its scope was too great for its effect to be appreciable. A couple of years later, when Stillingfleet issued his sermon on *The Mischief of Separation*, the public reaction was instantaneous and it initiated an intense discussion of the entire problem. Stillingfleet's work was not only brief (in itself an advantage) but was admirably calculated to achieve the maximum effect. In an age when invective often passed for argument, it relied on a calm and reasoned statement of a highly plausible case. Stillingfleet's argument was simple and straightforward. The nonconformists, he pointed out, conceded that the Church of England was a true church of Christ; they admitted that unjustifiable separation was sin, and yet they persisted in what was indistinguishable from sin. If it were permissible for them to attend church and even on occasion to receive communion, how could they justify an attitude which unquestionably weakened the national church? In this they merely advanced the cause of popery; though posing as the bitter enemies of Rome, they were acting as its best friends.[1]

With considerable skill, Stillingfleet turned the nonconformist arguments against the men who used them. Their response was immediate, and many of their ablest advocates came forward to explain and defend their position. They were not slow to point out that for all its apparent plausibility, Stillingfleet's work had left its author open to shrewd attack. He disclaimed a persecuting spirit, but he had preached his sermon not to those who might be turned from their error, but to those who would certainly treat it as an exhortation to apply the persecuting laws.[2] He had used a text which could only serve his purposes when its true meaning had been distorted by very questionable exegesis.[3] And without doubt many of his arguments proved to be dangerously two-edged weapons. Unity was the basic issue which Stillingfleet had raised; there cannot be more perfect agreement, he claimed, till 'men are convinced of the evil and danger of the present separation'. On the contrary, retorted Alsop, union is 'impossible to be attained till men are convinced of the evil and danger of the present impositions'.[4] Nor could the plea for unity be allowed to override spiritual obligations—for instance, loyalty to the truth or concern for men's souls.[5] In any case, could men really be blamed for separation when impositions were laid upon them against which their consciences rebelled?[6] The true schismatic is the man that makes 'communion impossible by his additions or impositions, or runs away from those that will not receive all his supernumeraries'.[1] Nor was the issue nearly as simple as Stilling-fleet made it appear. The nonconformists often went to parish churches, but not to all of them alike, since in some the conditions requisite for growth in grace were lacking. Everyone admitted that there were not enough parish churches to accommodate the people; was it wrong to supplement the insufficient ministrations they afforded? Many nonconformists maintained some kind of contact with the established church, but they were not prepared to concede that it could justly prohibit all other forms of religious association. Nor did they feel that Anglicanism had achieved within itself such a measure of unanimity that it was justified in visiting heavy penalties on those who could not subscribe to all the conditions it imposed.[2]

The attempt to distinguish between lay communion and minis-terial conformity—so central in Stillingfleet's approach—was dismissed as misleading and unreal. In principle, ministers and people were united; any differences between them sprang solely from the fact that Anglican impositions affected them in different ways.[3] To accuse the ministers of hypocrisy on the grounds that they concealed from their followers their genuine convictions and the nature of the situation that prevailed, revealed astonishing ignorance both of the character of nonconformist groups and of the published opinions of nonconformist leaders. The real reasons for separation were entirely different from what Stillingfleet had suggested. The nonconformists remained outside the national church because the requirements imposed upon them afforded no alternative. Until there was some way of resolving their doubts regarding the worship, doctrine, discipline and order of the church, the requirement of the church would continue to ex-clude them. That they desired peace was shown by their willing-ness to go as far as they could; to blame them for not going further was to ignore the simple fact that certain things are justi-fiable as an occasional gesture which would be intolerable as an invariable practice. Meanwhile they would adhere to principles which, as they firmly believed, could stand without fear 'before any bar where scripture and reason, not interest and prejudice, have the chair'. They would insist that particular churches have a right to choose their own pastors, and individual Christians the privilege of selecting their own church. They would affirm that it was 'the duty of every Christian to worship God not only in purity of heart but according to the purity of Gospel administrations', and 'to live in the use of all God's ordinances and commandments'. They would stand by their conviction that 'it is sinful to submit, subscribe or assent to dubious and obscure terms of communion', and in this, as in all other matters, 'it is a safe rule to remember that every Christian is obliged to walk with and in all the ways of God so far as they have attained'.[1]

Stillingfleet assumed that separate churches would not continue if schismatical ministers did not serve them. Even though the Act of Uniformity had created a large body of ministers who were debarred from serving in the parish churches, many Anglican apologists felt that it was perverse and unreasonable for them to persist in preaching. If they could not conform, let them keep silence. The legitimate sphere of ministerial service was the established church, and those who found themselves excluded from it must accept their disability with such grace as they could command. This was a claim which the nonconformists were at some pains to dispute. Baxter, indeed, with almost wearisome monotony reiterated the story of the self-imposed silence which for many years barred him from public preaching, but he was as willing as any man to insist that the nonconformist ministers had a commission which no external events could invalidate. The circumstances of the time emphasised their duty to work as they were able. 'Being deprived', said Calamy, 'in a time when debauchery came in like a flood, they could not abandon their ministry but exercise it as able.'[2] They were appalled at the immense numbers with which the city parishes struggled so inadequately. How could a church cope with a population five or ten or even twenty times as great as the capacity of that church? The urgency of the problem was not wholly created by the Fire of London, but it was certainly aggravated by it. When the people were 'as sheep having no shepherds', the nonconformists refused to believe that their efforts were entirely superfluous. But their conviction did not spring primarily from any external circumstances. To forsake their ministry would be to break their solemn ordination vows. If it was sacrilege to deflect to common uses the material objects set apart for God's service, it was surely a more grievous sin to throw into the discard living souls which had been consecrated to his ministry. Men who willingly had a share in such apostasy became guilty of the doom pronounced on the unfaithful steward, and cast away their expectation of salvation in Christ. They were removing the hand once set to the plough, and giving the people an example of pusillanimous flight. They were failing the charge to preach the gospel, and so they fought against Christ and for his antagonist the devil.

All this meant that there were some activities which even the force of law could not restrain. The call to preach was a mandate which no magistrate could disannul. Whatever earthly rulers might say, a man who was convinced that God had called him to proclaim the truth could not be silent. Moreover, the nonconformists felt that their persistence had been vindicated by the fruit with which God had crowned their efforts. It was no negligible satisfaction to observe that men had been 'turned from ignorance, worldliness, deceiving, lying, sensuality and fleshly lusts, to the serious belief of a world to come, and to love of God and man, and to the joyful hopes of glory and the obedience of Christ, and confidence in his salvation. We take this to be worth our labour and our lives. And would you have us so unthankful to God,... as to cast away our callings? Can you expect all threatenings of men, or the weekly reproach of pamphlet-writers, should make us wish all the sermons unpreached which we have preached, and all the books unwritten which we have written, and all the souls unconverted who have repented?'[1]

As we have already seen, hypocrisy was one of the causes often cited by antagonists for the continuance of nonconformity. The desire for gain was another. Some Anglicans insisted that the ministers would not inform their people of the true state of the matter, for fear the members of their congregations might join the church;[2] others added that the ministers' governing motive was their personal advantage. Separation was their livelihood;

therefore they perpetuated separation.[1] In both cases the nonconformists countered with appeals to plausibility and to experience. The members of their flock were not completely isolated from the rest of the community; even if the ministers wished to keep them in ignorance, they could not do so. But in any case it was unnecessary. Their people came to them because they desired a certain kind of worship. They looked for preaching which would match their sense of need with the full spiritual resources which the unfolding of the scriptures would afford. As long as the nonconformist ministers could satisfy a religious hunger which the parish churches failed to meet, they would have congregations; on no other basis could they either gather their people or hold them.

In the same way, they could counter the charge of avarice by an appeal to facts which were well-known to the whole community. Many of the ejected ministers had forfeited large incomes and had reconciled themselves to a life of poverty and need. Dr Burgess had resigned a living worth a thousand pounds a year, and had become dependent on the generosity of friends.[2] Many of his brethren were glad to 'live on brown bread and water', and great numbers of them 'were cast upon the charity of others for their own and families' subsistence'. Those willing or able to help them were few, while those in need were many; assistance was necessary, but its scope was sorely restricted. And in any case, it was a fixed rule among the dissenters to accept help only from those who offered it gladly.[3] These facts alone were a sufficient answer to accusation of greed. Could a man be charged with self-interest when he cut himself off from every material advantage, and 'lived obscurely amid contempt, on alms, . . . in great poverty'? Was it a mark of covetousness when a man chose a course which forced him into debt and left him in a position where he would 'have nothing to pay house rent, for clothes, bread etc., and to have a wife and many children to pacify, and to live on bread and water, or little more'?[4] Moreover, these were privations which the ejected ministers could easily have escaped. Various alternatives were open to them, all more profitable than ministering to nonconformist groups. In any case, was not this a charge which could readily be reversed? Apart from the anomaly of seeing highly placed ecclesiastics (and pluralists, at that) abuse for their greed men who had forfeited their livelihood, the accusation could much more plausibly be levelled against some who had too readily conformed. Philip Henry commented on the vagaries of fortune when he noticed that an Oxford contemporary (a republican before the Restoration, when Henry was a royalist) had become an ardent conformist after the king's return—when Henry was ejected. There were many, remarked Matthew Meade, who felt that it was 'better to baptise with the cross than to bear the cross....Thus many (it is to be feared) destroy their consciences to keep their places, and conform against their judgements to preserve their profits.' But this, he added sadly, 'is as if a man to save his hat should lose his head, or as if a man should sink the ship to avoid the storm'.[1] The Restoration era was a period in which controversialists seldom hesitated to attribute discreditable motives to their opponents, and neither side wholly resisted the temptation to pass judgement on the other.

The major controversies of the time naturally concerned the issues chiefly responsible for nonconformity. Few questions emerged so promptly, none were debated so bitterly or at such length, as the right ordering of church government and the proper form of church worship. The failure to achieve uniformity was the result of unreconciled differences in these areas.

As soon as the restoration of monarchy appeared inevitable, thoughtful men realised that the question of episcopacy would inevitably arise. Some Puritans strongly opposed any return to ancient forms of church government. This was due in part to bitter memories of Laud's high-handed methods, but not less to strong conviction regarding the scriptural sanction for alternative patterns of church life. But the incorrigibles were a minority. Most of the moderates admitted that episcopacy of some kind would be restored, but they hoped that entrenched abuses would not also be considered sacrosanct.[2] In the first days of the Restoration, even strong Cavaliers reported that many people hoped that in its extremer forms episcopal power would never return, and

Pepys, nervously observing the signs of restiveness around him, noted that the arrogant attitude of the bishops was threatening the stability of the system so recently restored.[1] A plea for a modified form of episcopacy seemed reasonable enough to Presbyterian leaders. At first it appeared that some of the Anglicans would meet them half-way. Stillingfleet admitted that the real issue was not what form of church government could claim the fullest measure of apostolic authority, but on what pattern all could now unite. It seemed to him important to preserve the benefits of congregational and presbyterial systems while recovering the advantages of episcopacy.[2] In the spate of pamphlets which Gauden issued in the months immediately after the Restoration, he assumed both that bishops would return and that their former powers would be curtailed.[3] Even Herbert Thorndike conceded that considerable changes might profitably be made.

Developments soon showed that the Anglicans who had been in exile were far less flexible than those who had stayed at home; moreover, they possessed the power to give effect to their more exacting demands. But for the moment, the Puritans could be pardoned for pressing their case. The permanently indecisive battles about New Testament texts were revived. Were Timothy and Titus bishops in the modern sense? Was the 'angel of the church of Ephesus' a bishop or a presbyter?—and in any case were the two offices originally distinguishable?[4] The crux of the whole matter, for many Puritans, lay in the fact that monarchical episcopacy had lost all resemblance to the primitive office of a bishop. As power and pomp had grown, the original functions had been lost or overlaid with irrelevant and worldly accretions. In becoming administrative, the bishop's task had ceased to be pastoral; as it had acquired worldly prestige it had forfeited spiritual effectiveness.[5]

Inevitably, therefore, a debate which started with theoretical questions passed to the consideration of practical problems. The Long Parliament had decided that bishops should not sit in parliament; after the Restoration that particular issue was not seriously in doubt, but it was hotly debated none the less. Of greater concern to most Puritans was the actual working of that form of episcopacy which had been characteristic of the English church. They felt that the dioceses were impossibly large. If the bishop were really to be the spiritual father of his people and the shepherd of their souls, he must establish some kind of personal contact with them. Even a conscientious bishop, with a high concept of the duty of residence, could have a very limited knowledge of the problems which beset individual parishes; he could give little help to his clergy or their people. To meet the difficulty the Puritans advocated the appointment of suffragans in numbers sufficient to make episcopal oversight a reality. They also complained that too much power was concentrated in one man's hands. Provision should be made, they claimed, for associating other ministers with the bishop, both in discussing ecclesiastical policy and in performing episcopal acts. Synods should be established, and presbyters should participate in ordinations. It was particularly irksome to the Puritans that though the bishops did so little to allow presbyters any share in the jurisdiction of the church, they delegated extensive powers to laymen. The position occupied by lay chancellors, and the functions they discharged, raised questions of the greatest gravity. The exercise of ecclesiastical discipline should be a ministerial function; presbyters were excluded from any effective part in it, and areas of crucial importance were controlled by laymen. The moderate Puritans repeatedly declared their willingness to accept a modified episcopacy. It was prelacy they opposed. They wanted to have bishops who would be preachers and pastors, not courtiers and peers; who would have a manageable sphere of responsibility, and would accept it as their primary task; who would find a place for presbyters in the government of the church and who would delegate disciplinary powers to ministers rather than to laymen. They felt that in Archbishop Ussher's 'reduction' they had a model to which they could safely appeal, since it carried the aura of episcopal authorship.[1] In the Restoration period any concessions to the Puritan party were remote because the bishops regarded any kind of changes as neither necessary nor desirable. The passage of time, however, has brought many of the modifications for which the Puritans asked in vain.

Inseparably connected with the question of episcopacy was the issue of reordination. A great many of the younger ministers had been ordained by presbyters. With many of them this had doubtless corresponded with their own convictions, but in any case for years past no alternative had been readily available. The re-established church insisted that only those with episcopal ordination could minister within its bounds. But could those who had already been ordained submit to a repetition of the same solemn rite? Some Anglicans suggested that the reordination could be treated as conditional; if you had not previously been ordained, you were now ordained.[1] To the Puritans this seemed a disingenuous proceeding, since neither party felt the uncertainty which the condition implied. Nor did the theory of 'an accumulation' of ministerial authority commend itself. The Puritans did not believe that their ministry was restricted in scope, and the arguments advanced by the Anglicans seemed to them thinly to disguise a belief that ordination by presbyters was not ordination at all.[2] The very fact that the bishops used the same service by which they set aside laymen proved that they were disregarding previous ordination.[3] And yet history provided no parallel to, and no authority for, such an attitude. To submit to reordination was to call in question the validity of the ordination you had already received, and so to cast aspersions on all the ministerial functions you had hitherto performed. Yet to doubt the validity of orders which God had blessed seemed a disloyalty bordering on blasphemy.[4] An ordinance of God could not be so slightly regarded, and in any case, the bare suggestion of reordination involved elements of fundamental incongruity; an unrepeatable act cannot be repeated. The inherent contradictions became clear as soon as the crucial terms were defined with reasonable care. Ordination, said Baxter, is 'that moral action by which a man is made a minister of Christ, which is, his solemn contract with Christ, expressed by his consent and by the ordainers' investing action. This is it which we mean in the controversy, which may not be done twice.'[5] The more carefully the Puritans studied the matter, the more surely were they driven to the conclusion that to submit to a second ordination was to admit either that they had not been sincere in their original intention or that the ministry they had exercised was radically defective and insufficient. In this implied repudiation they could not possibly participate. It was also necessary to consider the probable reaction of the public; to submit to a second ordination would seem an acknowledgement of prior insufficiency, a confession of an uneasy conscience, or a sign of sheer hypocrisy. Increasingly their proper course of action became apparent. 'My prayer', said Giles Firmin, 'is, Lord lead me not into temptation. But if it comes to this, that I must renounce my presbyterial ordination and be ordained by a bishop or I must be silenced, I shall desire grace from the Lord and resolve to lay down my ministry before I will my ordination.'[1]

On questions of worship the Puritans were by no means unanimous. They were all opposed to the Book of Common Prayer, but they objected to it for various reasons and in differing degree. To the more extreme sects, a liturgy of any kind was intolerable. No man, whether magistrate or minister, had the right to devise a form of worship and then impose it on others. No one had the infallibility of spirit necessary to produce a mandatory prayer book, and no blessing can be expected from the use of liturgies not commanded by God. For the more radical Puritan the crux of the matter was the issue of imposition. The free expression of man's devotional spirit was checked by the obligatory use of forms not authorised by scripture, and consequently growth in grace was seriously hindered. Human additions to the kind of worship authorised by the Bible seemed to many earnest men a serious obstacle to conformity; the weak were scandalised, the gospel was corrupted, powerful preaching was obstructed, and the honour of God was challenged. Moreover, 'ceremonies and human inventions in the worship of God' were popish in character, and reliance upon them opened the door by which the mass might finally enter.[2]

Most of the moderate Presbyterians were prepared to concede that the Book of Common Prayer would certainly be reintroduced. They were willing to admit that set forms might lawfully be used, but they believed that relatively slight changes would eliminate causes of offence, and they desired some opportunity for free prayer.[1] 'Pulpit prayers', and in particular a long prayer before the sermon, had become the most characteristic feature of Puritan worship. Anglicans vehemently attacked the practice, but permission to continue it was a concession earnestly desired by the moderates. Though they would not have chosen liturgical worship by preference, many who became nonconformists were prepared to accept the principle of set prayers as the price of peace; they were not necessarily opposed to 'a uniform pattern of appointed worship'. Baxter himself prepared, single-handed and with amazing rapidity, a complete liturgy. If some things might be regarded as permissive rather than obligatory, the features which gave offence need not create division.[2]

In any case the Puritans could see no reason why certain details in the Book of Common Prayer might not be altered. A careful revision, so far from detracting from the effectiveness of the liturgy, would greatly enhance it. They felt that the lectionary could be improved; certain unprofitable passages were prescribed, yet great chapters were never read. Parts of the Apocrypha were included—even 'ridiculous legends' like *Bel and the Dragon*—and the Puritans were satisfied that in their place neglected chapters of the Bible could be used with far greater profit to the people. The translation in which the Psalms were read seemed less exact as well as less felicitous than the King James version. Minor points in the phrasing of the prescribed forms raised theological questions which the seventeenth century could not ignore. The Puritans felt that in the service for the burial of the dead, the confident anticipation that the deceased was numbered among the saved meant, in certain cases, either a wilful blindness to basic moral facts or a usurpation of the divine right to judge men's conduct. The doctrine of baptismal regeneration implicit in certain phrases in the Prayer Book gave wide offence, while the unhesitating statement regarding the position of infants who died before baptism went far beyond the reverent hesitancy which the Puritans thought appropriate when confronted both with our ignorance and with the solemn mysteries of election.[3]

Objections to details were innumerable, and varied in some degree from writer to writer, but certain points became matters of prolonged debate.[1] Kneeling to receive the sacrament had always given offence to the Puritans. They associated it with superstitious and Romish worship of the host. It seemed to them an unnatural attitude, not necessarily related to the inherent character of the rite, and lacking the authority of scriptural warrant. When our Lord instituted his supper, did he not sit at table with his disciples; and is there any example that we could more fittingly follow?[2] Some, like Baxter, felt that the gesture itself was not a serious barrier, but they strongly objected when it was treated by the Anglicans as a point of major importance. Salvation was not determined by the physical attitude a man adopted when he received the sacrament; even if it could be proved that he was wrong, should he on that account be excommunicated, and driven from the fellowship of the church?[3]

Equally contentious was the sign of the cross in baptism. Many ministers refused to use it; many of their people disliked participating in a sacrament of which it formed a part.[4] The ever-present fear of popery was in large measure responsible. Distrust of Rome was so deep-seated that any echoes of its forms of thought or ways of worship were immediately detected and were regarded with inveterate suspicion. The Puritans did not object to the cross under all conditions, but they felt that it was not an appropriate symbol to use in baptism. It lacked both scriptural warrant and inherent suitability.[5] It seemed to suggest a meaning which the Puritans did not believe was properly derived from the nature of the rite itself. They were satisfied that it fulfilled all five conditions present when men falsely set up a covenant of grace.[6] Moreover, it added to an ordinance of God an element of purely human invention; 'we are neither to add nor diminish in the matter of God's worship, and particularly this holds good in the sacraments of the Gospel, which in their own nature are signs and ceremonies'.[7] But even granting that those who objected had exaggerated the dangers which lurked in the sign of the cross in baptism, did the penalties imposed upon them bear any reasonable relation to their offence? Was it right to deny baptism to children because the parents suffered from excessive scruples?[8]

For many earnest people the place assigned to godparents in

baptism created further difficulties. They felt that the practice
reduced a solemn religious sacrament to the level of a tawdry
farce. The very poor often hired a beggar to act as godparent, and
the customary fee (as Baxter tells us) was half a crown. Those
higher in the social scale would seek out a friend slightly richer
than themselves in the hope that the implied compliment would
prompt a generous gift. No one, however, accepted his responsibilities as a godparent in the literal sense, and it would
have been incongruous if he had. It was unreasonable for anyone
except the parents to take the vows which only the parents themselves could discharge. Godparents merely disguised the true
nature of the sacrament and concealed the obligations which it
entailed.[1] And yet those who claimed the privilege of accepting
their religious duty to their children were subject to the heavy
penalties of excommunication.

Since the early days of the Reformation the Puritans had
strongly resisted the use of the surplice, and with the Restoration
the debate was revived. The Puritans disliked its associations: it
seemed a popish garment. But the defence advanced by Anglicans
did not strike them as particularly convincing. It was all very
well to quote 1 Cor. xiv. 40, but decency and order by themselves did not postulate a garment of any particular shape or
colour. White linen was not even decent when it was dirty (as it
often was). On the other hand, a minister's customary habit
was neither incongruous nor unsuitable, and to dismiss it as
'profane' was to admit a dangerous distinction into the religious
life, and divide sacred things from common ones.[2] Similarly,
bowing toward the altar and bowing at the name of Jesus—
aspects of worship which the Puritans attacked—did not seem to
them decent and reverent gestures but dangerous relics of super-
stition. The frequent repetitions of the Lord's Prayer and of the
Gloria were also grounds of protest. So was the observation of
man-made holidays. Special festivals could appeal neither to the
practice of antiquity nor to the sanction of scripture. God had
appointed one particular day in the week on which we should
thankfully remember his mercies, and special occasions, so far
from promoting the cause of religion, militated against it. They

distracted men's minds from the things on which they ought to meditate and encouraged them in debauchery instead.[1]

Within a couple of years of the Restoration it became apparent that the Anglicans would not grant concessions and that the Puritan could not conform. This reduced the intensity of the debate on many of the issues, but it certainly did not terminate the controversies. The reasons for nonconformity continued to be stated; those who remained outside the church defended their position and their opponents constantly attacked it. But the situation which developed gave rise to a prolonged discussion of the issue which it thrust more and more insistently on the attention of thoughtful men. What standing in the community could be claimed by those whom conscience had forced into nonconformity? Had they any rights, and could they even be tolerated? Clearly the answer implicit in the penal legislation was *No*. But this was a position impossible for its victims to accept and increasingly difficult for its advocates to defend. Comprehension was sometimes urged and as often opposed, but throughout the period toleration was the solution most carefully canvassed. For nearly a generation the question was examined from every possible angle. There were many champions of an utterly inflexible position. Some of them based their arguments on theory, some on purely practical considerations. Toleration never had been feasible, they said, and it never would be. There was no lack of controversialists who were content with insisting that since the Puritans had formerly persecuted Anglicans, the Anglicans were now justified in persecuting Puritans. From the nonconformist side the rights of conscience were advocated in many forms and with great earnestness and ingenuity. As the years passed and the climate of opinion changed, a new type of champion emerged. The growing latitudinarianism made extremes seem indefensible, and a cooler spirit deprecated the heats of violent controversy. Practical considerations of trade and prosperity outweighed theoretical arguments hammered out in syllogistic form. The rational and empirical spirit of the eighteenth century was beginning to emerge, and Locke's letters on toleration, which in a sense ended the debate, were merely the most influential of a series of writings which aimed at creating a new approach to differences in religion.

The passing of the Toleration Act did not put an end to controversy, though it changed its character. Anglicans still attacked the nonconformists, who in turn replied in kind. The arguments of Hoadly and Ollyffe called forth the answers of Calamy and Peirce, and there was still a good deal of incidental abuse of each side by the other. But at least the nonconformists' right to a distinct legal existence had been recognised and consequently the form in which many of the issues had formerly been debated was no longer relevant. Controversy could not be treated as an adjunct to persecution; it might still be desirable to persuade the nonconformist to come back, but it was impossible to punish him if he refused to do so. You might abuse him for his obstinacy, but you could not accuse him of treasonable designs. Indeed, the dissenter suddenly found himself less vulnerable to the charge of seditious intent than many of the Anglicans who had so lately accused him of disloyalty to the king. In the altered atmosphere of the age of reason, controversy lost much of its unbridled violence. Moreover, it tended to cut across denominational lines rather than follow them. The Trinitarian debate might chiefly involve Anglicans, but it did not leave the dissenters untouched, and both alike were involved in the internal tensions introduced by Deism and Socinianism. As nonconformity gradually retired into that aloofness which, for more than a century, kept it withdrawn from the main currents of national life, it ceased to be the most eligible target for attack. It might still seem an object of contempt and so merit a passing rebuff, but it was not one of the issues in the forefront of the nation's intellectual life. The 'battle of the books' did not cease, but it was fought in a different spirit, with different weapons and for different ends.

CHAPTER IX

ON THE THRESHOLD OF TOLERATION

FOR a generation—from the end of the exile of Charles II till the beginning of the exile of his brother—the persecution of nonconformists was the official policy of England's rulers.[1] On the morrow of the Restoration the Puritans began to discover that they had little protection against the malice of their foes. Royalists who were eager for revenge felt justified in ignoring the conciliatory statements which the king found it expedient to make. Legislation against nonconformity was still on the statute books; the local authorities busied themselves enforcing it. In due course, new laws—the various stages of the 'Clarendon Code'—provided an instrument of repression so flexible in character and so inclusive in scope that those who persisted in dissent had little prospect of escape. The official policy, it is true, was not consistently applied. There were intervals when nonconformists enjoyed comparative security and there were districts where they were relatively undisturbed. When every allowance has been made, however, the fact remains that persecution pressed with cruel weight upon its victims. Though not enforced with sufficient ruthlessness to achieve its avowed objectives, it caused incalculable suffering to thousands of earnest men and women. What, we may ask, were the results of persecution, and what effect did it have on those who were compelled to endure it?

Events had clearly shown the ineffectiveness of repression. For centuries it had been assumed that men could be coerced into accepting correct beliefs. Latterly reflection had begun to undermine the comforting assurance that convictions could be controlled, but many people were still persuaded that uniformity of religious practice was a desirable minimum and could successfully be enforced. In England the Restoration experiment was the last serious attempt to produce religious uniformity by means of persecution. It was at best a half-hearted and intermittent effort. It is futile, said the critics, to use force for such a purpose, and they could fortify their arguments by an appeal to the lessons of experience. When Charles II issued his second Declaration of Indulgence in 1672, he pointed to 'the many and frequent ways of coercion that we have used for reducing all erring and dissenting persons, and for composing the unhappy differences in religion' which prevailed among the people, but it was 'evident', he continued, 'by the sad experience of twelve years, that there [was] very little fruit of all those forcible courses'.[1] As the period drew to a close, the ineffectiveness of persecution compelled all thoughtful men to re-examine the theoretical justification of repression, and the chief intellectual tendencies of the age predisposed them to find it insufficient. Latitudinarianism and the authority of the new science, the growing cult of reason and the scepticism which was beginning to chasten every kind of confident fanaticism made men more willing to question their own assumptions and consequently more hesitant to punish those of their fellow-men. It was not an accident that an era which opened with the Act of Uniformity ended with the Act of Toleration.

By 1688 it was clear that no useful purpose could be served by continuing the attempt to stamp out nonconformity. What was far from certain was the kind of relationship that would prevail between the two sections of the community—the majority that belonged to the established church and the minority that dissented from it. The closing months of James II's reign had created a new situation. Anglican and nonconformist alike realised that the king had tried to use each in turn in order to destroy the other. Lord Halifax, in the brilliant and persuasive pages of his *Letter to a Dissenter*, had warned the nonconformists of the peril of harbouring malice against the Anglicans, and had assured them that in the future the established church would be governed by a spirit wholly different from that which had induced it to resort to persecution. At a moment when they faced unquestioned peril, both sides had realised that Protestant solidarity was their only safeguard against the popish designs of James II. Generous promises

249

had been made, and corresponding hopes had been awakened. Would they be fulfilled?

There was no doubt that toleration, in some form, would be conceded. On that score the leaders of the Church of England (lay and clerical alike) had committed themselves so irrevocably that there was no room for retraction. Moreover, the political character of the Revolution made any other solution impossible. What had been achieved through the co-operation of both the great parties could not be celebrated by persecuting the supporters of either. When Nottingham introduced the Toleration Act, there was consequently little danger that it would be rejected.[1] Its terms, it is true, were not unduly generous. It did not repeal the persecuting acts; it merely suspended their operation in agreed cases. Nonconformists who would subscribe to the doctrinal articles of the Church of England and who would take the requisite oaths and engagements, might worship freely in places set apart for that purpose, provided they secured a licence and left the doors unlocked.[2] It was, as Macaulay pointed out, an illogical compromise, yet it proved to be a useful one.[3] Like most compromises, the Toleration Act left both sides dissatisfied. Many nonconformists were frankly disappointed.[4] Before long Anglicans were complaining that it not only encouraged dissent but also shielded indifference and debauchery.[5]

The promises which the popish peril had prompted certain leading Anglicans to make implied changes far more drastic than those effected by a measure so cautious as the Toleration Act. If it was dangerous for Protestants to be divided, steps should be taken to reunite them. Comprehension, so often advocated and so often rejected in the past, again became a living issue. But no sooner was the Revolution an accomplished fact than the ardour of many of the enthusiasts began to cool. High churchmen were quick to notice and to resent any indications that a Calvinist king might be disposed to encourage those who shared his views. Danby warned William that too generous an attitude to dissenters would forfeit the support of men whom the new régime could not afford to alienate.[6] The king's attempts to remove the barriers which excluded nonconformists from public service were decisively defeated.[1] There seemed little likelihood, therefore, that the promised measure to comprehend dissenters within the Church of England would ever be passed. It is true that one of Sancroft's last official acts was to draft a bill for this purpose, but the reaction against the recent conciliatory mood had already set in so strongly among the Tories that anything implying change or compromise was certain to be blocked.[2] When the Comprehension Bill was introduced into parliament, it was fiercely attacked and feebly defended; and when Burnet and Tillotson agreed that the question should be referred to Convocation, its fate was sealed. Many prominent Anglicans were genuinely disappointed; so were many of the leading nonconformists. But some of the dissenters shed no tears over the collapse of the suggested measure; they did not feel that a glorious opportunity had been lost. Members of the younger generation shared neither the experiences nor the hopes of older men like Baxter, Bates and Howe. They had grown reconciled to the prospect of a separate existence; the futility of the repeated efforts to secure comprehension left them indignant and exasperated. They felt that in recent months they had been manœuvred into a position at once indefensible and ignominious. But whatever their attitude to the main issue, all nonconformists bitterly resented the insinuation that they were to blame for the collapse of the scheme, and that consequently no apologies need be offered for promises which had been freely made but which would never be honoured.

Exclusion from the national church involved exclusion from many other phases of the national life. In the future nonconformists might be permitted to worship God as they chose, but (if their opponents had their way) they would not be free to serve the king at all. As far as possible they would be excluded from all positions of responsibility and trust. They would be prevented from sending their sons to the universities. They would have little share in the cultural life of the country. Increasingly they would find themselves relegated to a backwater of English life. From certain areas they could not effectively be debarred. Scientific investigation and mechanical invention were neither highly esteemed nor fully organised. Where the initiative of the individual counted for so much, the nonconformists could not readily be excluded, and in the years to come they would play a distinguished role. For the most part, however, the Revolution settlement accentuated forces already at work; though dissent was not subject to persecution, it became a body educationally handicapped and socially proscribed.

Persecution had affected relationships between nonconformist bodies, but it had pointed to no permanent solution of existing differences. Many of the smaller and more exotic sects had dwindled in size and seemed certain to disappear. The Quakers had sturdily maintained both their distinctive witness and their aloofness from all other groups. In spite of fierce repression, they had strengthened their internal organisation, and had achieved a measure of cohesion greater than anything they had known in earlier days.

Under the pressure of their common sufferings, the two largest groups of nonconformists—the Presbyterians and the Independents—had drawn closer together. The differences which had seemed so important during the Interregnum had dwindled into comparative insignificance. Persecution had increasingly compelled both parties to conform to a common pattern. Baxter himself pointed out the inexactness of the term 'Presbyterian'. To his contemporaries it conveyed a meaning similar to that of 'Puritan' in an earlier generation; it indicated a person seriously concerned about godliness and dissatisfied with the degree of reformation achieved in the national church.[1] Few of those who bore the name seriously hoped that the 'classical' system of church government would be introduced in England. There is little evidence that they even tried to rule their congregations with the help of lay elders. Moreover, persecution destroyed any chance of achieving any system of national church government. Circumstances compelled the Presbyterians to acquiesce in a practical congregationalism, and their corporate life differed little, if at all, from that of the Independents. Neighbouring congregations of differing persuasions found it easy to co-operate, and when conditions made the step appear advisable, they had no difficulty in uniting. Ministers as well as members passed easily from one group to the other, and designations were so inexactly used that a man could be described in one document as a Presbyterian and in another as an Independent.

When differences appeared so inconsequential, it was widely assumed that greater freedom would inevitably lead to more cordial relations. This, as a matter of fact, was the immediate result of toleration. Amid great rejoicing, the 'Happy Union' was consummated. This scheme for closer co-operation concerned, in the first instance, the ministers of both denominations in the immediate neighbourhood of London, but its example was widely followed throughout the country. The purpose of the Union was to promote the orderly government of congregations that could not conform; to eliminate anything in the way of terminology or practice that recalled former differences, and to put an end to all controversies among brethren. An immediate and practical consequence of the Happy Union was the creation of the Common Fund. A great deal of information was collected concerning needy ministers and their problems; contributions were solicited from well-wishers, and then assistance was given to those in special distress.[1]

The experiment in unity was short-lived. Within a few months controversies had broken out which destroyed the Happy Union and broke up the Common Fund. The Rev. Richard Davis of Northwell, Northants, provided the pretext for the initial dispute. He was a man of ardent temperament and of indefatigible missionary zeal. His methods of providing pastoral oversight for the scattered flock he had gathered caused some uneasiness, but it was his theological opinions which precipitated the controversy known by his name. Though not a profound thinker, nor even a man with the advantage of formal theological training, Davis did not hesitate to make pronouncements on intricate and disputed points of doctrine. After careful consideration, the London ministers concluded that he had overstepped the line which separated orthodoxy from Antinomianism, and rebuked him accordingly. The resultant controversy was bitter and prolonged. The differences which divided the moderate Calvinists from the high Calvinists were brought into sharp relief. Each party showed itself acutely sensitive to the dangers which lurked in the position of the other. Cleavages appeared which were deepened by time, and which ultimately carried the contestants far apart.

The controversy about the opinions of the Rev. Richard Davis divided the two denominations; the controversy about the writings of the late Dr Crisp effectually kept them apart. In the latter case, an apparently trivial matter touched off a catastrophic explosion. Dr Crisp had long been dead; a new edition of his works contained some hitherto unpublished items; were these really authentic? The dispute ranged far afield from the question which provoked it. Abstruse doctrines and problems of behaviour were fiercely debated. For the better part of a decade, relationships within nonconformity were embittered. A spate of intemperate and unprofitable works poured from the presses. The protagonists only forsook their wrangling about intricacies of doctrine in order to indulge in virulent personal abuse. This singularly sterile controversy served to emphasise still further the divisions within nonconformity. The Presbyterians were more moderate Calvinists than the Independents, and were aghast at the extravagant views which could apparently find shelter under the aegis of the strictest school of Calvinism. The Independents, on the other hand, while stoutly maintaining that they did not succumb to the temptations of Antinomianism, were so fearful of anything remotely reminiscent of Arminianism that they were inclined to treat indulgently the wilder excesses of the more rabid Calvinists. They felt that to make concessions at any point was certain to open the door to the insidious contamination of Socinianism.

The controversies induced by freedom were thus domestic quarrels within the household of Calvinism. Except to experts and partisans, the points so fiercely debated seemed hardly of sufficient importance to keep brethren apart. Yet the ten years of controversy did more than merely destroy all co-operative enterprises; they also proved that as yet nonconformists could agree among themselves only when external pressures compelled them to do so. The bitter years of Restoration persecution had persuaded them to sink their differences. Before long, when Queen Anne's reign revived old dangers in a new guise, the dissenters would again be driven into closer alliance. But meanwhile, in the free and favourable atmosphere of the days of William and Mary, they could indulge, with comparative safety, their passion for theological disputes. Squabbles of this kind did not present an edifying spectacle. It was little consolation to observe that the Church of England was simultaneously torn asunder by controversies that were equally ferocious. This merely emphasised the particularly wanton way in which the closing decade of the seventeenth century dissipated the spiritual resources which earlier generations had so painfully accumulated. A great age closed amid disputes which not merely denied the spirit of charity but were devoid even of any semblance of dignity.

It is not easy to assess the degree of vitality with which the nonconformists faced the new era. Persecution had tried them sorely, but it had certainly not left them crushed or even dispirited. With high hope they hailed the period of wider liberty, and immediately began to make plans for the freer life which was opening before them.[1] With an astonishing outburst of activity they proceeded to make the most of their opportunities. Everywhere new congregations were organised and new meeting-houses were built to accommodate them. Up to a point, this was natural and inevitable. Many a struggling group which under persecution had barely managed to survive now looked ahead with confidence; new conditions made it safe to give its life a constituted form, and it seemed feasible to take the trouble and meet the expense of erecting a building. But the movement which was thus inaugurated was more than merely a matter of making good lost opportunities. A new vitality surged through nonconformity. New causes sprang up where none had previously existed; contributions of money flowed in on a scale hitherto unknown, and hopeful young men began to offer themselves for the ministry. All over the country, the simple and austere meeting-houses so characteristic of that period of nonconformity began to spring up. The plain oblong room, with the pulpit overlooking the communion table and facing the simple box pews, often had a quiet dignity which at once reflected a Puritan heritage and anticipated the idiom of eighteenth-century architecture. Meanwhile, a new self-assurance matched the sign of outward progress. Critics complained bitterly of the confidence—the arrogance, they called it—which the nonconformists were manifesting. In many a corporation, election candidates found that it ill-behoved them to alienate the dissenters; without their support success might well be uncertain. Complacency, remarked Howe, was the sin to which the nonconformists were now chiefly exposed.[1]

But this was only half the story. Disconcerting symptoms began to multiply. What profit was there in all this material progress if the heart of nonconformity was dead within? The witness of earnest men is not always trustworthy; they measure the faults of their contemporaries by an ideal standard, not by a careful comparison with what has actually hitherto existed. Nevertheless, there seems little reason to doubt that those who now complained did so with good cause. Even before his death, John Owen had noted the prevalent signs of spiritual decay. He observed that the distinctive Puritan convictions were held with a tepid propriety that compared unfavourably with the enthusiasm of the days of old.[2] He was persuaded that there were 'great and woful decays in churches, in church members, in professors of all sorts, and in the gradual withdrawing of God from among us all on that account'. Many Christians, he explained, found it 'hard to keep up their former pitch'. An open want of love was manifest, as well as little delight or diligence in gospel worship. A worldly attitude was producing lethargy in the church; 'dead preachers' stood before 'dead hearers'.[3]

As time went on, complaints of this kind multiplied. Religion was 'upon its last legs'. Principles of all kinds were more laxly held; those who had once been keen republicans were now merely indifferent atheists. Religious worship was generally neglected, while drunkenness and immorality emphasised the extent of the moral collapse which was taking place.[4] An increase in debauchery, said Baxter, went hand in hand with an increase in heresy.[5] The outlook seemed dark, and nonconformists often described it in the most sombre terms. Religious enthusiasm was declining; weakness and degeneracy were now the marks of dissent.[6] For years the nonconformists had sought to induce a moderate attitude in their opponents; they had merely succeeded in creating a Laodicean spirit among themselves.[1] The great leaders of the first generation were disappearing from the scene, and their loss was sorely felt. Their successors might be very worthy men, but to many an anxious observer they seemed eminent neither for fervour nor for power.[2]

A less intense religious spirit was naturally reflected in a laxer corporate life. There was no conscious slackening of discipline, but alike in individual congregations and within the various denominations a relaxed sense of spiritual direction resulted in a life less amenable to religious control. When dissension broke out in a congregation, the constraints of brotherly love operated more feebly than in the days of old. Ill-will smouldered without the intensity which confers dignity, yet with a sullen persistence that defied attempts at mediation.[3] In more than one denomination a cooler faith connived at doctrinal aberrations which an earlier generation would have hotly condemned. The Baptists were divided about the Calvinism which had originally been their common faith, and at least one influential leader began to suggest deviations in Christology which created concern but which the denomination did not know how to control.[4] Within other groups as well the survivors of an earlier day viewed with dismay the speculative doctrines which the bolder spirits of the new age were tentatively advocating.[5] These anxious protests were more than an echo of the nervousness to which old men are prone; those who complained were calling attention to the tides which were sweeping Puritanism away from its ancient moorings. The eighteenth century had not yet dawned, but the seventeenth century, with its firm beliefs and its strong affirmations, was rapidly passing away.

It is therefore clear that though the policy of persecution had failed to achieve its primary purpose, it had nevertheless had far-reaching results. It had not exterminated nonconformity; it had not even forestalled a remarkable outward resurgence, but it had severely strained its inner resources. The old resiliency of spirit had disappeared. A buoyant certainty no longer fortified the dissenters against the corroding influences of a new age. Outward signs of vitality were not matched by a spiritual vigour sufficient to offset the seductions of the coming era. The nonconformists stood on the threshold of a period in which they would need wisdom as well as strength. The demands of the new age were perhaps greater than the resources available to meet them. As the dissenters felt their way forward, they discovered by trial and error the place in the nation's life which they could thenceforth expect to occupy. In the process it became apparent that the ardours of earlier Puritanism had spent themselves; the more subdued proprieties of eighteenth-century dissent gradually took their place. The twilight of Puritanism did not give way to darkness, but it was clearly the prelude to a more prosaic day.

ABBREVIATIONS USED IN THE NOTES

A.H.R.   *American Historical Review.*

Besse   *A Collection of the Sufferings of the People called Quakers,* by Joseph Besse.

Broadmead Records   *The Records of a Church of Christ Meeting in Broadmead, Bristol, A.D. 1640 to A.D. 1688,* by Edward Terrill. Ed. Nathaniel Haycroft.

C.H.E.L.   *Cambridge History of English Literature.*

C.J.   *Journals of the House of Commons.*

C.M.H.   *Cambridge Modern History.*

Cal.Clar.S.P.   *Calendar of Clarendon State Papers.*

Cal. Rev.   *Calamy Revised,* by A. G. Matthews.

Cal.S.P.Dom.   *Calendar of State Papers, Domestic.*

Cal.S.P.Ven.   *Calendar of State Papers, Venetian.*

Calamy, *Abridgment*   *An Abridgment of Mr Baxter's History of his Life and Times,* by E. Calamy.

Calamy, *Account*   *An Account of the Ministers...who were Ejected or Silenced,* by E. Calamy.

Calamy, *Continuation*   *A Continuation of the Account of the Ministers...who were Ejected or Silenced,* by E. Calamy.

Clar.S.P.   *Clarendon State Papers.*

Chaldler, *Parliamentary Debates*   *The History and Proceedings of the House of Commons* and *The History and Proceedings of the House of Lords from the Restoration to the Present time.*

Cobbett, *Parl. Hist.*   *Cobbett's Parliamentary History of England.*

D.N.B.   *Dictionary of National Biography.*

E.H.R.   *English Historical Review.*

E.R.E.   *Encyclopaedia of Religion and Ethics.*

Gould, *Documents*   *Documents Relating to the Settlement of the Church of England by the Act of Uniformity of 1662.*

Grey, *Debates*   *Debates of the House of Commons,* by Anchitel Grey. 10 vols.

Hist.MSS.C.R.   *Reports of the Historical Manuscripts Commission.*

L.J. Journals of the House of Lords.

Nonconf. Mem.   *The Nonconformists' Memorial,* by S. Palmer.

Parl. Hist.   *The Parliamentary or Constitutional History of England.*

Rel. Bax.   *Reliquiae Baxterianae,* by Richard Baxter.

S.P.Dom.   *State Papers Domestic.*

Thurloe.   *A Collection of the State Papers of John Thurloe, Esq.*

Turner, *Original Records*   *Original Records of Nonconformity under Persecution and Indulgence.* Ed. G. Lyon Turner.

NOTES

PAGE 3

1 *The Life of Adam Martindale*, p. 133; *Rel. Bax.* pt. I, p. 71; pt. II, p. 214.
2 Heywood, (*Life*), vol. I, p. 74.

PAGE 4

1 Cobbett, *Parl. Hist.* vol. IV, pp. 105 ff.; Clarendon, *Life and Continuation*, vol. I, pp. 398 ff.
2 For the trial of the regicides, see *State Trials*, vol. V, pp. 128 ff. and vol. VI, pp. 1 ff.; *The Speeches and Prayers of some of the King's late Judges*; Sir Heneage Finch, *An Exact and Most Impartial Account of the Indictment...of Twenty-nine Regicides.* For a time Milton was in hiding; something of his attitude can be gathered from *Samson Agonistes* (268-73, 692-6) and *Paradise Lost* (bk. VII, 25-33).

PAGE 5

1 Cf. the letters of James Sharp in Wodrow, *History of the Sufferings of the Church of Scotland*, vol. I, pp. 21, 49; Kennett, *A Register and Chronicle*, p. 205; *Hist.MSS.C.R.* XII, vii, p. 26.
2 Pearse, *The Conformist's Fourth Plea for the Nonconformists*, pp. 32 ff.
3 For a clear and very convincing exposition of Laudian aims and methods, see R. S. Bosher, *The Making of the Restoration Settlement*, pp. 154 ff.
4 *Rel. Bax.* pt. II, p. 279. The Declaration is given in full in Cobbett, *Parl. Hist.* vol. IV, cols. 131-41; also in Gould, *Documents*.

PAGE 6

1 Cobbett, *Parl. Hist.* vol. IV, cols. 141-2, 152-4; cf. *Cal.S.P.Dom.* 1660-1, p. 404.
2 *Cal.S.P.Dom.* 1660-1, pp. 545-67.
3 *Rel. Bax.* pt. II, p. 303.
4 Ranke, *History of England*, vol. III, p. 368; *History of the Tory Party*, p. 130.
5 Burnet, *History of my own Time*, vol. I, p. 321.

PAGE 7

1 *Rel. Bax.* pt. II, p. 384.
2 The full text of the Act is given in Gould, *Documents*, pp. 286-404.

PAGE 8

1 M. Frank, *The Grand Case of the Present Ministry, whether they may Lawfully Declare and Subscribe*, Preface.
2 M. Meade, *Spiritual Wisdom Improved*, p. 18; Henry, *Diaries and Letters*, pp. 77, 78, 101; Newcome, *Diary*, p. 41.

3 *The Life and Death of the Revd Joseph Alleine*, p. 66.
4 Pearse, *The Conformist's Plea for the Nonconformists*, p. 46.
5 Baxter MSS (Letters), vol. vi, f. 245; also Baxter's *The English Nonconformity*, pp. 5, 43 ff., *The Nonconformists' Advocate*, pp. 2–8; and *The Nonconformists Plea for Peace*, p. 207.
6 Calamy, *A Defence of Moderate Nonconformity*, pt. ii, pp. 100–1; Pearse, *The Conformist's Second Plea*, etc. p. 55; Locke, (*Letter to a Person of Quality*), vol. x, p. 204.
7 Troughton, *Apology for the Nonconformists*, p. 58.
8 Heywood, *op. cit.* p. 93.

PAGE 9

1 Baxter MSS (Letters), vol. ii, f. 93.
2 Calamy, *Abridgment*, p. 193.
3 Newcome, *Diary*, pp. 122, 127, 130, 133, 136; Henry, *op. cit.* pp. 137, 146–7; Heywood, *op. cit.* vol. i, p. 140; Calamy, *Account*, p. 383.
4 *The Life and Death of the Revd Joseph Alleine*, p. 67; *Rel. Bax.* pt. ii, p. 296.
5 On the problem of emigration, see Baxter MSS (Letters), vol. iii, ff. 261–2.

PAGE 10

1 Rawlinson MSS, 109, f. 87; *Rel. Bax.* pt. ii, pp. 429–30.

PAGE 11

1 Cf. Bennet's letter outlining the King's attitude in Lister, *Life and Administration of Edward, Earl of Clarendon*, vol. iii, pp. 198–201.
2 Cobbett, *Parl. Hist.* vol. iv, col. 257.
3 *Hist.MSS.C.R.* vii, App. pp. 167–8; Christie, *Life of Shaftesbury*, vol. i, pp. 266 ff. and App. vi; Harris, *Life of Sandwich*, vol. i, p. 244.
4 *Rel. Bax.* pt. ii, p. 436.

PAGE 12

1 For the terms of the Act, see Gould, *Documents*, pp. 477–88, or Besse, vol. i, pp. xiii–xx.
2 *Cal.S.P.Dom.* 1661–2, p. 316.
3 Cf. *State Trials*, vol. vi, pp. 226 ff.; *Cal.S.P.Dom.* 1661–2, pp. 85, 89, 258, 263, 287, 304, 397–8, 404, 411, 448, 523, 540–1, 546, 588, 600; 1663–4, pp. 360–89.

PAGE 13

1 Heywood, *Diaries*, vol. i, p. 183; Henry, *op. cit.* pp. 148, 149, 151, 173.
2 Halifax, (*Letter to a Dissenter*), p. 139.
3 Cf. W. C. Abbott, *English Conspiracy and Dissent*, in *A.H.R.* vol. xiv, p. 528.
4 Calamy, *Life of John Howe*, pp. 40, 42–3; *Account*, pp. 541, 709, and *Continuation*, p. 437; Henry, *op. cit.* p. 181; Heywood, (*Life*), vol. i, p. 119; *Rel. Bax.* pt. iii, pp. 3–14.
5 Crosby, *History of the English Baptists*, vol. ii, pp. 209, 214.
6 Baxter, *Apology for the Nonconformist's Ministry*, p. 101, and *Second True Defence of the Meer Nonconformists*, Historical Preface.

PAGE 14

1 *Cal.S.P.Dom.* 1671, p. 581; *Rel. Bax.* pt. III, p. 39.
2 Cf. W. C. Abbott, in *A.H.R.* vol. XIV, pp. 699 ff.
3 *Cal.S.P.Dom.* 1664–5, pp. 33, 52, 271.
4 *Ibid.* p. 286.
5 Ogg, *England in the Reign of Charles II*, vol. I, p. 205.
6 Harris, *op. cit.* vol. II, p. 189.
7 Cf. *Cal.S.P.Dom.* Nov. 1667–Sept. 1668, p. 259; *Rel. Bax.* pt. III, pp. 21–2.

PAGE 15

1 *Cal.S.P.Dom.* Apr.–Oct. 1667, pp. 9, 39, 167, 454; S. Patrick, *Autobiography*, p. 59.
2 References to nonconformist activity abound in *Cal.S.P.Dom.* for the years 1666–70.
3 *Cal.S.P.Dom.* Apr.–Oct. 1667, pp. 336, 552.
4 Newcome, *Diary*, p. 120; *Life of Adam Martindale*, p. 180; *Cal.S.P.Dom.* Apr.–Oct. 1667, p. 277; *Cal. Rev.* pp. 51, 55, 192.
5 *Rel. Bax.* pt. II, pp. 436–41.

PAGE 16

1 *Rel. Bax.* pt. III, pp. 24–36.
2 Grey, *Debates*, vol. I, pp. 146 ff., 160 ff.
3 *Ibid.* p. 146.
4 Baxter MSS (Letters), vol. II, f. 273 *a*, *b*.
5 See Grey, *op. cit.* vol. I, pp. 220 f., 227 f., 265.
6 Marvell, *Works*, vol. II, p. 316.
7 Grey, *op. cit.* vol. I, p. 228.

PAGE 17

1 For the terms of the Act, see Gould, *Documents*, pp. 491 ff.
2 *Cal.S.P.Dom.* 1670, p. 273.
3 *Ibid.* p. 233.

PAGE 18

1 Cf. Owen, *The State of the Kingdom with respect to the Present Bill against Conventicles*, passim.
2 *Hist.MSS.C.R.* XII, vii, p. 86.
3 *Hist.MSS.C.R.* XIV, ii. p. 322; *Cal.S.P.Dom.* Dec. 1671–May 1672, pp. 27–9, 44–6.

PAGE 19

1 Grant Robertson, *Select Statutes, Cases and Documents*, pp. 75–7.
2 *Rel. Bax.* pt. III, pp. 99 ff.; *The Life of Adam Martindale*, p. 198; Henry, *op. cit.* pp. 247–50.
3 *The Note Book of Thomas Jolly*, p. 6; *Cal.S.P.Dom.* Dec. 1671–May 1672, p. 567.
4 *Ibid.* pp. 272, 609.
5 Crosby, *op. cit.* vol. III, pp. 82–3.

PAGE 20

1 G. L. Turner, *Original Records of Nonconformity*, vol. III, *passim*.
2 *Minutes of the General Assembly of the General Baptist Churches*, p. xvii.
3 Hunter, *The Rise of the Old Dissent*, pp. 241–2.
4 Heywood, *Diaries*, vol. I, p. 346.
5 *The Memoirs of Sir John Reresby*, p. 86; *Cal.S.P.Dom.* May–Sept. 1672, p. 559, and Oct. 1672–Feb. 1673, p. 300.
6 Stillingfleet, *The Unreasonableness of Separation*, p. 23.
7 Rogers, *Life of John Howe*, p. 113.

PAGE 21

1 *C.J.* vol. IX, p. 248; *Letters of Sir Joseph Williamson*, vol. II, p. 59.
2 North, *Examen*, pp. 44–5.
3 *C.J.* vol. IX, p. 259; Grey, *op. cit.* vol. II, pp. 2–181.
4 Calamy, *Abridgment*, p. 336.
5 Calamy, *An Historical Account of my own Life*, vol. I, p. 71; *The Note Book of Thomas Jolly*, p. 16.

PAGE 22

1 Cf. Cobbett, *Parl. Hist.* vol. IV, cols. 854 ff., 861 ff., 964 ff., 990 ff., 1006 ff.
2 Owen, (*Posthumous Sermons*), vol. IX, pp. 5, 11–12.
3 Clarkson, (*Of Taking Up the Cross*), vol. I, p. 505; Heywood, *op. cit.* vol. III, p. 315.

PAGE 23

1 *Rel. Bax.* pt. III, pp. 109, 156–62; Calamy, *Life of John Howe*, pp. 71 f., and *Abridgment*, p. 347; *Hist.MSS.C.R.* IX, App. ii, p. 44.
2 L. F. Brown, *The First Earl of Shaftesbury*, pp. 132–3, 213, 302, 318, 320–1; *Memoirs of the Life of Mr Ambrose Barnes*, p. 186.
3 Pearse, *The Conformist's Third Plea for the Nonconformists*, p. 8; Luttrell, *Brief Historical Narration*, vol. I, p. 124.
4 Whiting, *Persecution Exposed*, p. 33; *The Hatton Correspondence*, vol. I, pp. 194, 209. There are frequent references in *Cal.S.P.Dom.*
5 *Letters of Early Friends*, p. 203; Whiting, *op. cit.* p. 33; J. Howe, *The Case of the Protestant Dissenters Represented and Argued*, p. 47.
6 *Cal.S.P.Dom.* 1682, pp. 8, 32, 138, 250, 357, 366.

PAGE 24

1 Heywood, *op. cit.* vol. II, p. 81; vol. III, p. 309.
2 Trevelyan, *The English Revolution*, p. 31.
3 *Cal.S.P.Dom.* 1682, p. 356.
4 *Letters of Gilbert Burnet*, p. 8.

PAGE 25

1 Note the increasingly frequent references in *Cal.S.P.Dom.*, especially during the years 1682 and 1683.

2 *Cal.S.P.Dom.* 1682, pp. 327, 328, 607; 1683, pp. 103, 216, 223, 279, 349.
3 *Ibid.* July–Sept. 1683, pp. 33, 36; Sept. 1683–Apr. 1684, pp. 141, 187.

PAGE 26

1 Calamy, *Life of John Howe*, p. 113.
2 Whiting, *op. cit.* pp. 76–7
3 Terrill, *Broadmead Records*, pp. 234–64; *The Diary of Ralph Thoresby*, vol. I, p. 153; *The Note Book of Thomas Jolly*, pp. 51, 54, 63, 66; Henry, *op. cit.* p. 325.

PAGE 27

1 *The Memoirs of Sir John Reresby*, pp. 326, 328.
2 Baxter MSS (Letters), vol. III, ff. 208–11; cf. also Baxter MSS (Treatises), vol. I, ff. 2–13, vol. VII, ff. 215–19.
3 *The Western Martyrology*, pp. 193–4, 203.
4 Henry, *op. cit.* pp. 325, 328.
5 Baxter, *The English Nonconformity*, f. 260.
6 Whitley, *A History of British Baptists*, p. 149.

PAGE 28

1 Baxter MSS (Treatises), vol. VII, f. 235; *The Diary of Sir John Bramston*, p. 267; Reresby, *op. cit.* p. 381; Burnet, *op. cit.* vol. III, pp. 161–7, 184–7, 193–5.

PAGE 29

1 *The Autobiography of Sir John Bramston*, p. 271; Luttrell, vol. I, pp. 402–3. Cf. the comments in the diaries of Thoresby (vol. I, p. 186), Reresby (p. 372), Heywood (vol. IV, pp. 124–5, 133–4), Whiting (p. 172).
2 *Life of William Kiffin*, pp. 84–5.
3 *The Memoirs of Sir John Reresby*.

PAGE 30

1 Calamy, *Life of John Howe*, p. 140.
2 Cardwell, *Documentary Annals*, vol. III, p. 375.
3 Calamy, *Abridgment*, pp. 366–7.

PAGE 31

1 *Broadmead Records*, p. 251. John Whiting counted six persecutions in the reign of Charles II (*Persecution Exposed*, p. 122).

PAGE 32

1 S. Parker, *History of his own Time*, p. 354; also pp. 357–8, 364, 368; Gauden, *Considerations touching the Liturgy of the Church of England*, p. 28.
2 W. Pope, *Life of Seth Ward*, p. 57.
3 Cobbett's *Parl. Hist.* vol. IV, p. 413. Cf. Judge Levin's charge to the Grand Jury at Stafford assizes, 1683: 'Where disagreement was admitted in the church, there could be no agreement in the state.' Besse, vol. I, p. 654.
4 Cf. Bunyan, (*Some Gospel Truths Opened*), vol. II, p. 131.

5 J. Gratton, *A Journal*, etc. pp. 125 f.; Calamy, *Account*, p. 647; letters to Sir Joseph Williamson, 11 Jan. 1670–1, *Cal.S.P.Dom.* 1671, p. 15; Heywood, *Diaries*, vol. IV, p. 91.

6 Cf. *Some Memoirs of the Life of John Roberts*, p. 58; Gratton, *op. cit.* pp. 134, 155; Besse, vol. I, pp. 27, 30. In certain cases inhumanity was prompted by annoyance at loss of customary dues—e.g. burial fees, Besse, vol. I, pp. 501, 654; Heywood, *op. cit.* vol. I, p. 356.

7 *The Diary of Dr Thomas Cartwright*, p. 66.

PAGE 33

1 Bunyan, (*Of Antichrist and His Ruin*), vol. II, p. 44, and (*Advice to Sufferers*), vol. II, pp. 696, 739; W. Bates, *A Funeral Sermon for the Reverend... Mr Richard Baxter*, p. 104; Henry, *Diaries and Letters*, p. 309; Baxter, *Cain and Abel Malignity*, to the Reader.

2 Halifax, (*A Letter to a Dissenter*), p. 136; *Rel. Bax.* pt. II, p. 385; Baxter, *The Nonconformists' Advocate*, p. 7.

3 *Hist.MSS.C.R.* XII, pt. vii, p. 28.

PAGE 34

1 Luttrell, *Brief Historical Relation*, vol. I, pp. 106, 124; Whiting, *Persecution Exposed*, p. 34; Calamy, *Memoirs of the Life of the Late Revd Mr John Howe*, pp. 135, 240–1; Sewell, *History of... the Quakers*, vol. II, p. 389.

2 *The Suffering Condition of the People called Quakers* (1685), p. 10; Besse, vol. I, pp. 240, 495, 585, 602; vol. II, p. 109; *Narrative of the late Proceedings of some Justices*, etc., p. 12; *An Account of the Convincement... of Richard Davies*, p. 141; *Record of the Sufferings of Quakers in Cornwall*, p. 89; Heywood on the activities of George Aisleby, *Diaries*, vol. III, p. 211.

PAGE 35

1 *Broadmead Records*, pp. 90–1, 130. Cf. *Life of Adam Martindale*, p. 165; *Memoirs of the Life of Mr Ambrose Barnes*, p. 191; *Rel. Bax.* pt. III, pp. 86, 172.

2 Cf. Episcopal Returns of 1669, reproduced in G. L. Turner, *Original Records of Early Nonconformity*, vol. I, pp. 13, 27, 34, 45, 46, 48, 50, 52, 53, 84–5, 91, 111, 150, 179, 187; Ellwood, *Life*, p. 187; R. Baxter, *The English Nonconformity*, p. 260.

3 *Life of Adam Martindale*, p. 194. Cf. Bishop Seth Ward's comment (1663/4) about ejected ministers in Exeter who 'lie gnawing at the root of government and religion'. Bodl. Add. MS. C. 5. 158.

4 *S.P.Dom.* 1663–4, 603, XCIX, 7.

PAGE 36

1 Besse, vol. II, p. 11; Cf. also vol. II, pp. 43, 210; Henry, *Diaries and Letters*, p. 149.

2 Henry, *op. cit.* pp. 173–4; Ellwood, *Life*, pp. 54, 58, 78, 207. Note the warning of the justice: 'He urged upon us that an insurrection had lately been made by armed men, who pretended to be more religious than others, that that

insurrection had been plotted and contrived in their meeting-house, where they assembled under colour of worshipping God; that in their meeting-house they hid their arms and armed themselves, and out of their meeting-house issued forth in arms, and killed many; so that the government could not be safe unless such meeting were suppressed' (p. 78).

3 *To the King, The Humble Address of the People Commonly Called Quakers* (1683).

4 Howe, (*Concerning Union among Protestants*), vol. IV, p. 150; *Some Memoirs of the Life of John Roberts*, p. 9; Stanford, *Joseph Alleine*, p. 206; Gratton, *A Journal*, etc. p. 49; *Nonconf. Mem.* vol. II, p. 130; *ibid.* p. 215; *Memoirs of the Life of Mr Ambrose Barnes*, p. 142.

PAGE 37

1 *Broadmead Records*, pp. 122–3; Heywood, *Diaries*, vol. IV, p. 42; *Some Memoirs of the Life of John Roberts*, pp. 46, 55; Calamy, *An Historical Account of my own Life*, vol. I, p. 88; Calamy, *Account*, p. 329; Thoresby, *Diary and Correspondence*, vol. III, p. 22; *Rel. Bax.* pt. III, p. 172; Pearse, *The Conformist's Third Plea for the Nonconformist*, p. 6.

2 *Hertford County Records*, vol. I, p. 128, vol. VI, p. 64; *Mercurius Publicus*, 22 March 1661/2; *Interest of Words in Prayer*, pp. 59 ff.; *Nonconf. Mem.* vol. II, p. 348; Pearse, *The Conformist's Fourth Plea*, p. 30; Calamy, *Account*, pp. 556, 597–9.

PAGE 38

1 O. Heywood, (*The General Assembly*), vol. V, p. 422; *Broadmead Records*, pp. 105–6, 135, 138; Barclay, *An Apology*, etc. p. 372; *The Hatton Correspondence*, vol. I, p. 58.

2 *A Monthly Intelligence, relating the affairs of the People Called Quakers in and near about the City of London* (1662); *For the King and both Houses of Parliament* (1664); *A Short Relation of the Barbarous Cruelties...* (1670); Fox, *Journal*, vol. II, p. 85; Ellwood, *Life*, p. 92; Calamy, *Account*, pp. 328, 331; *The Conformist's Fourth Plea for the Nonconformist*, p. 52; *Behold A Cry* (1662), *passim*; E. Burrough, *The Woeful Cry of Unjust Persecutions, Works*, p. 260.

3 *Broadmead Records*, pp. 124, 219, 221–2, 231; Barclay, *op. cit.* pp. 508–9; Luttrell, *Brief Historical Relation*, vol. I, p. 152; cf. *Cal.S.P.Dom.* 1682, p. 46.

PAGE 39

1 Roger Morrice MS Entering Book, Dr Williams's Library; *Broadmead Records*, pp. 222–3, 226.

2 Barclay, *op. cit.* pp. 372–4, 508; Besse, vol. I, p. 412; *Some Memoirs of the Life of John Roberts*, p. 55.

3 J. Griffith, *A Complaint of the Oppressed against the Oppressor*, p. 2; J. Sturgion, *A Plea for Toleration*, p. 7.

4 Calamy, *Continuation*, vol. I, p. 245–6. For a somewhat similar case, see Henry, *Diaries and Letters*, p. 227.

PAGE 40

1 (J. Hickes), *The True and Faithful Narrative of the Sufferings of Many Christians in Devon* (1671), pp. 12–13.
2 *Broadmead Records*, p. 273; Jessey, *The Lord's Loud Call to England*, p. 21.
3 *Broadmead Records*, pp. 229–30; cf. pp. 54, 103–4; *Depositions from York Castle*, p. 172; *Cal.S.P.Dom.* 1664–5, pp. 461, 476.
4 Pearse, *The Conformist's Third Plea*, pp. 6, 8; *Broadmead Records*, pp. 95–6, 126, 132, 142–3, 155–6.
5 Gratton, *A Journal*, pp. 105–6.

PAGE 41

1 Elwood, *op. cit.* pp. 83 f., 141.
2 *Broadmead Records*, pp. 107, 120–1, 128.
3 In *Cal.S.P.Dom.* 1682, p. 72, there is an interesting account of the precautions taken at Vincent's meeting in Southwark for the safety of both minister and people; cf. also *Cal.S.P.Dom.* 1670, p. 240.

PAGE 42

1 *Broadmead Records*, pp. 241, 247, 249, 257.
2 Ellwood, *op. cit.* p. 140; cf. Besse, vol. I, pp. 123, 143, 235–6, 266, 327, 642, 653–4; vol. II, p. 76.

PAGE 43

1 Calamy, *Account*, p. 448; Ellwood, *op. cit.* p. 104.

PAGE 44

1 *A Relation of the Imprisonment of Mr John Bunyan*, pp. 106–7.

PAGE 45

1 *Ibid.* pp. 105–10.
2 *Cal.S.P.Dom.* 1668–9, pp. 354, 373; *Broadmead Records*, p. 226; Slate, *Nonconformists' Remains*, pp. 200–1; Crosby, *op. cit.* vol. III, p. 132.
3 E. Burrough, *A Just and Righteous Plea*, *Works*, p. 782; Besse, vol. I, p. 626, vol. II, p. 106; Ellwood, *op. cit.* pp. 79, 204; Fox, *Journal*, vol. II, p. 148; Dewsbery, *op. cit.* p. 73; Calamy, *Continuation*, vol. I, p. 331; Ross, *Margaret Fell*, p. 131.

PAGE 46

1 Ellwood, *op. cit.* p. 79; Judge Wild complained that the Five Mile Act was so framed that it was extremely difficult to issue a valid mittimus, *Rel. Bax.* pt. III, p. 59.
2 *Broadmead Records*, pp. 54, 113, 213; Gratton, *A Journal*, etc., p. 121.

PAGE 47

1 Cf. Bunyan, (*Of the Resurrection of the Dead*), vol. II, pp. 108, 123; (*Pilgrim's Progress*), vol. III, pp. 129–30; (*The Holy War*), vol. III, pp. 310 ff., 366–8.
2 Calamy, *Continuation*, vol. I, p. 470. For other instances of considerate treat-

ment of nonconformists by the judges, see Calamy, *Account*, pp. 6, 167, 289, 305, 382, 578; *Continuation*, pp. 11, 232, 489, 558, 731; *Rel. Bax.* pt. III, p. 59.

3 Cf. *Hist.MSS.C.R.* XI, App. VII-3, p. 212; *Memoirs of the Life of Ambrose Barnes*, p. 141 a.

4 Letters from Daniel Fleming to Secretary Williamson, *Extracts from State Papers*, pp. 188–9, 277; Fox, *Journal*, vol. II, p. 242; Besse, vol. I, pp. 393, 403, 24–5. The oath of allegiance as an infallible trap for Quakers was the ground of constant complaint. E.g. A. Rigge, *A Standard of Righteousness*, etc. p. 149.

PAGE 48

1 Besse, vol. I, p. 403. When a man, fined twenty pounds for meeting, asked the magistrate if he were being fined for worshipping God, he got the answer, 'Yes, you are; you are fined twenty pounds for worshipping God'— *A Short Relation of...the Sad Suffering and Cruel Havoc and Spoil*, etc. p. 4.

2 Besse, vol. II, pp. 63–5, 66. What emerges most clearly from much Quaker literature is not merely the peculiar gift of the sufferers for stating their case in such a way as to antagonise those to whom they appealed, but also the fact that the kind of arguments they used belonged in a sense to the realm of law, but always transcended it. Cf. Fox, *Journal*, *passim*.

3 Dewsbery, *The Faithful Testimony*, etc. pp. 68 ff; cf. p. 38. The discussion might not be so amicably conducted, and it might not end so well. Cf. the case of John Otter, a London shoemaker arrested in 1663 at a meeting at Mile-end. When asked by the justices where he dwelt, he answered 'In a dwelling where neither thief, murderer nor persecutor can come.' When asked where that was, he answered 'In God.' Thereupon the justices sent him to Bridewell as a vagabond! Subsequently for similar answers to the same questions he was sentenced to banishment and was sold as a slave in Virginia. Besse, vol. I, p. 404. Cf. also pp. 369 ff.

PAGE 49

1 Letter of Tillotson to M. Sylvester, Baxter MSS (Letters), vol. II, ff. 76 a, b– 77 b. Full accounts of the trial are found in Baxter MSS (Letters), vol. III, ff. 208–11 (ostensibly by an eye-witness); Calamy, *An Abridgement of Mr Baxter's Life and Times*, vol. I, pp. 368 ff. (Calamy writes as a near-contemporary); in Orme, *Life of Baxter*, in Macaulay, and in *State Trials*, vol. XI, pp. 490 f.

2 Baxter's notes are preserved in the Baxter MSS (Treatises), vol. I, ff. 2 a–13 b; vol. VII, ff. 215 a–219 a.

3 *The People's Ancient and Just Liberties Asserted* (1670). Cf. also William Penn, *Works*, vol. I, pp. 486–521; *Correspondence of John Cosin*, vol. II, p. 252; Henry, *op. cit.* pp. 232–3.

PAGE 50

1 The Quaker provides the most extreme example, since his characteristic views exposed him to the punishments of the law at a greater number of points than anyone else; but all dissenters could be punished in a wide variety of ways and yet it could fall within the letter of the law. In George Fox,

Epistles, no. 386 (23 Feb. 1683/4) there is an interesting general summary of the grounds on which Quakers were being attacked during the height of the Tory reaction.

2 Grey, *Debates*, vol. II, pp. 92, 119; Fox, *Journal*, p. 563; Parker, *History of my own Time*, pp. 9, 17, 55, 81; *Cal.S.P.Dom.* 1660–1, pp. 80, 109, 224; 1661–2, pp. 80, 81, 89; 1664–5, pp. 33, 120, 183, 293, 517, 538.

1 Cf. *The Case of the Protestant Dissenters of late Persecuted on old Statutes made against Papists and Popish Recusants* (1680), *passim*; Burnet, *History of my own Time*, vol. II, p. 433; A. Grey, *Debates of the House of Commons*, vol. V, p. 252; vol. VI, p. 329; vol. VII, pp. 76, 422–5; vol. VIII, pp. 214–18; Fox, *Journal*, vol. II, pp. 214, 219.

2 *Some Remarkable Passages in the Life of William Kiffin*, pp. 118–20; Crosby, *op. cit.* vol. II, pp. 181–5. A Cambridgeshire nonconformist minister, Francis Holcroft, was sentenced under 35 Eliz. to take the oath of abjuration of the Kingdom, or be hanged, but his execution was stopped by the king. Heywood, *Diaries*, vol. III, pp. 83, 88.

1 *Broadmead Records*, pp. 240, 256, 263, 266; *Some Memoirs of the Life of John Roberts*, p. 8; *To the King... The Suffering Condition of the People Called Quakers*; Besse, vol. I, pp. 179, 318, 607; *Cal.S.P.Dom.* 1664–5, p. 39; Ellwood, *op. cit.* p. 175; Besse, vol. I, pp. 322, 442; Heywood, *Diaries*, vol. III, p. 96; *Narrative of the late Proceedings of Some Justices and others*, p. 15.

2 Fox, *Journal*, p. 430; Sewell, *op. cit.* vol. I, p. 406; Calamy, *Continuation*, vol. I, p. 574; Besse, vol. I, p. 358.

3 Cf. *Cal.S.P.Dom.* 1664–5, p. 206; Thoresby, *Diary and Correspondence*, vol. III, p. 47; Luttrell, *op. cit.* vol. I, pp. 320–1; Crosby, *op. cit.* vol. I, p. 371; Spence MSS, III, 186; Baxter, *The English Nonconformity*, Preface; Pearse, *The Conformist's Fourth Plea*, p. 32; Fox, *Journal*, vol. II, p. 245; Ellwood, *op.cit.* p. 104; *Cal.S.P.Dom.* 1664 (Letter from Dover, 25 April), p. 565.

1 In its original form the Meeting for Sufferings consisted of London Friends appointed to correspond with the various counties, together with members of the Morning Meeting (a committee of men 'ministers'), and one Friend from each county prepared to attend when necessary. A full meeting was held before each law term; each week a partial meeting was held on a system of rotation. The Meeting for Sufferings was instituted in order to provide legal aid for persecuted Quakers; its representative character and its proven usefulness made it in time the executive committee of the Society of Friends, and it still meets regularly.

2 The first fifteen volumes of the minutes of the Meeting for Sufferings (in the Friends Historical Library) contain an immense amount of illuminating material.

PAGE 55

1 The most celebrated case was that of the Hertford Quakers: The letter of John Rous to Margaret Fell, 6.vi.64, in Thirnbeck MSS, 3; W(illiam) S(tout), *A True, Short, Impartial Relation...of the Proceedings...at the Town of Hertford* (1664), and *A Second Relation from the Town of Hertford* (1664); Besse, vol. I, pp. 244–9. Cf. also Richard Crane, *God's Holy Name Magnified...by the Testimony of his Faithful Servants who have suffered...Banishment* (1665); Sewell, *op. cit.* vol. II, p. 171; George Whitehead, *Christian Progress*, pp. 286, 300; *Cal.S.P.Dom.* 1664–5, pp. 80, 164, 244, 373, 513. For a similar case involving Baptists, see Crosby, *op. cit.* vol. III, p. 120.

PAGE 56

1 *Middlesex County Records*, vol. IV, pp. 166, 174, 176, 178ff.; Turner MS, 30, Dr Williams's Library; Spence MSS, III, 1, 186; Pearse, *The Conformist's Third Plea*, p. 6.

PAGE 57

1 In Suffolk in May 1683, exchequer processes against Quakers for absence from worship amounted to £33,300; Besse, vol. I, p. 687. In Bristol, fines returned into court of exchequer amounted to £16,440, *ibid.* pp. 68–70. Cf. also pp. 135, 178–9, 226. Luttrell (*Brief Historical Relation*, vol. I, p. 216) reports that in Bristol in a single year the authorities anticipated a revenue from fines on nonconformists of £100,000. The losses suffered by the Puritans have been estimated at amounts varying from £2,000,000 to £14,000,000 (C. E. Whiting, *Studies in Restoration Puritanism*, p. 441).

2 P. Henry, *Diaries and Letters*, pp. 301–2, 307. Henry lost six wagon loads of hay (about 3 tons) ('and hay scarce and dear'), seven wagon loads of coal, a field of barley, the corn in his barn, and a good deal of farm equipment.

PAGE 58

1 Cf. Besse, vol. II, p. 42; *A True and Impartial Narrative of some Illegal and Arbitrary Proceedings...in and near the Town of Bedford.*

2 Besse, vol. I, pp. 94, 96, 155–6, 469, 631; *Broadmead Records*, pp. 260, 269. Cf. Fox, *Journal*, vol. II, p. 52.

3 Besse, vol. I, p. 95; cf. p. 556.

4 Cf. the case of Thomas Arthur in *A True and Impartial Narrative of Some Illegal and Arbitrary Proceedings*, etc.

5 *Broadmead Records*, pp. 224, 231; Spence MSS, III, 186; Besse, vol. I, p. 61; Heywood, *Diaries*, vol. II, pp. 124–8; Baxter, *A Breviate*, etc. p. 121; *The English Nonconformity*, Preface.

6 Besse, vol. I, p. 93; pp. 6, 238.

7 Spence MSS, III, 1; Margaret Fell, *Works*, p. 10.

PAGE 59

1 Besse, vol. I, pp. 93, 111, 217, 257.

2 Calamy, *Continuation*, vol. I, p. 486; *The Note Book of Thomas Jolly*, p. 17.

3 Gratton, *A Journal*, etc., pp. 142–4; cf. *Rel. Bax.* pt. III, pp. 155ff.

PAGE 60

1 Letter of Sarah Meade to Rachel Abraham, Spence MSS, III, 186; cf. also Baxter, *An End of Doctrinal Controversies*, p. vii.

2 Besse, vol. II, p. 120; vol. I, pp. 53, 188, 495, 725; 356; 204; xlii, 471; Ellwood, *op. cit.* pp. 173–5; Pearse, *The Conformist's Fourth Plea*, p. v; Margaret Fell, *Works*, p. 10; Luttrell, *op. cit.* vol. I, pp. 320-1.

PAGE 61

1 Bunyan, (*The Life and Death of Mr Badman*), vol. III, p. 625; Gratton, *A Journal*, etc. p. 121; Calamy, *Memorials of the Life of. . .John Howe*, p. 153; Besse, vol. I, p. 602; Pearse, *The Conformist's Third Plea*, pp. 6, 8; *Fourth Plea*, p. 15. Cf. the tracts against informers quoted in Fox, *Journal*; also J. Owen, (*The Present Distresses on Nonconformists Examined; A Word of Advice to the Citizens of London*), vol. XIII, pp. 582 and 591. One of the strongest attacks on informers ('the pests of society', etc.) was in a work by an Anglican rector, *A Sermon against Persecution*, by Samuel Bold.

2 Quoted in Besse, vol. I, p. 460.

PAGE 62

1 Thoresby, *Diary*, vol. I, p. 130; *Rel. Bax.* pt. II, p. 441; *Nonconf. Mem.* vol. II, p. 305. *Broadmead Records*, p. 262–3; Besse, vol. I, p. 502; Heywood, *Diaries*, vol. II, p. 223; vol. IV, p. 120; W. Pooley, *Part of the Sufferings of Leicestershire and Northamptonshire by Informers and Priests*, pp. 3–4; Besse, vol. I, pp. 63, 186, 471, 601; *Broadmead Records*, pp. 95–6, 133, 136. Cf. the case of the man who swore that he had heard a nonconformist whistle treason, R. Baxter, *The English Nonconformity*, p. 185.

2 Gratton, *op. cit.* p. 123; R. Davies, *An Account of the Convincement*, etc. pp. 141–6; Heywood, *op. cit.* vol. IV, p. 101; *Rel. Bax.* pt. III, p. 165.

3 Fox, *Journal*, vol. II, p. 80–1; *Cal.S.P.Dom.* 1682, p. 227.

4 *First Publishers of Truth*, p. 95.

5 Besse, vol. I, p. 188.

PAGE 63

1 Ellwood, *op. cit.* pp. 178f.

2 George Whitehead, *Christian Progress*, pp. 591–609; Luttrell, *Brief Historical Relation*, vol. I, p. 387.

3 Pearse, *The Conformist's Third Plea*, pp. 5ff.

4 *Ibid.* pp. xiv, 7ff. Cf. Fox, *Journal*, vol. II, p. 135.

5 The people of England, said a speaker in the House of Commons, 'are generous in their sympathies, and pity sufferers', Grey, *Debates*, vol. I, p. 127. Cf. also Lord Delamere, *Works* (1694), p. 416; Pearse, *The Conformist's Plea*, pp. 9–10; *Rel. Bax.* pt. III, p. 60.

PAGE 64

1 *Cal.S.P.Ven.* 1669–70, pp. 152–3; letter of Lloyd to Sancroft, Tanner MSS, cxlvi, 33. Cf. Baxter, *A Second True Defence of the Meer Nonconformists,*

Historical Preface; *Correspondence of John Cosin*, vol. II, p. 197; Grey, *Debates*, vol. VI, p. 286.

2 Pearse, *The Conformist's Third Plea*, pp. 4–5.

3 Cf. Pearse, *The Conformist's Fourth Plea*, pp. 10, 29f.; *Third Plea*, p. 5. Cf. the reaction of the public to the behaviour of the justices at one of Fox's trials: they murmured that this was reminiscent of the days of Queen Mary, *The Swarthmore Documents in America*, ed. by H. J. Cadbury, p. 78.

PAGE 65

1 J. Owen, (*A Peace-Offering*), vol. XIII, p. 556.

PAGE 66

1 Bunyan, *Grace Abounding*, §§324–330. Cf. Charnock on the danger of magnifying fears concerning the future (*A Discourse of Divine Providence*), vol. I, p. 118; and Henry on the temptation, in times of persecution, of falling into the sin of fearfulness, *Diaries and Letters*, p. 169.

PAGE 67

1 J. Alleine, *A Call to Archippus*, pp. 3–5, 12–13, 17–20, 24. Alleine's book owed its urgency to his keen awareness of the fact that ministers were tempted to shrink from the dangers that faced them.

2 Barclay, *Apology*, p. 509; Fox, *Epistles*, p. 5; Gratton, *A Journal*, pp. 28, 42, 49. Cf. Crosby, *The History of the English Baptists*, vol. III, p. 82.

PAGE 68

1 Bunyan, (*Advice to Sufferers*), vol. II, p. 726.

2 Baxter, *An Apology for the Nonconformists' Ministry*, p. 247.

3 Baxter, *Judgement of the Nonconformists*, p. 87.

4 Henry, *Diaries and Letters*, p. 288. 'He that flies', as he remarks, 'may fight again.'

5 Bunyan, *op. cit.* vol. II, p. 714.

6 T. Goodwin, (*Of Christ the Mediator*), vol. V, p. 202; also vol. XI, pp. 422–51.

7 J. Howe, (*Concerning Union Among Protestants*), vol. IV, p. 150; Jeremiah Burrough, *The Excellency of Holy Courage in Evil Times*, pp. 49–69.

PAGE 69

1 Bunyan, *op. cit.* vol. II, p. 715.

2 Baxter, *An Apology for the Nonconformists' Ministry*, p. 19.

PAGE 70

1 Bunyan, (*An Exposition of the First Ten Chapters of Genesis*), vol. II, p. 461.

2 Howe, (*Spiritual Advantages and Improvements by Sufferings*), vol. VI, p. 232.

3 Bunyan, (*Christian Behaviour*), vol. II, p. 553.

4 A. Rigge, *Constancy in the Truth Commended*, p. 55.

5 Charnock, (*A Discourse of Divine Providence*), vol. I, p. 114.

PAGE 71

1 E. Burrough, (*A Just and Righteous Plea*), pp. 788–93.

2 Owen, (*Of Toleration*), vol. VIII, p. 181.

3 E. Hookes, *The Spirit of the Martyrs Revived*, To the Reader; Heywood, (*Israel's Lamentation After the Lord*), vol. III, p. 401.
4 Howe, (*Funeral Sermon of Mrs Esther Simpson*), vol. IV, p. 204.
5 E. Burrough, (*The Woeful Case of Unjust Persecutions*), *Works*, pp. 267–74; A. Rigge, *The Good Old Way*, pp. 145, 169–70.
6 Clarkson, *op. cit.* vol. I, pp. 460, 501; Bunyan, *op. cit.* vol. II, pp. 692–3.
7 R. Alleine, *Vindiciae Pietatis*, p. 68.

PAGE 72

1 Owen, *op. cit.* vol. IX, p. 233.
2 Charnock, (*A Discourse Upon the Goodness of God*), vol. II, p. 361; Bunyan, *op. cit.* p. 693.
3 Heywood, *op. cit.* vol. III, p. 391.
4 E. Hookes, *op. cit.* p. 557.
5 Owen, *op. cit.* vol. IX, p. 240; Bunyan, (*An Exposition of the First Ten Chapters of Genesis*), vol. II, p. 494.

PAGE 73

1 Clarkson, *op. cit.* vol. I, p. 457; Owen, (*The Meaning of Conversion Explained*), vol. III, p. 347.
2 Baxter, *An Apology*, etc. p. 196.
3 Charnock, (*A Discourse Upon the Goodness of God*), vol. II, p. 361; Clarkson, (*Of Faith*), vol. I, pp. 104–5.
4 Bunyan, *op. cit.* vol. II, p. 483; Charnock, (*A Discourse of Divine Providence*), vol. I, p. 111.
5 Owen, (*An Exposition Upon Psalm cxxx*), vol. VI, p. 583.
6 Howe, (*Funeral Sermon of Mrs Esther Sampson*), vol. IV, p. 203; Heywood, (*Heart Treasure*), vol. II, p. 122.

PAGE 74

1 T. Goodwin, (*On Repentance*), vol. VII, p. 567; Clarkson, (*The Lord Rules Over All*), vol. II, p. 458, and (*God's End in Sending Calamities*), vol. II, p. 238; Owen, (*The Filth of Sin Purged*), vol. III, p. 447, and (*Watching Against Temptation*), vol. VI, p. 137.
2 T. Goodwin, (*Of Election*), vol. IX, p. 398.
3 Howe, (*Thirteen Sermons on Various Subjects*), vol. VI, p. 224; Fox, *Journal*, vol. II, p. 80.
4 Clarkson, (*God Rules Over All*), vol. II, p. 466.
5 Charnock, (*Upon God's Patience*), vol. II, p. 526.
6 Charnock, (*Upon the Goodness of God*), vol. II, p. 361.

PAGE 75

1 Clarkson, (*Sinners Under the Curse*), vol. II, p. 558.
2 Z. Crofton, *The Hard Way to Heaven*, p. 1.
3 Charnock, (*A Discourse Upon the Wisdom of God*), vol. II, p. 77.
4 Charnock, (*A Discourse Upon the Goodness of God*), vol. II, p. 361.

PAGE 76

1 Bunyan, *op. cit.* vol. II, p. 497.
2 E. Burrough, (*The Woeful Cry of Unjust Persecution*), pp. 265–6; J. Burrough, *The Excellency of Holy Courage in Evil Times*, ch. I.
3 Howe, (*A View of the late Considerations...about the Trinity*), vol. IV, p. 382.
4 Clarkson, (*Of Taking Up the Cross*), vol. I, p. 472; Howe, (*The Work of the Holy Spirit in Reference to the Christian Church*), vol. V, p. 358.
5 Baxter, (*A Christian Directory*), vol. I, p. 48.
6 Goodwin, (*Of Christ the Mediator*), vol. V, p. 207; Fox, *Journal*, vol. II, p.64.
7 Owen, (*The Holy Spirit and His Work*), vol. III, p. 37; E. Burrough, *op. cit* p. 266.
8 Charnock, (*God's Patience*), vol. II, p. 500.

PAGE 77

1 Howe, (*The Redeemer's Tears Wept Over Lost Souls*), vol. IV, pp. 4–5.
2 Charnock, (*A Discourse of Divine Providence*), vol. I, pp. 106–7.
3 J. Whiting, *Persecution Exposed*, Preface.

PAGE 78

1 *A Narrative of the Cruelties and Abuses Acted by Isaac Dennis, Keeper his Wife and Servants, in the Prison of Newgate in the City of Bristol*; also *Broadmead Records*, p. 259; *Some Memoirs of the Life of John Roberts*, p. 56; Defoe, *Review*, vol. IV, p. 368; Besse, vol. I, pp. 105, 111, 218, 240; vol. II, p. 151; Fox, *Journal*, vol. II, pp. 3, 7.
2 Clarkson, (*Of Repentance*), vol. I, p. 16; *The Diary of the Revd Ralph Josselin*, pp. 17, 18.
3 Gratton, *A Journal*, p. 195; J. Owen, (*The Nature and Cause of Apostasy*), vol. VII, p. 138.

PAGE 79

1 Bunyan, (*Advice to Sufferers*), vol. II, pp. 696, 703, 733; Owen, (*Of Communion with the Holy Ghost*), vol. II, p. 259.
2 Charnock, *op. cit.* vol. I, p. 59.
3 Charnock, (*The Wisdom of God*), vol. II, p. 85.
4 Baxter, *Second Part of the Defence of the Meer Nonconformists*, p. 202; Heywood, (*Life*); vol. I, p. 186 and *Diaries*, vol. III, p. 21.
5 Baxter, (*A Christian Directory*), vol. I, p. 48.
  Bunyan, *op. cit.* p. 738.
  Owen, (*Posthumous Sermons*), vol. IX, pp. 499 ff.
8 Baxter, *Judgment of the Nonconformists*, p. 53; also Baxter's letter (to a minister of state?), *c.* 1677–8, Baxter MSS (Letters), vol. VI, f. 199a.

PAGE 80

1 Baxter, *Answer to Dr Edward Stillingfleet's Charge of Separation*, p. 100.
2 Fox, *Journal*, vol. II, pp. 85, 86.
3 Charnock, (*A Discourse of Divine Providence*), vol. I, p. 113.

4 Clarkson, (*Justification by the Righteousness of Christ*), vol. I, p. 282; Owen, *op. cit.* p. 229.
5 E. Hookes, *A Brief View of the Great Sufferings and Living Testimonies of the True and Constant Martyrs*, p. 568.

PAGE 81

1 Charnock, *op. cit.* vol. I, pp. 101–2.
2 Clarkson, (*Of Taking Up the Cross*), vol. I, p. 479.
3 Bunyan, *Advice to Sufferers*, pp. 701, 702, 711, 736, 739, 740.

PAGE 82

1 Bunyan, *op. cit.* p. 721; Howe, (*Jerusalem Rebuilt in Troublous Times*), vol. VI, pp. 303–4.
2 Owen, (*The Person of Christ*), vol. I, p. 116; Fox, *Journal*, vol. II, p. 206; Owen, (*Of Communion with the Holy Ghost*), vol. II, p. 259; R. Alleine, *Vindiciae Pietatis*, p. 44; A. Rigge, *Constancy in the Truth Commended*, p. 62.

PAGE 83

1 Bunyan, (*An Exposition of the First Ten Chapters of Genesis*), vol. II, pp. 450, 451.
2 Charnock, (*Upon God's Dominion*), vol. II, p. 497; Charnock, (*Of Divine Providence*), vol. I, pp. 109, 110.
3 Charnock, (*The Immutability of God*), vol. I, p. 416.
4 Charnock, (*Upon the Goodness of God*), vol. II, p. 395; Charles Marshall, *Sion's Travellers*, p. 133; Clarkson, (*God's End in Sending Calamities and Afflictions on His People*), vol. II, p. 239.

PAGE 84

1 Charnock, (*A Discourse of the Power of God*), vol. II, pp. 180–1.
2 Charnock, (*Upon the Goodness of God*), vol. II, p. 389.
3 Charnock, (*Upon the Dominion of God*), vol. II, p. 482.
4 Charnock, (*Of Divine Providence*), vol. I, pp. 98 ff.; Bunyan, *op. cit.* pp. 722, 727–31.
5 Charnock, (*Upon God's Omnipresence*), vol. I, p. 451; Owen, (*Posthumous Sermons*), vol. IX, p. 439.
6 A. Rigge, *op. cit.* p. 344.
7 Owen, *op. cit.* p. 67.
8 Charnock, (*Upon the Wisdom of God*), vol. II, pp. 86–7; Clarkson, (*The Lord the Owner of all Things*), vol. I, p. 390.

PAGE 85

1 Whiting, *Persecution Exposed*, p. 58.
2 Bunyan, (*Advice to Sufferers*), vol. II, p. 699.
3 Charnock, (*Upon the Power of God*), vol. II, p. 175; Dewsbery, *The Faithful Testimony*, etc. p. 328.
4 Bunyan, (*The Saints' Knowledge of Christ's Love*), vol. II, p. 13; Clarkson,

18-2

(*Justification by the Righteousness of Christ*), vol. I, p. 319, and (*Men by Nature Unwilling to Come to Christ*), p. 388; (*Pray for Everything*), vol. II, p. 173.
5 Fox, *Journal*, vol. II, p. 87; Charnock, (*God's Knowledge*), vol. I, pp. 524, 536.

PAGE 86

1 Bunyan, (*Of Anti-Christ and his Ruin*), vol. II, p. 44; Howe, (*Thirteen Sermons on various Subjects*), vol. VI, pp. 189, 195; Owen (*Posthumous Sermons*), vol. IX, p. 247.
2 Charnock, (*Of Divine Providence*), pp. 95, 108.
3 T. Manton, (*Sermons Upon Romans viii*), vol. XII, p. 140.

PAGE 87

1 Baxter, *Apology for the Nonconformist's Ministry*, p. 198.
2 Charnock, *op. cit.* vol. I, p. 102.
3 A. Rigge, *A Standard of Righteousness Lifted unto the Nations*, pp. 156-7.

PAGE 88

1 Calamy, *Continuation*, etc. vol. I, p. 470; *Nonconf. Mem.* vol. II, p. 122. Cf. Crosby, *The History of the English Baptists*, vol. III, p. 81; Besse, vol. II, p. 68.

PAGE 89

1 Heywood, *Diaries*, vol. IV, p. 114; *The Life and Death of the Revd Joseph Alleine*, p. 72.
2 Baxter, *A Breviate*, etc. p. 113; also *Rel. Bax.* pt. III, pp. 50-1, 58. Baxter, of course, realised that he was very fortunate, and he knew how easily he might have met a very different fate.
3 Heywood, *Diaries*, vol. IV, p. 114. Mr Whitaker was a fellow-minister arrested at the same time.
4 Philip Henry, *Diaries and Letters*, p. 340.

PAGE 90

1 William Dewsbery, *The Faithful Testimony of that Ancient Servant of the Lord*, etc. pp. 344-9.

PAGE 91

1 Besse, vol. II, p. 101; vol. I, pp. 395, 586-7. In a letter to Richard Hickson, Francis Howgill mentions that at the end of March 1661 there were at least 500 Quakers in the London prisons, and nearly 4000 throughout the nation (*Cal.S.P.Dom.* 1660-1, p. 533).
2 Besse, vol. I, pp. 32, 52, 55, 56-7. For a terse description of congestion in prison, see *To the King, The Humble Petition of the People Commonly Called Quakers* (1683). Cf. also J. Sturgion, *A Plea for Toleration*, p. 7.
3 T. Ellwood, *Life*, p. 107.

PAGE 92

1 Besse, vol. I, pp. 366, 380-1; cf. Whiting, *Persecution Exposed*, pp. 126-8. For Judge Jeffrey's account of crowded prison conditions, see North, *Life of Guilford*, vol. II, p. 150.

2 J. Howard, *State of the Prisons in England and Wales* (1785), p. 283. In Howard's time, the prisoners still slept on straw, and the gaoler received an allowance of five pounds a year for its purchase.

3 Besse, vol. I, p. 491.

4 Calamy, *Account*, p. 377. Cf. Whiting, *Persecution Exposed*, pp. 15, 53; Rigge, *Constancy in the Truth Commended*, p. 11.

5 Spence MSS, III, 184.

PAGE 93

1 I. Ross, *Margaret Fell*, p. 191; Miller MSS, 75; Fox, *Journal*, vol. II, pp. 33–8.

PAGE 94

1 Margaret Fell, *Works*, p. 288.

2 Cf. Bunyan's graphic touch about felons and their chains, (*Of the Resurrection of the Dead*), vol. II, p. 107; *The Life and Death of the Revd Joseph Alleine*, p. 73. Cf. Bunyan's comment: 'The jail that thou seest with thine eye, and the felons that look out at the grate, they put thee in mind of the prison of hell, and of the dreadful state of those that are there' (*The Resurrection of the Dead*), vol. II, p. 11.

PAGE 95

1 R. Baxter, *The English Nonconformity*, Preface, and p. 304; *Church History of the Government of Bishops*, Preface; *Narrative of the Sufferings of Thomas Delaune*, p. 119. O. Heywood, (*The General Assembly*), vol. V, p. 423; A. Rigge, *The Good Old Way*, p. 211; Besse, vol. I, p. 692. In the common prison at Newgate, in London, an open drain ran down the middle of the flag-stone floor; when it became clogged, the whole room was awash with filth, and the straw became a sodden mass. Brockband, *Edward Burrough*, p. 143. Regarding women among the felons, cf. Ellwood, *Life*, p. 114. Ellwood remarks that the common prison was 'a type of hell upon earth'. For nonconformist ministers in the common gaol, see Baxter MSS (Letters), vol. VI, f. 199*a*.

PAGE 96

1 Cf. Calamy, *Continuation*, vol. I, p. 469; Besse, vol. I, pp. 100, 154, 257; *Cal.S.P.Dom.* 1683, p. 232; also pp. 260, 300; G. Fox, *Journal*, vol. I, p. 235.

PAGE 97

1 Whiting, *op. cit.* pp. 144–7; E. Burrough, (*The Woeful Cry of Unjust Persecutions*), *Works*, p. 260.

2 Philip Henry, *Diaries and Letters*, p. 324; M. Henry, *Life of Philip Henry*, pp. 84–5.

PAGE 98

1 Besse, vol. I, p. 724.

2 O. Heywood, *Diaries*, vol. IV, p. 118; note the reference to 'cannibal jailers' in *S.P.Dom.* vol. CLIV, 64, Cf. the graphic account of a gaoler's attitude to his

position and his prisoners in *An Account of the Convincement, Exercises, Services and Travels of that Ancient Servant of the Lord, Richard Davies*, p. 60.
3 Besse, vol. I, pp. 487, 509, 692.

PAGE 99

1 Quoted in Brown, *John Bunyan*, p. 172.
2 Sewell, *History of the Quakers*, vol. I, pp. 312–13; *Cal.S.P.Dom.* 1666–7, Preface, pp. xiv–xviii.

PAGE 100

1 Fox, *Journal*, vol. I, p. 161; *Some Memoirs of the Life of John Roberts*, p. 21; cf. also letter of George Taylor to Margaret Fell, Swarthmore MSS, I, 257.
2 *A Journal of that Ancient Servant of Christ, John Gratton*, p. 165.
3 *A Relation of the Imprisonment of Mr John Bunyan*, p. 128.

PAGE 101

1 Fox, *Journal*, vol. II, p. 46.
2 *The Household Account Book of Sarah Fell*, p. 300.

PAGE 102

1 *The Life and Death of the Revd Joseph Alleine*, p. 73.
2 Richard Davies, *An Account*, etc. p. 57.
3 J. Alleine, *Christian Letters*, no. XLIII.
4 R. Davies, *op. cit.* p. 66. Cf. also Fox, *Journal*, vol. II, p. 39; Ellwood, *Life*, p. 58.

PAGE 103

1 Bunyan, (*The Life and Death of Mr Badman*), vol. III, p. 610.
2 Letter of Thomas Lower, 7 January 1673/4, Abraham MSS. 17.

PAGE 104

1 *The Life and Death of the Revd Joseph Alleine*, p. 76.
2 O. Heywood, (*Life*), vol. I, p. 273.

PAGE 105

1 Cf. Bunyan, *Grace Abounding*, §§327–8; *Advice to Sufferers*, vol. II, pp. 722, 730. Also Fox, *Journal*, vol. II, pp. 20–1; Gratton, *A Journal*, etc. p. 84; J. Sturgion, *A Plea for Toleration*, p. 5.
2 Spence MSS, III, 85.

PAGE 106

1 *The Household Account Book of Sarah Fell*, p. 299.
2 *A Copy of a Letter Written from Leicester Gaol* (1660); Ellwood, *Life*, pp. 99, 101.
3 *For the King and Both Houses of Parliament* (1664), p. 27; Fox, *Journal*, vol. II, p. 38.

PAGE 107

1 *The Life and Death of the Revd Joseph Alleine*, p. 73.
2 P. Henry, *Diaries and Letters*, p. 341.
3 J. Howard, *op. cit*. p. 283.
4 *The Works of Edward Burrough*, Prefatory Testimony of Francis Howgill.

PAGE 108

1 Besse, vol. I, pp. 52, 56, 57, 58.
2 Calamy, *Account*, p. 328; cf. also p. 74.
3 Besse, vol. I, p. 407; cf. Thomas Taylor, *Works*, p. 63; *Cal.S.P.Dom*. 1666-7, p. 206.
4 Swarthmore MSS, II.
5 William Dewsbery, *The Faithful Testimony*, etc. p. 376.

PAGE 109

1 Fox, *Journal*, vol. II, p. 51.
2 Swarthmore MSS, IV, 150.
3 Besse, vol. II, p. 108. Cf. *Broadmead Records*, p. 227; Whiting, *Persecution Exposed*, p. 32; *Behold a Cry*, p. 10; Rigge, *The Good Old Way*, p. 211; Besse, vol. I, pp. 58-9, 395, 716; John Gratton, *A Journal*, etc. p. 196.

PAGE 110

1 Thomas Taylor, *Works*, p. 65. In *Broadmead Records*, p. 53 we read of a minister 'straining his voice in prison to preach...that the people that gathered together under the prison walls might hear, he being about 4 pair of stairs high from them...'.
2 *The Life and Death of Vavasor Powell* (1672), p. 125. Another case was that of John Turner, at Ilchester.
3 *Christ Confessed: Written by a preacher of the Gospel now a Prisoner* (1665). The author was Turner.

PAGE 111

1 Bunyan, (*The Holy City*), vol. III, pp. 397-8.

PAGE 112

1 Joseph Alleine, *Christian Letters*, p. 241. Note Ralph Ward's letter to his people, Calamy, *Continuation*, pp. 659-69, as an excellent example of correspondence prompted by a pastoral interest.

PAGE 113

1 Thomas Taylor, *Works*, Prefatory Testimony by Fox.
2 A. Rigge, *op. cit*. p. 24; John Gratton, *A Journal*, etc. p. 197.
3 John Whiting, *Persecution Exposed*, p. 26.

PAGE 114

1 John Gratton, *A Journal*, etc. p. 165.
2 Besse, vol. I, p. 631. Cf. also Fox, *Journal*, vol. II, p. 6.

PAGE 115

1 Gratton, *A Journal*, etc. p. 166. A story identical in almost every detail is told of John Bunyan. For an instance of the remarkable latitude allowed a prisoner under seventeenth-century conditions, see Toulmin, *A Review of the Life, Character, and Writings of the Revd John Biddle*, pp. 71–3.

2 Besse, vol. I, p. 588. Cf. the attitude of the keeper of Bridewell Prison to those coming to him from Newgate, Ellwood, *Life*, pp. 112, 115.

3 Letter of Daniel Abraham to Margaret Fox, Miller MSS, 75; Besse, vol. II, p. 164; *Broadmead Records*, p. 53; Richard Davies, *An Account*, etc. pp. 66, 82.

PAGE 116

1 R. Davies, *op. cit.* p. 55; Bunyan, (*A Confession of My Faith*), vol. II, p. 593.

2 Bunyan, *Grace Abounding*, §324.

PAGE 117

1 Heywood, *Works*, vol. I, p. 107. Also note Calamy, *Continuation*, p. 332.

2 Calamy, *Account*, etc. vol. II, p. 232.

3 Bunyan, (*The Saint's Knowledge of Christ's Love*), vol. II, p. 11; Gratton, *A Journal*, p. 166.

4 Bunyan, *Grace Abounding*, §§327–9.

5 Bunyan, (*Of Antichrist and His Ruin*), vol. II, p. 45. Cf. also p. 74; (*Advice to Sufferers*), vol. II, pp. 713, 738; Baxter, (*A Christian Directory*), vol. I, p. 48.

PAGE 118

1 J. Alleine, *Christian Letters*, p. 158. Cf. also *The Life and Death of the Revd Joseph Alleine*, pp. 76, 87–9; Bunyan, (*Advice to Sufferers*), vol. II, pp. 725, 739–40.

2 Bunyan, (*On Praying in the Spirit*), vol. I, p. 640.

3 Thomas Taylor, *Works*, pp. 67, 139, 148; William Dewsbery, *The Faithful Testimony*, etc. p. 189; G. Bishop, *A Little Treatise Concerning Sufferings*, p. 36.

4 Fox, *Journal*, vol. II, pp. 20, 21.

5 Bunyan, (*Of the Resurrection of the Dead*), vol. II, p. 105. Note the care with which Howe argues this question, (*The Principles of the Oracles of God*), vol. VII, pp. 127ff.

PAGE 119

1 D. Defoe, Preface to Delaune's *Plea for the Nonconformists*, pp. ii, vii.

2 *A Narrative of the Sufferings of Thomas Delaune*, pp. 57ff. Cf. also Baxter, *An End of Doctrinal Controversies*, p. vii; G. Bishop, *A Little Treatise Concerning Sufferings*, pp. 43–5.

3 Bunyan, (*The Saints' Knowledge of Christ's Love*), vol. II, p. 26.

4 Z. Crofton, *The Hard Way to Heaven*, p. 37.

PAGE 120

1 Besse, vol. I, p. 174. Cf. Spence MSS, 184; I. Pennington, *Works*, pt. I, p. 328; Ellwood, *Life*, pp. 64–5.

2 Letter from Friends in Ilchester prison to those in Newgate, London, 22nd of 9th mo., 1663, Besse, vol. I, pp. 594–5. Cf. also W. Dewsbery, *The Faithful Testimony*, etc., for a series of letters sent from one gaol to sufferers in another, especially pp. 220–62, 328. On the other hand, a man imprisoned for talking abusively against the ecclesiastical authorities could look for no countenance from the members of his congregation, since his attitude was contrary to the spirit and letter of the New Testament, *Broadmead Records*, p. 167.

3 Heywood, (*The Sure Mercies of David*), vol. II, p. 477: 'In case of persecutions, ...you may then improve these covenant mercies, and find abundance of sweetness, solace, and satisfaction therein. Were it not for these, the soul of a child of God would sink under his pressures....'

PAGE 121

1 *The Life and Death of the Revd Joseph Alleine*, p. 82.

2 Letter from prisoners at Bristol, to Yearly Meeting in London, 1684, Besse, vol. I, p. 73. Cf. the triumphant declaration of William Dewsbery: 'For this I can say, I never played the coward, but joyfully entered prisons as palaces...; and in the prison-house I sang praises to my God, and esteemed the bolts and locks put upon me as jewels and in the name of the Eternal God I always got the victory, for they could keep me no longer than the determined time of my God.' Dewsbery, *op. cit.* early unnumbered pages.

3 Caton MSS, III, 431. Cf. Bunyan, *op. cit.* pp. 727ff.; P. Henry, *Diaries and Letters*, p. 78.

PAGE 122

1 Thomas Taylor, *Works*, p. 137. Cf. Bunyan, *Grace Abounding*, §339; F. Bampfield, *A Letter to the Saints*. One of the fullest statements of the duty of the prisoner is Bunyan's *Advice to Sufferers* (vol. II, pp. 691–741).

PAGE 123

1 Bunyan, *A Relation of the Imprisonment of Mr John Bunyan*, pp. 124–8. Twisden (as the name is usually spelt) was a judge of whom many prominent dissenters had intimate and unhappy knowledge. Cf. Fox, *Journal*, vol. I, p. 375; vol. II, pp. 17, 18, 28, 34; P. Henry, *Diaries and Letters*, pp. 236–7.

PAGE 124

1 Cf. W. Dewsbery, *op. cit.* p. 301f.: 'Epistle to all enslaved, hard-hearted and unbelieving Jews in this nation.'

2 W. Dewsbery, *The Faithful Testimony*, etc. p. 188. Cf. M. Fell, *Works*, pp. 325–30; (G. Whitehead), *Christian Progress of that Ancient Servant and Minister of Jesus Christ, George Whitehead*, pp. 350–1.

PAGE 125

1 Letter of M. Fell to Alexander Parker and George Whitehead, Spence MSS, III, 146.

2 Fox, *Journal* (Camb. ed.), vol. I, pp. 372–3.

3 Margaret Fell, *Works*, pp. 5–6.
4 Spence MSS, III, 169.

PAGE 126

1 Bunyan, *A Relation*, etc. p. 416.

PAGE 127

1 Besse, vol. I, p. 256. For similar cases, cf. *ibid.* vol. I, pp. 77, 399.
2 Letter of Ralph Ward, Calamy, *Continuation*, vol. II, p. 668.
3 Letter of Thomas Browning, *Nonconf. Mem.* vol. III, p. 34.

PAGE 129

1 Calamy, *Memoirs of the Life of John Howe*, p. 238.
2 Baxter, (*The Christian Directory*), vol. I, p. 471; cf. also (*The Poor Man's Family Book*), vol. IV, p. 238.
3 Evelyn, *A Character of England*, p. 16.

PAGE 130

1 Thoresby, *Diary*, vol. I, pp. 3–10, 13, 17–18, 43, 125. Though Thoresby ultimately conformed, he was a nonconformist till about the beginning of the reign of Queen Anne.
2 Heywood, *Diaries*, vol. II, p. 295; vol. III, p. 19.
3 *The Autobiography of Anne Lady Halkett*, p. 7.

PAGE 131

1 The day's programme is worked out in great detail in Baxter, (*A Christian Directory*), vol. I, pp. 466–9.
2 E. Pledger, MSS, Autobiography and Diary, ff. 32*a*, 42*b*.
3 *The Diary of the Revd Ralph Josselin*, pp. 145 ff.

PAGE 132

1 Thoresby, *op. cit.* p. 74.
2 It was not always reckoned harmless; at Bedford complaints were made of 'the disorderly walking of Sister Walker and her son Hubert, the latter having played shuffle-board'—*Church Book of Bunyan Meeting*, f. 97.
3 Newcome, *Autobiography*, vol. I, pp. 81–2; *Diary*, p. 66.
4 Cf. Pepys, *Diary*, 21 Dec. 1663, vol. III, p. 385. Pepys reports that 'ordinary working folk' would lose '£10 to £20 a meeting'—large sums in those days.

PAGE 133

1 Baxter, *op. cit.* p. 386.
2 Barclay, *An Apology*, etc. pp. 536–8. Baxter, *op. cit.* pp. 240–2, includes 'pastimes, inordinate recreations, sports, plays' in one of the twelve categories of 'thieves or time-wasters to be watched against'.
3 Henry, *op. cit.* pp. 146–7.

PAGE 134

1 Newcome, *Autobiography*, vol. I, p. 157.

2 Heywood, *op. cit.* vol. IV, p. 86.

3 Baxter, *op. cit.* p. 468. Cf. also Baxter's comments in (*The Poor Man's Family Book*), vol. IV, p. 236.

4 The speaker was the Rev. Mr Sharp, minister of Mill Hill Chapel, Leeds, Thoresby, *op. cit.* p. 238.

5 Henry, *op. cit.* p. 152. This is a recurrent refrain. Cf. p. 168: 'As fast as time goes, eternity comes. The Lord help me to redeem time and to make ready for eternity.'

PAGE 135

1 Pledger, *op. cit.* ff. 41 b, 58 b.

2 Thoresby, *op. cit.* p. 282.

3 Baxter, (*A Christian Directory*), vol. I, p. 247. The whole question of time and its most profitable use is considered in 'directions for redeeming as well as improving time', pt. I, ch. v, pp. 230–46; cf. also (*The Redemption of Time*), vol. IV, pp. 1037 ff.

4 Baxter MSS (Letters), vol. v, f. 28 b.

5 Henry, *op. cit.* p. 102.

PAGE 136

1 Bunyan finds in 'a life of holiness' three phases: 'heart-holiness', 'family-holiness' and 'conversation-holiness in the world', (*The Pilgrim's Progress*), vol. III, p. 124.

PAGE 137

1 Henry, *op. cit.* p. 217.

2 Heywood, *op. cit.* vol. III, p. 138; cf. vol. I, p. 147.

PAGE 138

1 Newcome, *op. cit.* vol. I, p. 23.

PAGE 139

1 William Thomas, in *A Preservative of Piety* (1662), makes these the distinguishing marks of a well-ordered household, and examines them one by one.

2 Clarkson, (*The Excellent Knowledge of Christ*), vol. I, pp. 258–9. Cf. Baxter, (*The Catechising of Families*), vol. IV, pp. 65–164.

PAGE 140

1 Orme, *Life of Richard Baxter*, p. 118. Bunyan believed that the distinguishing sounds heard in a godly community were 'good words, prayers, the singing of psalms', (*The Holy War*), vol. III, p. 347.

2 Cf. Baxter, *Gildas Salvianus*, pp. 446 ff.

3 Howe, *op. cit.* vol. v, pp. 382, 400–3, 422–3; Baxter, (*A Christian Directory*), vol. I, pp. 410, 414 f.

4 *Ibid.* pp. 422–3. Cf. also Baxter, (*The Poor Man's Family Book*), vol. IV, pp. 236, 237; Howe, *op. cit.* vol. v, pp. 415–18.

1 M. Henry, *op. cit.* pp. 45–9.

1 Heywood, *op. cit.* vol. III, pp. 225–6.
2 Heywood, *op. cit.* vol. II, p. 47.
3 Henry, *Diary and Letters*, pp. 161 f. Cf. p. 172.

1 Heywood, *op. cit.* vol. III, p. 115.
2 *The Note-Book of Thomas Jolly*, pp. 10, 11, 12.
3 Rigge, (*Constancy in the Truth Commended*), pp. 230f.
4 R. Alleine, *Vindiciae Pietatis*, p. 69.
5 Clarkson, (*Men by Nature Unwilling to Come to Christ*), vol. I, p. 338; Alleine, *op. cit.* pp. 2–3, 33–4.
6 Bunyan, (*A Holy Life the Beauty of Christianity*), vol. II, p. 545.

1 Whiting, *Persecution Exposed*, p. 122.
2 Henry, *op. cit.* p. 143.
3 W. Kiffin, *Remarkable Passages in the Life of William Kiffin*, p. 50.

1 Heywood, *op. cit.* vol. III, p. 334; vol. IV, pp. 139–40.
2 MSS Diary of Mrs Stockton (Dr Williams's Library), f. 18. Even to the end faith and fear were in doubtful balance.
3 Pledger, MSS Autobiography and Diary, ff. 73 b–74 a. Cf. also his record of his wife's death, f. 84 a.
4 Baxter, *A Breviate*, etc. p. 61.

1 Heywood, (*Life*), vol. I, p. 79.
2 Baxter, (*A Christian Directory*), vol. I, p. 467; cf. also (*The Poor Man's Family Book*), vol. IV, p. 236.
3 *The Life and Death of the Revd Joseph Alleine*, p. 106. Cf. the practice of Mr Ignatius Jordan, of Exeter, described by Howe, *op. cit.* vol. V, p. 426. On a minister who regularly began his day's work at 2 a.m., see D. Williams, *Practical Discourses on Several Important Subjects*, vol. II, p. 227.
4 Heywood, *Diaries*, vol. III, p. 222.

1 Baxter, (*A Christian Directory*), vol. I, p. 56.
2 M. Meade, *Spiritual Wisdom Improved*, pp. 16f.
3 MSS Diary of Mrs Stockton, f. 5.
4 *Ibid.* ff. 10, 13, 16, 18; cf. MSS Diary of Owen Stockton, f. 1.
5 Baxter, *op. cit.* p. 57.

PAGE 149

1 MSS Diary of Mrs Stockton, f. 22.

PAGE 150

1 Heywood, *op. cit.* vol. I, pp. 333–43; vol. III, pp. 224–6.

PAGE 151

1 Pledger, MSS Autobiography and Diary, f. 59*b*. Cf. MSS Diary of Owen Stockton, f. 1.
2 Baxter, *op. cit.* p. 492.
3 Henry, *op. cit.* pp. 96, 145.
4 Heywood, *op. cit.* vol. IV, p. 185.

PAGE 152

1 Heywood, *op. cit.* vol. I, pp. 300–2, 307–32; vol. III, pp. 123–4; Henry, *op. cit.* pp. 159, 199; MSS Diary of Mrs Stockton, ff. 4, 5.

PAGE 154

1 Heywood, *op. cit.* vol. III, pp. 298–9; cf. also pp. 264, 273, 286.

PAGE 155

1 Heywood, *op. cit.* vol. III, p. 262. This account belongs to the later and more sedentary period of Heywood's life. In his prime he had been an indefatigable itinerant, travelling thousands of miles and preaching hundreds of sermons every year.

PAGE 157

1 The words were used of Bishop Laney's attitude to S. Ainsworth, Calamy, *Account*, p. 496.
2 *Rel. Bax.* pt. III, p. 46.

PAGE 158

1 *The Life of Adam Martindale*, p. 176; Heywood, *op. cit.* vol. I, p. 270. Cf. Calamy, *op. cit.* p. 143.
2 *Broadmead Records*, p. 264. Cf. *Cal.S.P.Dom.* 1683, pp. 358, 415.
3 Heywood, *Diaries*, vol. III, pp. 114, 136.
4 *Broadmead Records*, p. 75. The result was 'one square room, 16 yards long and 15 yards broad'.
5 J. Gratton, *A Journal*, etc. p. 69; *Church Book of Amersham*, p. 209; Heywood, *op. cit.* vol. I, p. 287; vol. II, p. 238.

PAGE 159

1 Heywood, *op. cit.* vol. I, pp. 187–8; vol. III, p. 346.
2 Heywood, *op. cit.* vol. III, p. 110; cf. also p. 154; *Broadmead Records*, p. 244; *The Correspondence of John Cosin*, vol. II, pp. 200–5.
3 Cf. the evidence of *The Church Book of Bunyan Meeting*, ff. 25–6; *Broadmead Records*, pp. 57, 144, 274.

4 *Cal. Rev.* p. 2.

5 Owen, (*Posthumous Sermons*), vol. IX, p. 228.

PAGE 160

1 Turner, *Original Records*, vol. I, pp. 14, 27, 36, 38, 72, 84, 104–5, 138; vol. III, pp. 80, 98, 101; *Cal.S.P.Dom.* 1664–5, p. 47.

2 Turner, *op. cit.* vol. I, pp. 5, 6, 7, 43, 46, 49, 61, 85 ff., 106, 110, 146; cf. *Cal.S.P.Dom.* 1668–9, pp. 354, 373, and 1670, p. 25; *Hist.MSS.C.R.* Report XI, App. VII, pp. 15–16.

3 Clarkson, (*Hearing the Word*), vol. I, p. 434.

PAGE 161

1 Heywood, *op. cit.* vol. III, pp. 327, 337; *Cal.S.P.Dom.* 1666–7, p. 12; *ibid.* 1683, pp. 358, 415; *Hist. MSS.C.R.* XI, App. VII, p. 20; *Depositions from York Castle*, p. 172.

2 Heywood, *op. cit.* vol. II, p. 64; the service lasted six hours, and Heywood concluded his entry with the words 'not weary, blessed be God'. Whether this also applied to the congregation he does not say. Sometimes a minister regretfully noted that he had not made full use of his opportunity: he 'might have preached longer'—Newcome, *Diary*, p. 4.

3 Calamy, *The Life of ... Mr John Howe*, p. 14. Towards the end of our period, Philip Henry kept publicly appointed fast days on the same uncompromising scale. His son tells us that he began at 9 a.m. and did not leave the pulpit till 4 p.m.—preaching, praying, expounding, and singing all the time. M. Henry, *Life of the Revd Philip Henry*, p. 108.

PAGE 163

1 Baxter, *Church History of the Government of Bishops*, etc. Preface. The value of knowledge as a bulwark against popery is particularly stressed.

2 Owen, *op. cit.* p. 320.

3 *Church Book of Amersham*, p. 217.

PAGE 164

1 Cf. Heywood, *op. cit.* vol. II, pp. 227–8. Over a 30-year period, the totals are Fasts, 1076; Days of Thanksgiving, 171. After 1686, days of thanksgiving became more frequent.

PAGE 165

1 Elias Pledger, Autobiography and Diary (Dr Williams's Library MSS (25) 4), ff. 15 b f., 24 a, 25 b, 27 a–b, 30 b, 50 a; Heywood, *op. cit.* vol. III, p. 121; vol. IV, p. 72.

2 Heywood, *Diaries*, vol. III, 214; vol. IV, pp. 86, 121–2, 141, 184, 191; cf. M. Henry, *Life of the Revd Philip Henry*, pp. 104–5.

3 *Church Book of Ford*, pp. 1, 11, 16, 48.

PAGE 166

1 Baxter, *A Breviate*, etc. pp. 115–19; Heywood, *op. cit.* vol. III, p. 234; vol. IV, pp. 128, 131; *The Note-Book of Thomas Jolly*, p. 43.

2 *Broadmead Records*, pp. 73, 189–91. For a similar account of a 'solemn lifting up of...hands' when Bunyan was chosen pastor of the Bedford meeting, see *Church Book of Bunyan Meeting*, f. 50.

3 *Broadmead Records*, pp. 76, 181.

PAGE 167

1 *Broadmead Records*, pp. 181, 183, 212. Cf. *Church Book of Amersham*, p. 214.

2 *Church Book of Ford*, p. 29; *Broadmead Records*, p. 186. In Bedford it was customary to receive an application at one meeting and act upon it at the next. Only under exceptional circumstances (and with explicit warning that a precedent was not thereby established) could a member be received as soon as his request for admission was presented—*Church Book of Bunyan Meeting*, ff. 85, 95.

3 Baxter, *The English Nonconformity*, p. 231.

4 Owen, (*A Brief Instruction in the Worship of God*), vol. xv, p. 512. In the succeeding twelve pages Owen gives, in catechetical form, a detailed exposition of the Puritan conception of discipline.

5 Owen, (*Concerning Evangelical Love, Church Peace and Unity*), vol. xv, p. 119.

PAGE 168

1 *Ibid*. p. 120.

2 For a full discussion of the proper exercise of discipline, see T. Goodwin, (*The Constitution, Right Order and Government of the Churches of Christ*), vol. xi, pp. 43 f. Cf. Owen, *op. cit.* vol. xv, p. 104.

3 Bunyan, (*An Exhortation to Peace and Unity*), vol. ii, p. 745.

4 Cf. *Broadmead Records*, p. 13; *Church Book of Ford*, p. 8; *Rel. Bax.* pt. ii, pp. 148, 163, 233.

5 Heywood, *op. cit.* vol. i, p. 171.

6 Henry, *Diaries and Letters*, pp. 84, 98. That this practice of excluding from the sacrament those who did not satisfy the minister's requirements involved serious dangers was recognised, and was clearly stated by Baxter, *Defence of the Principles of Love*, p. 50.

PAGE 169

1 Bunyan, (*A Holy Life the Beauty of Christianity*), vol. ii, pp. 527, 544.

2 *Minutes of the General Assembly of the General Baptists*, p. 15; see also *Church Book of Bunyan Meeting*, ff. 2–3, 54, 66, 97, 103.

3 Heywood, *op. cit.* vol. iv, pp. 50–1; cf. vol. ii, p. 277.

4 Bunyan, (*A Reason of My Practice in Worship*), vol. ii, p. 615.

5 Baxter, *An End of Doctrinal Controversies*, p. 6.

6 This was particularly true as the period progressed. The fact that able men were cut off from participation in civic and national life meant that they were exposed to the temptation to tyrannise over the local congregation. Of this there is occasional evidence in the *Church Book of Ford* and in the *Church Book of Bunyan Meeting*.

1 It must be added, however, that it is easy to see in the seventeenth-century records the seeds of that spirit which ultimately brought discipline into disrepute. Many of the societies were small groups, living an in-grown life in a very narrow orbit. When other interests were few, it was easy to make the most of the failures of your neighbours.

1 *Broadmead Records*, especially pp. 156–8, 167–70; cf. also *Church Book of Bunyan Meeting*, ff. 28, 34, 43, 54, 68, 96, 100, 131; *The Note-Book of Thomas Jolly*, pp. 40–1.

2 Cf. *Broadmead Records*, pp. 171–2. For the formula of ejection used at Bedford, see *Church Book of Bunyan Meeting*, f. 66: a man's conduct having been to 'the great reproach of the Gospel and people of God', 'therefore for the vindication of God's name and showing our dislike of his sins, and also for his soul's health, we did then and there cast him out of the church and deliver him up to Satan, for the destruction of the flesh, and that his spirit may be saved in the day of the Lord Jesus'.

1 *Church Book of Ford*, p. 72; cf. Calamy, *Account*, p. 71.

2 *Ibid.* pp. 2, 7, 10, 22; cf. *Church Book of Amersham*, p. 218.

3 *Church Book of Bunyan Meeting*, ff. 27, 29, 30–9, 43–5. From Robert Nelson the congregation withdrew for the following reasons: '1. He forsook the church with the order of the Gospel therein. 2. In a great assembly of the Church of England, he was openly and profanely bishoped, after the anti-Christian order of that generation, to the great profanation of God's order and heart-breaking of his Christian brethren. For these he hath been often admonished,...but hath condemned and slighted the same' (f. 45).

1 *Church Book of Ford*, pp. 23, 51, 61, 64; *of Amersham*, p. 227; *Minutes of the General Assembly of the General Baptists*, pp. 23 f., 26, 39, 52; Charles Marshall, *An Epistle to the Flock of Jesus Christ* (reprinted in *Sion's Travellers Comforted*), pp. 16–17; *Church Book of Bunyan Meeting*, ff. 96, 97, 100.

2 Cf. Ford, *A Gospel Church: or God's Holy Temple Opened*, p. 343; *Broadmead Records*, pp. 201–2; *Church Book of Bunyan Meeting*, ff. 44, 53, 54, 66, 101, 107, 117, etc. Note the sad case of John Stanton (*ibid.* f. 68) who, 'being divers times admonished of his sin and wickedness in beating his wife often, and other abuses towards her, he being impenitent, not hearing the church', was cast out.

1 *Church Book of Ford*, p. 75.

2 For an example of the solemn decision of a church to admonish a member for drunkenness, see Baxter MSS (Letters), vol. IV. f. 132 *a*.

PAGE 176

1 *Broadmead Records*, p. 200; also pp. 156-8, 164, 176-7, 177-8, 179. John Rush was 'cast out' of the Bunyan Meeting for being drunk 'above the ordinary rate of drunkards, for he could not be carried home from the Swan to his own house without the help of no less than three persons, who when they had brought him home could not present him as one alive to his family, he was so dead drunk'—*Church Book of Bunyan Meeting*, f. 53.

2 Heywood, *op. cit.* vol. II, p. 279; vol. III, p. 102; cf. pp. 206-7.

3 Baxter, *Church History of the Government of Bishops and their Councils Abbreviated*, Preface.

PAGE 177

1 *Broadmead Records*, pp. 195-200. For a case of fornication in Bunyan Meeting, see *The Church Book*, f. 66.

PAGE 178

1 Heywood, *op. cit.* vol. I, p. 47; vol. III, p. 318; vol. IV, p. 86; cf. also vol. III, p. 236.

2 Heywood, *op. cit.* vol. I, p. 178. But at least one man was furious at what he regarded as an intrusion into the privacy of his family life, *ibid.* vol. IV, p. 104. For Baxter's own experience, see *Rel. Bax.* pt. I, p. 115; pt. II, p. 179, and *An Apology*, etc. pp. 22, 56-7; also Bates, *A Funeral Sermon for...Richard Baxter*, 92-3.

3 *The Life of Adam Martindale*, p. 122. Concerning the importance attached to teaching both of children and of adults, see Bunyan, (*Instruction for the Ignorant*), vol. II, p. 675.

PAGE 179

1 *Minutes of the General Assembly of the General Baptist Churches in England*, pp. xxxi-xxxiii.

PAGE 180

1 *Broadmead Records*, pp. 76-9.

2 Cf. Gordon, *Freedom After Ejection*, *passim*.

PAGE 181

1 *The Persecution of Agnes Beaumon* gives a vivid picture of the constant dangers to which gossip exposed nonconformist congregations and their members and affords interesting side-lights on Bunyan and his people.

2 *Memoirs of...Ambrose Barnes*, pp. 138-9.

3 *Church Book of Amersham*, pp. 207-8.

PAGE 182

1 *Church Book of Ford*, pp. 35, 37, 37-8, 49, 58-9, 62; *Minutes of General Assembly of the General Baptists*, pp. xxii, 39, 43, 45, 51, 88-90; *The Diary of Ralph Thoresby*, vol. I, p. 242.

2 *Memoirs...of Ambrose Barnes*, p. 149; Howe, (*The Carnality of Religious Contention*), vol. IV, pp. 82ff.

19   289   CP

3 *Church Book of Ford*, p. 79. A similar case is recorded in the *Church Book of Bunyan Meeting*, f. 72.

PAGE 184

1 *Broadmead Records*, pp. 95, 98, 114–20, 147; Bunyan, (*Differences in Judgement about Water Baptism*), vol. II, pp. 617, 619, and (*Peaceable Principles and True*), p. 657.
2 *The Life of Adam Martindale*, p. 198.
3 Owen, *op. cit.* vol. IX, pp. 327, 470; Baxter's controversy with Penn led (after the customary initial acrimony) to unusually cordial expressions of respect and good will, Baxter MSS (Letters), vol. II; cf. also Baxter MSS (Treatises), vols. II, IV, V. It was, of course, a common thing for the civil and ecclesiastical authorities to see a disguised Jesuit in every Quaker.
4 Cf. Whiting, *Persecution Exposed*, p. 240; Fox, *Journal*, vol. II, pp. 99, 132; Ellwood, *Life*, pp. 168–9, 189–91; Crosby, *op. cit.* vol. II, pp. 231ff., 294ff.; *Broadmead Records*, pp. 36, 37, 47, 81, 83.

PAGE 185

1 Baxter MSS (Letters), vol. VI, ff. 244–5b; for Jolly's attempt to bring Owen and Baxter to a greater measure of agreement, see his *Note-Book*, p. 28.
2 Heywood, *op. cit.* vol. IV, p. 178. On the lamentable effect of nonconformist controversies, cf. the letter of Revd Richard Stretton in Thoresby, *Diary and Correspondence*, vol. III, p. 196.

PAGE 186

1 *The Life of Adam Martindale*, pp. 187–90. Cf. *The Autobiography of Henry Newcome*, vol. I, p. 163.
2 Calamy, *Historical Account of my own Life*, pp. 147ff.; also his *Defence of Moderate Nonconformity*, pt. I, p. 30 and *The Principles and Practices of Moderate Nonconformists*, p. 44; Heywood, *Diaries*, vol. I, p. 321; Thoresby, *Diary and Correspondence*, vol. III, p. 112.

PAGE 187

1 E. Pledger, MSS Autobiography and Diary, ff. 3–4.
2 (S. Wesley), *A Letter from a Country Divine... Concerning the Education of the Dissenters in their Private Academies*, pp. 3–4.
3 Cf. MSS Account of the Dissenting Academies (Dr Williams's Library), ff. 1, 33, 73. In a debate in the House of Lords in 1705, when many Anglican leaders were clamouring for the suppression of the academies, Lord Wharton twitted Archbishop Sharp with having sent his own sons to such a school— *The History and Proceedings of the House of Lords* (1742), vol. II, p. 158. Cf. *ibid.* p. 423.

PAGE 188

1 Defoe, *The Present State of Parties*, pp. 316–17; cf. also Defoe's comments in *More Short Ways With the Dissenters* (in *A Second Volume of the Writings*, etc.), pp. 276–7.

PAGE 189

1 Heywood, *op. cit.* vol. IV, pp. 306–21.
2 Thoresby, *Diary and Correspondence*, vol. III, p. 290.

PAGE 190

1 Frankland to Thoresby, Thoresby, *op. cit.* vol. III, pp. 172–4; cf. also p. 286.
2 Birch, *Life of Tillotson*, pp. 296–7.
3 Cf. Calamy, *Account*, p. 145.

PAGE 191

1 (S. Wesley), *A Letter from a Country Divine*... (1703); S. Palmer, *A Defence of the Dissenters' Education in their Private Academies* (1703). For later stages of the controversy, cf. Bogue and Bennett, *History of the Dissenters*, vol. II, pp. 90–1.
2 *Hist.MSS.C.R.* Portland MSS. (Welbeck Papers), V, 444.
3 Frankland to Heywood, Thoresby, *op. cit.* vol. III, pp. 175 f.

PAGE 192

1 Heywood, *op. cit.* vol. II, p. 194; also vol. III, p. 115.
2 The moderator, of course, never ordained without the assistance of other ministers. Cf. Calamy, *Account*, p. 191.
3 Heywood, *op. cit.* vol. II, pp. 199 ff.; also pp. 21 ff., 67, 204, 209. Cf. vol. III, pp. 115, 228; vol. IV, p. 126.

PAGE 193

1 Lloyd, *Quaker Social History*, p. 77; Raistrick, *Quakers in Science and Industry*, p. 29.
2 *The Church Book of Bunyan Meeting*, p. viii.

PAGE 194

1 *Rel. Bax.* pt. II, p. 207.

PAGE 195

1 Baxter, *Church History of Bishops and their Councils Abridged*, p. 5.
2 Charnock, (*Upon the Power of God*), vol. II, p. 164.
3 R. Alleine, *Vindiciae Pietatis*, p. 69.
4 Owen, (*A Discourse Concerning the Holy Spirit*), vol. III, p. 64; cf. Owen's comment in *Of Communion with the Holy Ghost*: 'The divine nature is the reason and cause of all worship', vol. II, p. 268.

PAGE 196

1 Charnock, (*Upon God's Dominion*), vol. II, p. 485.
2 Charnock, (*Upon God's Wisdom*), vol. II, p. 78.
3 Baxter, *The Second Part Against Schism*, p. 8.
4 Owen, (*Posthumous Sermons*), vol. IX, p. 55.

PAGE 197

1 *Ibid.* p. 59; Charnock, (*God the Author of Reconciliation*), vol. III, p. 471; Owen, *op. cit.* p. 74.
2 *Ibid.* p. 56; cf. also p. 63.
3 Owen, *op. cit.* p. 56.
4 Howe, (*The Work of the Holy Spirit in Reference to Particular Persons*), vol. v, pp. 186–7.

PAGE 198

1 Owen, (*Posthumous Sermons*), vol. IX, p. 70; Bunyan, (*The Pharisee and the Publican*), vol. II, p. 219, and (*Instruction for the Ignorant*), vol. II, p. 680.
2 Charnock, vol. II, pp. 81, 82.
3 Howe, (*Thirteen Sermons on Various Subjects*), vol. VI, p. 361.
4 *Rel. Bax.* pt. II, p. 306. Baxter claims that in most of the churches where he worshipped, the nonconformists used 'most of the liturgy', *The English Nonconformity*, p. 296.

PAGE 199

1 Charnock, vol. II, p. 466.
2 Howe, (*The Carnality of Religious Contention*), vol. IV, p. 90.
3 Owen, (*A Discourse of the Work of the Holy Spirit in Prayer*), vol. IV, p. 301.
4 Baxter, *The English Nonconformity*, p. 11; *Second Part of the Nonconformist's Plea for Peace*, pp. 141–2; Baxter, *Five Disputations of Church Government and Worship*, pp. 47, 383; Owen, *op. cit.* pp. 243 f., 283, 344.

PAGE 200

1 Bunyan, (*The Pharisee and the Publican*), vol. II, p. 225; Baxter, *A Second True Defence of the Meer Nonconformists*, p. 15.
2 Manton, (*A Practical Exposition of the Lord's Prayer*), vol. I, p. 33.
3 Baxter, *The English Nonconformity*, p. 301.

PAGE 201

1 Howe, (*A Letter Written out of the Country to a Person of Quality in the City*), vol. IV, p. 445.
2 Clarkson, *op. cit.* vol. I, p. 508.
3 Bunyan, (*Doctrine of the Law and Grace*), vol. I, p. 493.

PAGE 202

1 Clarkson, (*Of Faith*), vol. I, p. 96; Bunyan, (*Instruction for the Ignorant*), vol. II, p. 684; R. Alleine, *Vindiciae Pietatis*, pp. 114–15, 118 ff.; Bunyan, (*The Holy War*), vol. III, p. 329.
2 Bunyan, (*On Praying in the Spirit*), vol. I, pp. 628 ff.; Owen, (*Of the Dominion of Sin and Grace*), vol. VII, p. 544.
3 Bunyan, (*The Straight Gate*), vol. I, p. 368; (*The Doctrine of the Law and Grace Unfolded*), vol. I, pp. 500 ff.
4 Clarkson, vol. I, p. xii.

5 George Newton, *A Sermon Preached at the Funeral of Mr Joseph Alleine*, p. 30.
6 Bunyan, (*Instruction for the Ignorant*), vol. II, p. 675.

PAGE 203

1 Clarkson, (*Of Faith*), vol. I, p. 140; Howe, (*The Principles of the Oracles of God*), vol. VII, p. 39; Bunyan, (*Of the Resurrection of the Dead*), vol. II, p. 123.
2 Bunyan, *op. cit.* p. 100.
3 Clarkson, *op. cit.* vol. I, pp. 170f.
4 Clarkson, (*The Excellent Knowledge of Christ*), vol. I, p. 262.
5 Clarkson, (*Of Faith*), vol. I, p. 141; T. Goodwin uses much the same words, (*The Constitution, Right Order and Government of the Churches of Christ*), vol. XI, p. 364.
6 Owen, *op. cit.* pp. 328, 453; Bunyan, (*The Holy War*), vol. III, p. 348; Howe, (*On the Love of God and our Brother*), vol. VI, p. 13.
7 Calamy, *The Principles and Practice of Moderate Nonconformists...*, p. 33.

PAGE 204

1 Bunyan, (*Doctrine of the Law*), vol. I, p. 495.
2 Bunyan, *Grace Abounding*, §276.
3 *The Life of Adam Martindale*, p. 36.
4 Owen, (*Concerning Evangelical Love, Church Peace and Unity*), vol. XV, p. 118.

PAGE 205

1 R. Alleine, *Vindiciae Pietatis*, pp. 123, 168f., 172.
2 Howe, *Works*, vol. VI, p. 375.

PAGE 206

1 Charnock, *op. cit.* vol. II, pp. 33, 35. Cf. also Howe's vindication of the justice of God from charges arising from the depravity of man, (*The Principles of the Oracles of God*), vol. VII, pp. 476ff.
2 Charnock, (*Upon the Goodness of God*), vol. II, p. 391.
3 Charnock, (*Upon the Wisdom of God*), vol. II, pp. 8, 33–5, 43, 78.
4 Clarkson, (*Of Living By Faith*), vol. I, p. 189.
5 *The Life and Death of the Revd Joseph Alleine*, p. 40; cf. Josselin's efforts, *Diary*, pp. 59–60; Newcome, *Diary*, pp. 2, 9. John Quick aimed to begin the day's work in his study at 2 a.m.—Daniel Williams, *Practical Discourses on Several Important Subjects*, vol. II, p. 227.

PAGE 207

1 Adams and Veal, *Works of Charnock*, To the Reader. Owen, however, pointed out one of the characteristic dangers of a scholarly ministry: a man becomes too preoccupied with study, (*Posthumous Sermons*), vol. IX, p. 448.
2 John Spademan, *A Sermon Upon the Occasion of the Justly Lamented Death of the truly Reverend Mr John Howe*.
3 Adams and Veal, *op. cit.*

PAGE 208

1 Howe, vol. VI, p. 347. Cf. an almost identical pattern in Charnock, vol. II, p. 282. But with few variants, it was characteristic of all Puritan preaching. In one of Philip Henry's sermons, there are forty-three divisions and sub-divisions (*What Christ is made to Believers*, pp. 9 ff.).

2 Cf. Bunyan, (*Come and Welcome to Jesus*), vol. I, p. 240.

3 South, *Sermons*, vol. III, p. 35.

PAGE 209

1 Howe, vol. IV, pp. 82 ff.

2 Howe, (*Thirteen Sermons on Various Subjects*), vol. VI, p. 195; Heywood, (*Life*), vol. I, p. 150; Bunyan, (*The Holy War*), vol. III, p. 347.

3 Charnock, (*A Discourse of Divine Providence*), vol. I, p. 49; cf. Bunyan, *op. cit.* vol. III, pp. 328–9; Baxter, *An Apology for the Nonconformist's Ministry*, p. 18.

4 Bunyan, *Grace Abounding*, §§276, 278, 280.

PAGE 210

1 Horton Davies, *The Worship of the Puritans*, p. 191.

2 Howe, (*The Principles of the Oracles of God*), vol. VII, p. 205; Bunyan, (*Of the Resurrection of the Dead*), vol. II, p. 111; Bunyan, (*The Saints' Knowledge of Christ's Love*), vol. II, pp. 28, 39; Charnock, (*Upon the Goodness of God*), vol. II, pp. 364–94; (*Upon God's Dominion*), pp. 461 ff.

3 Howe, *op. cit.* vol. VII, pp. 144 ff., 476 ff.

4 *The Life of Adam Martindale*, p. 216.

PAGE 211

1 Baxter, *A Saint or A Brute*, Introd. Ep.; *A Sermon of Repentance*, Preface; *Rel. Bax.* pt. I, pp. 114, 124–5.

2 Bunyan, *Grace Abounding*, Preface.

3 Bunyan, (*Law and Grace*), vol. I, p. 495.

PAGE 212

1 Charnock, (*Practical Atheism*), vol. I, p. 242.

2 Bunyan, (*Christian Behaviour*), vol. II, p. 574. Cf. also pp. 114, 126.

3 Bunyan, (*Come and Welcome to Jesus*), vol. I, p. 252; (*The Jerusalem Sinner Saved*), p. 89.

4 Charnock, (*Upon the Wisdom of God*), vol. II, p. 55.

5 Howe, (*The Redeemer's Tears Wept Over Lost Souls*), vol. IV, p. 46; (*Of the Love of God and Our Brother*), vol. VI, p. 23; Clarkson, (*Of Faith*), vol. I, p. 172.

PAGE 213

1 Calamy, *The Church and the Dissenters Compared*, p. 6.

2 South, *Sermons*, vol. IV, p. 48; cf. also Robert Steppens, *Rex Theologus*, Ep. ded.; Patrick, *A Friendly Debate*, pp. 14–16. As examples of the use of simple

language and a natural and unaffected voice by nonconformist preachers, Calamy cites Dr Bates and Dr Gilpin, *Account*, pp. 49, 155.

3 Bunyan, (*The Pharisee and the Publican*), vol. II, p. 271.

4 Baxter, *The English Nonconformity*, p. 15.

5 Heywood, (*Life*), vol. I, p. 113; also *Diaries*, vol. I, pp. 167, 193, 197, 282, 341; vol. III, pp. 126, 129; Horton, *Rich Treasure in Earthen Vessels*, p. 17; Calamy, *Account*, p. 541.

6 *The Note-Book of Thomas Jolly*, p. 57.

PAGE 214

1 Pope, *Life of Seth Ward*, p. 148.

2 Clarke and Foxcroft, *The Life of Gilbert Burnet*, p. 142.

3 Gilbert Burnet, *Pastoral Care*. Dean Granville also advised his curates to preach for half an hour, *Remains*, vol. II, p. 144.

4 Thoresby, *op. cit.* vol. I, p. 130. The time had been verified both by 'Mr W.'s and church clock', so it was not a random guess. The length was not resented, but it was noticed.

5 Bunyan, (*A Holy Life the Beauty of Christianity*), vol. II, p. 539.

PAGE 215

1 Bunyan, (*An Exhortation of Peace and Unity*), vol. II, p. 750.

2 Letter of Penry to Norton, Oxford, 1672, in Baxter MSS (Letters).

3 *The Autobiography of Lady Anne Halkett*, p. 115.

PAGE 216

1 I. Mather, *Practical Truths tending to Promote the Power of Godliness*, pp. 209 ff. Mather returned to New England in 1662, and the book in question was published in Boston. There is no reason to think that his hearers in old England had been essentially different.

2 Clarkson, (*Hearing the Word*), vol. I, p. 430.

3 Clarkson, *op. cit.* p. 429.

4 Bunyan (*Instruction for the Ignorant*), vol. II, p. 679.

5 Howe, (*On Hearing the Word*), vol. VI, pp. 259–61.

6 Clarkson, *op. cit.* vol. I, pp. 431, 435.

PAGE 217

1 Bunyan, (*The Saint's Knowledge of Christ's Love*), vol. II, p. 3; Bunyan, (*Instruction for the Ignorant*), vol. II, p. 683; Owen, (*Posthumous Sermons*), vol. IX, p. 328; Baxter, (*A Christian Directory*), vol. I, pp. 44, 633. Much of this practical advice is found in Howe, *op. cit.* vol. VI, pp. 253 ff. and Clarkson, vol. I, pp. 440 ff.; Baxter, *op. cit.* pp. 473–7.

2 Baxter, *op. cit.* pp. 474–5.

PAGE 218

1 Clarkson, (*Of Faith*), vol. I, p. 173; Henry, *op. cit.* p. 330; O. Heywood, *Diaries*, vol. I, p. 46; *Rel. Bax.* pt. II, p. 249; Heywood, *op. cit.* vol. I, p. 247; vol. II, pp. 87, 97, 103; vol. IV, p. 22.

PAGE 219

1 Bunyan, *Grace Abounding*, §282.

PAGE 221

1 Baxter MSS (Letters), vol. VI, f. 41.
2 *Ibid.* vol. VI, f. 199 a.
3 *The Hatton Correspondence*, vol. I, p. 128.
4 Pepys, *Diary*, 31 July 1663 (vol. III, p. 234). The pamphlet was *Cabala* (reprinted in *Somers' Tracts*, vol. VII, pp. 567 f.).
5 Luttrell, *Brief Historical Relation*, vol. VI, pp. 67–8, 98. For the inference that the reading public expected a little violence from controversialists, see V. Alsop's sly thrust in *The Mischief of Impositions*, p. xxxi.
6 Corbet, *An Account Given of the Principles and Practices of Several Nonconformists*, p. 15; Baxter, *The English Nonconformity*, Preface; *Answer to Dr Edward Stillingfleet's Charge*, etc. Preface; *The Judgment of the Nonconformists*, p. 83.

PAGE 222

1 Baxter, *The English Nonconformity*, p. 209.
2 Baxter, *The Judgment of the Nonconformists*, pp. 21–45.
3 Baxter, *An Apology*, etc. pp. 143, 147; V. Alsop, *The Mischief of Impositions*, p. 93.

PAGE 223

1 Calamy, *Defence of Moderate Nonconformity*, pt. I, pp. x–xi.
2 Calamy, *op. cit.* p. 11; Baxter, *The Judgment of the Nonconformists*, pp. 116–22. Baxter lists fifteen respects in which the nonconformists felt that oaths, promises, and declarations could not be so laxly interpreted as was common among the more careless conformists.
3 Baxter, *The English Nonconformity*, p. 5.
4 Baxter, *The English Nonconformity*, p. 209; *An Apology for the Nonconformist's Ministry*, pp. 147 ff.; *Answer to Dr Edward Stillingfleet's Charge...*, p. 27.

PAGE 224

1 Baxter, *The Second Part of the Nonconformist's Plea for Peace*, pp. 23–8, 164, 172–8.
2 Corbet, *The Interest of England* and *The Second Part of the Interest of England*.

PAGE 225

1 Calamy, *op. cit.* pt. I, pp. 16–28.
2 Baxter, *Second True Defence of the Meer Nonconformists*, pp. 39, 56.
3 (C. Burgess), *Reasons Shewing the Necessity of Reformation of the Public: 1. Doctrine, 2. Worship, 3. Rites and Ceremonies, 4. Church Government and Discipline.* The title is almost a synopsis of the controversial questions which divided Anglican and Nonconformist.
4 Baxter, *Answer to Dr Edward Stillingfleet's Charge*, Preface; *The English Nonconformity*, pp. 36–7.

PAGE 226

1 Z. Crofton, Ἀνάληψις, Ἀνελήφθη, *The Fastening of St Peter's Fetters.*

PAGE 227

1 Gauden, ΆΝΑΛΥΣΙΣ, *The Loosening of St Peter's Bonds*, pp. 3–4, 6–10, 13, 20, 21–2.
2 Calamy, *op. cit.* pt. I, p. 2. Cf. *A Private Conference between a Rich Alderman and a Poor Country Vicar made Public*, p. 192.
3 Baxter, *Apology*, etc. pp. 111–12, and *The English Nonconformity*, pp. 125 ff.

PAGE 228

1 Clarkson, (*Of Taking Up the Cross*), vol. I, p. 506.
2 Baxter, *The Judgment of the Nonconformists*, p. 113.
3 Cf. Patrick, *A Friendly Debate*, p. 57; L'Estrange, *The Dissenters' Sayings* (the second part), pp. 29f., 34–6, 39–44, 55.

PAGE 229

1 M. Meade, *Spiritual Wisdom Improved against Temptation*, Ep. ded. In times of intense persecution, the omission of the king from the prayer before the sermon could be construed as evidence that a nonconformist minister was guilty of sedition—*Cal.S.P.Dom.* 1682, pp. 86, 104.
2 Baxter, *The Second Part of the Nonconformist's Plea for Peace*, Preface; Delamere, *Works*, p. 415; cf. A. Marvell, (*The Rehearsal Transprosed*, pt. I), vol. III, pp. 176–7.

PAGE 230

1 Cf. James Jones, *Nonconformity not Inconsistent with Loyalty* (1684).
2 John Owen, (*Truth and Innocence Vindicated*), vol. XIII, p. 369–439.
3 Baxter, *The English Nonconformity*, p. 262; Corbet, *An Account Given of the Principles and Practices of Several Nonconformists*, pp. 8–14; Henry, *Diaries and Letters*, pp. 368 f.; Baxter, *The Second Part of the Nonconformist's Plea for Peace*, pp. 35, 37.

PAGE 231

1 Baxter, *Second Part of the…Plea for Peace*, pp. 38–9.
2 *Ibid.* pp. 40–8. Chapter III of this work (Of the Power of Kings and the People's Obedience) is arranged, with characteristic Baxterian exactitude and thoroughness, under sixty-nine propositions. There is also an interesting statement of the Puritan view of the subject's rightful obedience to rulers in Baxter's *Christian Directory*, pt. III, ch. III, (*Practical Works*), vol. I, pp. 744–68.

PAGE 232

1 Calamy, *Account*, p. 549.
2 Peirce, *A Vindication of the Dissenters*, pp. 313–15, 322–5.

PAGE 233

1 Stillingfleet, *The Mischief of Separation, passim.* Stillingfleet subsequently expanded his sermon into a work of much more ambitious scope, *The Unreasonableness of Separation.*

2 V. Alsop, *The Mischief of Impositions,* p. iv.

3 Owen, (*A Brief Vindication of the Nonconformists from the Charge of Schism*), vol. XIII, p. 309; Alsop, *op. cit.* pp. 6–7.

4 *Ibid.* p. vi.

5 Howe, (*A Letter Out of the Country,* etc.), vol. IV, p. 441.

6 Alsop, *op. cit.* pp. 2, 12, 31, 47–8.

PAGE 234

1 Baxter, *An Apology,* etc. p. 130; cf. Owen, *op. cit.* pp. 319–21.

2 Baxter, *Second True Defence,* p. 26, *Answer to . . . Stillingfleet's Charge,* pp. 45–6; Alsop, *op. cit.* pp. xxi, 31.

3 Owen, vol. XIII, p. 313; Baxter, *Answer to . . . Stillingfleet's Charge,* p. 43; *The English Nonconformity,* pp. 163–5; Alsop, *op. cit.* pp. 64f.

PAGE 235

1 Alsop, *op. cit.* pp. xi–xviii.

2 Calamy, *op. cit.* p. 28.

PAGE 236

1 Baxter, *The English Nonconformity,* p. 301. Cf. also pp. 154–5; also *Answer to . . . Stillingfleet's Charge,* pp. 20–1, and *An Apology,* etc. pp. 14, 33–9.

2 William Assheton, in *The Cases of Scandal and Persecution* (1674), p. 71; note also the charge that pride and reluctance to yield accounted for the nonconformists' attitude, Gauden, *Considerations touching the Liturgy,* p. 5; Stillingfleet, *The Mischief of Separation,* pp. 3, 56–7; Patrick, *A Friendly Debate,* pp. 3, 96, 110f.

PAGE 237

1 Baxter MSS (Letters), vol. VI, f. 199a.

2 *Cal.S.P.Dom.* 1663–4, p. 64.

3 Baxter, *An Apology,* etc. pp. 16, 142, 177–8.

4 Baxter, *An Answer to . . . Stillingfleet's Charge,* pp. 97, 99–100.

PAGE 238

1 Meade, *Spiritual Wisdom Improved against Temptation,* pp. 19–20.

2 For an example of the point of view widely held among moderate Puritans, see the letter of Hicks to Baxter, Baxter MSS (Letters), vol. VI, f. 163a, b. Cf. Barwick, *Life of John Barwick,* p. 256.

PAGE 239

1 Pepys, *Diary,* vol. II, pp. 264, 271, 391, 434. Cf. *Cal.S.P.Dom.* 1660–1, p. 542.

2 Stillingfleet, *Irenicum,* p. xiii.

3 Gauden, *op. cit.* p. 14: '...primitive, reformed and regular episcopacy, so reduced to an efficacious conjunction with Presbytery as the most reverend primate of Armagh proposed....'

4 C. Jessop, *The Angel of the Church of Ephesus No Bishop of Ephesus, distinguished in order from and Superior in Power to a Presbytery* (1660); for a characteristic statement of the nonconformist position regarding the relation of presbyters and bishops, see Corbet, *The Nonconformist's Plea for Lay-Communion,* pp. 12–14, 20–24. Cf. also Clarkson, *No Evidence for Diocesan Churches* (1681) and *Diocesan Churches not yet Discovered in the Primitive Times* (1682).

5 Baxter, *Church History of the Government of Bishops,* etc., *passim. Rel. Bax.* pt. II, pp. 234, 237–8, 267–8.

PAGE 240

1 Corbet, *Interest of England,* pt. I, pp. 67–82; Firmin, *The Liturgical Considerator Considered,* p. 3; Baxter, *The English Nonconformity,* pp. 14, 31, 36–8, *Answer to...Stillingfleet's charge,* pp. 73–4; *Rel. Bax.* pt. II, in the documents drawn up for the Savoy Conference, presents many of the nonconformist arguments.

PAGE 241

1 Cf. Cosin to Frankland, Calamy, *Account,* p. 286. But some bishops demanded an explicit repudiation of Presbyterian ordination—Henry, *Life of the Revd Philip Henry,* p. 58.

2 *Rel. Bax.* pt. II, pp. 273, 422; pt. III, p. 30, and Appendix, p. 101; Baxter, *The English Nonconformity,* p. 24; Z. Crofton, *A Serious Review of Presbyter's Re-ordination by Bishops,* pp. 2–4, 11; J. Humfrey, *The Question of Re-ordination,* pp. 18–20, 34; Calamy, *Abridgment,* p. 196–200; Newcome, *Diary,* p. 88.

3 (Henry Hickman), Χειροθεσία τοῦ πρεσβυτερίου, p. 3.

4 G. Firmin, *Presbyterian Ordination Vindicated,* p. 25; *Terms of Accommodation,* p. 9; Corbet, *Of the Church,* pp. 70–2; Humfrey, *op. cit.* p. 51.

5 Baxter, *op. cit.* p. 24. Cf. pp. 242–3.

PAGE 242

1 G. Firmin, *op. cit.* p. 29. One of the most interesting cases was that of John Humfrey, who in his first book on the subject, argued that reordination was permissible, and was reordained. He then bitterly repented, disavowed his action, repudiated his new orders, and became a nonconformist. Calamy printed a number of documents which Humfrey had transmitted to him— *Account,* pp. 615–20.

2 Vavasor Powell, *Common Prayer Book No Divine Service,* pp. 1, 4, 7, 12–14; Bunyan, *(Advice to Sufferers),* vol. II, p. 714; Clarkson, *(Of Taking Up the Cross),* vol. I, pp. 491, 505–10; Corbet, *Interest of England,* pt. I, p. 89.

PAGE 243

1 *The Grand Debate between the most Reverend the Bishops and the Presbyterian Divines* (as reprinted in Gould, *Documents*), pp. 206–10, 218–28, 258, 262.

Concerning the legitimacy of a liturgy, Baxter had never been in doubt—see his dissertation on *Whether it be lawful to use Set forms of Prayer*, Baxter MSS (Treatises), vol. III, ff. 1 *ab*–2 *ab*.

2 Baxter, *The Second Part of the Nonconformist's Plea for Peace*, pp. 142, 157–8; also, *An Apology*, etc. p. 4; *Rel. Bax.* pt. II, p. 306. The liturgy is printed in Baxter, *Practical Works*, vol. I, pp. 922–48.

3 G. Firmin, *The Liturgical Considerator Considered*, Epistle to the Reader (by Crofton); Baxter, *The Nonconformist's Advocate*, pp. 10, 64 ff. and *The Christian Directory*, p. 717, and *Rel. Bax.* pt. II, p. 254; Peirce, *Vindication of the Dissenters*, pp. 537–46; V. Powell, *op. cit.* p. 16; Calamy, *A Defence of Moderate Nonconformity*, pt. I, p. 338; Corbet, *Remains*, p. 161.

PAGE 244

1 At the beginning of the period, most of the points at issue were stated clearly and at length in the papers issued preparatory to or in connection with the Savoy Conference; *Rel. Bax.* pt. II, pp. 308–33, 369–72. Calamy provided an excellent summary of the arguments used by both sides (as seen, of course, from the nonconformist position) in his *Abridgment*, pp. 203–37, and in *A Defence of Moderate Nonconformity*, especially part II.

2 Peirce, *op. cit.* pp. 489 ff.

3 Baxter, *The English Nonconformity*, pp. 61 ff., 79, 193; *Rel. Bax.* pt. II, pp. 236, 273, 346–9; Baxter MSS (Letters), vol. V, f. 210 *ab*.

4 Howe, (*A Letter Written Out of the Country*), vol. IV, p. 417.

5 Baxter, *The Judgment of the Nonconformists*, pp. 103–4; Baxter, *The Second Part of the Nonconformist's Plea for Peace*, p. 30; cf. *Rel. Bax.* pt. II, pp. 257, 327–8.

6 Baxter, *The English Nonconformity*, pp. 12, 18, 74.

7 Baxter, *The Nonconformist's Advocate*, p. 16.

8 Baxter, *The English Nonconformity*, pp. 75–7. The Puritans did not ask that the sign of the cross in baptism be abolished, but that it should not be imposed. In 1689, in the debates of the ecclesiastical commission, it was decided that the matter should be left 'indifferent'. S. Patrick, *Autobiography*, p. 149.

PAGE 245

1 Baxter, *The English Nonconformity*, p. 66; Howe, (*A Letter Written Out o, the Country*), vol. IV, pp. 417–18; Baxter, *Second True Defence of the Meer Nonconformist*, p. 167; Taylor, *op. cit.* p. 70.

2 Peirce, *op. cit.* pp. 476 ff.

PAGE 246

1 D. Cawdrey, *Bowing Toward the Altar...Impleaded as grossly Superstitious* (1661); Crofton, *Altar-Worship, or Bowing to the Communion Table Considered as to the Novelty, Vanity, Iniquity, Malignity Charged upon it* (1661); Peirce, *op. cit.* pp. 501 ff.; *The Diary of the Revd Ralph Josselin*, p. 23.

PAGE 248

1 Both kings tried to change the policy; nothing, however, showed the weakness of their constitutional position so clearly as their inability to defy at this point the wishes of the country gentlemen, who were increasingly asserting their political power. As members of parliament they made the laws; as justices of the peace they enforced them, and royal interference was not tolerated.

PAGE 249

1 Cobbett, *Parl. Hist.* vol. IV, col. 516.

PAGE 250

1 *L.J.* vol. XIV, pp. 134, 217; Cobbett, *Parl. Hist.* vol. V, cols. 263–6; for the text of the Act, see Gould, *Documents*, pp. 507ff.
2 Roman Catholics and Unitarians were exempted from the benefits of the Act.
3 Macaulay, *History of England*, vol. I, pp. 697–8.
4 Cf. the letter to Matthew Henry in P. Henry, *Diaries and Letters*, p. 362.
5 *The Letters of Humphrey Prideaux*, p. 153.
6 *Memoirs of Sir John Reresby*, pp. 425, 441; cf. Evelyn, *Diary* (26 Apr. 1689), vol. II, p. 300.

PAGE 251

1 *L.J.* vol. XV, pp. 150, 156–7; Grey, *Debates*, vol. IX, pp. 110–11; Cobbett, *op. cit.* vol. V, cols. 184, 196–8.
2 Cf. Patrick, *Autobiography*, p. 149.

PAGE 252

1 *Rel. Bax.* pt. II, p. 278.

PAGE 253

1 Calamy gives a good deal of information about the Happy Union. Regarding the Common Fund, see A. G. Gordon, *Freedom After Ejection*, *passim*.

PAGE 255

1 Heywood, *Diaries*, vol. III, pp. 260–1.

PAGE 256

1 Howe, (*The Carnality of Religious Contention*), vol. IV, p. 120.
2 Owen, (*Posthumous Sermons*), vol. IX, pp. 331, 459.
3 *Ibid.* pp. 510–15. Cf. Clarkson, (*Of Living by Faith*), vol. I, p. 173, and (*Faith in Prayer*), p. 204.
4 *The Life of Ambrose Barnes*, p. 5; *The Letters of Humphrey Prideaux*, pp. 154, 160–2.
5 Baxter, *An End of Doctrinal Controversies*, p. vii.
6 *The Diary of Ralph Thoresby*, vol. I, p. 57; Crosby, *History of the English Baptists*, vol. IV, pp. 5, 16.

1 *The Life of Ambrose Barnes*, p. 9.
2 Calamy, MS sermon on Gospel Ministers the Salt of the Earth, f. 2; *Letters of Eminent Men to Ralph Thoresby*, vol. III, p. 240; *The Life of Adam Martindale*, p. 236.
3 Calamy, *Historical Account of my own Life*, vol. I, pp. 303 f.
4 *Minutes of the General Assembly of the General Baptists*, pp. 37, 39, 43, 67; Underwood, *History of English Baptists*, pp. 126, 128. There were two varieties of Baptists at the time (General and Particular), but their problems were largely the same.
5 Hunter, *The Rise of the Old Dissent*, p. 400.

BIBLIOGRAPHY

(This is not a bibliography of the period, but merely a list of those books directly referred to in this work. Unless otherwise indicated, the place of publication is London.)

I. MANUSCRIPTS

Dr Williams's Library, London:
  Baxter MSS (Letters).
  Baxter MSS (Treatises).
  Turner MSS.
  Roger Morrice MS Entering Book.
  The Journal of Elias Pledger.
  The Diary of Owen Stockton.
  The Diary of Mrs Stockton.
  The Conformity of those that the Vulgar call Independents with the Ancient
    Christians.
  An Account of the Dissenting Academies from the Restoration of Charles II.
  E. Calamy, D.D. Gospel Ministers the Salt of the Earth.

British Museum:
  Lansdowne MSS.
  Additional MSS.

Bodleian Library:
  Tanner MSS.
  Western MSS.
  Rawlinson MSS.
  Walker MSS.

Friends Historical Library, London:
  Abraham MSS.
  Canton MSS.
  Gibson MSS.
  Record of Sufferings.
  Spence MSS.
  Thirnbeck MSS.

II. PRIMARY

Adis, Henry. *A Fanatick's Letter*. 1660.
——— *A Fanatick's Address*. 1661.
——— *A Fanatick's Alarm*. 1661.
——— *A Fanatick's Testimony against Swearing*. 1661.

Agas, B. *An Antidote against Dr Edward Stillingfleet's Unreasonableness of Separation.* 1681.

Alleine, J. *A Call to Archippus.* 1664.

—— *The Voice of God in His Promises.* 1666.

—— *The Believer's Triumph in God.* 1666.

—— *Christian Letters.*

Alleine, R. *The Godly Man's Portion and Sanctuary.* 1663.

—— *Heaven Opened.* 1666.

—— *Vindiciae Pietatis.* 1684.

(Alleine, Mrs T. and others.) *The Life and Death of the Revd Joseph Alleine.* New York, 1840.

Alsop, V. *The Mischief of Impositions,* 1680.

—— *Melius Inquirendum.* 1681.

—— *A Faithful Rebuke to a False Report.* 1693.

An Abstract of the Sufferings of the People called Quakers. 3 vols. 1738.

An Address to Persons of Fashion.

An Apology of some called Anabaptists in and about the City of London. 1660.

An Appeal from the Country to the City, for the Preservation of his Majesty's Person, etc. 1679.

Assheton, W. *Toleration Disapproved and Condemned.* 1670.

—— *The Cases of Scandal and Persecution.* 1674.

'ΑΣΥΣΤΑΤΑ. *The Repugnancy and Inconsistency of the Maintenance of an Orthodox Ministry, and Toleration of Heretical Opinions.* 1659.

Aubrey, J. *Brief Lives, Chiefly of Contemporaries.* Ed. A. Clark. 2 vols. Oxford, 1898.

(Bagshaw, Edward.) *The Great Question concerning things indifferent in Religious Worship.* 1660.

Baillie, R. *The Letters and Journals of Robert Baillie.* 3 vols. Edinburgh, 1824.

Baker, Richard. *Chronicle.* 1670.

Barclay, Robert. *An Apology for the True Christian Divinity.* Philadelphia, 1775.

(Barnes.) *Memoirs of the Life of Mr Ambrose Barnes, 1627–1710.* Surtees Society, vol. L. Durham, 1867.

Barwick, P. *Life of John Barwick* (English edition). 1724.

Bates, William. *A Funeral Sermon for the Reverend, Holy, and Excellent Divine, Mr Richard Baxter.* 1692.

Baxter, Richard. *The Quaker's Catechism.* 1656.

—— *Gildas Salvianus* (1656). 1860.

—— *Five Disputations of Church Government and Worship.* 1659.

—— *A Key for Catholics.* 1659.

—— *Universal Concord.* 1660.

—— *The Life of Faith, as it is the Evidence of things unseen.* 1660.

—— *A Sermon of Repentance.* 1660.

—— *Right Rejoicing.* 1660.

Baxter, Richard. *Two Papers of Proposals concerning the Discipline and Ceremonies of the Church of England.* 1661.
—— *A Saint or a Brute.* 1662.
—— *A Defence of the Principles of Love.* 1671.
—— *The Judgment of the Nonconformists.* 1676.
—— *The Second Part of the Nonconformist's Plea for Peace.* 1680.
—— *The Nonconformist's Advocate.* 1680.
—— *Answer to Dr Edward Stillingfleet's Charge of Separation.* 1680.
—— *An Apology for the Nonconformist's Ministry.* 1681.
—— *Church-History of the Government of Bishops and their Councils Abbreviated.* 1681.
—— *A Search for the English Schismatic.* 1681.
—— *A Second True Defence of the Meer Nonconformists.* 1681.
—— *A Funeral Sermon for Sir Henry Ashurst.* 1681.
—— *Catholic Communion Defended.* 1684.
—— *The Second Part against Schism.* 1684.
—— *R.B.'s Sense of the Subscribed Articles of Religion.* 1689.
—— *Cain and Abel Malignity.* 1689.
—— *The English Nonconformity as under King Charles II and King James II truly Stated and Argued.* 1689.
—— *An End of Doctrinal Controversies,* 1691.
—— *Reliquiae Baxterianae.* 1696.
—— *The Practical Works.* 4 vols. 1854.
—— *A Breviate of the Life of Margaret...Baxter* (1681). 1928.
(Beaumont.) *The Persecution of Agnes Beaumont.* Ed. G. B. Harrison. N.d.
Behold A Cry; or a true relation of the inhuman and violent outrages of divers soldiers, constables and others, practised upon many of the Lord's People...called Anabaptists.
Bellers, John. *Writings.* Ed. Ruth Fry. 1935.
Be Merry and Wise. 1660.
Besse, Joseph. *A Collection of the Sufferings of the People called Quakers.* 2 vols. 1753.
Bethell, Slingsby. *The Most Material Debates in that pretended Parliament called by Richard Cromwell.* 1680.
Bishop, George. *The Burden of Babylon and the Triumph of Zion.* 1661.
—— *A Little Treatise concerning Sufferings.* 1663.
—— *The Warnings of the Lord to the King of England and his Parliament.* 1667.
Bold, S. *A Sermon against Persecution.* 1682.
Bolde, Thomas. *Rhetorick Restrained.* 1660.
Bramston, J. *The Autobiography of Sir John Bramston.* Camden Society. 1845.
A Brief Confession or Declaration of Faith [Anabaptist]. 1660.
Bunyan, John. *The Whole Works.* Ed. George Offor. 3 vols. Glasgow, 1862.
(Bunyan.) *A Relation of the Imprisonment of Mr John Bunyan* (usually printed as a pendant to *Grace Abounding*).
(Burgess, C.) *Reasons Shewing the Necessity of Reformation of the Public. 1. Doctrine, 2. Worship, 3. Rites and Ceremonies, 4. Church Government and Discipline.* 1660.

Burrough, Edward. *Works.* 1672.

Burrough, Jeremiah. *The Excellency of Holy Courage in Evil Times.* 1661.

Burnet, G. *An Apology for the Church of England with Relation to the Spirit of Persecution.* 1688.

—— *A Discourse of the Pastoral Care.* 1692.

—— *History of my own Time* (Reign of Charles II. Ed. O. Airy). 2 vols. Oxford, 1897.

—— *History of my own Time.* 6 vols. Oxford, 1833.

—— *Some Unpublished Letters of Gilbert Burnet, the Historian.* Camden Miscellany, vol. XI. 1907.

Butler, S. *Hudibras.* 1811.

(Butler, S.?) *A Proposal Humbly Offered for the Farming of Liberty of Conscience.* 1662.

Calamy, Edmund. *Eli Trembling for the Ark.* Oxford. 1662.

Calamy, Edmund ('E.F. and N.'). *A Defence of Moderate Nonconformity.* Pt. I, 1703; Pt. II, 1704; Pt. III, 1705.

—— *Comfort and Counsel to Protestant Dissenters.* 1712.

—— *An Account of the Ministers who were Ejected after the Restoration.* 1713.

—— *An Abridgment of Mr Baxter's History of his Life and Times.* 2 vols. 1713.

—— *The Principles and Practice of Moderate Nonconformists with Respect to Ordination.* 1717.

—— *The Church and the Dissenters Compared, as to Persecution.* 1719.

—— *Memoirs of the Life of the Late Revd Mr John Howe.* 1724.

—— *A Continuation of the Account.* 2 vols. 1727.

—— *An Historical Account of my own Life.* 2 vols. 1829.

(Calamy.) *Master Edmund Calamies Leading Case.* 1663.

(Cartwright.) *The Diary of Thomas Cartwright, Bishop of Chester.* Camden Society. 1843.

The Case of Protestant Dissenters, of late Persecuted on old Statutes made against Papists and Popish Recusants. 1680.

The Cause of God and these Nations. 1659.

Cawdrey, D. *Bowing toward the Altar...Impleaded as grossly Superstitious.* 1661.

Charnock, S. *Complete Works.* 5 vols. Edinburgh, 1864–6.

The Church Book of Bunyan Meeting. Fascimile edition, ed. G. B. Harrison. 1928.

The Church Books of Ford or Cuddington and Amersham. Ed. W. T. Whitley. 1912.

The Church-Lurcher Unkennelled. 1660.

Clarendon. *History of the Great Rebellion.* 6 vols. Oxford, 1807.

—— *Life and Continuation.* 2 vols. Oxford, 1857.

Clarendon. *Calendar of the Clarendon State Papers,* vol. IV. Ed. F. J. Routledge. Oxford, 1932.

The Clarke Papers. Ed. C. H. Firth, vols. III and IV. Camden Society. 1899, 1901.

Clarkson, D. *No Evidence for Diocesan Churches.* 1681.
—— *Diocesan Churches not yet Discovered in the Primitive Times.* 1682.
—— *A Funeral Sermon on the Revd John Owen.* 1683.
—— *Practical Works.* 3 vols. Edinburgh, 1864–5.
Cobbett's Parliamentary History of England, vol. IV. 1808.
A Coffin for the Good Old Cause. 1660.
A Commonwealth and Commonwealths-Men Asserted and Vindicated. 1659.
Conyers, T. *A Pattern of Mercy Opened.* 1660.
The Copy of a Letter from a Lincolnshire Gentleman. 1660.
A Copy of the Proceedings of some Noteworthy and Learned Divines Touching Innovations, etc. 1660.
Corbet, John. *The Interest of England in the Matter of Religion.* 1660
—— *The Second Part of the Interest of England,* etc. 1660
—— *An Account Given of the Principles and Practices of Several Nonconformists.* 1682.
—— *The Non-Conformists' Plea for Lay-Communion with the Church of England.* 1683.
—— *Of the Church.* 1684.
—— *Remains.* 1684.
A Cordial Recipe, for causing adherence to the Parliament. 1659.
Cosin, J. *The Correspondence of John Cosin, Lord Bishop of Durham.* 2 vols. Surtees Society, vols. LII and LV. 1869, 1872.
Councill Humbly Propounded for the Speedy Settlement of these Long Disturbed Nations. 1660.
Crane, R. *God's Holy Name Magnified...by the Testimony of his Faithful Servants who have suffered...Banishment.* 1665.
(Croft, H.) *The Naked Truth, or the true state of the Primitive Church* (1675). 1919.
Crofton, Z. *A Serious Review of Presbyters Re-ordination by Bishops.* 1660.
—— ’Ανάληψις, *or Saint Peter's Bonds Abide.* 1660.
—— ’Ανάληψις ’Ανελήφθη, *The Fastening of St Peter's Fetters.* 1660.
—— *Altar Worship, or Bowing to the Communion Table Considered as to the Novelty, Vanity, Iniquity, Malignity Charged upon it.* 1661.
—— *The Hard Way to Heaven.* 1662.
—— *Reformation not Separation.* 1662.
Crosby, T. *The History of the English Baptists.* 4 vols. 1738–1740.

Davenant, Charles. *Essays Upon Peace at Home and War Abroad.* 1703.
Davies, Richard. *An Account of the Convincement, Exercises, Services and Travels of that Ancient Servant of the Lord, Richard Davies.*
(Davis.) *The Last Legacy of Mr Joseph Davis, Senior.* 1720.
D(awbery), H(enry). *A Sober and Temperate Discourse concerning the Interests of words in Prayer.* 1661.
A Declaration of the Faithful Soldiers of the Army. 1659.
Defoe, D. *The Present State of the Parties.* 1712.
Delamere, Lord. *Works.* 1694.

Delaune, Thomas. *Plea for the Nonconformists.* 1706.

Depositions from York Castle. Ed. J. Raine. Surtees Society, no. 40. 1861.

Dewsbery, William. *The Faithful Testimony of that Ancient Servant of the Lord and minister of the Everlasting Gospel, William Dewsbery.* 1689.

A Discourse Concerning Liberty of Conscience. 1661.

Dryden, J. *Poetical Works.* Oxford, 1910.

The Due Account and Humble Petition of the Ministers of the Gospel lately Commissioned for the Review and Alteration of the Liturgy. 1661.

Ellwood, Thomas. *The History of the Life of Thomas Ellwood.* Ed. C. G. Crump. 1900.

Evelyn, John. *Diary.* 2 vols. Everyman's Library.

——— *A Character of England.* 1659.

Extracts from State Papers. 1913.

Fair Warning, or XXV Reasons against Toleration, etc. 1663.

Farewell Sermons, An Exact Collection of.... 1662.

Farewell Sermons, A Complete Collection of.... 1663.

F(arnsworth), R(ichard). *Christian Religious Meetings allowed by the Liturgy are no Seditious Conventicles.* 1664.

The Farington Papers. Chetham Society. Manchester, 1856.

Fell, Margaret. *A Brief Collection of Remarkable Passages,* etc. (referred to as *Works*). 1710.

Fell, Sarah. *The Household Account Book of Sarah Fell.* Ed. N. Penney. Cambridge, 1920.

F(irmin), G(iles). *Presbyterial Ordination Vindicated.* 1660.

Firmin, Giles. *The Liturgical Considerator Considered.* 1661.

First Publishers of Truth. Ed. N. Penney. 1903.

Flavel, J. *Remains.* 1701.

For the King and both Houses of Parliament. 1664.

Ford, S. *A Gospel Church: or God's Holy Temple Opened.* 1675.

Foulis, H. *The Wicked Plots and Conspiracies of Our Pretended Saints.* 1662.

(Fowler, E.) *Dirt Wip't Off: or a Manifest Discovery of the Gross Ignorance, Erroneousness, and most unchristian and wicked spirit of one John Bunyan....* 1672.

Fox, George. *Book of Miracles.* Ed. H. J. Cadbury. Cambridge, 1948.

——— *A Declaration...Against all Sedition Plotters and Fighters in the world.* 1660.

——— *A Battle-Door for Teachers and Professors.* 1660.

——— *Epistles.* 1698.

——— *Journals.* 2 vols. (7th edition). 1852.

——— *Journal.* Ed. N. Penney. Cambridge, 1911.

——— *Journal.* Ed. J. L. Nickalls. Cambridge, 1952.

Frank, M. *The Grand Case of the Present Ministry, whether they may Lawfully Declare and Subscribe.* 1662.

The Fresh Suit Against Independency. 1661.

Gauden, John. 'ΑΝΑΛΥΣΙΣ, *The Loosing of St Peter's Bonds.* 1660.
—— *Considerations touching the Liturgy of the Church of England.* 1661.
Godwyn, Thomas. *Phanatical-Tenderness, or the Charity of the Nonconformists Exemplified.* 1684.
Goodwin, Thomas. *Works.* 12 vols. Edinburgh, 1861–5.
Gould, George, *Documents Relating to the Settlement of the Church of England by the Act of Uniformity of 1662.* 1862.
The Grand Debate between the Most Reverend the Bishops and the Presbyterian Divines. 1661.
The Grand Rebels Detected, or the Presbyter Unmasked. 1660.
(Granville.) *The Remains of Dennis Granville, D.D., Dean and Archdeacon of Durham.* 2 vols. Surtees Society. 1860 and 1865.
Gratton, J. *A Journal of the Life of that Ancient Servant of Christ, John Gratton.* Stranford, New York, 1805.
Grey, Architell. *Debates of the House of Commons, from the year 1667 to the year 1694.* 10 vols. 1763.
Griffith, John. *A Complaint of the Oppressed against the Oppressors.* 1661.
—— *The Case of Mr John Griffith, Minister of the Gospel and now prisoner in Newgate.* 1683.
—— *The Sacrifice of Gratitude.* 1703.
Grumble, T. *Life of General Monk.* 1671.

Halifax. *The Complete Works of George Savile, First Marquis of Halifax.* Ed. W. Raleigh. Oxford, 1912.
(Halkett.) *The Autobiography of Anne Lady Halkett.* Camden Society. 1875.
Hamilton, W. *Some Necessity of Reformation of the Public Doctrine of the Church of England.* 1660.
Sir Arthur Haselrig's Last Will and Testimony, with a Brief Survey of His Life and Death. 1661.
The Hatton Correspondence. 2 vols. Camden Society. 1878.
Hell Broke Loose. 1661.
Henry, Matthew. *The Life of the Revd Philip Henry.* Ed. Sir J. B. Williams, 1839.
Henry, P. *Diaries and Letters of Philip Henry, M.A.* Ed. M. H. Lee. 1882.
Hertford County Records. Compiled by W. J. Hardy. Hertford, 1905–.
Heywood, Oliver. *His Autobiography, Diaries, Anecdote and Event Books.* Ed. J. Horsfall Turner. 4 vols. Brighouse and Bingley, 1882–5.
Heywood, *The Whole Works of the Revd Oliver Heywood, B.A.* 5 vols. Idle, 1827.
Hickes, G. *Jovian, or an Answer to Julian the Apostate.* 1683.
(Hickes, J.) *The True and Faithful Narrative of the Sufferings of many Christians in Devon.* 1671.
(Hickman, Henry.) Χειροθεσία τοῦ πρεσβυτερίου. 1661.
His Majesty's Gracious Speech to Both Houses of Parliament...at the Passing of the Act of Free Pardon, Indemnity and Oblivion. 1660.

Hookes, Ellis. *The Spirit of the Martyrs Revived.* Edition of 1719.
—— *A Brief View of the Great Sufferings and Living Testimonies of the True and Constant Martyrs.* 1719.
—— *An Account of the Just Judgments of God Inflicted upon Persecutors.* 1719.
—— *A Christian Plea Against Persecution for the Cause of Conscience.* 1719.
Horton, T. *Rich Treasure in Earthen Vessels.* 1663.
Howard, J. *State of the Prisons in England and Wales* (3rd edition). 1785.
Howe. *The Whole Works of the Revd John Howe, M.A.* 7 vols. 1813.
The Humble Apology of Some Commonly Called Anabaptists. 1660.
The Humble Petition and Representation of Sufferings of Several Peaceable and Innocent Subjects, etc. 1660.
Humfrey, John. *The Question of Reordination.* 1661.
(Hyde, Henry.) *Second Thoughts; or the Case of a Limited Toleration Stated.* 1660.

Interest of Words in Prayer. 1661.

Jenner, D. *Beaufrons, or a New Discovery of Treason.* 1683.
Jessey, Henry. *The Lord's Loud Call to England.* 1660.
Jessop, C. *The Angel of the Church of Ephesus no Bishop of Ephesus, distinguished in order from and Superior in Power to a Presbytery.* 1660.
(Jolly.) *The Note-Book of the Revd Thomas Jolly, 1671–1693.* Chetham Society. Manchester, 1895.
Jones, James. *Nonconformity not Inconsistent with Loyalty.* 1684.
Jones, Sir William. *A Just and Modest Vindication of the Proceedings of the Last Two Parliaments of King Charles II.* 1681.
(Josselin.) *The Diary of the Revd Ralph Josselin, 1616–1683.* Camden Society. 1908.
(Juxon, Abp.) Χάρις καὶ Εἰρήνη, *or Some Considerations Upon the Act of Uniformity.* 1662.

Kennett, White. *History of England* (2nd edition). 1717.
—— *A Register and Chronicle, Ecclesiastical and Civil.* 1728.
Kiffin. *Some Remarkable Passages in the Life of William Kiffin, Written by Himself.* Ed. William Orme. 1823.

Langbaine, G. *A Review of the Covenant.* 1661.
The Late Proposal of Union Among Protestants Reviewed and Rectified. 1679.
L'Estrange, R. *Mistaken Interest, or the Holy Cheat.* 1661.
—— *The Relaps'd Apostate.* 1661.
—— *State Divinity.* 1661.
—— *Toleration Discussed.* 1670.
—— *Citt and Bumkin.* 1680.
—— *The Dissenters Sayings* (the Second Part). 1681.
A Letter from a Gentleman in Gray's Inn, to a Justice of the Peace in the Country, Explaining the Act of Uniformity. 1662.

A Letter from a Gentleman in the City to a Friend in the Country, about the Odious-
   ness of Persecution. 1675.
A Letter from the Devil to the Pope and his Prelates. 1670.
Liberty of Conscience upon its true and proper grounds asserted and vindicated. 1668.
A Lively Pourtraict of Our New Cavaliers, Commonly Called Presbyterians. 1661.
Lobb, S. *Report of the Present State of the Differences in Doctrinals between some*
   Dissenting Ministers in London. 1690.
Locke, J. *Works.* 10 vols. 1812.
Ludlow. *The Memoirs of Edmund Ludlow.* Ed. C. H. Firth. 2 vols. Oxford,
   1894.
Luttrell, N. *Brief Historical Relation of State Affairs.* 6 vols. Oxford, 1857.

Manton, Thomas. *The Complete Works.* 12 vols. 1870–3.
Marlborough, Sarah, Duchess of. *Private Correspondence.* 2 vols. 1838.
Marshall, Charles. *Sion's Travellers Comforted.* 1704.
(Martindale.) *The Life of Adam Martindale, written by himself.* Chetham Society.
   1845.
(Martin.) *Letters of Dr Edward Martin.* 1662.
Marvell, Andrew. *Complete Works.* Ed. A. B. Grosart. 4 vols. 1873.
—— *The Poems and Letters of Andrew Marvell.* Ed. H. M. Margoliouth. 2 vols.
   Oxford, 1927.
Mather, I. *Practical Truths Tending to Promote the Power of Godliness.* Boston,
   1682.
Meade, M. *Spiritual Wisdom Improve against Temptation.* 1660.
The Memorial of the Church of England. 1705.
Mercurius Publicus. Published weekly during the period.
Middlesex County Records. Ed. J. C. Jeaffreson. 4 vols. 1882–92.
Milton, John. *Poetical Works.* Ed. W. Aldis Wright. Cambridge, 1903.
—— *Works* (Columbia edition). 13 vols. New York, 1931–8.
Minutes of the General Assembly of the General Baptist Churches in England. Ed.
   W. T. Whitley. 1909.
Moderation, or Arguments and Motives Tending Thereto. 1660.
A Modest and Peaceable Letter concerning Comprehension, etc. 1668.
A Monthly Intelligence, relating the Affairs of the People called Quakers in and near
   about the City of London. 1662.
Mordaunt. *The Letter Book of John, Viscount Mordaunt.* Camden Society. 1945.
The Mystery and Iniquity of Nonconformity. 1664.
The Mystery of the Good Old Cause briefly Unfolded. 1660.

Nalson, J. *The Project of Peace.* 1678.
A Narrative of the Cruelties and Abuses Acted by Isaac Dennis, Keeper, his Wife and
   Servants, in the Prison of Newgate in the City of Bristol. 1672.
A Narrative of the late Proceedings of some Justices and others. 1670.
A Narrative of the Sufferings of Thomas Delaune. 1706.
Neal, D. *History of the Puritans.* 5 vols. Edition of 1822.

Nedham, Marchamont. *The Character of a Rigid Presbyter.* 1661.
(Newcome.) *The Diary of the Revd Henry Newcome.* Chetham Society. 1849.
The Autobiography of Henry Newcome. 2 vols. Chetham Society. 1852.
Newton, George. *A Sermon Preached at the Funeral of Mr Joseph Alleine,* 1672.
The Nicholas Papers. Camden Society. 1920.
North, Roger. *Examen.* 1740.
—— *The Life of the Right Honourable Francis North, Baron of Guilford.* 1742.
—— *The Lives of the Norths.* 3 vols. 1826.
(Nye, Stephen.) *The Life of Mr Thomas Firmin* (1698) (reprinted in Unitarian Tracts, vol. IV). 1791.

Oates, Constant. *The Character of a Good and Bad Subject.* 1682.
Owen, John. *Works.* Ed. W. H. Gould. 16 vols. Edinburgh, 1850–3.

The Parliamentary or Constitutional History of England, vols. XXI, XXII. 1760.
Palmer, S. *A Defence of the Dissenters' Education in their Private Academies.* 1703.
—— *The Nonconformist's Memorial, Originally written by Edmund Calamy* (2nd edition). 3 vols. 1802.
Parker, S. *A Discourse of Ecclesiastical Polity.* 1669?/70.
—— *History of his own Time* (English translation by T. Newling). 1727.
Patrick, S. *A Friendly Debate between a Conformist and a Nonconformist* (3rd edition). 1669.
—— *Autobiography.* Oxford. 1839.
Pearse, Edward. *The Conformist's Plea for the Nonconformists.* 1681.
—— *The Conformist's Second Plea for the Nonconformists.* 1682.
—— *The Conformist's Third Plea for the Nonconformists.* 1682.
—— *The Conformist's Fourth Plea for the Nonconformists.* 1683.
Pearson, John. *No Necessity of Reformation of the Public Doctrine of the Church of England.* 1660.
Peirce, James. *A Vindication of the Dissenters* (2nd edition). 1718.
Penn, William. *Works.* 2 vols. 1726.
Penington, I. *Works.* 1681.
The People's Ancient and Just Liberties Asserted. 1670.
Pepys, S. *The Diary.* Ed. H. B. Wheatley. 8 vols. 1904.
—— *The Tangier Papers of Samuel Pepys.* Ed. E. Chappell. Navy Records Society. 1935.
A Pertinent Speech made by an honourable Member of the House of Commons, tending to the Establishment of Kingly Government. 1660.
(Peters, Hugh.) 'Peter Cornelius.' *The Way to the Peace and Settlement of these Nations.* 1659.
Peters, Hugh (?). *A Dying Father's Last Legacy to an only Child.* 1661.
Pinney, J. *Letters of John Pinney, 1679–1699.* Ed. G. F. Nuttall. Oxford, 1939.
A Plea for Ministers in Sequestrations. 1660.
Pooley, William. *Part of the Sufferings of Leicestershire and Northamptonshire by Informers and Priests.* 1683.

Pope, W. *Life of Seth Ward, Bishop of Salisbury*. 1697.

Powell, Vavasor. *Common Prayer Book no Divine Service*. 1660.

—— *Sinful and Sinless Swearing*. 1661.

(Powell, Vavasor.) *The Life and Death of Vavasor Powell*. 1671.

—— *The Sufferer's Catechism*. 1664.

Price, J. *The Mystery and Method of His Majesty's Happy Restoration*. 1680.

The Letters of Humphrey Prideaux...to John Ellis, 1674–1722. Camden Society. 1875.

A Private Conference between a Rich Alderman and a poor Country Vicar made Public. 1670.

Prynne, W. *The Unbishoping of Timothy and Titus* (2nd edition). 1660.

—— *A Short Sober Pacific Examination of Some Exuberances in and Ceremonial Appurtenances to the Common Prayer*. 1661.

Ralph, J. *History of England*. 1744.

Rapin, P. *History of England*. 1743.

Record of the Sufferings of Quakers in Cornwall, 1655–1686. Transcribed and edited by N. Penney. London and Philadelphia, 1928.

Regicides no Saints. 1660.

(Reresby.) *The Memoirs of Sir John Reresby*. 1875.

Reynolds, E. *The Author and Subject of Healing in the Church*. 1660.

Rigge, Ambrose. *A Standard of Righteousness Lifted unto the Nations*. 1663.

—— *The Good Old Way*. 1669.

—— *Constancy in the Truth Commended*. 1710.

(Roberts.) *Some Memoirs of the Life of John Roberts*. n.d.

Royal Proclamations. 1660–1664.

(Russell.) *The Last Speech and Behaviour of William, late Lord Russell*. 1683.

'Salem Philalathes.' *The Moderate Independent, Proposing a Word in Season to the Gathered Churches, the Episcopal and Presbyterian Parties*. 1660.

The Savile Correspondence. Letters to and from Henry Savile. Camden Society. 1858.

Semper Idem: or a Parallel betwixt the Ancient and Modern Phanatics. 1661.

Serious Quiries against the late Act of Parliament relative to Meetings. 1670.

Sewell, William. *The History of the Rise, Increase, and Progress of Christian People called Quakers*. 2 vols. Philadelphia, n.d.

(Shaftesbury.) *A Letter from a Parliament-man to his Friend*. 1675.

Shaw. *Memoirs of John Shaw* (in 'Yorkshire Diaries and Autobiographies in the Seventeenth and Eighteenth Centuries'). Surtees Society. 1877.

Sherlock, W. *A Discourse about Church Unity*. 1681.

A Short Relation of the Barbarous Cruelties Inflicted on the People of God Called Quakers. 1670.

A Short Relation of some part of the Sad Sufferings and Cruel Havoc and Spoil Inflicted on the Persons and Estates of the People of God in scorn called Quakers. 1674.

Sion's Groans for her Distressed. 1661.

Skinner, Thomas. *Life of General Monk.* 1723.
A Sober and Seasonable Discourse, etc. 1681.
South, Robert. *Sermons* (3rd edition). 6 vols. 1704.
Spademan, J. *A Sermon upon the Occasion of the Justly Lamented Death of the truly Reverend Mr John Howe* (reprinted in Howe, *Works,* vol. IV).
The Speeches and Prayers of some of the King's late Judges. 1660.
The Speeches and Prayers of John Barkstead, John Okey and Miles Corbet. 1662.
Steppens, R. *Rex Theologus.* 1664.
Stillingfleet, E. *Irenicum* (2nd edition). 1662.
—— *Origines Sacrae* (3rd edition). 1666.
—— *The Mischief of Separation.* 1680.
—— *The Unreasonableness of Separation.* 1680/1.
—— *Ecclesiastical Cases.* 1695.
Stockton, Owen. *A Rebuke of the Informers.* 1675.
S(tout), W(illiam). *A True, Short, Impartial Relation...of the Proceedings...at the Town of Hertford.* 1664.
—— *A Second Relation from the Town of Hertford.* 1664.
Stuart Tracts, 1603–1693. (An English Garner.) Ed. C. H. Firth. 1903.
Sturgion, J. *A Plea for Toleration.* 1661.
The Sufferings of the Quakers in Nottinghamshire. Ed. P. J. Cropper. 1892.
The Swarthmore Documents in America. Ed. H. J. Cadbury. London and Philadelphia, 1940.

(Taswell.) *Autobiography and Anecdotes by William Taswell.* Camden Miscellany, vol. II. 1853.
Taylor, Thomas. *Works.* 1697.
Terms of Accommodation between those of the Episcopall and their Brethren of the Presbyterian Perswasions. 1661.
Terrill, Edward. *The Records of a Church of Christ Meeting in Broadmead, Bristol, A.D. 1640 to A.D. 1688.* Ed. Nathaniel Haycroft. 1865.
Thomas, William. *A Preservative of Piety.* 1662.
Thoresby. *The Diary of Ralph Thoresby, F.R.S. (1677–1724).* 2 vols. 1830.
—— *Letters of Eminent Men Addressed to Ralph Thoresby.* 2 vols. 1832.
Thorndike, H. *The True Way of Composing the Differences on Foot.* 1660.
(Thurloe.) *A Collection of the State Papers of John Thurloe, Esq.* 7 vols. 1724.
Tillotson, John. *A Sermon preached at the Funeral of the Revd Mr Thomas George.* 1682.
Toleration and Liberty of Conscience Considered and Proved Impracticable, Impossible, and even in the Opinion of Dissenters Sinful and Unlawful. 1685.
Tombes, John. *Saints no Smiters.* 1664.
To the King. The Humble Address of the People Commonly called Quakers. 1683.
To the King. The Humble Petition of the People Commonly called Quakers. 1683.
Townshend, H. *Diary of Henry Townshend, 1640–1663.* Ed. J. W. Willis Bund. Worcestershire Historical Society. 1920.
Trelawney Papers. Camden Miscellany, vol. II. 1853.

Troughton, J. *An Apology for the Nonconformists.* 1681.

A *True and Impartial Narrative of some Illegal and Arbitrary Proceedings by Certain Justices of the Peace and others, against several innocent and peaceable Nonconformists in and near the Town of Bedford.* 1670.

The True Presbyterian without Disguise. 1661.

Turner, F. *Animadversions upon a late Pamphlet entitled the Naked Truth.* 1676.

Turner, G. Lyon (ed.). *Original Records of Early Nonconformity.* 3 vols. 1911–14.

Turner, J. *Christ Confessed: Written by a Preacher of the Gospel now a Prisoner.* 1665.

(Vane.) *The Substance of what Sr Henry Vane Intended to have Spoken upon the Scaffold.* 1662.

—— *The Trial of Sir Henry Vane at the King's Bench.* 1662.

Wanley, Nath. *Peace and Rest for the Upright.* 1681.

Watson, T. *A Pastor's Love Expressed to a Loving People.* 1662.

(Wesley.) *A Letter from a Country Divine...Concerning the Education of the Dissenters in their Private Academies.* 1703.

The Western Martyrology: or Bloody Assizes (5th edition). 1705.

Whitehead, George. *Christian Progress of that Ancient Servant and Minister of Jesus Christ, George Whitehead.*

Whiting, John. *Persecution Exposed.* 1715.

Williams, Daniel. *Gospel Truth Stated and Vindicated.* 1691.

—— *Defence of the Gospel Truth.* 1693.

—— *Man Made Righteous.* 1694.

—— *Peace With Truth, or an End to Discord.* 1699.

—— *Practical Discourses on Several Important Subjects.* 2 vols. 1738.

Williamson. *Letters to Sir Joseph Williamson.* 2 vols. Camden Society. 1874.

Wodrow, R. *The History of the Sufferings of the Church of Scotland from the Restoration to the Revolution.* 7 vols. Glasgow, 1828.

(Woodcock.) *Extracts from the Papers to Thomas Woodcock.* Camden Miscellany, vol. XI. 1907.

A Word in Season for Christian Union To all Protestant Dissenters. 1680.

Wornock, L. *The Solemn League and Covenant Arraigned and Condemned.* 1661.

—— *Pulpit-Conceptions, Popular-Deceptions.* 1662.

Yarranton, A. *A Full Discovery of the First Presbyterian Sham Plot.* 1681.

III. COLLECTIONS OF DOCUMENTS

Browning, A. (ed). *English Historical Documents,* vol. VIII (1660–1714). 1953.

Calendar of Clarendon State Papers. 4 vols. Oxford, 1869–1932.

Calendar of State Papers, Domestic: (Charles II) 28 vols. 1860–1938; (William and Mary, and William III) 11 vols. 1895–1937; and (Anne) vols. I and II. 1916, 1924.

Calendar of State Papers, Venetian (1659–75). 7 vols. 1931–1947.
Clarendon State Papers. Ed. R. Scrope and T. Monkhouse. 3 vols. Oxford, 1767–86.
Cobbett's Parliamentary History of England, vols. IV, V. 1808.
Collection of Original Letters and Papers of the Duke of Ormonde. Ed. T. Carte. 1739.
A Collection of the State Papers of John Thurloe, Esq. Ed. T. Birch. 7 vols. 1742.
Dictionary of National Biography.
Gould. *Documents Relating to the Settlement of the Church of England by the Act of Uniformity of 1662.* 1862.
The History and Proceedings of the House of Commons from the Restoration to the Present Day. 1742.
The History and Proceedings of the House of Lords from the Restoration to the Present Day. 1742.
Journals of the House of Commons, vols. VII–XVII. n.d.
Journals of the House of Lords, vols. XI–XIX. n.d.
The Parliamentary or Constitutional History of England, vols. XXI, XXII. 1760.
Reports of the Historical Manuscripts Commission (e.g., the Le Fleming MSS, the Ormonde MSS, the Sutherland MSS, the Dartmouth MSS, the Leeds MSS, MSS of the House of Lords). Various dates.
C. Grant Robertson. *Selected Statutes, Cases and Documents.* 2nd ed., 1913.
Wilkins, D. *Concilia Magnae Britanniae.* 4 vols. 1737.

IV. SECONDARY

Abbey, C. J. and Overton, J. H. *The English Church in the Eighteenth Century.* 2 vols. 1878.
Abbott, W. C. *English Conspiracy and Dissent* (*American Historical Review*, vol. XIV). 1908–9.
—— *The Origin of English Political Parties* (*American Historical Review*, vol. XXIV). 1918–9.
Acton, Lord. *Lectures on Modern History.* 1906.
Ashley, M. *John Wildman.* 1947.
—— *England in the Seventeenth Century.* 1952.
—— *Cromwell's Generals.* 1954.

Bate, Frank. *The Declaration of Indulgence, 1672.* 1908.
Bayne, Peter. *English Puritanism: Its Character and History.* 1862.
Birch, T. *Life of Dr John Tillotson, Archbishop of Canterbury.* 1820.
Blaxland, B. *The Struggle with Puritanism.* 1910.
Bosher, R. S. *The Making of the Restoration Settlement, 1649–1662.* New York, 1951.
Brailsford, M. R. *The Making of William Penn.* 1930.
Braithwaite, W. C. *The Beginnings of Quakerism.* 1912. (Second ed. Cambridge, 1955.)
—— *The Second Period of Quakerism.* 1919.
Brockband, E. *Edward Burrough.* 1949.

Brown, John. *John Bunyan* (Tercentenary edition). 1928.
Brown, Louise F. *The First Earl of Shafesbury.* New York, 1933.
Browning, Andrew. *Life of Thomas Osborne, Earl of Danby.* 3 vols. Glasgow, 1944–51.
Browning, Andrew (ed.). *English Historical Documents*, vol. VIII (1660–1714). 1953.
Brunton, D. and Pennington, D. H. *Members of the Long Parliament.* 1954.
Bryant, A. *King Charles II.* 1931.
—— *Samuel Pepys, The Man in the Making.* Cambridge, 1933.
—— *Samuel Pepys, The Years of Peril.* Cambridge, 1935.
—— *Samuel Pepys, The Saviour of the Navy.* Cambridge, 1938.
Buchan, John. *Oliver Cromwell.* 1934.
Bush, D. *English Literature in the Earlier Seventeenth Century.* Oxford, 1945.

Cadbury, H. J. *Annual Catalogue of George Fox's Papers.* 1939.
Cambridge History of English Literature, vols. VII (Cavalier and Puritan), VIII (The Age of Dryden), IX (Steele and Addison to Pope and Swift). Cambridge, 1911–12.
Cambridge Modern History, vol. V. Cambridge.
Campbell, John, Lord. *Lives of the Lord Chancellors and Keepers of the Great Seal of England* (4th edition). 1857.
Cardwell, E. *Documentary Annals of the Reformed Church of England.* 2 vols. 1839.
—— *History of Conferences and other Proceedings Connected with the Revision of the Book of Common Prayer.* 1840.
—— *Synodalia, A Collection of Articles of Religion, Canons and Proceedings of Convocations of Canterbury.* 2 vols. 1842.
Chapman, H. W. *Great Villiers, A Life of the Second Duke of Buckingham.* 1948.
Christie, W. D. *A Life of Anthony Ashley Cooper, First Earl of Shaftesbury.* 2 vols. 1871.
Clarke, G. Kitson. *The English Inheritance.* 1950.
Clarke, G. N. *The Seventeenth Century.* Oxford, 1929.
—— *The Later Stuarts.* Oxford, 1934.
Clarke, Henry W. *History of English Nonconformity.* 2 vols. 1911–13.
Clarke, T. E. S. and Foxcroft, H. C. *Life of Gilbert Burnet.* Cambridge, 1911.
Craik, Henry. *The Life of Edward, Earl of Clarendon.* 2 vols. 1911.

Dale, R. W. *History of English Congregationalism.* 1907.
Dalrymple, J. *Memoirs of Great Britain and Ireland.* 3 vols. 1790.
Davies, G. (ed). *Bibliography of British History.* Stuart Period, 1603–1714. Oxford, 1928.
Davies, G. *The Early Stuarts.* Oxford, 1937.
—— *The Army and the Downfall of Richard Cromwell* (*Huntingdon Library Bulletin*, no. 7).
Davies, Horton. *The Worship of the English Puritans.* 1948.
—— *The English Free Churches.*

317

Davies, J. H. *The Life of Richard Baxter.* 1887.

Dudley, A. C. *Nonconformity under the Clarendon Code (American Historical Review,* vol. XVIII), 1912–13.

Drysdale, A. H. *History of the Presbyterians in England.* 1889.

Feiling, Keith. *England under the Tudors and Stuarts.* n.d.

—— *History of the Tory Party.* Oxford, 1924.

—— *Clarendon and the Act of Uniformity (English Historical Review,* vol. XVIII). 1929.

Figgis, J. N. *The Divine Right of Kings* (2nd edition). Cambridge, 1914.

Firth, C. H. *Oliver Cromwell and the Rule of the Puritans in England* (3rd edition). 1924.

—— *Cromwell's Army.* 1902.

—— *The Last Years of the Protectorate, 1656–1658.* 2 vols. 1909.

—— *Essays, Historical and Literary.* Oxford, 1938.

Fletcher, J. *History of Independency in England.* 4 vols. 1862.

Foxcroft, H. C. *Life and Letters of Sir George Savile, First Marquis of Halifax.* 2 vols. 1898.

Gardiner, S. R. *Cromwell's Place in History.* 1891.

Gordon, Alex. *Freedom After Ejection.* Manchester, 1917.

Grubb, E. *Social Aspects of the Quaker Faith.* 1899.

Guizot, M. *History of Richard Cromwell and the Restoration of Charles II* (English translation). 2 vols. 1856.

Gwatkin, H. M. *Church and State in England to the Death of Queen Anne.* 1917.

Hanbury, B. *Memorials of the Independents.* 3 vols. 1839–44.

Harris, F. R. *The Life of Edward Montagu, First Earl of Sandwich.* 2 vols. 1912.

Harris, W. *Memoirs of Thomas Manton.* 1725.

Hart, A. T. *William Lloyd.* 1952.

Holdsworth, W. S. *A History of English Law,* vol. VI, 1924; vol. VIII, 1925.

Horton, R. F. *John Howe* (new edition). 1905.

Hunt, J. *Religious Thought in England.* 3 vols. 1870.

Hunter, Joseph. *The Rise of the Old Dissent, exemplified in the Life of Oliver Heywood.* 1842.

Hutton, W. H. *A History of the English Church from the Accession of Charles I to the Death of Anne.* 1903.

Hyde, H. M. *Judge Jeffreys.* 1948.

Jones, I. Deane. *The English Revolution, 1603–1714.* 1931.

Kent, C. B. R. *The Early History of the Tories.* 1908.

Keir, D. L. *The Constitutional History of Modern Britain* (4th edition). 1950.

Kitchin, G. *Roger L'Estrange.* 1913.

Knox, R. A. *Enthusiasm.* Oxford, 1950.

Ladell, A. R. *Richard Baxter, Puritan and Mystic.* 1925.
Latimer, J. *Annals of Bristol in the Seventeenth Century.* Bristol, 1900.
Lecky, W. E. H. *A History of England in the Eighteenth Century,* vol. i. 1878.
Lewis, H. E. (ed.). *The Ejectment of 1662 and the Free Churches.* 1912.
Lister, T. H. *Life and Administration of Edward, first Earl of Clarendon.* 3 vols. 1838.
Lloyd, A. *Quaker Social History, 1669-1738.* 1950.
Lodge, R. *The History of England from the Restoration to the Death of William III* (new impression). 1918.

Macaulay, T. B. *The History of England* (two-volume edition). 1873.
Mackintosh, Sir James. *History of the Revolution in England, 1688.* 1834.
MacLachlan, H. J. *Socinianism in Seventeenth Century England.* Oxford, 1951.
McLachlan, H. *English Education under the Test Acts.* 1931.
Marriott, J. A. R. *The Crisis of English Liberty.* Oxford, 1930.
Masson, D. *The Life of Milton,* vols. v and vi. 1877.
Matthews, A. G. *Calamy Revised.* Oxford, 1934.
Miller, Perry and Johnson, T. H. *The Puritans.* New York, 1938.
Mitchell, W. F. *English Pulpit Oratory from Andrewes to Tillotson.* 1932.
Montague, F. C. *The Political History of England, 1603-1660* (3rd edition). 1916.
Morgan, I. *The Nonconformity of Richard Baxter.* 1946.
Morley, J. *Oliver Cromwell.* 1904.
Muddiman, J. G. *The Bloody Assize.* 1929.

Nightingale, B. *The Ejected of 1662 in Cumberland and Westmorland.* 2 vols. Manchester, 1911.
—— *Lancashire Nonconformity.* 6 vols. 1890-3.

Ogg, D. *England in the Reign of Charles II.* 2 vols. Oxford, 1934.
Orme, W. *Life of Richard Baxter* (vol. i of the Practical Works of Richard Baxter, 23-volume edition). 1830.
—— *Life of John Owen.* 1826.

Parker, I. *Dissenting Academies in England.* Cambridge, 1914.
Payne, E. A. *The Baptists of Berkshire.* 1951.
Plum, H. G. *Restoration Puritanism.* Chapel Hill, N.C., 1943.
Plummer, A. *English Church, 1649-1702.* Edinburgh, 1907.
Powicke, F. J. *A Life of the Revd Richard Baxter.* 1924.
—— *The Revd Richard Baxter under the Cross.* 1927.

Raistrick, A. *Quakers in Science and Industry.* 1950.
—— *Dynasty of Ironfounders.* 1953.
Ranke, L. von. *History of England, principally in the Seventeenth Century.* 6 vols. Oxford, 1875.
Rees, T. *History of Nonconformity in Wales.* 1861.

Rogers, Henry. *The Life and Character of John Howe.* n.d.
Ross, I. *Margaret Fell, Mother of Quakerism.* 1949.
Russell Smith, H. F. *The Theory of Religious Toleration under Charles II and James II.* Cambridge, 1911.

Schlatter, R. D. *Social Ideas of Religious Leaders, 1660 to 1688.* Oxford, 1940.
Seaton, A. A. *The Theory of Toleration under the Later Stuarts.* Cambridge, 1911.
Simpkinson, C. H. *Thomas Harrison, Regicide and Major-General.* 1905.
Slate, R. *Select Nonconformists' Remains.* 1814.
Smyth, C. H. *The Art of Preaching.* 1940.
Staley, V. *The Life and Times of Gilbert Sheldon.* 1913.
Stanford, Charles. *Joseph Alleine, His Companions and Times.* 1861.
Stoughton, J. *The Ecclesiastical History of England.* 6 vols. (revised edition). 1881.
Swainson, C. A. *The Parliamentary History of the Act of Uniformity.* 1875.

Talon, H. *John Bunyan* (English translation). 1951.
Toulmin, Joshua. *A Review of the Life, Character and Writings of the Revd John Biddle.* 1789.
—— *Historical View of the State of the Protestant Dissenters in England.* 1814.
Trevelyan, G. M. *England Under the Stuarts.* 1904.
—— *The English Revolution.* 1938.
—— *The History of England.* 1926.
Troeltsch, E. *The Social Teaching of the Christian Churches* (English translation). 2 vols. 1931.
Tulloch, J. *Rational Theology and Christian Philosophy in England in the Seventeenth Century.* 2 vols. (2nd edition). Edinburgh, 1874.

Underwood, A. C. *A History of the English Baptists.* 1947.

Vaughan, R. *English Nonconformity.* 1862.

Ward, E. F. *Christopher Monck, Duke of Albemarle.* 1915.
(White, W. H.) *John Bunyan,* by the Author of *Mark Rutherford.* N.d.
Whitelocke, R. H. *Memoirs of Bulstrode Whitelock.* 1860.
Whitley, W. T. *A Baptist Bibliography,* vol. 1. 1916.
—— *A History of British Baptists.* 1923.
Whiting, C. E. *Studies in English Puritanism from the Restoration to the Revolution, 1660–1688.* 1931.
Willcocks, M. P. *Bunyan Calling.* 1943.
Willey, B. *The Seventeenth Century Background.* 1934.
Wormald, B. H. G. *Clarendon: Politics, History and Religion, 1640–1660.* Cambridge, 1951.

INDEX

Abjuring the realm, 51
Academies, dissenting, 186–91
Adams, Richard, 159
Alleine, Joseph, 8, 36, 88, 94, 103, 109, 112, 121, 138, 147
Alleine, Mrs T., 102, 106, 147
Alsop, V., 233
Amusements, 132–3, 135
Andrews, L., 211
Anne, Queen, 254
Antinomianism, 253, 254
Appeals (legal), 54
Apprentices, 137
Arminianism, 254
Arrest, 40 ff.
Assizes, 46
Aylesbury, 52

Bad company, 174
Banishment, 55
Baptism, 183, 184
Baptists, 2, 8, 19, 51, 52, 54, 90, 102, 181, 183, 184, 257
  General, 172–3, 179, 189
  Seventh-day, 184
Barclay, Robert, 133
Barnes, Ambrose, 182
Barrow, Isaac, 208, 213
Bates, William, 15, 251
Batt, Jasper, 114
Baxter, Mrs Margaret, 144, 146
Baxter, Richard, 5, 15, 16, 27, 49, 89, 129, 131, 133, 134, 135, 138, 140, 144, 146, 147, 152, 176, 178, 185, 189, 196, 198, 199, 200, 207, 211, 217, 221, 224, 227, 235, 241, 243, 251, 252, 256
Bedford, 92, 110
Bereavement, 146
Betting and gambling, 132, 192
Bible, 148, 198, 207
Bishop, George, 108
Book of Common Prayer, *see* Common Prayer, Book of
Books, 138, 148–9
Bowing, 245
Boyse, Joseph, 189
Bragge, Robert ('Eternal'), 205
Bridgman, Lord Keeper, 15, 35

Bristol, 34, 38, 54
Broadmead Congregation, Bristol, 40, 41, 158, 176, 179, 191
Browne, Sir Richard, 33
Browning, Thomas, 127
Bunyan, 44–5, 61, 66, 68, 100, 103, 104, 109–10, 116, 117, 118, 122–3, 126, 128, 138, 184, 199, 209, 211, 213, 218–19, 220
Burgess, Cornelius, 225, 237
Burnet, Gilbert, 214, 251
Burrough, Edward, 107
Butler, Bp. Joseph, 187

Cabal, The, 21
Calamy, E., 149, 161, 203, 222–3, 226, 235, 247
Calling a minister, 166
Calvinism, 181–2, 253–4, 257
Cambridge, 185, 186
  Emmanuel College, 186
Cards, 132
Carleton, Bp. Guy, 34–5
Caryl, J., 149
Catechising, 129, 139, 178
Catholics, Roman, 19, 28
Ceremonies, 225, 228
Chains, imprisonment in, 96
Chancellors, lay, 240
Charles I, King, 2, 4, 226, 249
Charles II, King, 4, 10, 11, 16, 18, 19, 22–4, 26, 52, 124–5, 208, 225, 248, 249
Charnock, S., 149, 205, 206, 212, 215
Chester, 96
Chichester, 97
Christ, Person of, 182, 257
Church, importance of, 156 ff.
Church meetings, 165 f.
Clarendon, Edward Hyde, Earl of, 5, 14
Clarkson, David, 160, 211, 215, 216, 228
Cock-fighting, 132, 193
Colchester, 62
Common Fund, The, 253
Common Prayer, Book of, 6, 7, 37, 242 ff.
Commons, House of, 4, 7, 11, 16, 18, 19, 21

21   321   C P

Gratton, John 40, 59, 61, 77, 100, 109, 113, 115
Guests, 137

Hale, Sir Matthew, 16, 54, 123
Halifax, 176
Halifax, George Savile, Marquis of, 29, 220, 249
Handbills, 138
'Happy Union', 253
Hardcastle, T., 179
Harwich, 99
Hatton, Charles, 221
Henry, Matthew, 141, 200
Henry, Philip, 57, 89, 97, 107, 133, 134, 141, 142, 144, 151, 152, 153, 168, 178, 238
Hewley, Lady, 180
Heywood, E., 142
  John, 142
  Oliver, 3, 8, 88, 89, 98, 104, 116–17, 134, 135, 137, 142, 145, 146, 147, 150, 151–5, 158, 160, 165, 176, 177, 178, 180, 213
  Mrs O., 89, 104, 145
Hildersham, A., 149
Hillier, George, 38
Hoadly, B., 222, 247
Holland, 14, 18, 186
Horrockes, Thomas, 88
Horse racing, 132
Houses, worship in, 157–8
Howard, John, 107
Howe, John, 61, 161, 201, 205, 207, 208, 209, 210, 212, 213, 216, 251, 256
Howgill, Francis, 35
Hughes, George, 117
Husband and wife, 144f.
Hyde, Edward, see Clarendon
Hypocrisy, 236

Ilchester gaol, 88, 90, 91, 102, 109, 110
Impositions, 223
Imprisonment, see Prison
Independents, 1, 4, 102, 182, 188, 252, 254
Indulgence, Declarations of, see Declarations
Informers, 34, 35, 57, 60–3, 184, 191
Intimidation of juries, 49
  of prisoners, 48
Irresponsibility, 171

James II, King, 26, 28, 29, 63, 231, 249
Jeffreys, Chief Justice George, 27, 49, 97

Jolly, Thomas, 153, 191, 213
Josselin, Ralph, 131
Judges, 47f., 53
Juries, 49–50
Justices of the Peace, 18, 37, 40, 46, 59, 63–4, 77, 97, 109, 114, 122, 124, 189, 236
  prisoners' appearances before, 43f.

Kaber Rigg Plot, 12
Kennett, Bp. White, 227
Kidderminster, 140, 207
Kiffin, William, 144
Kneeling at communion, 244

Lancaster, castle, 93, 109, 114
Langley, H., 215
Latitudinarianism, 249
Laud, William, 238
Laudian party, 5, 7, 225, 239
Launceston, 92, 96
Laws invoked against dissenters, 50–2
Leadbeater, Thomas, 137
Learning, value placed on, 207
Lectures, 163, 183, 210
Legal advice, 53–4
Leominster, 96
Licences to preach, 19–21
Listening, training in, 216
Liturgy, 225
Locke, John, 246
London, City of, 2
Long Parliament, 239
Lords, House of, 11, 18, 21, 23

Macaulay, Lord, 250
Magistrates, see Justices of the Peace
Manton, Thomas, 15, 16, 149, 160, 205
Martindale, Adam, 133, 178, 204, 210
Marvell, Andrew, 16, 220, 221
Mathematics, 187
Maypoles, 132
Mead, Matthew, 49, 229, 238
Meditation, 149
Meeting for Sufferings, 54
Minister, place of, 177–8, 183
Ministerial support, 178–80
Mittimus, 45–6
Mixed marriages, 172–3
Monmouth, Duke of, 23, 27
Monmouth Rebellion, 27
Moore, Thomas, 125
Moral lapses, 173 ff.
Morton, Charles, 187, 190

323

324

Private prayer, 150–1
Probation of ministers, 191
Protectoralists, 1
Psalm-singing, 41, 140, 163, 183
'Pulpit prayers', 243
Puritanism
  lack of unity within, 1
  political bankruptcy of, 2

Racing, 132, 192
Ransacking of homes, 40
Reception of members, 166–7
Recreations, 132–3
Reformation as a Puritan ideal, 194, 224–5, 252
Relationships among dissenters, 151, 252 ff.
Reordination, 241–2
Repetition of sermons, 129, 139, 217–18
Republicans, 1
Restoration of 1660, 2 ff., 33, 36, 60, 248
Revenge, desire for, 4, 18, 33, 226, 248
Revolution of 1688, 250
Rigge, A., 84, 113
Roberts, John, 100
Rumours, prevalence of, 12
Rutherford, Samuel, 149
Rye House Plot, 25

Sacrament, admission to, 168
St Bartholomew's Day, 1662, 7, 8
Sancroft, Abp. William, 30, 61, 251
Savoy Conference, 6–7
Scarborough Castle, 93, 101
Schism, 232–5
Science, 187, 249, 251
Scotland, 186
Scroggs, Chief Justice, 49
Secker, Abp. 187
Sedition, 36
Self-discipline, 147
Self-examination, 149–50
Sentence, 55
Sermons, length of, 213–14
  structure of, 207–8, 217
Servants, 136, 143
Services, length of, 161
  special kinds of, 164
Sexual immorality, 176–7
Shaftesbury, Earl of, 23–4
Sharp, Abp. John, 189–90
Sheldon, Abp. G., 10
Sibbes, Richard, 138, 149, 186
Sign of the cross, 244

Size of congregations, 160
Sleep, due regulation of, 131, 135
Smith, Francis, 99
Social status of dissenters, 160, 193
Socinianism, 247, 254
Soldiers, 88, 97
Solemn League and Covenant, 7, 8
South, Robert, 208, 212
Spademan, John, 207
Stockton, Mrs Owen, 146, 149
Story, Thomas, 144
Strictness of life, 143
Study, 206
Style, 211–13
Suffragan bishops, 240
Sunday, 129 f.
Supervision of members, 169
Sureties, 45
Surplice, 245
Swarthmore Hall, 105, 114
Switzerland, 186
Synods, 240

Taylor, Jeremy, 211
Taylor, Thomas, 113, 118
Temporal affairs, 165 f.
Terrill, Edward, 40, 175, 176, 177
Theatre, 193
Thoresby, Ralph, 129, 135, 138, 149, 214, 217
Thorndike, Herbert, 239
Tillotson, Abp. John, 190, 251
Time, value of, 134–5
Toleration, 31, 65, 246, 253
Toleration, Act of, 247, 249, 250
Tories, 24–6, 34, 230, 231, 251
Totnes, 95
Transportation (as a punishment), 51
Treason, accusations of, 12, 228–30, 247
Trial
  difficulty of securing fair, 53
  of Richard Baxter, 27
  of the Seven Bishops, 29
Trinitarian Controversy, 247
Trosse, George, 205
Turner, Francis, 221
Twisden, Judge, 123

Uniformity, 222
Uniformity, Act of, 1662, 7, 11, 52, 56, 185, 188, 230, 235, 249
United action, 183
Unity, Puritan lack of, 1, 185
Universities, 185, 251
Ussher, Abp. James, 240

325